D1267200

Witch Craze

Witch Craze

Terror and Fantasy in Baroque Germany

Lyndal Roper

YALE UNIVERSITY PRESS
NEW HAVEN AND LONDON

For information about this and other Yale University Press publications, please contact:
U.S. Office: sales.press@yale.edu   yalebooks.com
Europe Office: sales@yaleup.co.uk   www.yalebooks.co.uk

Set in Minion by Fakenham Photosetting
Printed in Great Britain by St Edmundsbury Press, Bury St Edmunds

ISBN 0–300–10335–2
Library of Congress Control Number 2004111947

A catalogue record for this book is available from the British Library.

10 9 8 7 6 5 4 3 2 1

Contents

Illustrations

Preface

The bus tour of the 'Romantic Road' through the highlights of baroque southern Germany stops for little more than quarter of an hour in Nördlingen, just long enough to take in the town hall, the beautifully restored half-timbered tanners' houses and the medieval skyline dominated by the high tower of St George's, Nördlingen's single parish church. In the middle of the flat Ries plain, with its almost perfectly circular city walls, Nördlingen rises from the distance as the quintessential small south German town.

The archive where I worked in Nördlingen was housed in a fine sixteenth-century building on the quiet Wine Market Square, surrounded by quaint medieval inns. Yet in the course of the closing decade of the sixteenth century, Nördlingen saw a particularly vicious witch hunt in which thirty-five of the town dwellers perished in the flames. Nothing could seem further from the tranquility of life in Nördlingen today. The building in which I sat has a history too: one of its previous inhabitants was Rebekka Lemp, who was executed as a witch and whose anguished farewell letter to her husband has survived. Around the Wine Market, eleven women and one man met their deaths in the witch panic, and from every tavern on that square a woman was accused of witchcraft.

Nördlingen has learnt to live with its past, and even to celebrate it. Most summers, the open-air theatre that performs within the old city wall presents a play about Maria Holl, the woman who did not confess to witchcraft despite sixty-two applications of torture. Holl is the town's heroine and her story dramatizes courageous resistance to authority, a powerful message in post-war Germany. But the play is based on a novel first written during the Third Reich, in which Maria has a rival who brings about her denunciation, and who is brown-eyed, swarthy-skinned and has dark curly hair. Recognizably Jewish, she has been excised from the stage version. Even in a novel designed to present the witch as a rebel against the power of the sleekly prosperous town councillors, the author could not escape demonizing another woman, a Jewess. And the play, which appears to be a triumphal reclamation of Maria Holl's civic courage, cannot help trying to bury the town's Nazi past.

When I began working on witchcraft, I was drawn less to the stories of resistance, of women like Maria Holl or Rebekka Lemp whose refusal to be branded as witches made them easy to identify with. Rather, I wanted to comprehend how their neighbours, people who had known them for decades and had eaten and drunk with them, came to believe that these women were witches and were prepared to denounce them. I wanted, too, to make sense of women I could not understand at all, those who came to confess they were witches. I wanted to discover how they could confess to sex with the Devil, flying to the sabbath or participating in Satanic rituals.

What surprised me most when I began to read the detailed trial records of women who were accused of witchcraft was that they talked not about sex and forbidden desire, but about birth; about breastmilk that dried up, about babies who sickened and died, and about the room where the woman spent her 'lying in', the period of six weeks after the birth of a child. These were areas of human experience that I had not encountered before in the historical record, and my training as a historian had not equipped me to think about them. They overturned my preconceptions about why people act, forcing me to consider unconscious motivations and aspects of life that seemed so fundamental as to be scarcely historical at all. So, when I first encountered this material over a decade ago, I was drawn to using psychoanalytic theory because it seemed to offer the best way of explaining the deeply disturbing themes of such confessions. Often, accusations of witchcraft were made by young mothers against the old women who were closest to them, the lying-in maids who cared intimately for mother and baby. They could easily be blamed if mother or baby failed to thrive. Cases like this concerned emotions closely connected with the bond between mother and child, and they seemed to cry out for a psychoanalytic exploration. This is what I attempted to develop in some of the articles I published in my earlier book, *Oedipus and the Devil* (1994).

My own approach to witchcraft, however, has changed over the years. While the present book has been deeply influenced by psychoanalytic ideas, it is a historical, not a psychoanalytic study. My original interest had been in the subjectivity of the individuals accused of witchcraft, the area to which Freud himself contributed one of the most original studies in his account of the possessed painter Christoph Haitzmann. I wanted to explore the relationship between interrogators and the accused, and to understand something Freud was less helpful in explaining, namely why maternal themes were so prominent in witches' confessions. But psychoanalysis is less useful once one tries to deal with a whole society and comprehend why fears about witches were so widespread in the towns and villages of sixteenth- and seventeenth-century Germany. Nor could psychoanalysis easily account for a phenomenon like witch-hunting in Europe, which was not geographically universal and whose worst excesses occurred in a specific epoch, the late sixteenth and early seventeenth centuries.

The problem I faced was how to build the detail of subjectivity and the sheer power of unconscious forces as they emerge in the confessions into a history that would be about a whole society and not just about individuals, and that would deal with historical change. The way historians of sixteenth- and seventeenth-century Europe have commonly tried to do this is to make use of anthropology, employing accounts of ritual, concepts of pollution and notions of space to delineate a collective mentality. But I was not drawn to this solution, because it seemed to allow too little space for the unconscious, or for individuality. The overwhelming emotions that gripped individuals at the centre of these dramas still seem to me to offer the most powerful evidence we have of the cultural values threatened by witchcraft. Such passions were aroused in whole communities – and in the end even in the witches themselves – only because the fantasies of witchcraft also spoke to the central determinants of life in sixteenth- and seventeenth-century Germany.

As I discovered, the fears that surrounded witches were not just about the deaths of infants and the early weeks of motherhood, but featured animals and crops, in short, fertility itself. These terrors were credible because of the realities of life in a precarious economy. Marriage often had to be postponed, and many could never afford to wed. To be a fertile wife with plenty of children was to be honoured and respected. To be an old woman frequently meant poverty, infirmity and humiliating dependence on the young. How a society organizes marriage, how the physical processes of ageing were experienced in the past and how religious fragmentation in the epoch after the Reformation and Counter-Reformation seared small communities therefore had to be part of the story of the emotions of the witch craze. As a result, this book is not just about trials for witchcraft, but about art, literature, politics and religious life in baroque Germany.

What I hope to have achieved here is to have incorporated areas of human experience that often elude the historical record, realms such as fantasy, envy and terror, or the apparently ahistorical sphere of the bond between mother and baby. I would argue that these dimensions of life are also historical factors of causation and that if we ignore them we will fail to understand fully why and how societies change. I hope, too, to open a window onto a world that seems strange and foreign, where people believed that if you fell into melancholy, the Devil might appear in person to tempt you to despair and so steal your soul; or that angels might visit you in dreams and visions. There have been countless books on witchcraft that have looked at the demographic distribution of the victims, the geographical patterns, the sociology of witchcraft accusation, or the gender dimensions of the witch hunt, and this book could not have been written without them. But at the heart of the story, I believe, must lie the emotional dynamic of envy, dependence and terror, which for over two hundred years issued in acts of appalling ferocity against apparently harmless old women.

When I started this project fourteen years ago, I had no conception of how long it would take me, or how my own life would change during the course of writing it. Becoming a mother has transformed my life; it has given me a sense of how much time things take to grow, how little of life one can plan, how deep rooted sexual identity seems to be and how surprisingly unimportant language is in establishing primary human relationships. It has also given me a longer sense of the future. I hope this book therefore conveys the importance of generations, the slowness of the pace at which many major historical changes happen, and the limits of conscious control most people, then and now, have over their actions. I hope, too, that some readers will recognize, as I did, common human experience in the testimonies of women who lived in very different times.

Acknowledgements

Many people and institutions have helped me to write this book. The German Academic Exchange service funded the initial period of research, and a year at the Wissenschaftskolleg in Berlin enabled me to start thinking about how to use the records. A Humboldt Foundation award provided a year in Göttingen in which to research and explore ideas with colleagues at the Max Planck Institute for History, while an attachment at the Australian National University in the Women's Studies department and repeated visits to the University of Western Australia and to the University of Melbourne made it possible for me to discuss the project with colleagues there. A grant from the British Academy helped fund research expenses in Germany. At Royal Holloway, my department generously gave me additional sabbatical leave, and from the Leverhulme Foundation I received a year's fellowship, which gave me time to write the manuscript. My colleagues at Balliol College and at the University of Oxford offered a wonderfully co-operative environment in which to finish it. An early version of chapter 3 appeared as 'Kinder ausgraben, Kinder essen: Zur psychischen Dynamik von Hexenprozessen in der Frühen Neuzeit' in Nada Boskovska Leimgruber (ed.), *Die Frühe Neuzeit in der Geschichtswissenschaft*; I am grateful to Schöningh Verlag for permission to reprint this, while *Past and Present*, to which I am grateful for much else besides, allowed me to reprint parts of 'Evil Imaginings and Fantasies. Child-Witches and the End of the Witch-Craze' (*Past and Present* 167, 2000, pp. 107-39) in chapter 9.

Audiences to whom I've given papers over the years have asked challenging and helpful questions, which have found their way into the book, and students at Royal Holloway and at Oxford who have taken my courses on witchcraft will also recognize how much I have been influenced by what they have said. I have learnt from conversations with many friends and colleagues, and amongst them I would like to thank in particular, Ingrid Bàtori, Willem de Blécourt, Ruth Bottigheimer, the late Alan Bray, Philip Broadhead, Stuart Clark, Natalie Zemon Davis, Cyril Edwards, Georg Feuerer, Liz Fidlon, Karl Figlio, Anthony Fletcher, Etienne François, Klaus Graf (who runs the excellent witchcraft on-line discussion forum), Valentin Groebner, Rebekka Habermas, Olivia Harris, Bridget Heal, Amos Hetz, Clive Holmes, Michael Hunter, Lorna Hutson, Bernd Jussen, Hans-Jörg Künast, Eva Labouvie, Hartmut Lehmann, Alf Lüdtke, Hans Medick, Aslan Mordecai, Maria E. Müller, Jinty Nelson, Caroline Oates, Adam Philips, Alison Phipps, Daniel Pick, Jörg Rasche, the late Gareth Roberts, Alison Rowlands, Miri Rubin, Hans-Christoph Rublack, Norbert Schindler, Jürgen Schlumbohm, Peter Schöttler, Regina Schulte, Gerd Schwerhoff, the late Bob Scribner, Pam Selwyn, Alex Shepard, Peter Sillem, Pat Simons, Ulrike Strasser, Kathy Stuart, Ann Tlusty, Amanda Vickery, Dietmar Voges, Bernd Weisbrod, Johannes Wilhelm, Heide Wunder and Amy Wygant. Rainer Beck, Machteld Löwensteyn, Peter Morgan and Richard Sheppard all shared their expertise with me. Wolfgang Behringer has given constant advice and help throughout this project, and I have learnt greatly from my former doctoral student Jonathan Durrant's work on witchcraft in Eichstätt. I was inspired to work on sixteenth- and seventeenth-century Germany by Charles Zika: uncannily, the themes of our work continue to echo each other. Patricia Crawford, Laura Gowing, Olwen Hufton, Alison Light and Barbara Taylor all read and commented on draft sections of the manuscript; Robin Briggs, Daniel Pick, Ailsa Roper, Mike Roper and Ulinka Rublack read and helped to form the whole thing; and Erik Midelfort kindly undertook the massive task of detailed reading, saving me from many an error. Julia von dem Knesebeck proved an indefatiguable picture sleuth, Simone Laqua compiled the bibliography and Danielle Barbour undertook a super final copy-edit. Clare Alexander, my agent, read and pencil-edited a baggy manuscript, grasped what it was about, and gave encouragement when I needed it most. Adam Freudenheim was a superbly perceptive and sympathetic editor, and I am grateful to Robert Baldock, Kevin Brown and Ewan Thompson at Yale who saw the book through the final stages; and to Hazel Hutchison, whose idea it was, when we both became mothers at the same time, that one day she should do its publicity. This book could not have been written without the editorial help and unstinting generosity of three people: Iain Pears, who savaged the book into shape, Ruth Harris, to whom my intellectual debt is immense, and Nick Stargardt, who commented incisively on every draft and pre-draft, and whose love and support made it possible.

Prologue
The Witch at the Smithy

1623 Marchtal

It was just on twilight and the Ave Maria bell sounded from the monastery tower across the fields, but the dancers outside Martin Hundersinger's house ignored it. They were stamping and whirling to the sound of the fiddle, for it was September and the harvest was in. As the festivity reached its height, the figure of an old woman could be seen, sidling by the dancers and coming to a halt just in front of Hundersinger's cowshed. A girl screamed at her 'Be gone!' and the old crone scuttled away, but soon she returned again, taking up her post in front of the cowshed. Shortly after, Hundersinger's wife, the mistress of the house, came out. There was little love lost between the two women. Seeing her near the cowshed, Hundersinger's wife was overcome with fear and rage. She had already lost one fine horse when the old hag had cursed as it crossed her path, and only eight weeks before, a sturdy two-year-old red bull had sickened mysteriously and they had been forced to dispose of it; she did not want to say it was witchcraft, but what else could it have been? Now the old woman was loitering next to her cows, and who knew what she was muttering or what she might be strewing in their hay? Provoked beyond endurance, Hundersinger's wife screamed out 'You shitty witch!' and the old woman fled home.

It was done now: a public insult, the words uttered to her face, and heard by the audience of village revellers. There was no going back. Ursula Götz had been branded a witch, and only a trial could settle the issue. It was to take four years, but that trial sent the old woman to her death.

Ursula Götz had been born and raised in the smithy. She must have known every horse for miles around. Never married, she had stayed on in her brother's household keeping house for him in his widowhood, until he died and the smithy passed to his son. She had remained, and had eventually done the same for her nephew when he too became a widower, caring for his little daughter. A pretty, healthy child, she was named Ursula too, after her great-aunt.

But when she was only three, little Ursula sickened and would not eat for nine days. She became paralysed on the left side, and now she could neither walk nor lift her arm. Jerg Götz, her father, blamed the girl's great-aunt. It must have been she who had caused his daughter's incapacity, for had not all her food been given her by old Ursula alone?

It was early evening in the village ten or twenty years before, and it was nearly time for the evening meal. Outside, underneath the smithy, Master Jacob the barber, Veit Brunnen and Jerg Götz and his father stood talking together. Götz's father was a widower at that time and so Ursula cooked for him. Dinner was ready and Ursula ran down to call the men to table. But the old man did not come at once, preferring to chat with his companions a while longer. Suddenly they heard a fearful commotion that sounded like hooves pounding down the village street and passing by the smithy. It sounded like a frightened horse, dragging the span of a cart behind it. But nothing was to be seen. After this, they had no wish to continue their conversation. They were all made uneasy by the riderless horse and those scraping sounds. Who knew what they might portend?

Shortly before Carnival ten years before Ursula was accused of witchcraft, her maid Waldburga fell ill and was confined to bed for three days. The maid's sister came to fetch her home, but Ursula would not let the girl leave, saying, 'Why take the girl from a full kitchen to an empty one?' All the same, Waldburga's sister took her home to her family. The Saturday before, the girl had begged her mother to bake her a cake. No sooner had she done so than Ursula appeared, bearing a rival tray of *Streuselkuchen* and apple slices, and saying, 'Why should you eat the *Streuselkuchen* and leave the good cake to go to waste?'

When Ursula was out of the house, the ill maid had cried at once: 'You must throw what Ursula baked away! Give it to the cats or dogs to eat!' The following Sunday the girl took a turn for the worse, and she died that Monday.

The village mayor, who had taken Ursula Götz into custody and noted down all the accusations against her, had been certain it would not be easy to get Götz to admit she was a witch. Against all the evidence, he wrote, she stubbornly behaved as if 'she was as clear as glass', and confessed 'neither much nor little'. The only way, he advised his superiors, was to tell her exactly what she had done, and what had happened; or else to confront her with her accusers face to face.

But in the event, Götz confessed readily once she was threatened with torture and the rigours of a full criminal trial; or at least that is what the surviving protocols of the interrogation report. She told how she had first met her personal devil, called Federlin ('Little Feather'), some thirty years before. He was dressed as a farm servant in clothes of many colours, and came into her bed. When she asked him what he was doing, he replied simply that he was there. A week later she consented to sexual intercourse with him, and signed the pact that made her the Devil's own. He had given her a black salve to harm humans, horses, pigs and cows. Freely she confessed how she had been sitting with a group of other women one evening at the smithy on Our Lady's Candlemas Eve, the festival when candles were blessed and the house protected against evil magic. She had put little Ursula to bed, but instead of blessing her, had laid her down in the name of the Devil. Then she had stroked her arm, whereupon the little girl became lame.[1]

Accused of numerous murders, Ursula went on to confess them all. She listed no fewer than eighty-eight animals she had attacked, describing colour, owner and age. To the last, she remained a shrewd observer of livestock, learned from her years in the smithy. And she confessed not only to harming little Ursula, but to killing little Ursula's mother and baby sister Marielin, aged eleven weeks. She had sucked out the blood of young children to use in her diabolic salves, and she had sucked out her little great-niece's blood completely.

On the intercession of the abbot and monastery who ruled the territory of Obermarchtal, Ursula Götz was granted mercy. She was beheaded, not burnt alive for her crimes, and her body was then consigned to the flames. She perished alongside two other witches in the year 1627.[2]

. . .

These scenes from village life were played out in Obermarchtal, a small monastery village nestled near the Danube in south-western Germany. Such scenes were repeated in hundreds of towns and villages across Germany during the period of the witch hunt, from the sixteenth to the seventeenth centuries. It is difficult to comprehend the sheer viciousness of the way villagers and townsfolk attacked those they held to be witches. Often, these people were well known to their accusers. They were neighbours or kin, people whose food they had shared, with whom they had sat sewing in the evenings, or who had cared for their children. The violence was rarely direct – lynchings were resorted to only occasionally – but everyone knew what was in store when an accused witch was taken away to be interrogated under torture. As one woman put it, her enemies were sending her 'to the butcher's slab'. Women convicted of witchcraft were burnt in public, and their deaths were a spectacle. The details of the crimes, read out in public, or even circulated as broadsheets, were seared into the memories of all who subsequently saw them perish. A woman like Martin Hundersinger's wife knew from her own family what fate awaited a witch, for she had been a child in the 1580s when witch pyres had been burning in the territory, and was just entering her teens when the last witches had been burnt in the 1590s. And yet she was willing to testify against a woman who was almost certainly her half-sister, who was her neighbour and whom she had known all her life.

Often, as in the case of Ursula Götz, those accused of witchcraft were old. They were women who had raised children, who had spent long years caring for others, and on whose housekeeping and social skills the community depended. Their very solicitude was interpreted as proof that they had caused illness or death. The puzzle for the historian of witchcraft is why – to our eyes – apparently harmless women like Götz should have elicited such murderous hatred, and how a society could have treated them so cruelly. It was as if something in the nature of human intimacy, in the very work of caring for the sick, dependent and children, made these women's attentions seem malign and their presence insufferable.

Much of Ursula Götz's trial concerned gifts and food, like the cake that made her servant ill. The word 'Gift', wonderfully ambiguous in German, is related to the verb 'to give' but also means 'poison'. From court to hamlet, gifts were the currency of politics and patronage, obligating the recipient and expressing the donor's power: only a counter-gift could restore equality. Gifts were not what they seemed. Like the Trojan horse, the gift was an object imbued with the donor's essence, placed in the receiver's proximity, from where it could exert harmful magical powers. Neither was charity always what it appeared, for it was well known that you should give a suspected witch something to break her power. Yet as a sign of amity, a gift could not easily be refused, even if it were clearly aggressive in its intention.

In such interactions, objects which might seem trifling were invested with immense emotional significance. They acted as the litmus test of relations between people. This was why so much of the substance of witchcraft testimony apparently concerns the giving of objects of minute value. It was not that accused witches begged for charity from their neighbours and were refused it, thus causing their accusers to feel guilt and therefore to expect and experience retaliation, as has so often been argued.[3] Rather, witchcraft allegations were implicated in a system of exchanges between people – of small amounts of money, food and household supplies – through which they constantly sought to negotiate the nature of their relationships. With the witch, giving went wrong. Yet human society itself depends on gifts and exchanges. Without the exchange of union between the sexes, without the capacity to give and to receive, there can be no fertility; without trade there can be no society.

· · ·

This book tells the story of those, like Ursula Götz, who died as witches; and the story of their accusers. If we are to understand why sixteenth- and seventeenth-century Germany unleashed such relentless hatred, we need to grasp the fears of women like Hundersinger's wife, women who saw their livestock stricken one after the other with death and disease, and who saw their hope of a plentiful farmstead and a well-stocked barn shrivel before their eyes. We need to sense the wretchedness of seeing a beloved sister sicken in a strange household, take to her bed and die; or the powerlessness of watching a pretty toddler face life crippled by injury, with little prospect of marriage and heirs, destined to be a lifelong drain on stretched household resources. When Ursula Götz crept by the cowshed, her neighbours did not see a pitiful old woman, fondly petting their cows, but a death-dealing sorceress whose envious malice would bring destruction on all who crossed her path.

Ursula Götz was suspect not least because of her age. Seventy-two years old when she came to trial, she probably knew that she was likely to lose her case and her life. Her near male relatives – her father and brother – were dead. Her mother had been accused of witchcraft during a major witch hunt a generation before, and since witchcraft ran in the blood, this made her an even more likely suspect. Milk thieves, as witches were known in some parts of Germany, harmed people and animals, and made them fall ill with strange diseases. They attacked men's potency. They killed suckling infants and children. Threatening life itself, they attacked fertility in the natural and the human world.

Small wonder, then, that Hundersinger's wife watched the cowshed with such dread, and could not keep her insults to herself. Or that, years later, the men would suddenly recall the uncanny sounds of the invisible wild horse as night fell and Ursula called the smith in to dinner. Or that Waldburga's sister remembered – or thought she remembered – how the sick girl had cried for the cakes to be fed to the cats and dogs, the sure test for discovering whether the food was poisoned. When little Ursula fell ill, suspicion fell on her great-aunt, the girl's close relative and mother-substitute. And it was by telling the stories again and again, pondering, saving them up and poring over them, that allegations came to be made, as people revisited events from the past and came to see them as an unbroken chain of witchcraft.

Hardest to recover is how Ursula Götz herself saw her world. How was she transformed from stubborn defender of her innocence to pliable confessor of every conceivable misdeed, from sex with the Devil to harming eighty-eight cows, pigs and horses? What led her to name two other women as her accomplices, who would also be tried, found guilty and their bodies burnt with hers on that summer day? Part of the reason is certainly torture; part of the reason, perhaps, the tactic the mayor proposed, that Ursula should simply be told the crimes to which she ought to confess. But that will not explain how she came to tell her story of life with the Devil, giving it her own individual colouring, nor will it tell us why she was accused of such crimes in the first place.

The nature of the surviving documentation affects what we can know about any witch. In the case of Ursula Götz, what purports to be the protocol of her formal interrogation covers three days, 22 to 24 March 1627, and contains crossings-out and alterations in different hands. A suspiciously large amount of it, however, is in a clear, even and flowing hand which suggests it may not have been compiled at the time. We do not have a record of what questions were asked, or when torture was used, and the records of the case as a whole are patchy. Yet in other cases the records do permit us to reconstruct the process by which victim and interrogator gradually, over a period of weeks and months, arrived at an account which revealed the Satanic drama beneath the mundane details of the accused's daily existence, and explained the seething envies and hatreds that motivated her deeds. Whilst in no sense literally 'true', such confessions do document what people believed, and they form a kind of life history, albeit one extorted under torture or its threat. These tales offer a way of exploring the mentalities of people of this era, who left few if any other traces behind them, and some of whom may well have come to believe that they truly were the Devil's own.

. . .

Witch hunts were not exclusively directed at old women. Throughout the period, young women, children and adult men also found themselves accused. As many as 20 per cent of the victims of a witch craze in Germany might be men, and those who wrote tracts about how to eradicate the heresy were always careful to remind their readers that even the most upstanding men could become prey to the Devil. The story of Faust, printed for the first time in Frankfurt in 1587 but well known as a popular tale throughout southern Germany, concerns the dealings of a man with the Demon: it provided much of the material for Christopher Marlowe's famous play the following year. The figure of the witch was never just a predictable stereotype, for the Devil set his snares to trap any unwary Christian into joining his service. It is difficult to discern universal patterns amongst those condemned, and no single pattern fits all cases. However, as contemporaries were aware, the largest group amongst the victims were women, predominantly women aged over forty. This was a group not otherwise likely to become embroiled in the criminal justice system: it was men, especially young men, who were the majority of those executed for crimes like theft and murder, while young women might be convicted of theft, prostitution or infanticide.

Over the course of the witch hunt, upwards of perhaps 50,000 people died. We will never know the exact figure because in many places the records of their interrogations have simply been destroyed, with allusions made only to 'hundreds' of witches killed. We do know, however, that the persecutions were not evenly spread across Europe. The lands of what is now Germany saw by far the greatest numbers of executions, around 25,000, fully half the total number. Any study of the witch craze must therefore begin by asking why the witch hunts were so heavily concentrated in the German-speaking lands of the Holy Roman Empire. It must also ask why – in a pattern of persecution stretching from the late fifteenth century until the era of the Enlightenment in the eighteenth century, which reached its height in Germany in the late sixteenth and early seventeenth centuries – so many victims were women. The shocking predominance of old women amongst those executed in the witch hunt suggests that this was a settled cultural pattern, whose resonances can be found in literature, art, theology and popular culture as well as amongst demonologists, that special group of professional witch-hunters who wrote about the science of witches and demons.

The hatred and terror that drove people to such violence were shaped by social tensions and religious beliefs, but the passions themselves derived from deeply rooted fantasies, extravagant in their evocation of demonic lovers and Satanic revels. These fantasies shared, for the most part, a standard structure and a similar set of primary themes. Time and again, they turned on motherhood, the bodies of ageing women, and fertility. Ursula Götz was an old woman no longer able to have children herself. With no direct descendants in the village, marooned with a niece who was unmarriageable, she represented a life that did not lead into the future, but only to death. Fertility, after all, depended on marriage and a union between a man and a woman from different families. It was this successful integration into the world of village exchanges that sprang from marriage which Ursula so desperately desired – why else the frenzied, competitive baking? – and so comprehensively failed to attain. Unfruitful herself, she was accused of attacking the fertility of all around her, by killing cattle, maiming and killing horses, harming babies, poisoning the sick; even crippling her own niece.

In all its essentials her trial hardly differed from many other cases of witchcraft pursued in Marchtal or many other towns and villages dotted across Germany at any time between the sixteenth and the eighteenth centuries. Lurid as the details of her case may seem, they were demonic cliché. By the time Ursula Götz made her confession, its outlines were familiar because confessions like hers had been heard so often before. The hostilities between neighbours which led to the court case were standard village fare. Yet they remain deeply puzzling. In so uncertain a world, riven by wars, famines and plagues villagers were helpless to prevent, they must have been singularly ill prepared to meet such external challenges if their relationships with each other were marked more by hatred than trust. How then could such trials happen? How could it become acceptable in many areas of Europe to burn as witches people whom their community had known as intimates and neighbours? And why, ultimately, did the image of the old hag gradually cease to terrify

Europeans? The answers to such questions cannot be found in statistical surveys of witch-hunting. They demand that we venture into the passions of the unconscious, exploring the terrors and images which contemporaries found hard to put into words; the fears that were founded around their obsession with the bodies of old women and made people behave in apparently brutal, voyeuristic and cynical ways. How people succumbed to such terrors, and how, in the eighteenth century, they gradually freed themselves from their grip, is the subject of this book.

My interest lies in the psychological workings of the witch hunt, in the fantasies which propelled it, and in the skewed emotional exchanges it generated. Fantasies come and go. Different terrors and obsessions may seize societies in different periods. Fantasies must also relate to experience, for only when a fantasy accords to some degree with our concerns can it be credible enough to grip our minds. In the case of witchcraft, the idea that old women were plotting to root out Christian folk and destroy Christendom made sense to people who were already worried about how their society could reproduce itself and continue. They lived in an age in which resources were limited, and men and women tried to control fertility by waiting, delaying the age at which they married or even giving up the hope of marriage if they had insufficient resources to set up their own household. Society lay on a knife-edge balance. Too great a restriction on fertility could imperil reproduction entirely; too little could result in vast numbers of beggars and the improvident. In many towns and territories, laws were passed to prevent the marriage of those who could not support themselves. This also meant that women who were married and fertile carried the burden of ensuring that the next generation would continue. Everything was done to safeguard their child-bearing and they were held in great honour and esteem. This protective attitude towards married women, however, had its darker side. People could become inclined to see threats to fertility lurking everywhere, and to expect older women to envy the fecund young. A society which regulated marriage as its main means of controlling fertility, where overpopulation seemed to threaten in the second half of the sixteenth century, and which then suffered the demographic catastrophe of the Thirty Years War, was not surprisingly obsessed with the fear of barrenness in both the human and the natural world.

This does not mean that the demographic regime of Western Europe caused the witch hunt, nor even that it was chief amongst a series of causal factors. It was a condition, but many regions subject to the same circumstances avoided witch hunts; indeed, sometimes areas next to places where severe witch persecution had occurred escaped a single case of witchcraft. Nor did that demographic regime end with the witch persecutions: well into the nineteenth century, people delayed marriage for economic reasons and governments continued to issue restrictive laws. Even during the worst incidents of witch-hunting, there were sceptical voices. Alongside demography, any explanation of the witch hunt has to consider factors such as the willingness of the authorities to prosecute, the legal framework, the role of individual witch-hunters, and the particular features of the phenomenon of mass witch-hunting, such as was experienced in Würzburg or Lorraine, where hundreds of individuals were sent to their deaths. There cannot be a single causal explanation.

One dimension which did play a vital part in the unfolding of witchcraft persecutions was that of the imagination. We cannot understand why witches were hunted unless we take the fears of those who hunted witches seriously. We must enter the nightmare world of those who believed in witchcraft and of those who found themselves accused. We have to suspend, at least for a moment, the comforting rationality of a society that claims no longer to believe in witches; and to immerse ourselves in the disorienting world of witches' stories, if we are to discover why this particular set of fantasies could be so powerful and persuasive at the time.

Witchcraft was an intensely *physical* experience. People attacked by witches said that their milk dried up, that their babies became ill and wasted away before their eyes, that they were suddenly pressed down upon as they slept. Their animals sickened; the crops shrivelled. Witches made men impotent and women infertile; they visited strange, inexplicable sicknesses on those they cursed, illnesses which did not obey the normal course of nature. Just how frightening such suffering was, how helpless one might feel as death scythed down one's loved ones or – perhaps still worse in that era – left one with cripples to care for, cannot really be grasped through the study of intellectual beliefs alone. The language of witchcraft was about suffering and it tells us as much about people's experience of pain, illness and despair as it does about what they could articulate. What made the witch recognizable for what she was were signs in her body. She had the tell-tale 'Devil's mark' or darkened mole or bump, she defecated when a so-called 'witch smoke' was lit, and her sexual organs were well used.

The harm witches were believed to accomplish was directed principally against pregnant women, babies, children and fertility in the natural world. As the Jesuit and demonologist Martin del Rio (1558–1608) put it, summarizing decades of research on witches, they 'poison people merely by breathing or blowing on them. This is how they are accustomed to cause miscarriages.' He went on to note gruesomely that they 'suffocate very small children during the night by smothering them with the mattress; or they kill them by thrusting a needle behind their ear .... They snatch children from the cradle and rend them in pieces; or they use them to make their ointments ... or they eat them, a food they find very pleasing ....'[4] The *Malleus Maleficarum*, first published in 1486, still the most infamous work of demonology and the first to bring beliefs about witchcraft into a lengthy, compelling synthesis, tarred midwives in particular as witches. The author provides a string of gripping tales about vicious midwives, like the one who confessed before she was burnt in the diocese of Basle that 'she had killed more than forty children, by sticking a needle through the crowns of their heads into their brains, as they came out from the womb'.[5] The connection between witchcraft and childbed had a long pedigree. Childbed had always been surrounded by the magical and the dangerous, often requiring the use of blessed girdles on the mother's heaving stomach and protective candles to guard the new child. As the preacher Johannes Geiler of Keisersberg noted in an apparently sceptical sermon of 1508, more women than men were witches, and women seemed to suffer from witchcraft particularly during childbed, when moisture climbed into their heads causing evil thoughts and, in an interesting use of the word in this context, 'fantasies' (*Fantaseien*).[6]

But this was not all. The witch might attack the act of generation itself. Del Rio elaborated in great detail how a witch might inhibit the operation of the male sexual member by tying knots in a string. Women might be affected too, but men were most often the victims, especially when, as Del Rio said, 'there are more female workers of harmful magic (*maleficiae*) than male (*malefici*)'.[7] Witches assaulted the very possibility of life, plenty and futurity. They were believed capable of causing such harm through their alliance with the Devil, an alliance cemented by diabolic intercourse. Unlike human intercourse, which led to increase and generation as the male and female seeds commingled in the active heat of coition, sex with the Devil was cold. The Devil's member was hard. Diabolic intercourse was unpleasurable and it led to no issue.

Witchcraft was a fantasy.[8] This does not mean that it was trivial or unreal. Rather, it had deep roots in the unconscious. The fantasies of witchcraft were formed in a particular period of European culture, but they drew their force from their relationship to the primary material of infantile experience, feelings about feeding and eating, about where the body of the child begins and the mother's ends, about emptiness and death. Beliefs and apprehensions about witches who flew to sabbaths, fornicated with Satan, made men impotent and cooked and ate dead infants formed a 'fantasy' in the sense that they gave a structure to wordless terrors and grief, translating them into a recognizable narrative. They seemed real, and so, in psychological terms, they were real. And they provided a moral account of who was to blame for deaths and illnesses that might otherwise have seemed cruelly random. It therefore becomes important to ask how a society – or at least a powerful cross-section of it – could become persuaded of the truth of such a fantasy.

What follows is an exploration of the fantasy of witchcraft, the reasons for its persuasiveness in the sixteenth and seventeenth centuries, and its gradual decline until, by 1800, witchcraft was no longer credible to most Europeans. To persuade those accused to supply the confessions, torture was used; and the confessions bear all the marks of the pain and degradation involved. They also required interrogators, often men who were educated in law and theology, cultured intellectuals, as well as village jurors or civic fathers. What went on in their minds, why they were prepared to question suspects exhaustively, often for many weeks, is just as important as what the witches' accusers believed. And what they heard was truly shocking. They heard about cannibalistic witches and sex with the Devil, and they uncovered a world of dark and sinister ceremonies that blasphemed against every Christian value. It was incredible. It was also riveting. When demonologists, the intellectuals who systematized beliefs about witches and the Devil, came to write their treatises, the sheer fascination of the material often got the better of them. They were not the only ones: the material of the witchcraft fantasy sparked some of the most dazzling literary and visual creations of the period, from Baldung Grien's extraordinary erotic sketches of witches, to Marlowe's *Dr Faustus*.

Why did such fantasies focus so relentlessly on women, old women in particular? The answer lies in how society of the sixteenth and seventeenth centuries conceived of female nature. It involves more than confronting the vein of deep misogyny towards older women that issued in the witch craze. It also requires an understanding of how a woman's status shifted through her life cycle, from maid to mother to crone. Tracing these ages of woman will take us on a voyage through demography, medical ideas, woodcuts and paintings, rituals and customs, and popular literature. It will lead us, too, into the humdrum town squares and tiny village streets where witchcraft accusations bred, and which became transformed, as the accused made their confessions, into the nightmare landscapes of the sabbath feast. For every witch who confessed had to make that story her own, furnishing it with the details of place and character that could persuade her hearers it was all true. And witch after witch did just that, strengthening the conviction that a vast sect of witches was in league with Satan to destroy all that Christians held dear.

There were many reasons why the witch craze ended. People began to doubt the truth of confessions produced under prolonged torture, and were shocked by the means executioners and interrogators used to make the accused confess.[9] New scientific and intellectual ideas began to undermine belief in authority and in revelation, and thereby sowed doubt about magic and supernatural intervention, though it still proved possible to integrate ideas about spirits and demons into the new philosophy.[10] Areas which had suffered major panics were sometimes cauterized by the experience, ceasing ever to hunt witches again – though occasionally the legacy was another hunt a generation later.

Gradually, changes in the law sealed the end of the witch craze, but often, repeal of the statutes followed long after the last cases. In Britain, the statutes remained in place until 1736, while in south-east Germany they were not abolished until 1813.[11] As late as the 1760s, the question of the reality of witchcraft could still ignite a major intellectual pamphlet war in Bavaria and south-east Germany.[12] People did not entirely cease to believe in magic and witchcraft even when persecutions stopped.

But one reason why the witch craze gradually receded was a change in what people feared. As people no longer saw the hand of witches in death and disease, they ceased to fear old women as they had once done, and the shadowy fantasies which had once clustered around them lifted. The new world of enlightened sensibility had its own interests and dark obsessions, but they centred on childhood, sexuality and the way character developed through infancy and youth. The witch, who had never been just an old woman, but who could lurk as a rich and powerful man, a child or even a young woman, shrivelled into a caricature of herself, an old, toothless, fairytale hag to scare children.

Part One
Persecution

Chapter One

The Baroque Landscape

Germany in the epoch of the witch hunt was not a unified state, and did not become so until the nineteenth century. It was a patchwork of jurisdictions and political entities of varied size and structure. Obermarchtal, for instance, where Ursula Götz was accused, was little more than a village, the administrative seat of a minute territory governed by a monastery. Across Germany, ecclesiastical boundaries, areas of legal jurisdiction, lordship and political boundaries rarely coincided, a confusion that left its mark on the witch hunt. A bishop might be a secular ruler of one part of his dominion, with full judicial power, but wield only religious authority in other parts of his diocese and lack the power to instigate trials. It is striking that most of the mass persecutions took place in just such territories, lands ruled by Catholic prince-bishops.[1] A town, large or small, might enjoy the status of imperial city, with no overlord other than the Emperor, a judicial island in a network of surrounding territories. A village court might make its own judgments, the village jurors untrained in the science of law but schooled in local tradition. Or all such cases might have to be referred to the territorial overlord, where decisions would be made in consultation with university-trained jurists. Sometimes appeals to a higher court were possible, sometimes not; and while in theory cases might be appealed to the Imperial Court of the whole Empire, which sat at Speyer, this rarely happened in practice.[2]

Within Germany, witch hunts followed different patterns. In some areas, one, two or more witches were burnt every few years, a regular if always terrifying occurrence; in others, none were. But in some regions, mass witch hunts of extraordinary ferocity took place where hundreds and even thousands of individuals lost their lives. Under Ferdinand of Bavaria, in the electorate of Cologne (1612–37), 2,000 people were killed; Johann Georg II Fuchs presided over 600 executions during his decade in Bamberg (1623–33). Witch-hunting encompassed more 'routine' cases, each episode terrifying in the demonstration it gave of the power of the Devil to lead people astray, and mass persecutions where the fear of witchcraft scythed its way through an entire society, killing friends, neighbours and kin.

What made these complex legal and political boundaries dangerous were the religious passions of the period. The Reformation of the early sixteenth century had set towns and territories at war with themselves, as the new faith gradually established a foothold. In the wake of the victory of the Catholic Emperor Charles V over the Protestant Schmalkaldic League in 1548, a new territorial principle was established that linked politics and religion together: the religion of the ruler is the religion of the territory. In the years that followed, this was to lead to a series of fateful struggles between Protestantism and Catholicism as rulers underwent conversions, dynasties changed, or towns tried to reach accommodations between Catholic minorities and Protestant majorities. Then, in the second half of the sixteenth century, the Counter-Reformation began to win back ground in Germany for the Catholic faith, led by militant prince-bishops and powered by the intellectual energies of the recently established Jesuit order. These men saw themselves as fighting Satan's agents. The statue on the new Jesuit church in Munich, showing a victorious St Michael brandishing his sword over the defeated Lucifer of Protestantism, conveys their sense of urgency.[3] Protestants, for their part, believed that Catholics were emissaries of the Devil and that the Pope was none other than the Antichrist – later illustrated editions of the Lutheran Bible show the Whore of Babylon sporting the papal tiara as she rides the seven-headed beast of the Apocalypse.[4] Religious passions became all the more volatile because Catholic, Calvinist and Lutheran territories lay cheek by jowl. The godless enemies of salvation were not distant foes but neighbours, and so religious hatreds were murderously immediate as well as apocalyptic in significance. In some towns, these tensions were overcome and different confessions managed to live more or less harmoniously together; but if this equilibrium was upset, powers outside the town walls could rapidly exploit the situation. Dynastic accident or political turns of events might mean that a change of ruler brought a change of confession, which was then imposed on the population. Religious tensions had the potential to touch off far wider geo-political struggles, eventually culminating in the disastrous Thirty Years War (1618–48), in which Catholic, Lutheran and Calvinist armies from all over Europe fought one another on German soil, leaving cities sacked, villages destroyed, the countryside ravaged and thousands dead.

The hundred years from 1550 to 1650 was one of the most terrible periods in Germany's history. It was also the epoch of the witch craze. Witch-hunting began there in serious numbers in the fifteenth century, but went through something of a lull in the first half of the sixteenth century, years which also saw the Reformation. It was in the second half of the sixteenth century, as the Counter-Reformation began its advance and as the second generation of the Reformation (those who had grown up under a permanently divided Christendom) came to power, that the witch craze took off. Starting in the 1560s, witch hunts grew in numbers to reach a dramatic peak in the 1580s and

1. Illustration to Apocalypse 17, in *Das Newe Testament Deutzsch*, Sept. 1522.

1590s. This wave of persecution was followed by another around a generation later, in the 1610s, 1620s and into the 1630s, which saw mass hunts of extraordinary severity.

Why Germany? Germany was not the only region in Europe to hunt witches: there were outbreaks of large witch persecutions in Scotland, Lorraine, Sweden and even Essex in England, as well as ongoing trials of one or two witches every decade or so. It is very difficult to explain why witch-hunting in parts of Germany was so horrific and why it produced so many more victims. Global religious explanations will not work: in Germany, Catholic prince-bishoprics were the most fearsome witch-hunters, but in Catholic Italy, Portugal and Spain, where the Inquisition played an important role in trying witches, the numbers of deaths were comparatively small. Calvinist Scotland suffered a very serious witch hunt and Lutheran Sweden had a late outbreak of witch-hunting in which many children were involved.[5]

Across Europe, the image of the witch was remarkably consistent: she was an old woman, and she attacked young children. The vast majority of those

executed, around 75–80 per cent, were women. There were of course exceptions to this rule: in the very first trials in Switzerland, men outnumbered
women, but they soon fell behind; in France, the proportions of men whose
appeals against conviction for witchcraft were heard by the Parlement of Paris
were always high. In Normandy, the world was turned upside-down: there,
men made up three-quarters of those convicted, though many were actually
priests misusing sacred objects for weather magic.[6] But in England, as in
Scotland, witches tended to be old women who cursed their neighbours, killed
their cattle and made children ill when their requests for alms were not met;
in Italy, old hags killed babies and made men impotent; in Lorraine, they took
revenge on their neighbours for every petty slight.[7] In some areas, women
made up 90 per cent or more of the victims. The themes of the witch trials
recur with monotonous regularity across Western Europe, featuring sex with
the Devil, harm to women in childbed, and threats to fertility, all issues which
touch centrally on women's experience.

It was in Germany that these fears found their most terrifying expression
and resulted in the largest numbers of deaths. There, the image of the cannibalistic, death-dealing witch who attends sabbaths and brews up storms
reached its apotheosis as witch after witch confessed. The very fragmentation
of political and legal authority in Germany made it possible for panics to get
out of hand, while the intensity of the religious struggle, with the forces of the
Reformation and Counter-Reformation confronting each other directly,
nourished a kind of moral fundamentalism that saw the Devil's hand at work
in all opponents. But the form such fears took and the kinds of fantasy to
which they gave rise had a great deal to do with local conditions; with religion,
history and law in baroque Germany. To understand how such persecutions
could happen, we need to explore the landscape, both physical and mental, in
which they took place.

By the period of what we might loosely call the baroque, stretching from the
newly reinvigorated Catholicism of the Counter-Reformation to its apogee in
the early eighteenth century, German culture was characterized by intense
emotionality, a profound religious sensibility, and a predilection for extremes
and opposites. This era saw the building of churches that were overwhelming
in their forthright, totalizing theological vision of a supremely brilliant heavenly court and of depraved mortal man – not for nothing did these churches
show skeletons, skulls and even rats eating away at corpses. The profuse orna-
mentation and the rhapsodic elaboration of details drawn from nature spring
from the same mindset as that of the bureaucrats who documented the bizarre
outpourings of witches, producing huge lists of questions, dizzying in their
ambition to capture every detail of the witches' experiences. These men
recorded the responses of those whom they interrogated in page after page of
flowery handwriting, the gracious, energetic curves of the script mirroring the

extravagant Latinate language formed by their study of the classics and law. Princes and intellectuals created 'cabinets of curiosities' – collections including rocks and crystals, exotic objects from the New World, even unicorns' horns, in a promiscuous mixture of science and fable, the rational and irrational. Scientists, as fascinated by transformation in nature as were demonologists by the shape-shifting of witches, tried to turn base metals into gold; writers like Grimmelshausen penned vast, baggy epics, crammed with crowds of extraordinary characters as one incredible incident follows breathlessly on another, and fed the same appetite for the uncanny as did stories of witchcraft. Baroque culture aimed to interpret the whole world, the Old and the New; the natural and the supernatural; it revelled in cosmic statements about man's place in the world and the universe.[8]

Yet it was also a highly local culture. When Sebastian Franck came to describe Germany in 1534 as part of his ambitious ethnography of the whole world, he resorted to series of descriptions of local rituals, landscapes and beliefs in Franconia, Swabia and so on.[9] So too, when people sought divine grace they visited the shrine of a local saint, or attended the sermon of their local minister; and when they encountered the Devil, they met him on the road to the next village, or in their own parlour. We can only uncover the baroque sensibility of the witch craze in all its baffling contrariety by exploring how it worked at local level, by uncovering how people made the totalizing moral vision of the baroque into their own understanding of life in town, village or hamlet. For although it was a Europe-wide phenomenon, the witch craze only took hold by persuading people that the apocalyptic battle between God and Satan, man and the Devil, was taking place in their very own villages, that witches were dancing in the woods where they gathered their firewood, or holding sabbaths on the hills, or congregating under the very streets of their towns.

Some of the most serious outbreaks of witch-hunting took place in southern Germany, the cradle of the German baroque, in what are now the states of Baden-Württemberg and Bavaria. Together these regions were responsible for perhaps 9,000 deaths, over a third of the German total. To take just four contrasting localities from this region: in the prince-bishopric of Würzburg, upwards of 1,200 people were killed in one of the largest European hunts. The small rural Catholic territory of Marchtal in Württemberg saw a small, but, for its size, large number of victims and witnessed panics in both the 1590s and the 1620s. The medium-sized Lutheran town of Nördlingen executed thirty-five in the space of a brief but bitter hunt. Finally, even the large imperial bi-confessional city of Augsburg, which saw no witch craze, executed around seventeen witches over a timespan of seventy years. It was a grim period, and witch-hunting encompassed burgher and peasant, Catholic and Protestant alike. From the late sixteenth century to around 1630, Europe endured the 'little ice age' – a combination of perishingly cold winters and wet summers and autumns which brought bad harvests as the grain rotted. It must have seemed as if the four horsemen of the Apocalypse were on the loose, bringing war, hunger, disease and death.[10]

The formal legal framework for the witch hunt in the Holy Roman Empire was provided by the Carolina, the Imperial Law Code which Charles V promulgated in 1532, and to which he gave his name. It was the nearest thing to a system of law valid throughout the Empire. But justice remained local: each of the four areas featured in this book had its own legal code and was virtually sovereign in matters of criminal justice, and though appeals to the Imperial Court were in principle possible, they were rarely made. The Carolina itself provided the barest skeleton for proceedings against witches, even though it was perpetually cited by jurists throughout the period and into the eighteenth century in support of sentencing and punishing witches.[11]

All the Carolina stipulated was that evidence of harm had to be supplied before torture might be used and that witches deserved to be executed 'with fire'. Hardly a witch-hunter's charter, it gave no details about what witches might be thought to do. Its provisions, limited though they were, should have prevented the kinds of witch panic where denunciations by other witches were enough to convict a suspected witch: at least the Carolina insisted there must be evidence of the malefice the witch was alleged to have caused. Some regions issued special mandates against witches – Bavaria published a lengthy ordinance in 1611, when the worst excesses of its witch hunt were over. Other regions simply prosecuted using a mixture of precedent and adaptation of existing criminal procedure.[12]

One of the shocking features of the European witch craze is that some of the most highly trained lawyers and sophisticated intellectuals of the age were its keenest proponents. The brilliant lawyer and political theorist Jean Bodin (1529/30–96) provides a telling example. His *Six Books of a Commonweal*, written in 1576 at the height of the French Wars of Religion, attacks the idea that there can be any justification for revolt against authority and develops the idea of the state.[13] It remains a key text of political theory. Order in the domestic and political realms was one of his prime concerns, and he is famous for providing the philosophical underpinning of absolutist monarchy. Bodin also, however, wrote a work of demonology championing the most ruthless campaign against witches, and he took part in witch trials himself. A subtle thinker capable of works of the utmost intellectual penetration, he was a seeker after truth whose religious beliefs are hard to pin down – it has even been speculated that he converted to Judaism. But on the question of witchcraft he was unambiguous, a hardline persecutor, determined to root out the enemies of Christendom and the state and punish them with fire.

In Bodin's case, we have a rare insight into the inner world of a witch-hunter. He recorded a dream, which he includes in the chapter of his *Démonomanie des sorciers* devoted to the relationship between witches and evil spirits. After a lengthy discussion of the nature of the relationship between a witch and her demon, there follows an extraordinary treatment of its opposite, the relation between an angel and a human. Bodin relates how a good friend of his – or perhaps Bodin himself – was constantly accompanied by a good spirit, who would regularly wake him at two or three in the morning: 'Then he had the real dreams about what he was to do, or believe, concerning doubts that he had, or what was to happen to him.'[14] The spirit immediately informed him in his sleep if ever he did something wrong. Bodin also reports a dream of red and white horses which, he said, foretold the dreamer's future.

These dreams, whether his or not, clearly meant a great deal to Bodin, who was convinced that the world was a battleground between the forces of good and evil and who was ready to see each individual soul in dualist terms. Who better to assure you of the rightness of your course of action than your own personal angel, ready to police your dreams, settle doubts about the future and advise you whenever you deviate from the path of goodness? It is no accident that this passage appears immediately after his long commentary on witches and devils. Whether consciously or not, Bodin recognized the kinship of the angelic spirit to its opposite, the witch's demon.

The angel offered authority, and reassured him that he had not been sucked into the world of the witch. And well might the witch-hunter have craved such an assurance. After all, even the infamous work of demonology *Malleus Maleficarum* (or *Hexenhammer*, *The Hammer of Witches*), the so-called witches' handbook compiled in 1486 by Heinrich Kramer and the inspiration of Bodin's work, has it both ways: on the one hand, the *Malleus* reassures judges that they are invariably immune from the attacks of witches because they are carrying out God's work; on the other, it offers them a series of pro-phylactic religious rituals to ward off harm. They 'must not allow themselves to be touched physically by the witch, especially in any contact of their bare arms or hands; but they must always carry about them some salt consecrated on Palm Sunday and some Blessed Herbs'; the witch 'should be led backward into the presence of the Judge and his assessors. And not only at the present point, but in all that has preceded or shall follow it, let him cross himself and approach her manfully.'[15] As Bodin well knew, judges could certainly be subject to the vicious attacks of witches, and they might even succumb to the Devil's blandishments. After all, they were exposed to him on a daily basis when they interrogated his creature, the witch.

Witch-hunters were not psychological monsters, but individuals with astute psychological insight and even highly developed sympathy. Nicolas Rémy (1530–1612) was responsible for the deaths of over 800 individuals, most of them women, in Lorraine, but his published work of demonology, *Demonolatry*, well known and influential in Germany, is far from the vicious excoriation of the evils of womankind one might expect. What fuels the tract is his ardent concern to 'save' the witches' souls. Rémy was not a simple misogynist. A skilled story-teller, he recreates women's anxieties and records with some understanding the terrible dilemmas that made them susceptible to the Devil:

> They were preparing the instruments of torture in order to extract from Barbe Gilet (Huecourt, Sept. 1587) a confession of this crime, when she, looking calmly on, spoke as follows: 'What madness it is to suppose that you can extort a confession from me by force! For if I wished I could easily stultify your utmost attempts by means of the power which is at my command to endure every torture. But I gladly spare you all that trouble. For because my Master does not cease to importune me to deliver into his power my four young children which still survive of many that I have borne, I would far rather submit myself to the cruellest death if by that means I may save my little ones from such a miserable fate as I have myself suffered all this time. For if I am acquitted of this charge it remains for me to choose either to suffer an even more terrible death at the hands of my Master, or sorely against my will to perform his demands with regard to my children.'[16]

Gilet wished to be executed as a witch because she did not want to turn her children over to the Devil: here was a woman who gladly submitted to justice because of motherly love. By executing witches after their full confession, Rémy gave them the chance to die in a Christian manner, to escape their terrible service to the Devil, and to be saved. By recording Gilet's story, Rémy ensured that the world knew that this vile witch was at least redeemed by her maternal devotion. This, of course, was Rémy's sincerely held conscious belief about what he was doing, not his unconscious motivation. And this is his version of what Gilet said, not her own account. An explanation of what drove Rémy would have to start by recognizing that he was a man with deeply sadistic impulses against women. But he was also a sincerely pious Counter-Reformation layman with a striking capacity for empathy, even with lowly village women.

Bodin and Rémy were not isolated cases. What makes them unusual is not that they hunted witches, but that they wrote about it. Their works of demonology – rapidly translated into German – can give us some clue as to what may have motivated men like them.[17] In Germany, a small band of identifiable jurists and clerics are to be found at work in several of the major witch hunts: the jurist Johann Simon Wagnereckh (c. 1565–1617) and his ally the jurist Dr Cosmas Vagh, both passionate witch-hunters, managed to unseat the Bavarian court chancellor by means of an intrigue. These two men saw themselves as engaged in a divinely sanctioned battle against godless aristocrats who were soft on witches and lax on crime, and both advanced their careers in part through their pursuit of witches.[18] Witch hunts regularly crossed political boundaries because a single case might implicate witches in another territory: the authorities would then supply each other with relevant documentation, thus further fanning the flames of persecution. Like all early modern authorities, witch-hunters corresponded. Even executioners, some of the key protagonists in the witch hunt because they knew how to identify witches, met regularly to discuss interrogation techniques. Hans Vollmair and his son-in-law Christoph Hiert, hangmen from the small town of Biberach, became famous for their skill and were called in to help get witches to confess in a series of vicious witch hunts all over southern Germany.[19] At all levels, bureaucrats could give free rein to their obsessions with witchcraft while building their professional networks.[20]

But the most remarkable politicians of the witch craze were to be found amongst the Catholic prince-bishops. These men came from the leading noble and princely families of the region, and family politics often loomed large at their courts. Absolute authorities in religion as well as politics, they could not, of course, bequeath that power to their families: it died with them. Just nine such individuals were between them responsible for well over 6,000 deaths, a quarter of those who died in Germany as a whole over the entire period. Some made careers out of witch-hunting: Johann Christoph von Westerstetten cut his teeth as prince-provost on the witch hunt in Ellwangen and then went on to preside over a major witch hunt as Bishop of Eichstätt.[21]

One of the nine prince-bishops was Julius Echter of Mespelbrunn, ruler of Würzburg. He was determined to win back his territory from the Protestant heresy. Behaving like the model reform bishop according to Trent, he sent his representatives to conduct a painstaking visitation of the diocese in which the level of religious standards, church attendance, knowledge of the fundamentals of the faith, and behaviour of the clergy were all investigated. Julius Echter established the university which bore his name and sought to raise standards of education and conduct among the clergy. Systematically, he re-established Catholicism in the territory and won the city of Würzburg back to the old faith through a combination of Jesuit-led missions and outright banishment of some who refused to convert. He started the programme of building that would eventually make Würzburg one of the most beautiful of the southern German baroque cities, and began the remodelling of the parish churches of its territory in line with the new religious aesthetic, their pointy red towers permanently altering the skyline. He modernized the administration of the territory and gave his name to the new hospital in the town, the Juliusspital, famed for its particular concern with the mentally ill, as well as with orphans, pilgrims and the sick. The symmetrical architecture of the Juliusspital, its

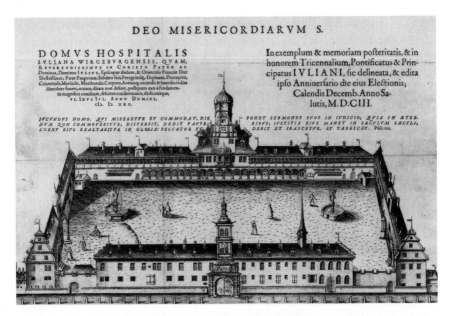

2. Johann Leypolt, the Juliusspital, 1603, copper etching based on a painting by Georg Rudolph Henneberg.

regular courtyard and elegant colonnade reflected his preferred vision of Christianity as ordered humility. The bishop himself liked to spend time there and he helped distribute food to the pensioners and washed their feet on Maundy Thursday. When a book commemorating his thirty-year reign was published during his lifetime, it featured a dedicatory page with four female figures embodying his virtuous achievements. One is Misericordia, compassion; and her shield carries a depiction of the Juliusspital.[22]

One might expect that such sensitivity to the poor and to the plight of the insane, a group often excluded from the reach of charity, would incline Bishop Echter to regard the ravings of women accused of witchcraft with sympathy, and to consider such women objects for compassion rather than for the machinery of justice. But such was not the case. Not long after the reimposition of Catholicism, Echter presided over a massive witch hunt. Three hundred witches were reportedly executed in the last year of his reign alone.[23] Because of the scale of the outbreak and the loss or destruction of many of the documents, we will probably never know with certainty how many died in this panic, one of the largest yet seen in Europe. Echter's passionate devotion to the Virgin Mary, his banishment of women from his court, his strict imposition of celibacy on his clergy and his determination to hunt witches were surely connected. This was a man who, like Rémy and Bodin, saw women as especially prey to the Devil's wiles, and who believed that female lust could

3. Title page of
*Encaenia et Tricenalia
Juliana*, the commem-
orative volume to
honour Bishop Julius,
with copper etchings
by Johann Leypolt,
1603.

undermine social and religious order; indeed, could destroy Christendom itself. He was also a man who idealized womankind in the shape of Mary.[24]

These were only the beginnings of the witch craze in Würzburg. The persecutions continued vigorously under Echter's successor Bishop Johann Gottfried von Aschhausen (1617–22). During the reign of Philipp Adolf of Ehrenberg (1623–31) the panic reached its height, even striking into the heart of the bishop's own administration: the former examiner Dr Johann Friedrich Burkhardt was accused of being a witch, and some of those accused claimed to have seen the bishop himself at the witches' dance; 219 of those executed during his reign came from the town of Würzburg itself. There were accusations that witchcraft was afoot in the Juliusspital. Allegations exploded in this closed institution, developing a dynamic of their own, and between 1627 and 1629, 160 people were executed, including 41 children.[25] Witch hunts of this type had much in common with panics in another kind of enclosed institution – convents. The most famous of these occurred in Loudun in France in 1634, the subject of Aldous Huxley's novel, *Devils of Loudun*.[26] As this panic scythed its way through the hospital's inmates, individuals who did not

4. Portrait of Julius Echter, 1587, oil
painting.

remotely fit the stereotypes of the witch found themselves convicted. And
towards its end, the panic began to encircle the clergy themselves. Now clerics,
a group who had been centrally involved in the campaign against sin and
witchcraft, were named as witches, and as many as fifty of them, including
prominent, well-educated members of Würzburg's city clergy and vicars from
the cathedral, perished in forty-two public burnings between 1627 and 1629.
Towards the end, over half those being burnt were clergy, most of them of
apparently exemplary life: to the watchers, it must have seemed a world turned
upside-down, where the Devil had corrupted even those who had appeared to
be the most doughty fighters against sin, ignorance and Protestantism.[27] In all, a
staggering 900 people were reportedly put to death for witchcraft during
Ehrenberg's reign, and only an imperial mandate of 1629 put a stop to the trials.
Even then, witch persecution continued on a reduced scale until the advent of
Bishop Johann Philipp von Schönborn (1642–73), who was persuaded by the
work of the Jesuit Friedrich Spee of the innocence of those executed.[28]

Whatever the importance of individual witch-hunters, an individual alone
could not carry out such a hunt. The witch hunt in Würzburg was pursued by
a whole cohort of Counter-Reformation clergy and legal advisers, who had
little in common with the peasants they ruled. There was bad weather and
poor harvests in 1600, 1616 and 1626. It must have seemed as if Würzburg's

authorities were being confronted with the overwhelming, urgent needs of a rural world suffering hunger, disease and death. No wonder apocalyptic visions of a society under assault from the Devil made sense. The inhabitants of this rural nightmare were the people the Catholic Reformation wanted to educate, weaning them off their pagan superstitions, shielding them from the poison of Lutheran heresy and teaching them their catechism. They were the 'European Indians', as one Spanish Catholic theologian put it, linking the campaign to convert the inhabitants of the New World with the attempt to Christianize Europe's own rural masses. Ironically, the witch craze in Würzburg, far from being an expression of authoritarian rulers riding rough-shod over their cowed populace, was at first an attempt by officials to take seriously peasant fears concerning sick cows, outbreaks of hail, mysterious insects and various diseases. As the panic reached its height, witches began to be interrogated and executed in Würzburg or with the advice of Würzburg officials even when they were actually subject to local courts. Here, the fact that a central court oversaw the verdicts of local authorities did not damp down the witch craze, as it often did elsewhere in Europe, but added fuel to the fire.[29]

5. Matthäus Merian, Franconian Circle, 1648: this shows most of the territory of the bishopric of Würzburg.

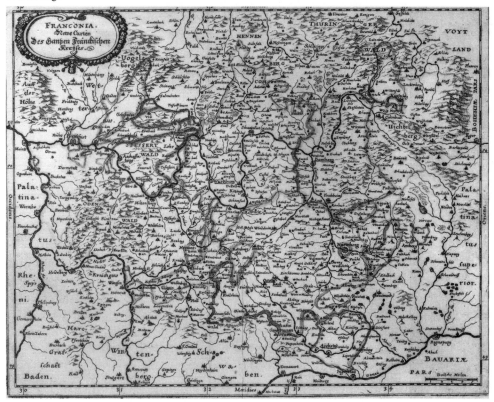

6. The town of Würzburg during the time of Julius Echter: woodcut from the
Cosmography of Sebastian Münster, Basle 1550.

Pressure to carry out the trials in Würzburg came not only from the bishops
and their administators but from the populace itself. It could often be difficult
to know quite what was afoot in the distant corners of the sprawling territory,
several days' ride away from the bishop's palace at Würzburg. The land ruled
by the bishop encompassed very different kinds of social units, from the
myriad small villages and hamlets, many with fewer than a hundred inhabitants, to small towns like Karlstadt or Gemünden, through to the
medium-sized town of Würzburg itself.[30]

In 1627, in the town of Ochsenfurt, rumours about witchcraft had
involved the allegation that a child had been eaten; while just a decade
earlier, a midwife had been questioned on suspicion of witchcraft.[31] Later
that same year, 150 citizens gathered in force to complain about 'the enemies
of their livelihood, and vermin and witchcraft',[32] demanding that action be
taken. The mayor and Council were strictly forbidden by Würzburg to
engage in any further assemblies. But they took matters into their own
hands, and arrested those they thought were to blame for the bad weather.
One girl died after being tortured and then 'sleeping' for twenty-eight hours:
she was buried in unconsecrated ground as if she were a witch, even though
she had not confessed. By June 1627, five more were in prison, and one
woman was not let out until 7 September, after enduring four rounds of

torture. During one of these, her right arm was ripped out of its socket 'with a great crack'.[33] In a case like this, the bishop's administration was simply unable to prevent a witchcraft trial. Popular outrage about what was perceived as the bishop's failure to act was enough to generate the potent threat of an uprising against Würzburg's rule. Rumours of cannibalism and fears about the weather and pests came together in general panic about witchcraft, which the bishop could not afford to ignore.

In this chaotic landscape, the rulers of Würzburg had to provide a framework that would order, explain and purify. They replaced lynchings with judicial process; they explained how the witch's mundane malice formed part of the divine struggle against Satan; they identified and executed the witches who were to blame. They translated the amorphous fears of the peasants into an organized, exhaustive questionnaire for suspected witches that omitted no element of the witchcraft fantasy. Just as the baroque church of the Catholic Counter-Reformation gave architectural order to the profusion of peasant belief, lining up the multiplicity of shrines and cults into a coherent vision, so also the baroque structure of the witchcraft interrogation gave shape to peasant fears about witches. A full witchcraft questionnaire could, by the seventeenth century, run to well over a hundred questions, dealing systematically with each aspect of witchcraft, from feasting on infant flesh, to dishonouring the Host, weather magic and harm caused to animals.[34]

Nor did belief in witches die out with the end of the mass trials. In 1744, a woman was questioned at Würzburg on suspicion of having caused a boy to be possessed. He had sneezed out three wolf's teeth through his nose, and fox's teeth, dog's teeth, nails, knife blades, straw and even leather had turned up in his snot, urine and excrement. These were all the old signs of real, physical possession, paraded in their usual lurid form. As late as 1749, the seventy-one-year-old nun Maria Renata Singer, sub-prioress of the convent of Unterzell near Würzburg, was condemned in an infamous case.[35] She was executed, her body was burnt to ashes and her head was impaled on a post looking towards the Unterzell convent. The Jesuit Georg Gaar preached a sermon on this occasion, defending the need to burn witches and insisting that Maria Renata had forsworn the Devil and had prepared for a good death. The aftermath of the case unleashed debate amongst intellectuals which finally undermined the witch hunt in educated circles in Bavaria, a process long since accomplished elsewhere.[36] But the episode did not mark the end of accusations. In 1769 a Catholic woman aged thirty-one who started talking about the experience of sex with the Devil in great detail was – by a strange twist of fate – confined in the Juliusspital. Fortunately for her, she was found to be free of witchcraft but 'confused in imagination and weak in understanding'.[37] There cannot be one single explanation for the witch cases in the prince-bishopric of Würzburg. Some followed the more usual patterns of village witchcraft, others sprang from tensions in civic institutions, while yet others owe more to the psychology of interrogation and persecution itself.[38]

The territory ruled by another religious institution, the Premonstratensian abbey of Marchtal, looks on the face of it like Würzburg writ small. It spanned little more than 15 kilometres north to south and was mostly a corridor about 5 kilometres wide stretching from the valleys of the upper Danube to the high plateau of the Federsee lake. On horseback, it could be traversed comfortably in half a day. As in Würzburg, a religious figure acted as both religious and political ruler. Marchtal, like Würzburg, felt the impact of the Counter-Reformation and the tiny town saw a renovation of the monastery church, which was given imposing new baroque altars to house its relics.

The size of the territory, however, made a difference to the experience of rule. In Marchtal the monks of the monastery often worked as parish priests in the small villages. They knew their flocks more intimately than the noble prelates of Würzburg knew theirs. The monastery was the main landowner in the area; its farm leases were each named after a saint. The abbots were locals, tending on the whole to come from the immediate area around the monastery – few, even in the years following the Counter-Reformation, had been educated at university or had visited such engines of the Counter-Reformation as the Collegium Romanum in Rome. The institutions of government in Marchtal were under-developed, indeed perhaps shambolic. It did not even have its own hangman, and had to hire one from Biberach, the nearest town. Biberach was self-governing, an imperial city. It was bi-confessional, and Lutherans outnumbered Catholics there. When Marchtal peasants went to Biberach's market for supplies, they came into contact with the new religion, and saw a town with a learned, cultured civic middle class.[39]

The first witch hunts in Marchtal formed part of a wave of persecutions in the region of Swabia, spreading right through Württemberg and beyond. They put the small territory's judicial system under immense strain, as notaries had to record hours of confessions and take statements from witnesses. This was more crime than Marchtal had ever seen: 46 witches condemned in the decade 1586–96, in a territory of around 700 inhabitants.[40] In the villages of Alleshausen and Seekirch alone, 13 people went to their deaths. The confessions which have survived are summary documents that give little sense either of village life or of full-blooded Satanic revels. It is as if the scribe lacked the time or patience to note it all down. In the 1620s, again in a clear echo of witch-hunting patterns outside Marchtal itself, at least five more people lost their lives.[41] The persecutions, though far less severe, unearthed persistent witch beliefs in the area which did not result in trials. It is also apparent that the village headman went about encouraging suspicion by taking people through a list of leading questions about witchcraft. Suspicion was long-lived and tenacious. Long after the witch craze in most of Germany was well and truly over, in the Age of the Enlightenment, the region saw an outbreak of

7. Map of Marchtal, 1796. The villages of the territory look like bunches of grapes on a vine, the branches all sprouting from the monastery of Obermarchtal at the bottom. The Federsee Lake can be seen top right, and below it, the villages of Alleshausen and Seekirch.

witch-hunting in which five people died; and a decade later, women were still being interrogated. Several of the women who lost their lives in the panic of 1747 came from Alleshausen and Seekirch, the very same villages which had been hotbeds of witchcraft allegation a century and a half before.

Most of the victims of the craze were women, but men also found themselves accused, especially during the course of a large panic like that in the area ruled by the Prince-Bishop of Würzburg, where there were well over a thousand victims. Though there were clear patterns amongst the women, it is very difficult to discern patterns amongst the men. However, it is striking that many were married or related to women who were accused of witchcraft. In the territory of Würzburg, the proportion of male victims was between 20 and 25 per cent, and we know that at least half of these men were related to women tried for witchcraft. So, for example, at Gerolzhofen, five men from the Kern family were tried, one of whom fled, while twelve Kern women were also caught up in the witch panic. These men seem to have become involved because their female relatives had been burnt for witchcraft, tainting the whole family.[42]

A very different pattern emerges in the subset of cases from the town of Würzburg itself, the bishop's seat, where men made up a large proportion of those tried: 120 women were tried but so were 90 men, and there were 45 children who also became caught up in the trials, most of them from the Juliusspital. Here the involvement of men seems to relate to the particular dynamics of the panic in the town, which in its final stages turned against the city's clerics, so that even senior clergy from leading churches were accused of witchcraft, and broadsheets alleged that Würzburg priests were baptizing babies in the Devil's name.[43] Other male victims included council members, former mayors, nobles, other members of the ruling elite, and civic syndic Dr Johann Friedrich Burkhardt, who had been actively involved in the interrogations at Grünsfeld and Lauda.[44] These two episodes reveal much about how a witch hunt could explode in a closed institution, or how it might even attack the group from which the interrogators were drawn. The character of these cases is unlike the bulk of the trials in the territory of Würzburg.

In the other trials considered in this book, the association between witchcraft and gender was much closer. In Nördlingen, where 34 women lost their lives, there was only one male victim, and he was married to another victim; in Marchtal there were 54 women and two men; while in Augsburg there was only one man amongst 17 individuals executed. The two men from Marchtal were not only guilty of witchcraft: Hans Hepp was condemned for many crimes, including fish-poaching and murder, and witchcraft was not the main accusation against him; while Conrad Merck also confessed to committing bestiality.[45] Overall, therefore, it seems that cases against men may be connected less with features of masculinity than with the dynamics of the trials themselves. This is not the case with accusations against women, which do form clearer patterns related to age and gender.[46]

Why so many women were executed demands explanation. The answer lies in what witches were believed to do: attack fertility. This theme emerges repeatedly in witch trials, though the form it took in town and country was slightly different. In rural areas, witchcraft encompassed the entire natural world, as witches brought harm to crops, and illness and death to humans and animals. Witches attacked the fertility of the earth, the animals and people. They were in league with midwives to harm the newborn. In Würzburg, witches were known as 'milk thieves'; for they stole milk from animals just as they disrupted mothers' nursing. Witches from towns tend to have left fuller confessions, making it possible to try to recreate in more detail the emotional conflicts and dilemmas from which accusations grew in more detail. It is far harder to penetrate the mentality of small village trials – indeed, the historian is in something of the same position as the puzzled bureaucrats who compiled the records, faced with the collective silence of villagers who had their own sense of the workings of the supernatural and their own apprehensions of the divine.[47]

In towns, witchcraft tended to centre more on harm caused to people, especially to young infants and women in childbed. As the witch craze gained a grip on the city of Würzburg itself in 1627, the figure of the midwife played a key role: the 'crafty midwife' is listed amongst those condemned, and the scribe has added in the margin the comment, 'The whole business comes from her.'[48] One midwife confessed to killing 50 mothers and children; another, to having killed over 200 newborn babies by pressing in their skulls. These horrific crimes placed them in the annals of the worst mass murderers, like Herod's pitiless soldiers slaughtering the innocents.

These fears can be seen at work in the witchcraft cases in Augsburg, even though the city only experienced a series of episodic witch trials, never a witch panic. On the eve of the Thirty Years War, Augsburg reached its peak. A metropolis boasting over 45,000 inhabitants, it was one of the largest cities in Germany, drawing large numbers of countryfolk into its walls to work as servants. Famed for its baroque churches, its splendid string of civic fountains and its new town hall, completed in 1620, Augsburg was a centre of printing, culture and scholarship. Gold and silversmiths produced ornate, intricately worked plate for an international market; clockmakers' and instrument-makers' products were exported around the world. It was a powerful imperial city that could still play a forceful political role, even as the towns were being gradually eclipsed by the principalities and dukedoms that could call on greater resources and had the military muscle to survive the Thirty Years War.

The city had little rural territory outside its walls, but the world of the peasants impinged upon it none the less. Many of its inhabitants had grown up in the countryside; peasants converged on its markets; rich urban families like the famed banking family, the Fuggers, owned landed estates beyond the town; while townsfolk of all social classes went to the country for recreation, for trips to taverns, for shooting matches or dalliances. Religiously, the town was split between Catholics and Protestants. A Catholic minority, which included many of the town's patricians, shared government with Lutherans and many civic posts were parcelled out to be undertaken by both a Catholic and a Protestant. The Bishop of Augsburg, whose seat was in Dillingen, had a residence and officials in the town; his church courts claimed jurisdiction over Augsburg Catholics in marital matters. Lutherans were governed on religious matters by a synod of Protestant clergy covering Augsburg alone, with a superintendent chief pastor.[49]

In the late sixteenth century, Augsburg did not hunt witches, and though there were trials for the illicit use of magic, the city executed no one for witchcraft until 1625.[50] Yet the surrounding region under the jurisdiction of the Bishop of Augsburg saw a serious wave of trials beginning in 1586 in which 150 people were put to death.[51] The city fathers were too concerned with trying to keep the peace between the rival confessions that preached in the same town

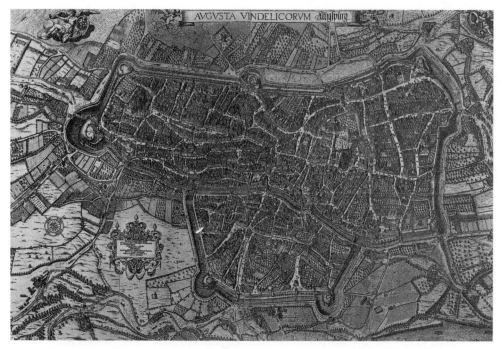

8. Wolfgang Kilian, *A bird's-eye view map of Augsburg*, 1626, copper etching of 9 plates.

to engage in witch-hunting. Superstition, it might have seemed, was what separated town from country.

Such a conclusion would be deceptive. Magical belief and witchcraft suspicion certainly existed in the town as well; and in the second half of the seventeenth century, a small but steady stream of witch trials began. In total, seventeen individuals were executed. As many again were interrogated and released, leaving aside one episode that focused on the orphanage in the second decade of the eighteenth century. Nearly all the cases took place after 1650, as the city was recovering from the ravages of the Thirty Years War in which it had lost as much as a third of its population. Sometimes two or three witches, who were either related to one another or whose stories interlocked, might be executed together. But the kind of momentum seen at Marchtal or Würzburg did not develop. Instead, each case unfolded at its own pace, leaving the historian with a very full record.[52]

In Augsburg, too, we find men like Julius Echter or Jean Bodin, with the same lethal combination of moral fervour, sensitivity to suffering and psychological acumen. But we find them amongst Protestants as well as Catholics. Radical Lutheran Pietists could be equally convinced of the reality of witchcraft and just as determined to extirpate it. A vigorous Pietist like Gottlieb Spitzel of Augsburg, who also corresponded with Leibniz, wrote with some acumen on the upbringing of children and was well aware that children tended to mistake dreams about the Devil for reality. Tough on sin, he had a lively sense of the motivations of the human heart. But this also inclined him not, as one might expect, to ponder the effects of the emotions on the behaviour of humans, but to persecute evil in the shape of witches. He was even convinced that children might be witches. The formative experience of his life was probably his encounter with Regina Schiller, a young woman who claimed she was possessed and had made a pact with the Devil – she could even produce copies of the document signed in her own blood. Spitzel became her spiritual adviser and for many years vainly tried to free her from the snares of the Devil. But his very public failure to do so seemed to underline the inferior nature of Lutheran clergy, who could not perform the exorcisms that a Catholic priest could undertake: a bitter pill to swallow in a town where Catholics and Lutherans lived side by side. For the rest of his life he was obsessed with the question of how young women like her might fall prey to the Devil and how they might be freed from Satan's snares with the help of sympathetic pastors such as himself. In fact, of course, it was precisely pastoral attentions of this kind that helped suck such young women into the emotional morass where they could be accused of witchcraft, as Schiller herself eventually was. Even contemporaries could grasp what made Spitzel tick: one woman he accused of witchcraft had the wit to sack him as her personal confessor. She shrewdly taunted him: 'I am not that Regina-witch'.[53]

Yet though the psychological susceptibilities of individuals were important, witch-hunting in Augsburg was a collective endeavour. Any councillor might find himself interrogating a witch. We can only guess at what this experience might mean for the councillor concerned. In Augsburg in 1689, Councillors Theodor Ilsung and Justus Breuning questioned Juditha Wagner, a young girl who was accused of killing her half-brother and half-sister by means of witchcraft. The trial was highly emotional: Wagner's father testified against her, Juditha claimed to see the Devil in the interrogation chamber itself and the final two key interrogations of Juditha and her father took place on Christmas Eve. Juditha herself consistently and emotionally appealed to the councillors as merciful 'lords' and even begged them for death.[54]

Ilsung was a Catholic patrician, a scion of one of the oldest Augsburg families; Breuning, a Lutheran, belonged to the next social group who intermarried and socialized with the patricians. As in all criminal cases in this city, men of opposing religious faith had to learn to work together. Ilsung and Breuning had joined the Council in 1682, Ilsung after some experience on the town court. Classic middle-ranking functionaries, neither made much of a political career.[55] Interrogations like these must have given these ordinary councillors an unforgettable sense of what it meant to be a 'city father', invested with the ultimate power to punish and shouldering the supreme paternal responsibility, their office a reflection – if pale – of God himself. Here they were being asked to act in place of a father who had manifestly failed to discipline his daughter. Whether the experience made them confident patriarchs or seared them emotionally forever we cannot tell.

Lutheran Nördlingen, by contrast, was a town that witnessed a short but ferocious witch hunt. But unlike the hunts at Würzburg or Marchtal, most of the victims were from the city's elite.[56] Again, particular individuals seem to have played crucial roles. By a striking coincidence, the trials began in the year Johannes Pferinger, a new politician on the make, first held the office of mayor in rotation, and he remained mayor in rotation during the entire period of the craze.[57] Pferinger had joined the Council only five years before rising to its highest office, but he had had to wait until the age of fifty-one before becoming a councillor. Perhaps he wanted to get back at the wives and relatives of the councillors who ran the old oligarchy, some of whom were named or interrogated as witches. Several women described seeing a devil seated in a large chair, wearing the mayoral chain of office. It may be that they were trying to point the finger at the mayor as the real source of the diabolic conspiracy; if so, this did not work and Pferinger was never accused of witchcraft. Dr Sebastian Röttinger and Dr Wolfgang Graf, legal consultants in the town, sat in on interrogations which resulted in the execution of thirty-four women and one man, many from the families with whom they socialized. Röttinger is commemorated by an elaborate memorial on the wall of the single parish church, St George's, which features a painting of the sufferings of Job, while above stand female statues depicting Tenderness and Justice (two further figures depicting Faith and Innocence have been lost).[58] Though it may seem so today, the memorial was not ironic. Witch-hunting was a natural expression of his work to defend the innocent and further justice, just as it was for the Catholic Bishop Echter.

But the individual psychology of mavericks like Echter, Bodin or Pferinger does not explain the witch craze. In Augsburg and in Nördlingen, councillors were assigned to witch cases in strict turns. In Nördlingen, around a dozen councillors, every functionary eligible for the job, carried out the interrogations in rotation in the panic years of 1589–90 and 1593–94;[59] Mayor Pferinger himself did not attend. All the councillors were therefore collectively responsible for the deaths of thirty-four of their fellow citizens as witches.

What sort of town could purge so many wives, widows and daughters of its own leading citizens? Nördlingen was a medium-sized town, home to between 7,000 and 11,000 inhabitants in the 1580s. It was a free imperial city and, as such, it was subject directly to the Emperor and boasted its own law code. In its centre stood the town hall, to which an elegantly sculpted Renaissance stairway was added in 1618, shielding the heads of the councillors from rain or snow as they filed into the council chambers. A Latin inscription reminded them to leave behind 'at the threshold passion and violence, anger, hatred, friendship and partisanship. For as others find in you a just or unjust judge, so also must you experience and endure the judgment of God.'[60]

9. Nördlingen viewed from the Kaiserwiese, from *Der curieuse Passagier*, Frankfurt and Leipzig 1725.

Nördlingen's skyline was dominated by St George's, the main parish church, staunchly Protestant since the early years of the Reformation. But the town lay in the middle of the Ries plain, where there were territories ruled by several lords, principal amongst them the counts of Öttingen: Ludwig XV had become Lutheran but his son Friedrich took the lineage of Öttingen-Wallerstein back to Catholicism, leaving the family divided ever after. There were Jewish communities in the Ries, though the town's own Jews had been banished at the beginning of the sixteenth century. Monastic institutions like Kaisheim Abbey or the Teutonic order still retained houses in the city to deal with their tenants in the Ries, a substantial Catholic presence in the Lutheran town. Monks living in the collection house of Kaisheim Abbey were allowed to celebrate Mass.[61] Though the town might at first have seemed religiously, economically and politically self-contained, secure in its city walls, appearances were deceptive. As well as containing buildings which belonged to Catholic institutions, the town also had jurisdiction over some 500 or so peasant heads of household in its own rural territories. Some of those who were caught up in the witch persecutions of 1589–94 were in fact from the countryside.[62] And Nördlingen's hunt proceeded in an atmosphere of panic about witches, as the nearby Catholic Counts of Öttingen-Wallerstein carried out large persecutions.[63]

Scratch the surface of even such an apparently sleepy oasis of religious conformity as Nördlingen, and a seething world of magic and fractured religious legacies appears. The generation imbued with the values of the Reformation and Counter-Reformation planned to change all this. Catholics and Protestants alike attempted to impose religious orthodoxy on their subjects, to inculcate doctrinal knowledge and train a generation of disciplined clergy. They aimed to punish prostitutes and rid the world of harlotry, to crack down on adulterers, to shame pregnant brides, to prescribe death for infanticidal mothers. Both saw these campaigns as a war against Satan, and witch-hunting as a natural extension of the fight. Not all of our demonologists' contemporaries shared their views on witches: part of the vigour of these men's attacks came from their sense of belonging to a beleaguered minority who understood the peril their society faced better than the common herd.

Yet in spite of the militant hostility between Catholics and Protestants, there were similarities in the lines both took on witchcraft. A Jesuit demonologist like Martin del Rio could at one moment spout the purest confessional bile, relating stories about how the Devil had caused Luther to suffer from diarrhoea, or how 'in Geila in Brabant, when Luther died, evil spirits flew from those they had possessed to Luther's funeral', but he was not above lifting the work of a Lutheran demonologist like Johann Gödelmann wholesale when it suited his purposes.[64] Protestants and Catholics both shamelessly plundered the work of the pre-Reformation demonologist Heinrich Kramer in his *Hammer of Witches*. Both confessions were obsessed with magic. Indeed, so taken up with it were they that the Calvinist Christoph Zimmerman spent his entire life railing against the superstitious practices of his rural congregation, in the process providing the historian with a superb ethnology of peasant magical practice. He suffered one of his most bitter defeats when, despairing of his hopelessly ineducable flock, he suffered a mental collapse – only to find his parishioners engaging in magical prayer at three pulpits simultaneously to ensure his recovery.[65]

The Catholic Del Rio was equally critical of magical practice, and his compendious *Six Books of Investigations into Magic* (1595; 1599–1600) sets out in considerable detail the varieties of magical and superstitious behaviour of which he disapproved, from touching one's teeth while reciting 'a particular verse of the Passion from the Gospel' to finding a thief by marking a glass with the sign of the cross.[66] His massive tome functions as a virtual encyclopaedia of the vast range of contemporary practices of magical healing and divining. Nor was Del Rio the only demonologist to fall into such a trap. Reginald Scot, an English Protestant gentleman, wrote *The Discoverie of Witchcraft* (1584) as a powerful assault on the belief in witchcraft altogether: at least Del Rio's text remained safely in Latin. Scot systematically set out what he held to be the erroneous prayers, spells and practices of those who dabbled in the magical arts. To convince the reader, he described what they did in detail to demonstrate once and for all just how foolish and superstitious their actions were. He would surely have turned in his grave to discover that his work was the most commonly owned volume in the libraries of seventeenth- and eighteenth-century

English conjurors. By a miraculous irony of history, Scot's book accomplished the task of transmitting in print the recipes of occult magical tradition to succeeding generations.[67]

For Protestants, Catholics were superstitious because they believed that the sacred could be manifest in objects in the material world. Lutherans held that the elements of bread and wine truly became Christ's body and blood, but they did not revere them outside the moment of communion. Calvinists held that the bread and wine only signified the body and blood of Jesus, who could never be reduced to mere material substances. Protestants abolished the wealth of blessings, processions, pilgrimages and holy objects. With a sharper sense of the distance between the natural and supernatural world, Protestants fought magic and Catholic belief because both epitomized this mistaken understanding of the sacred. To them, Catholic belief was a species of magic. But Protestants found it difficult to shift their view of the divine, as their own frequent lapses into magical thinking show. For example, Lutherans were happy to recount the story of the magical picture of Luther which refused to burn when Luther's birth-house went up in smoke, because this proved the truth of Luther's doctrine. Protestants could treat family bibles with the reverence that Catholics might accord relics.[68] It proved hard to give up entirely the idea that the sacred could inhabit objects.

For Catholics, the issue of magic was even more tricky. A Catholic demonologist such as Del Rio was just as concerned as Protestants to combat popular superstition. He chastised those, for example, who blamed witchcraft when they were afflicted with passionate love for another person. As Del Rio explained, love magic required the tacit agreement of the victim to work, for the passions can only be swayed with the individual's free will. Here, Del Rio seems to be debunking the idea that love can be caused by enchantment, and suggesting that accusations of love magic are the last refuge of the scoundrel. But he also believed that the Devil could move the passions, and recounted how the Virgin Mary had miraculously freed a man who had made a pact with the Devil to win a woman's love. Del Rio's catalogue of superstitious and magical practices is as compendious an assault on popular error as the Protestant diatribes. Yet he also maintained that the Church had an arsenal of sacred objects, blessings and pious practices which were efficacious against witchcraft. What was difficult was knowing where to draw the line. On the one hand, he commended the young lover who had carried out penance for three days, fasting, wearing a hair shirt and praying prostrate before the Virgin at Loretto; on the other, he condemned the use of magical prayers, such as praying for a sick person on a Friday while making them face east. Because witchcraft posed the question of the nature of magic, it also forced Catholics to define the central features of their faith, the nature of the divine and the power of Mary. Witchcraft raised issues that lay at the heart of religious identity.[69]

But it was not only the passions arising from the clash of Protestants and Catholics that shaped the religious sensibilities of the witch hunt. Witchcraft beliefs were also connected to much older and more amorphous beliefs about Jews, beliefs which latched on to inchoate fears about magic, blood and sacrifice. Many contemporaries believed that Jews were a magical people who knew how to work wonders with the Word and practised secret cabbalistic rituals. Anti-Semitism had a long tradition in southern Germany, and it could be closely linked to venerating Mary. In 1519, when the entire community of Jews in Regensburg was killed or banished from the city, a pilgrimage church honouring the Virgin was built on the site of the demolished synagogue. A woodcut by Michael Ostendorfer illustrating the Regensburg pilgrimage shows the statue of the Beautiful Virgin outside the church on a pillar. Around her pilgrims flock, and the sick, in various attitudes of distress, pray for healing. A mother sits at the foot of the pillar, cradling her sick child as she appeals to the merciful Mother of God for aid; a pious virgin folds her hands in devout prayer in the foreground of the image; while in the background one can make out the remains of the Jewish ghetto.[70] It was common for chapels and churches dedicated to the Virgin to be built on sites that had formerly belonged to Jews, and in Nuremberg, Bamberg and Rothenburg ob der Tauber, Marian chapels were built where the synagogue had once stood. In the market-place in Würzburg, a chapel to Mary was begun on the site of the former synagogue in 1377, its tower completed in 1479.

Adulation of Mary, hatred of Jews and witch-hunting: all three can be found under Julius Echter. The Juliusspital itself was built on the site of the Jewish cemetery, despite the vigorous protests of the Jewish community. An oil painting of 1611 shows the bishop attending the baptism of three Jewish converts in the chapel of the hospital dedicated to St Kilian, patron saint of the diocese. 'Christian charity', we might say, was to be confined to the body of Christians. Indeed, in this case the institutionalization of charity rested not only on forcibly dispossessing the Jews, who were viewed as enemies of the Gospel, but obliterating the traces of their community's past and their collective dead. Another central plank of Echter's programme of re-Catholicization throughout the bishopric was pilgrimage; in particular, pilgrimage to the Virgin. Echter made the Marian shrine of Dettelbach the most important pilgrimage church in lower Franconia, building a new, imposing church to replace the old Gothic structure in 1610–13. The church was consecrated in 1613 on the Feast of the Virgin Mary, when 4,000 pilgrims assembled in seven special tents.[71] Marian devotion, charity and powerful anti-Semitism thus fed off one other. Mary, the Mother of God, represented mercy and inspired charity, but she could also become a vengeful mother towards those who, like the Jews, denied the divinity of her Son. This was a dynamic that dated back to the expulsions of Jewish communities from southern Germany in the fourteenth and fifteenth centuries.[72]

10. Michael Ostendorfer,
*Pilgrimage to the Beautiful
Virgin of Regensburg*, 1520.

Catholics did not hold a monopoly on anti-Semitism. In 1574 in Protestant Strasbourg, for instance, a woodcut was published about a Jewish woman from Binswangen near Augsburg who had supposedly given birth to twin piglets, a miracle which according to the author proved the stubborn blindness of the Jews in refusing to recognize Christ. The Jews were sunk in fleshliness and sin, 'smeared in sow-grease', and the piglets were a sign of their true lubricious nature. This crude polemic mixed the genre of wondrous birth pamphlets, a common theme of sixteenth-century woodcuts, with the staples of anti-Semitic polemic. It is an inversion of the libel that Jews are suckled by sows and eat pig-shit, an old myth which was also drawn upon in anti-Protestant polemic of the time (and revealed the depths of Christian ignorance of Jewish beliefs and taboos).[73] The illustration shows the mother recovering in bed with an attendant while in the foreground a Jewish woman with a prominent nose displays the two piglets; on the left, Jewish men bury the hideous offspring. Here, Jews are linked to deformed births.

Such themes could mutate, forming new lethal combinations. In Nördlingen, the witch hunt drew on the old idea that Jews stole Christian children to torture and kill them so that they could use their blood in Jewish holy rites.

11. Bernhard Jobin, *A Jewess Giving Birth to Two Piglets*, 12 Sept. 1574, in Binswangen, c. 1574.

Stories like these were some of the most potent and enduring myths of anti-Semitism, and they had sparked off bloody riots against Jews for hundreds of years, leading to lynchings and to the expulsion of entire Jewish communities. Jews had been expelled from Nördlingen in 1507. But they had not disappeared from the region around the town, and communities of Jews still lived in the

12. Christopher Murer, *Allegory of Good Government and the Justice of the Nuremberg City Councillors*, 1598, stained glass (detail).

Ries.[74] What happened in Nördlingen, as in many other places, was that these hoary stories were reworked into tales about witches, who became suspected of killing and devouring children. Nor was this connection unique to Nördlingen. In Nuremberg in 1598, the Council commissioned a stained-glass window as an 'Allegory on Good Government and the Justice of the Nuremberg City Councillors'. It depicts a scene of ritual murder where a knife-holding Jew, about to kill the Christian child, is assisted by a witch.[75] Just as torture had played a key role in getting accused Jews and heretics to confess to the most heinous crimes, so too in the case of witchcraft, the process of interrogation began to take on a momentum of its own and new groups of people admitted to carrying out foul deeds and plotting against Christianity.

The witch-hunters of the baroque saw themselves as soldiers, sworn to fight the Devil and his minions, and as Christians entrusted with the duty of saving witches' souls. They saw no contradiction here. They belonged to generations formed in the years of bitter religious antagonism between Catholic and Protestant, when unremitting struggle against the forces of evil was integral to the religious imagination on both sides of the confessional divide. When individuals with highly developed consciences, with tendencies both to adulate and to denigrate women, or with an overweening sense of their own importance as judges were let loose, the result could be witch hunts of extreme ferocity. But though the intensity of religious division may help to answer the question why the witch hunt was concentrated in Germany, it does not tell us why whole communities could become convulsed in witch-hunting, denouncing neighbours and accusing relatives of the same faith. It does not explain how the religious imagination of the baroque could develop a persecutory dynamic. And it does not explain why this persecuting mentality chose women as its object, or why fertility became its central obsession. To understand how this happened, we need to examine the process at the heart of the witch craze: the interrogation.

Chapter Two
Interrogation and Torture

In 1595, Gertrauta Conrad from the village of Ober Wittighausen, widow of Kilian Conrad, confessed how the Devil had come to her dressed 'in a black hat, with a black feather, during the day on her meadow'. He had demanded that she should do his will, and she had acceded, the first time in her chamber, the second in her kitchen in a corner. His sexual organ was cold. He had given her 15 shillings, half a *batzen* and three kreuzer, which she kept in a corner in an old butter churn, and her servants knew nothing about it.[1]

Torture played a key part in driving women to confessions like these. We can sometimes get an inkling of how they were extracted in the occasional cases where the scribe noted how torture was applied and then remarked on its effect. Gertrauta Conrad's account of her dealings with the Devil came after several earlier interrogations. This particular session had begun without torture, and Conrad had been stoutly denying that she was a witch, rejecting all the accusations put to her. As the scribe notes, she was then left hanging on the rack from eight in the morning until 1 p.m., presumably when the interrogators came back from lunch. This was unusual enough for the scribe to record it. At this point, he notes, she said that she had learned to fly.

This confession was not directly connected to the specific points on which she was being interrogated, and it was not a clear statement that she was a witch. It seems to reflect a state of dissociation and alienation from her own body, most likely the result of the tortures she had endured. The rack or strappado was used commonly in witchcraft trials, normally for specified intervals of a quarter or half an hour. The victim would be suspended from the rack, her arms tied behind her back and lifted above her head, her shoulders pulled back until they might become dislocated from bearing the weight of her whole body, and the pain would be intensified by attaching weights to her feet. Presumably – given the five hours she endured – Conrad had been just left hanging, without weights. Flying is a physical experience in which the normal limits on what human bodies can do no longer apply. Mystics, under the inspiration of divine visions, might also levitate. The suspension, both mental and physical, involved in flight might well express what it felt like to endure this kind of torture, literally unable to touch the ground.

After this, the scribe notes, Conrad did not know what to say. Even in the scribe's rushed notation, her disorientation is palpable. She continued, 'one should read out to her the articles to which Apollonia Crafft confessed, she would confess it', as if she was proposing to confess whatever this fellow-accused woman had admitted. To the modern reader this seems to prove that the woman's 'confession' was gained by breaking her will through pain, to the point that she renounced her own individuality along with her wish to live and agreed to confess anything at all. She was forced to use another woman's script because she had no idea what she needed to tell her interrogators to get them to stop.[2]

Yet her interrogators would not have been content with a recitation of another woman's story of witchcraft. In this case, interrogation would almost certainly have continued for further sessions until Gertrauta Conrad had supplied a long and distinctive narrative of her life with the Devil, but the full record of her interrogation does not survive.[3] In the eyes of the scribe, this prolonged period of torture was the turning point in the interrogation. The outcome – her confession – justified the use of an exceptional technique. He was able to record it in detail because he had no reason to anticipate the sceptical response of a later generation. As he would have seen it, torture enabled her tongue to be loosened. It allowed her to escape the power of the Devil, first by confessing that she had indeed learned to fly; then by supplying detailed, convincing accounts of her encounter with the Devil (how could she have made up that detail about keeping the Devil's money in the old butter churn?), and ultimately, by confessing she was a witch. As her interrogators saw it, this transformation of the witch's stubborn spirit into a willingness to co-operate was for her own good. Only then might she be saved, by confessing her misdeeds as a witch and so weakening the Devil's power over her. Only through confession and execution could she be reconciled with the Church.

The problems historians face in dealing with such material are reminiscent of those historians of Stalinist Russia encounter in relation to the 'confessions' made at the show trials. Convincing and detailed as their narratives might be, they were clearly the product of psychological and physical torture. They were designed to relegate the accused to the ranks of non-persons, enemies of the people; and as evidence of 'real' plots against Stalin they are useless. But unlike at least some of the Stalinist judges, witchcraft interrogators were generally not cynical about the process of getting confessions. Though they had a rough idea of what witches normally did, they relied on the accused witches to furnish the story of their experiences with the Devil. Witchcraft confessions do not report real historical events. They do, however, tell us what their hearers believed that witches did, and so they help us to understand why the interrogators were so passionately determined to root out the terrible sect of witches.

Immense judicial effort was expended in extracting a full confession from the accused witch. Judicial procedure was dominated by Roman law and the legal code of Charles V, the Carolina (1532), and on the continent it was based not on the balance of probabilities as determined by a jury but on the confession of the accused criminal.[4] This was the most certain proof. It meant that the convicted felon had to provide a confession of his or her crimes; and so the criminal had to go a certain way towards agreeing to his or her own execution, or at least, had to appear to be doing so. Torture was an inherent part of the entire judicial system, not a feature of witch hunts alone. It was in theory not to be used indiscriminately, but only when there were 'strong indications' of the guilt of the accused, including material evidence. Any admission made under torture had to be confirmed later in the absence of torture.[5] Judicial authorities, the executioner and his assistants who carried out torture, and the scribes who recorded what was said were all used to carrying out 'painful questioning', as it was known, and they were also aware that torture might lead people to make false confessions. They saw torture as a means of arriving at the truth, not as a cynical system for forcing people to confess whatever was needed. The widespread conviction that pain freed the tongue of the criminal was a cornerstone not only of the legitimacy of the witch hunt, but of the entire legal edifice of the time.[6]

Witchcraft confessions often amount to detailed life histories of individuals, their motivation and the reasons for their 'fall'. The extensive, psychologically detailed confession was not new. Confessions of this kind can be found in the case records of many criminals, including in particular prostitutes, cross-dressers and sexual offenders of all types, especially women, and they existed even before the Carolina had established clear procedures for this type of questioning and for the use of torture. Culprits would be asked about their parents; about who had first seduced them; where and when intercourse had taken place; what they had been promised. In this way, accused women gave information that enabled the authorities to construct a basic personal profile explaining why she had fallen into sin, whether her mother had pressed her into prostitution, who had first corrupted her, whether it was love of money or material goods which had led her astray. Early sixteenth-century questioning techniques thus anticipated the sophisticated psychological probing to which witches would later be subjected as the witch hunt accelerated later in the century.[7] They also created the judicial framework in which women talked about sex with the Devil: had marriage been promised? Had she been seduced, and how? Had her mother been present? What had the Devil given her?

Confessions mattered so much in the case of witchcraft because the criminal acts could by definition not be witnessed. The stories about flight with the Devil, diabolic dances and sex with the Devil had to come from the

13. Questioning the accused; in the background, the execution scene. Woodcut illustration to the second edition of Spee's *Cautio criminalis.*

witch's mouth, or from fellow witches, for only participants in the diabolic assemblies could observe such things. And because witches harmed in secret, strewing their poison where it might least be expected, one could only presume that there was a connection between a meeting with an alleged witch and a later misfortune. It was up to the accused witch to confess that her diabolic lover had made her carry out an act of malefice.

In many of the interrogations it is apparent that the techniques of questioning and of torture were designed to bring the accused witch to a crisis, when she would finally admit at least an element of guilt. It was believed that the Devil would assist his minions to withstand torture without confessing. Torture therefore had to be applied until her resistance collapsed. When Barbara Stecher was interrogated at Nördlingen in 1590, the application of torture brought her to beg for a day's grace before she confessed. The next day, after torture, she would confess only to a small fraud; and when interrogation resumed three days later she would confess to nothing and asked for a further day's grace. Next day, after a fruitless morning, she asked for a drink 'so that she could say it', and then admitted that she had given diabolic salve to a little boy who had died. In the following three interrogations, however, she denied this story, which her interrogators put down to her 'obstinate persistence and denial'. They continued interrogating her with alternate use of the boots and thumbscrews, and finally the bench. The thumbscrews were usually the first

resort of the executioner, particularly in the case of women, because they produced only localized pain. But they could be applied until the blood ran. The
legscrews, or boots as they were known in Nördlingen, used the same technique but imprisoned the whole lower leg, and could result in serious injuries.
Torture on the bench involved tying the accused to the bench and whipping
her.

In the case of Barbara Stecher, after all three methods had been tried, they
ceased interrogations for nearly two weeks. Another week later, she at first
confessed to killing three children with her salve, but when she was tortured
on the bench yet again, she recanted the confession they had just prised from
her. The next day, she was hauled up on a rope, with her arms twisted behind
her back and her shoulders carrying her full weight. Now she confessed to
seeing the Devil in the night on the meadows near a mill, but nothing followed
on this promising beginning. In the subsequent session of interrogation she
confessed merely to the theft of two gulden thirty years ago, and no more was
to be got from her, even though she was drawn up on the rope no fewer than
four times. A repetition of this torture the following day brought the confession that she had given her child a powder against mites, and that he had died
four days later. Yet though she confessed that the Evil One had made her do
it, this was still not a proper witchcraft confession. It was not until two days
later, in her fifteenth interrogation, that she finally produced a story about her
seduction by the Devil, a confession made without the use of torture. From
then on, she produced a series of long narratives about her life as a witch, all
given without any use of torture, as the scribe triumphantly noted.[8]

It is evident that the interrogators deliberately left Stecher alone for long
periods, and then built up tension by carrying out question sessions daily,
sometimes in both the mornings and the afternoons. They resorted to a range
of different types of torture, from methods involving the compression of parts
of the body, to repeated use of suspension and painful stretching. In theory,
there was an order of degrees of torture, designed to progress through grades
of pain in a systematic manner, known and accepted throughout the Empire
by jurists and by the executioners who carried out torture. The first degree
consisted in merely exhibiting the instruments of torture and ordering the
accused to confess. Often, however, especially during witch-hunting panics,
these meticulous rules were overridden. In any case, each executioner had his
own knowledge and predilection for certain types of instruments. Probably
more important than orderly progression through the degrees of torture was
the use of particular kinds of instruments, the alternation of methods, and the
conscious use of intervals between bouts of torture.

In addition to physical pain, witchcraft interrogations exploited the
psychological disorientation brought about by confinement for unlimited
periods in darkness without a clear sense of the passage of time. The nature

of imprisonment varied from place to place. As private businesses, jails relied on a good deal of contact between the prisoner and the outside world: relatives might even be expected to feed the prisoner. Where a special prison was built to house witches, as it was in 1618 in Würzburg,[9] rumours were rife and accused witches could readily discover what others had confessed. Jailers also played an important part in advising the accused on what to say or in letting them know what others had confessed. They were also charged with reporting on the behaviour of the accused to the authorities. Very occasionally the records give hints of the role they played, and of the nature of the relationship that could build up between warders and witches. In eighteenth-century Augsburg during a panic where a number of children were accused of witchcraft, the children began to confide their stories about flight to the witches' sabbath to the prison warders. In another early eighteenth-century case there, a young girl who confessed to witchcraft was clearly receiving advice from a sympathetic jailer's wife on what not to say under interrogation.[10]

When an admission was not forthcoming, torture might develop a brutal dynamic of its own. As late as 1747 Magdalena Bollmann of Marchtal was interrogated on suspicion of witchcraft. She did not confess. Since it was determined that there were sufficient indications against her to license torture, the thumbscrews were applied. In subsequent interrogations, Bollmann was tortured with thumbscrews, on the rack, and on the 'bock', the bench on which she was stretched and whipped. She was stripped and shaved, and needles were inserted into areas around her genitals to see if she experienced sensation. Subsequently, her genital area was discovered to be quite swollen. Torture continued. On 16 October, ten weeks after torture had first been used, she was found apparently unconscious and half dead. She sat in front of the judges' chair for the space of two Our Fathers saying nothing, with a 'rigid body'. To rouse her from her insensible state, the interrogators 'found themselves forced to double the strokes with the blessed whip'. When this brought no results, they tied her arms with a rope and dragged her on the floor and down the stairs. At 2.30 on the same day, it was reported that she had been found 'stone dead' in her cell. Her body was burnt as that of a witch and the ashes buried under the gallows, the most dishonourable place possible, as an additional punishment (and to confirm that the allegations against her were true). The historian can only conclude that the interrogators had determined to torture the woman to death since she would not confess. Yet throughout, they represented their behaviour as a religious act. They hung her up, her hands tied behind her back, and let her hang there 'for the duration of five or six Our Fathers', and burnt her with the blessed Easter candle 'partly under her nose, partly under her two big toes'. The way in which they employed holy objects looks less like confidence in the sanctity of their office than an attempt to employ the counter-magic of the Church to shield themselves, not only from the power of the Devil, but also from a full awareness of what they were doing: they could believe they were carrying out religious rituals, not inflicting pain.[11]

The case of Bollmann is extraordinary, unusual both in the late date at which it occurred and in the savagery with which torture was applied. It is not, however, unique. In Nördlingen in the sixteenth century, at least one woman died from the effects of torture without having fully confessed; but she was buried as a witch all the same because the 'indications' against her were so strong. Yet there are examples of accused witches who managed not to break under torture. Maria Holl of Nördlingen resisted sixty-two applications of torture and her steadfastness eventually undermined the basis of the Nördlingen panic. Since she would not name accomplices, she brought the hunt to a standstill. But she was not the only woman from Nördlingen who managed not to confess. Seventeen other accused women withstood torture and thus apparently satisfied their persecutors that they were innocent. They too were let free.[12]

Yet even once an initial admission of guilt had been secured, the interrogation was not over. The process of building a coherent and, to a certain degree, consistent account of the individual witch's experiences with the Devil now began. In some places, such as Augsburg, this could take many sessions, as each varied account proffered by the witch was compared with her previous answers and the reports of her accusers until a story was arrived at to which all parties – the authorities, the witnesses and the witch – could assent. A trial for witchcraft usually lasted around six weeks, but might take many months or even years.

Only in conditions of mass panic did trials become summary matters, and even then, trials in Nördlingen, Würzburg or Marchtal still took several weeks. In Würzburg it is not possible to be certain how many of these confessions were extracted, for the sources we have mostly provide a 'clean', systematic, organized account of the witches' life, summarized in accord with a standardized pro forma document. It appears as if the confession arrived in flowing, organized form over a brief period of interrogation. This could not have been the case, as we know from the sheer confusion of the way in which confessions were usually gained. The tortuous process of denials, argument, altered stories, contradictions and repeated questioning through which the witch's confession was normally developed has been smoothed out here, in all likelihood, at the end of the trial. In sixteenth-century cases from Marchtal, for instance, just a page or two of 'protocol' sufficed to record the confession and condemnation of a witch, but by the eighteenth century each accused witch from that territory generated hundreds of closely written pages. So formalized had procedures become in seventeenth-century Augsburg and eighteenth-century Marchtal that each point of information was carefully numbered and

14. Torture: in the foreground, the application of the 'boots'; in the background, 'stretching'. Woodcut illustration to the second edition of Spee's *Cautio criminalis*.

checked back in a painstaking routine. First the witnesses would be questioned, then the accused, then the replies would be put to the witnesses, until a sufficient degree of consistency was attained. Yet consistency was only ever a matter of degree. In every witch's interrogation there remain pieces of the story which are left unfinished, small inconsistencies, slips and contradictions.

The desire to find out the truth and to uncover yet more detailed information about the Devil is evident throughout the interrogations. Only rarely, during mass panics, did questioning become a matter of routine. There was always more to find out about the Devil: aspects of his appearance or details of his habits which were novel. The interrogators did not terminate the interrogation when they had enough of a confession to justify an execution but continued until the witch had confessed all she knew. Even then, her confession had to be freely confirmed in the absence of torture.

As the work of the seasoned witch-hunter Nicolas Rémy from Lorraine shows, they incorporated what they learned from interrogation into their knowledge about the Devil. Rémy was sure that the idea that the Devil could make women pregnant was 'ridiculous', but it was unquestionably true that the Devil could sweep men up in whirlwinds and convey them through the air, a fact attested by his own experiences and the confessions of numerous witches.[13]

Even the most diehard interrogator could never take belief in witchcraft for granted among the people of his jurisdiction. There were always counter-voices, muted though they often were: a preacher preaching against the trials in Nördlingen, a husband in Eichstätt convinced of his wife's innocence and determined to sue the authorities who had imprisoned her without cause.[14] The attitude of scepticism towards witchcraft was not an invention of the Enlightenment, but was present throughout the witch hunt.[15] Witch-hunters struggled with the demons of doubt. Not all a witch said might be true. The Devil, the master of lies, might lead her to make false denunciations.

Above all, the witch's confession had to convince the interrogator. She had to provide those details which only she could know. Her description of the Devil had to be vivid enough to persuade interrogators that she really had encountered him, and to do this, she had to incorporate her story about the Devil into the tissue of everyday life. This is what makes the confessions such remarkable documents. To an extent, they conform to the broad out-lines of what a sound grounding in the principles of demonology might have led one to expect a witch to say. But they are peppered with detail drawn from the witch's own experience and coloured by her own emotions, like the old butter churn where Gertrauta Conrad hid the Devil's money from her servants, or the meadow where she met the dark stranger. And they empha-size parts of the witch fantasy which were not necessarily those which demonology stressed. In turn, demonology changed in the light of witches' confessions. After all, it was to a large degree a science founded on the evi-dence of experience.

Those normally present at a trial varied in accordance with the legal custom of each area. In Augsburg, for example, criminal trials were on the whole con-ducted by two interrogators. A scribe was present; and the executioner who carried out torture, sometimes with an assistant, was called in when appro-priate. In Nördlingen, groups of council representatives would frequently interrogate together in groups of two or three, Dr Graf, the Council's legal adviser, attending most of the interrogations. In Würzburg, Dr Georg Diettman was an aficionado of witch trials, attending many. It is possible that the 'Dr Kolb' whose name occasionally appears is the same Dr Kolb who was a driving force behind the large witch trials in Eichstätt, moving on in 1628 to the service of the counts of Öttingen-Wallerstein and finally to the employ-ment of the Duke of Bavaria. He made a substantial career out of witch-hunting.[16] In local trials, particular combinations of interrogators are noticeable, though they did not follow a rigid schedule. For a time, in Würzburg and Eichstätt, special standing witch-hunting commissions were set up, and these small groups became expert in how to judge a witch, accelerating the panics. Sharing experience of this order must have greatly strengthened the bonds between interrogators, giving them an almost intuitive knowledge of how their colleagues would react to each admission or denial of the witch. It also gave them a heightened sense of their mission.

Such an audience of men, probably dressed (with the exception of the executioner) in the sombre black favoured by men of mature years in powerful professional positions, must surely have overawed the accused witch. Nicolas Rémy, who worked as a judge in the trials at Lorraine, remarks on how demons often turned themselves into men of good standing, wearing the black cloak 'such as is worn only by honoured men of substance', so as to seduce the gullible more easily. It is as if Rémy were at some level aware of the possible confusion between the 'men of authority' like himself dressed in black, and the Devil, whose colour it was. How was the witch to know that her interrogator was not himself Satanic?[17] Indeed, it seems likely that for some witches, their confrontation with the judges may have led them to tell stories about a devil dressed in just this way, whose authority brooked no demur. Sometimes the judges' own awareness of their judicial majesty and divine function may have made them sensitive to any assault on their position. In 1744, towards the end of the witch hunt, one judge in Würzburg complained that witches had been stealing his wig. For him, this was no laughing matter. There could hardly have been a better symbolic item to steal: the wig, worn by all officials, was not peasant garb. By the eighteenth century, it was their wigs that made the faces of the elite look different from those of the rustics whom they ruled.[18]

The other key participants in the interrogation process were the hangman and his assistants. A dishonourable person, the hangman could pollute by his very touch. Executioners' children were banned from entering honourable trades, and they could only marry people who were also dishonourable, like knackers or hangmen's assistants. As a result, dynasties of executioners developed, linked by blood and marriage. They might be social pariahs, but executioners could make good money. They had a strong sense of self-confidence and professional mastery. The executioner of Nuremberg kept a diary in which he proudly listed all the judicial executions he had carried out, complete with brief descriptions of the felons' crimes, while in eighteenth-century Augsburg a local beadle kept count of all the executioner's handiwork and published his tally.[19] Where interrogators wore sombre colours, hangmen were renowned for their bright, flamboyant clothing.

Hangmen from all over southern Germany gathered at key trials in the late 1580s, and this meant that advice and information about witches was exchanged.[20] Just as some jurists specialized in witch-hunting, so also some executioners became involved in a series of witch hunts, developing careers and reputations in the process. They too might fear witches. Margareta Strenger confessed that she had attacked the wife of the executioner, Master Hans from Biberach, notorious for his involvement in witch-hunting over the whole of southern Germany. She had passed her hand over his wife's stomach, attempting to kill the child in her belly. Margareta's mother had been executed as a witch, so she had every reason to retaliate; and the executioner had every reason to expect her revenge. In Augsburg in 1685, the executioner's arm withered when he tried to execute a witch.[21]

To be convicted, a witch usually had to be brought to confess.[22] But the signs of witchcraft could also be found on the witch's body. These signs were the province of the executioner. In Würzburg, the mere threat that the executioner would shave the witch's body and investigate any apparent marks was often enough to precipitate a confession.[23] It was not only the dread of what might be discovered, but also the touch of the executioner that terrified: women feared being exposed to a dishonourable man, and knew that his touch would make them socially dishonourable too. There was clearly a sexual element as well, for diabolic marks were often found around the genital area. One desperate woman suspected of witchcraft in Augsburg even visited the hangman herself, to ask whether hers were witch's marks or not.[24] In Nördlingen, Barbara Stecher resorted to self-help techniques: she pricked the mark that she found on her foot 'to test whether she was [a witch]'.[25] It was believed that the demon could secrete himself in the folds of a witch's clothing, enabling her to withstand the interrogators or even do them harm. She had, therefore, to be undressed. One's craft, marital standing and class could all be read from one's clothes, and so taking off a witch's clothes also stripped her of social status. She might then be dressed in special clothes designed to humiliate while she was interrogated, or even left naked.[26]

The interrogators did not themselves inflict pain on the suspect. They merely determined when torture was appropriate and what degree should be applied; and even this decision was often not in their hands but was set out beforehand by the Council. Perhaps this occasionally led the accused witch to distinguish between the executioner, who caused her pain, and the interrogator who wanted to know all the details of her life. Certainly some witches seem to have thought of the interrogators as protective father figures, an attitude which complemented the councillors' own vision of themselves as city fathers, responsible for the good of all their subject citizens. When the witch was psychologically broken by torture, this might lead her to develop a bond with the torturer himself. Euphrosina Endriss begged not to be executed by the visiting executioner from Memmingen, but rather by the local Augsburg executioner, because she knew him.[27] Or she might make no distinction at all between interrogators and executioners, spitting at them, cursing them – expressions of impotent rage which confirmed the interrogators' view that they were dealing with Satanic forces.[28] When women retaliated in such a physical way, breaking the taboos on normal modest comportment, the interrogators could hardly remain untouched by the experience. Extreme physical and emotional states were part of the routine of witch-hunting.

15. Exorcism of an accused witch as part of the interrogation procedure. Woodcut illustration to the second edition of Spee's *Cautio criminalis.*

In Catholic areas, interrogators constantly made use of holy objects while they exercised their sacred role as judges sworn to defeat the enemies of Christendom. In Eichstätt, the bells were tolled during interrogation. (Church bells were known to have power against the Devil: they would be rung during thunderstorms to protect crops and animals from witches' sorcery.)[29] Trial proceedings there began with the executioner ordering the accused to strip naked, cramming 'consecrated salt in her mouth, as much as he can hold between two fingers' and giving her holy water and baptismal water to drink.[30] In Würzburg, interrogators would often start a session of questioning by asking the witch to cross herself, or by checking that she knew her prayers. If she was unable to make the sign of the cross, or could not say the prayers, it was a strong sign of her guilt. Such practices were also a form of counter-magic, protecting the interrogators from evil influences. Convinced that they were engaged in a battle against the powers of evil, their every act and question carried a religious significance, inclining them to see signs and miracles everywhere. Anna Zott was given holy water to drink, causing her to confess that the Devil had come to her in her cell only yesterday. This miraculous loosening of her tongue could be ascribed to the dose of blessed water she had received.[31] Ursula Götz was given holy water in cooking and to drink to see whether she would vomit it up, a sure sign that she was a witch.[32]

The Devil himself might visit the witch in prison and attempt to make her recant the confessions she had made. Prison officials watched for every sign of his presence. So for instance the prison officials in Augsburg noted how one young woman was having sex with the Devil by means of a candle. In Obermarchtal, the Devil appeared to Rosina Baur and instructed her not to confess.[33] Just how intense the emotional involvement in the case might be, and how all those who questioned a witch might become convinced that they were engaged in a divine mission, is evident in a miracle reported from Würzburg in 1590, during the interrogation of Anna, wife of Hans Schinleder. Her lover the Devil appeared to her just before dawn, saying he would take her off to the woods to a secret spot by a hollow stone where he would have his way with her. As the scribe notes, there was indeed such a hollow stone 'underneath which many rascals used to hang out years ago, but no more than a hundred people know the place'. It was clear what the Devil was up to: he must have wanted to kill her at the desolate place. But, the report continued, 'God, who created the soul and who suffered for her did not want to have this, and he put it into our minds that we should go into her cell at 5 a.m. to commence the inquisition whereas normally we do not begin before 7 a.m.'[34] Anna Schinleder probably wanted to commit suicide. Because the bureaucrats were so intensely absorbed by her case, they interrupted their normal procedure. This, in their view, allowed them to foil the Devil and rob him of his victim, saving her for the execution pyre.[35]

Accused witches might also attempt to understand the trial as a divine drama. Some tried to comprehend the pain they were experiencing as an imitation of Christ, in which they shared in His sufferings. In Protestant Nördlingen, when Katharina Keßler was bound and put into the 'boots' or legscrews, she said 'she must suffer and reign with Him'.[36] She used the interrogation to express her guilt and sorrow about minor sins she had committed, especially about her feelings towards others. Maria Schöpperlin insisted on her innocence and said that God should help her to endure the torture; Apollonia Aißlinger said 'she would to God that she could rip open her heart, so that the Council could see it, she knows that she is innocent, and will commend herself to the authorities and above all to God'.[37]

Other accused women, however, felt despair and alienation from God. These feelings were in themselves a sign, proof that they had forfeited God's grace. In such cases, the sense of being abandoned by God convinced the women that they were damned, and this often precipitated them into confessing to witchcraft. The same woman might alternate between religious exaltation and despair. After she had been tortured, and had implicated another woman, Apollonia Aißlinger said 'her heart felt heavier and heavier, it was a heavy thing. She could find nothing more in her heart, she was sorely troubled. She prayed always that God should come with His angels and make everything right.' She trembled in her whole body, could not lie, eat or drink, and was worried that if she had falsely accused the other woman, then 'she might become damned, or be damned [already]'. Four days later, she began her interrogation without torture, screaming and raging wildly that 'she could not believe anything, she did not know whether God was with her or not. She had done nothing, she just could not believe in Christ, or pray an "Our Father". There were thoughts in her heart, she was damned, damned, damned, and even if she screamed Jesus, it had no effect.'[38] To her interrogators, all this was proof that torture was effective in overcoming her heaviness of heart and leading her to confess. They continued to torture her in further sessions of interrogation to get more names and details from her, even after she had admitted that she was a witch.

It is tempting to presume that the interrogators had no human fellow feeling with the witch; that they regarded her as less than human. Detachment might be thought necessary for one human being to inflict such pain upon another, and in the end to order the killing of a person who was, after the weeks it took to try a witch had passed, an individual they knew well. Certainly the beliefs of the interrogators led them to view the witch as a member of the Satanic sect, sworn to do harm to her fellow Christians. Beliefs of this kind, one might argue, could predispose a judge to reckon such men and women to be literally beyond the pale of the Christian community and so make him capable of inflicting such treatment on them.

Yet this would be to miss the degree of moral commitment required of a witchcraft investigator. The interrogator had a high view of his sacred office, which was to save the soul of the witch by bringing her to renounce Satan and confess her sins. This was true of criminal trials in general, which were concerned not only with retribution and 'making an example' to warn others against sin, but also with ensuring that the fullest confession possible had been made, so that the individual might attain salvation. The interrogator's role was like that of a priestly confessor. In the case of witches, who had given themselves to the Devil, the fight for the soul of the witch became paramount. When the interrogator attempted to 'loosen her tongue', he was fighting Satan, the diabolic adversary who desired at all costs to prevent the witch admitting the truth. To rescue the witch and extricate her from Satan's clutches, the interrogator was therefore compelled to use the instruments of pain. This was a craft. The interrogators had to know when to repeat a question, when to insist on an answer, and when to desist.

It might seem paradoxical that one and the same person could be both a compassionate philanthropist and a ruthless witch-hunter. Yet witch-hunting may have required a particular kind of empathy. Those who had a certain sensitivity to the mental states of others, who had the capacity to enter into their emotional worlds, often made the best persecutors. They had to take seriously the concerns of peasant communities about soured milk, blighted crops and stricken beasts, to listen to the stories of the victims of the witch and respond to their suffering. Their capacity to sympathize with the victims of witchcraft provided the most powerful impetus to witch-hunting; a psychological trait which could lead the same individual, like Bishop Julius Echter of Würzburg or Sebastian Röttinger in Nördlingen, to make benefactions to the poor and outcast and to hunt witches.

Good interrogators created a relationship with those they interrogated. They did so not only by asking the witch questions and listening to her responses. Unconscious communication between the two was vital to eliciting the confession and to creating the kind of atmosphere in which fantasies of this dark and lurid kind could be developed. To understand what drove witch-hunting, therefore, we have to understand the psychology not only of the witch, but also of her interrogators. Both were needed to produce a confession.

No witch hunt can be attributed to a single individual. Executions for witchcraft require at least the tacit support of a section of the populace prepared to denounce a witch and send her 'to the raven stone', the vivid name for the execution block. They required the participation of a series of political, legal, medical and ecclesiastical professionals, each of whom played an essential part in the trial procedure. And yet the interrogator's role was peculiarly important.

At the heart of the witch craze lay the unequal and ambivalent relationship between the interrogators and the suspect. It was a brutally unequal partnership. The interrogators shaped the story that the witch confessed, even if they did not consciously believe themselves to be doing so; the witch, though she provided the substance and detail of the material, was not free to provide any narrative she liked. Consciously or unconsciously, she learned what she had to say.

The nature of this relationship has long fascinated observers. For Freud, who noted with amusement the similarities of his own relationship to his hysterical patients with that of the witches' inquisitors as he first began to develop the science of the 'talking cure', it was obvious that emotional participation was required on both sides.[39] The therapeutic uses to which this dynamic of identification and emotional attachment could be put prompted him to develop the theory of transference and counter-transference, which remains a helpful tool for understanding how an accused individual and interrogator might together provide a witch 'fantasy'. The projections of the accused on to the interlocutor allow deeply buried emotional experiences to be expressed. As she or he begins to know the interrogator and unconsciously to identify with his needs, so it becomes possible for her to produce the kind of story he wants to hear. In the case of the witch interrogations, we are seeing not an attempt at healing, but a collusion with a destructive fantasy which will result in the accused's death.

Yet this does not quite capture the dynamic of interrogation. What took place was connected with the psychology of sadism. The sadistic dynamic could take over in conditions of mass panic, when fives, tens – or even hundreds – of witches were interrogated; or in individual cases where an accused refused to confess and the interrogation lasted weeks, months or even longer. And it could proceed when the interrogators were not forced to stick to carefully prescribed routines for the application of torture, but were allowed to use physical intervention as they thought fit. So in Nördlingen, in yet another case, that of Katharina Keßler, first the thumbscrews, then the boots were applied and finally the bench was used, as if they were experimenting with every means available.[40] The point of the pain was to extract more of the story from the witch. Yet the story which the interrogators heard – as in so many sexual obsessions – was in outline always the same.

The sadism of the exchange also had a sexual component which could engulf not only the interrogators but prison officials as well. We have already noted how prison warders observed the sexual activity they believed they beheld between witch and Devil, the excited language of their reports conveying their voyeurism. It is certainly likely that many women in solitary imprisonment did masturbate in an attempt to seek comfort from their own bodies and so deal with their fears and confinement. To their keepers, this behaviour constituted clear evidence that the Devil was visiting the witch and renewing his sexual contract with her. So for example Anna Bernegker was constantly visited by the Devil in jail, so that, according to the authorities, 'she was found undressed in the mornings and quite naked and terrible, and it also made her ill and utterly weak'.[41] Something of the same excitement is evident during the interrogations themselves in those moments when the Devil was believed to be actually present in the interrogation room. The stories the women told about sex with the Devil, the undressing of the witch for investigation and the inspection of her genital area before questioning, certainly suggest that sexual fantasies were likely to circulate around witches. We know that in eighteenth-century Marchtal suspected witches were found by the executioner to have swollen genital areas, evidence, according to the torturer, of their lubricious lives with the Devil. But it is also possible that the swollen genital areas were the result of rape or of torture carried out during the course of the trial. It is rare to find the existence of sexual fantasies surrounding the witches directly confirmed in the records. It is virtually impossible to find direct traces of sexual interference on the part of the interrogators, but this does not mean that such things did not happen.

We do know that in Eichstätt a group of prison warders raped the accused witches under their supervision. Lorenz Fendt, who 'had rubbed his virile

16. The burning of the witches. Woodcut illustration to the second edition of Spee's *Cautio criminalis.*

member three times' on one of the witches, said that one of the other warders had gone into a witch's cell when drunk, and had fallen on her, grabbed the cloth concealing her breasts, and said 'You old whore, you must let yourself be fucked'.[42] This is unlikely to have been an isolated case. What sexual fantasies might have been at work here, as warders had sex with women whom they probably believed also to have had intercourse with the Devil? Did fear trigger lust? Yet what could it mean to rape someone who one believed to be sworn to the Devil, determined to harm her fellow Christians, especially any who caused her injury?

Each successful trial moved to a climax of admission, continuing until a full narrative had been secured, and then finishing with the execution of the witch, the community purged of her maleficent presence. Yet, though the curiosity of the interrogators was constantly piqued by the new and unorthodox information about the Devil that each witch supplied, the interrogators 'knew', more or less, what they were going to hear. They also needed to hear it again. In conditions of mass panic, a practised interrogator might hear the story literally hundreds of times. This was also, of course, true of all kinds of criminal cases: one case of theft reads very much like another. But in witchcraft cases the story was all. The length of time required to produce a story and convict the witch, the shocking nature of the admissions she had to provide, the fact that witches might come from any walk of life, not necessarily from a criminal underclass, and that she might denounce even the most unlikely suspects, all lent witchcraft interrogations a peculiar intensity. This leads one to suspect that part of the dynamic involved the compulsions of repetition, of hearing the same terrible story once more. In hearing such tales, one might speculate, witch-hunters could tease themselves with horrific visions and then master their anxiety by defeating the witch.

The process of interrogation provided lurid, persuasive fantasies that spoke of pain, love and longing. The emotions and the psychological conflicts which such tales conveyed were not invented. Once a 'conversation' of this kind developed between the two sides, resting on deep exchange, the witch was able to produce the compelling narratives which fuelled the witch craze. Such an emotional combustion did not always take place, however. Some accused witches remained taciturn, admitting their guilt but providing almost no details of their experiences. But in most witch panics there were at least several witches who would become key witnesses. Their gruesome accounts fostered the addictive fascination of the interrogators that stoked the persecutory dynamic. The feeling of emotional truth which such central confessions generated was enough to persuade interrogators of the veracity of the accounts of other witches who might be less forthcoming. Few witches failed to provide at least some confessional material that came from experience and drew on the details of daily life.

Occasionally, accused witches went so far as to identify with their persecutors, to the point that they praised them for their severity. Lucia Vischer 'gave thanks and praise to God' that she had been arrested before she had been able to carry out the many acts of malefice that the Devil had wanted her to do.[43] Walpurg Stainach, interrogated by the Würzburg authorities in 1603, concluded her interrogation by giving 'the Master [that is, the executioner] her hand.... She forgave him the pain which he had done her, he had acted justly towards her, because she had been so hard and had not wanted to confess'. She thanked the interrogators, saying 'she had long wanted to confess that it had come to that, but she had not known how she should make a start'.[44] Reactions such as hers, carefully noted in the protocol, greatly strengthened the judges in the belief that torture was not only justified but would even help the witch, by assisting her to confess and escape the Devil's clutches.

The witch had to be brought to recognize her own evil character. Something of the role that envy and anger played both in witches' understanding of themselves and in how they were perceived can be caught in the summary confession from Barbara Schluchter of Krautheim in 1617, during the mass panic in Würzburg. She described how she had fallen into the Devil's clutches five years before, when 'she was seduced during her widowhood through anger, and let herself be persuaded. And forswore herself in anger, when she was in dispute with the neighbours, and she said "If she gave way on this then let her be of the Devil's'". Schluchter had therefore become a witch because she had angrily invoked the Devil when her neighbours tried to cheat her of her land. However, she immediately went on to contradict herself, telling how she had been seduced not five but fifteen years before, while out grazing her animals. A man in green clothing had suddenly appeared behind her, saying 'What are you doing?', to which she had replied 'Well, I'm grazing'. He offered to help her lift up the bundle of grass, but then 'sat down upon it, and she picked up the bundle and wanted to go off, and the green chap said, "Wait put your bundle down again, I have more to say to you", and he then seduced her, saying it would be "no sin"'.[45] The second story is a vivid but conventional account of being seduced by the Devil, the story all witches had to provide; in the first, less usual tale, the scribe uses the word anger three times. Anger is the nub of the case, the emotion which alienated her from the community. Convinced that her claim for the land was just, she had invoked the Devil, saying 'If she yielded, let her go to the Devil!'

There were deep cultural sanctions against envy, anger and hatred in early modern European societies. Those who were in a state of enmity with their fellow Christians were not admitted to communion. People were regularly excluded from the Lord's Supper on these grounds, or took their own decision not to participate in the sacrament because they felt themselves to be guilty of hatred and enmity. Interrogators repeatedly quizzed witches on their treatment of the Host, trying to discover whether they had dishonoured it, trampled on it or stolen it: this was a classic blasphemy to expect of a witch because it showed her contempt for the substance which was God and which represented the fellowship of the community of Christians. Having once confessed to envy or hatred of her fellows, the accused witch would typically launch into a raft of confessions to killing animals, children and people. Envy, hatred and anger were felt to be literally murderous. Once she had admitted to them, there was little option for the witch but to confess to all the maleficent acts which must of necessity – so it was believed – follow from such destructive emotions.

The actual dynamics at work in cases against alleged witches were the exact opposite. In reality, it was the witches' denouncers and interrogators who were driven by anger and hostility towards the witch, and who sought to kill her. As they knew, successful prosecution meant the confiscation of a portion or all of the witches' assets – her animals and possessions. In many cases it is evident that the witch, the woman who allegedly felt envy, was herself its target. Evidence from Scotland and New England has shown that a significant minority of suspects were heiresses and women of good fortune; and in Würzburg property to the value of over 100,000 gulden had been declared confiscated from witches by 1629.[46] This was not universally true; after all, most witches

17. The rack: from *Constitutio Criminalis Theresiana*, Vienna 1768.

were poor. But envy certainly played its part in many accusations, as it did in Nördlingen. Witchcraft accusations were a hall of mirrors where neighbours saw their own fear and greed in the shape of the witch.

Not surprisingly, these emotional dynamics could be very unstable. In the psychology of the persecutors, lurid emotions were overlaid with a rigid moralism; their inner worlds were peopled with agents of divine authority like angels and just judges. Only ceaseless struggle against the forces of evil could maintain the precarious psychological balance. In this moral universe, the mixture of good and evil, an inherent part of social relations, could simply not be tolerated. Indeed, a strict separation of good and evil, an inability to admit to feeling envy, anger or hostility, and the conviction that these emotions were deeply destructive – destructive of life itself – look very like the phenomena the psychoanalyst Melanie Klein has described as being connected to one another in infant psychology. Perhaps what we see in the witch craze is a moralism which has failed to integrate the mixture of good and bad elements that are part of human life itself.[47]

The relationship between convicted witch and interrogator ended in death. Once sentence was passed, the date of execution would be set. On the day itself, the criminal would be handed over to the executioner. From that point on, the condemned person was no longer a member of the community. He or she was led away in public procession in a cart to the gallows outside the town or village. The rituals of execution served to emphasize the gulf that separated the judges from the grubby business of, as the expression put it, 'laying hands on' the condemned person. Instead, the condemned was surrendered to the dishonourable touch of the executioner.

The act of killing was also a kind of festival. As with executions of all criminals, a festive meal was held for the executioner and his men at the commune's or city's expense; and the repast could be substantial. In Nördlingen in 1590, when three witches were burnt together, a princely 15 gulden was lavished on the banquet; by comparison, a midwife earned a pension of only 2 gulden per quarter. Quite a civic feast, it must have impressed the other executioners and their henchmen from outside the town who had given their assistance in the witch hunt. Such an orgy of eating and drinking blotted out the guilt of killing and strengthened the bonds of fellowship amongst those dishonourable folk charged with the duty of carrying out the judgment of the law. The city fathers paid for this excess of feasting, and in some cases attended it, along with clergy, judges and even the condemned criminal.[48]

The witch was a sworn enemy of Christendom, whose evil deeds were an affront to Christ's body and a mockery of His sacrificial death. Yet the execution offered her the chance, should she truly repent, of expiating her sin and attaining salvation. This created a dilemma for clergy. All condemned criminals had to be offered confession and communion before execution; but many clerics who wrote about witches sought to make an exception in their case. After all, witches habitually purloined hosts and mistreated them, so might they not dishonour Christ's body if it was given to them? The Jesuit demonologist and suffragan Bishop of Trier Peter Binsfeld (died 1598), the leading light in the mass persecutions there, insisted (in one of the rare passages where he resorts to the first person) that he regularly advised that genuinely penitent witches ought to be given communion. But they should receive it four hours before execution, so that it should be digested and no dishonour would therefore be done to the Host.[49] The issue was such a thorny one for clergy because the witch's crimes were a direct affront to the Eucharist – she was guilty, after all, of wishing harm to others and this state of enmity itself precluded her from taking communion. Witches were believed to trample the Host underfoot, their sabbaths were a travesty of the Mass and their use of the bodies of dead children drew part of its horror from its perversion of the central Christian mystery. Yet the priest also had a prime pastoral duty to encourage all sinners to confession and contrition, as Catholic and Protestant reformers insisted in unison. This made the witch the supreme example of the priest's duty to minister to all, even to such wretches.

At the execution, a record of the witch's crimes would be read out to the assembled onlookers, and then she would be burnt in public. Sometimes she would already have been garrotted so that she would not fall into despair because of the pain and so forfeit the chance of salvation. In late seventeenth-century Augsburg, most witches were given the 'merciful' and honourable punishment of execution by the sword, which at least spared them the executioner's touch. But their bodies were still burnt in public for all to see at the place of execution. In cases where the witches' crimes were particularly heinous, the punishment was compounded by mutilation. One lying-in maid in Augsburg, the servant hired to help mother and baby during the lying-in after birth, who had killed young children was burnt with glowing tongs on her breast before execution. The part of her body symbolically associated with motherhood was thus branded in retaliation for the mothers she had harmed.[50] Executions were a species of theatre, held on raised platforms so as to be visible to all. The witch would exhibit penitence and perhaps even make her touching final confession to a priest or pastor in full view of the public. Often, witches would be executed in clutches of three to six or so, a procedure that not only saved money but increased the drama.

There was an appetite for the salacious details of the witch's crimes and her fearful end: woodcuts and pamphlets were soon on the market in the wake of an execution, immortalizing the spectacle in print. Many of those who accused others of witchcraft or who were themselves accused recalled executions they had witnessed, or included in their confessions details from those public denunciations which had been seared into their memory. But though the witch might be executed, her body turned to ashes so that nothing remained, and though everything might be done to excise her from the community of Christians, she was not so easily forgotten. She lived on in print, in pictures, and in the stories people told.

In the long term, it was the experience of ministering to condemned witches which was to generate the most powerful assaults on the whole belief system of witchcraft. In 1631 the Jesuit Friedrich Spee published his *Cautio criminalis* anonymously, and without the permission of the order. This book was a systematic demolition of the entire process of interrogation which went to the heart of the psychology of questioning, and it was so devastating because it came from experience. Hearing the pre-mortem confessions of condemned witches who still insisted they were innocent convinced Spee that they had been wrongfully convicted. For Spee, it was the confessional that provided the yardstick by which secular inquisition should be judged. Spee repeatedly returns to the biblical image of the wheat and the tares, arguing that torture itself must be abolished because of the danger that, so far from purifying the community, in witch-hunting the wheat will be pulled up with the tares. Systematically he describes the ways in which hangmen got around the system

– since an hour's torture is permitted, they divide the hour into two or three parts and stretch it over several days; or they evade restrictions on repeated torture by arguing that since more than one offence has been committed, the accused can be tortured again on a different point. And Spee is well aware that many 'find such pleasure in the cruelty, that they consider neither the bodies of others nor their own consciences'.[51] With this observation, Spee went to the psychological heart of the dynamic of interrogation.

Yet Spee does not describe what the witches confessed to, or how people could become so frightened of witches that they were willing to override natural human feelings of sympathy and deviate from what Spee repeatedly refers to as 'healthy reason'. Why so many could fall prey to prurient fantasies about witches, why witch panics could take hold of a whole community, and what made the stories witches told so compelling, is the subject of the next chapter.

Part Two

Fantasy

Chapter Three

Cannibalism

In 1590 Barbara Lierheimer confessed that she had attended a banquet at a friend's house. At first she claimed not to know what they had eaten, but then she admitted that, though she did not know who cooked it or where it had come from, the meat was 'a roasted child's little foot'.

Lierheimer was one of thirty-five witches executed in the town of Nördlingen between 1590 and 1598, in the course of a wave of persecution which was repeated in a host of southern German towns and villages in those years.[1] There, women confessed to cannibalism and grave desecration, as one after another told how they had dug up the bodies of children and cooked them. Birth and motherhood featured in all their stories: Lierheimer was a midwife, many of the accused mentioned another mysterious midwife who officiated at the feasts, and nearly all of the women who died during the panic had themselves given birth.[2]

What makes a mother confess to digging up dead babies and cooking and eating them? More than any other crime, witchcraft depends on producing stories, and so, in a panic like that in Nördlingen, torture was used repeatedly to make women talk. When Barbara Lierheimer told how she killed her husband after a dance on the command of the Devil but then hesitated before continuing her story, the interrogators ordered torture.[3] When, in the eighth interrogation, she denied her story, the executioner was summoned. By the time he arrived, she was admitting everything.[4] When she denied visiting one witch's house, she was bound by the executioner. So she repeated the story about eating a cooked child, but since she offered few new details, weights were attached and she was stretched. She called herself a lying rascal, and so the 'boots' were put on. At this point she said – as always in criminal records, her words were reported by the scribe in the third person – 'The more one tortures her the more she lies, one was simply forcing her to lie'.[5] The bench was then tried; but this too brought no further story. Like a coin in the slot, physical pain was being used to keep the story going. In this case, it killed her. Barbara Lierheimer died in prison as a result of torture and her corpse was burnt at the scaffold.

What made the encounter between Lierheimer and the executioner particularly bitter was the fact that Lierheimer was a midwife, and had failed to attend

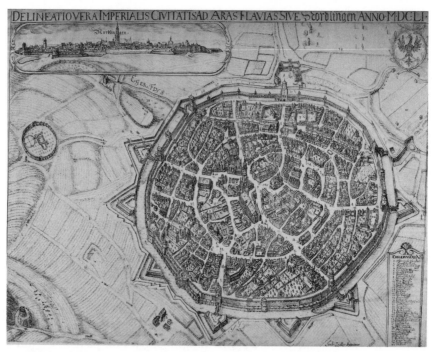

18. Andreas Zeidler, A bird's-eye view map of Nördlingen, 1651, etching.

when the executioner's wife was giving birth. She had pleaded a prior engagement, but, since all contact with an executioner was dishonouring, he may well
have suspected that she simply did not wish to help his wife in her hour of
need. He certainly had his revenge: Lierheimer had angrily let it be known 'it
would be no surprise if she were to stick a knife into him, because he had
ruined her livelihood by putting it about that she was a witch'. A pious
Lutheran, her first reaction to interrogation was to search her mind for her
sins, confessing that 'she had sinned gravely against God' because she had felt
envy and hatred against a woman who accused her of stealing baptismal fees.
Her son was a Lutheran preacher, and, in a story that might have come from
a Lutheran broadside, when she saw the Devil, he was dressed as a Catholic
monk who tried to seduce her. Yet she was stubborn: though her son had tried
to get her away from the town because of the rumours, she had refused to
leave. She was also proud of her professional skill. Even when she was finally
broken to the point of confessing, she insisted that none of the children
injured or eaten had been born under her care.[6]

Lierheimer was interrogated when the panic in Nördlingen was well under
way, and she was not the only solid citizen to be caught up in the craze.
Rebekka Lemp, wife of the high-ranking civic official Peter Lemp, was also
brutally forced to supply a confession against her will. Her letter to her

husband, smuggled out of prison, and written in a hand made unsteady by the effects of torture, explains what happened:

> O my chosen treasure, must I thus be torn in all innocence from you? That will cry out to God for all time. They force one, they make one talk; they have tortured me. I am as innocent as God in heaven. If I knew as much as one iota of these things, then I would deserve that God should deny me paradise .... Father, send me something so that I die, otherwise I will break down under torture.[7]

We know that the Nördlingen councillors carefully chose their moment to imprison her, waiting until her husband had left town on business. He was unable to save her, and she was burnt as a witch. She had lived in a substantial house on the Wine Market Square, where the city's archive is now housed. From house after house around that square, women were accused as witches.

The witch-hunting mania in Nördlingen was fuelled by the horrors of these women's confessions, the idea that Protestant citizens, even widows of councillors and wives of officials,[8] were cooking infant flesh in copper pots and banqueting in their quiet parlours, in cellars beneath the town, on the Wine Market Square or even in the town hall.[9] Those accused of the crimes were executed on the 'hill' just outside the town.[10] The other 'hill', the only relief from the endless flatness of the Ries plain surrounding the city with its circular walls, was the graveyard where the infants had allegedly been dug up.[11]

Cannibalism was a sixteenth-century preoccupation. For Montaigne, writing about anthropophagi in his *Essais*, it was the test case of tolerance, proof of the sheer variety of human life forms. It was a subject not for moral

19. Engraving of the Wine Market Square, Nördlingen: the house where Rebekka Lemp lodged can be seen on the left.

outrage but for sober reflection on the nature of man. Cannibalism was a feature of the New World, of the exotic or the innocent; of a world where, as the sixteenth-century German woodcuts show them, half-clad women could adorn their bodies with bizarre feathers as if they were subject to no dictates of modesty or convention. Originally, cannibalism was linked with heresy, but later this charge became an established part of the repertoire of witches. During the French Wars of Religion, images of butchered, mutilated or eaten human bodies allowed their Protestant opponents to excoriate Catholics as inhuman, as people who infringed the deepest civilized taboo; and later it was rumours of cannibalism in the Thirty Years War which expressed the terrifying disorientation and collapse of German society. Allegations of cannibalism were usually directed at social outsiders, religious opponents or other races. But in witchcraft trials they targeted neighbours, friends and kinsfolk.[12]

Nördlingen was certainly not the only place where witches confessed to cannibalism: similar admissions are found in trials in Würzburg, Marchtal and elsewhere. The *Malleus* mentions cannibalism, witchcraft interrogatories often devote an entire section to the phenomenon, and it was widely believed that the witches' salve was made of child-flesh.[13] Yet each stereotype, like all profound myths, found its local variant. In Nördlingen, the eating of children, grave desecration, murderous attacks on children, even one's own, and local town hall politics formed a compelling whole. It made sense of all that was known about witches. The meal provided occasion for witches to meet (and so the list of those present formed the lists of suspects), the leftover flesh was used to make the witches' salve, the bones were ground to form the witches' powder and the broth became the water witches stirred to raise storms. But the power of the myth to convince depended in turn at least in part on the persuasiveness of the witches' testimony.[14]

Nördlingen was a city of tanners and leatherworkers, a town where people knew how to transform carcasses into other products.[15] Residents of Nördlingen were acquainted with the processes of bodily decomposition, and recognized the smells of boiling flesh and bone. For a buried child to be dug up and then eaten required a suspension of the normal natural processes of decay. It was as if – even in Protestant Nördlingen – the body of the dead baby were like that of a saint, which does not decay in the grave but emits a pleasant odour. The Nördlingen judges themselves appear to have been genuinely confused about the relationship of truth to evidence. They dutifully interrogated the gravedigger when the first confessions of grave desecration were made.[16] When the gravedigger said he had noticed nothing amiss, they did not mount a search to see for themselves, but nor did they conclude that the allegations were unfounded.

In this, they were in line with Protestant understandings of how the Devil operated in the world: he might not do things in reality, but use only tricks and illusion.[17] If nothing was disturbed in the cemetery, this did not mean that the Devil had not appeared to the witches and made them think that they ate human flesh. Like the miracle of communion, which Lutherans believed was transformed into Christ's body and blood and still remained true bread and wine, this diabolic feast could have taken place without leaving physical proof behind. Nor, in the end, did the allegations of cannibalism seem to be crucial for the conviction: it was not always one of the crimes read out over the witch at her execution. Instead, the authorities contented themselves with merely referring to the fact that one witch 'had not spared the birth of her own body, against nature'. That she allegedly stewed and ate her own child was not mentioned.[18]

Cannibalism in witch cases in Nördlingen had a long pedigree. As early as 1478, in the first reported case of a witchcraft allegation in the town, Else Schwab was accused of being a witch and said to have cooked and eaten exhumed children.[19] In the case which sparked off the panic in 1589, Ursula Haider was accused of having killed a young child in her care. The child's body was seen to bleed as she approached the bier; a second child died soon before and the third died straight after the funeral. Her story of maleficence towards children then became transposed into a narrative of cannibalism: by the fourth interrogation, she was recounting how she had seen the Devil dig up children, and by the fifth, how the 'Evil One' had 'roasted' the child which had been dug up, and how the meal had lasted four hours. The participants at the feast named by Haider were then interrogated, and each ultimately produced a variety of cannibalistic fantasies. One confessed only that she saw something black lying in a bowl.[20]

The power of the myth of cannibalism in Lutheran Nördlingen was clearly related to communion and it is striking that the issue of receiving the Host emerges as a theme in nearly all the testimonies. One woman insisted that she had received the Host worthily, another, attempting to limit her guilt, said that 'she did not go often to communion'. If she had gone, she would have done something evil with the Host. After confessing that she had given birth to a child out of wedlock, Barbara Stecher added that the experience 'tempted her, and when she went to communion, she thought that her sins had not been forgiven'. Her conviction meant that she had eaten communion unworthily, to her own damnation. Thus, stories of sin, motherhood and Host desecration began to converge. Stecher eventually confessed to stealing her own child and giving it to the Devil, just as in communion she stole the body of another child, Jesus, for her diabolic master.[21]

There are strong parallels between the cannibalistic and Host imagery. The connection between the two was already uncomfortably evident to contemporaries. Confronted with Aztec cannibalistic sacrifice, sixteenth-century Spaniards were aware that eating the Host might appear to be a kind of cannibalism. Indeed, one of the taunts the Swiss Protestant reformer Zwingli, who did not believe in the Real Presence, hurled against his opponents was that to believe one truly ate the body of Christ in the Eucharist was to believe oneself a cannibal. The flesh of the babies had to be processed, dug up, roasted or stewed, and then the bones ground; the concrete, housewifely manner in which this is imagined has something in common with early sixteenth-century woodcut images of Christ being put through the mill, processed and turned into hosts; or of Christ in the winepress, His blood making the communion wine. Many witches describe the standard fare at diabolic feasts as infant flesh and wine; the meat was always consumed by groups of witches, whose bonds with one another were strengthened thereby, just as the Christian congregation becomes one body.[22]

The element of cannibalism in the central Christian mystery found its most vivid variant in the myth of Jewish ritual murder.[23] In these cases, an innocent Christian child becomes the victim of Jewish lust for Christian blood. As the myth took shape, that child became a male child and the myth became a version of Christ's own sacrifice. Its moral was clear: Jews kill Christ and Christians. Nördlingen's inhabitants would have known such stories, and they would also have known Jews, for although the town's Jews had been expelled in 1507, there were Jewish communities dotted about the countryside and Jews continued to trade in the town, probably even to live there. There were also bitter memories, for there had been a pogrom of Jews in 1384, organized by some of the leading citizens of the town.[24]

All these associations shaped the broad outlines of the witches' confessions. But each individual witch also had her own idiosyncratic version of the story. To get a witch craze going, enough witches had to provide the kind of specific, riveting detail which – contradictory as it was – could spur the interrogators on.

The confessions which the Council elicited from the women were disturbingly reminiscent of the sensory experiences of motherhood. The witches reported that the infant flesh tasted 'sweet'. They remembered the precise age of the corpses, details which fixed size and made imagination precise; they remembered a little child and a 'little foot' (*Füsslin*), diminutives which evoked maternal tenderness. The confessions also circled around themes of eating and cutting. Susanna Mair recounted how the midwife had once baked a child in her house, and said that 'she should come to visit her, she had something good to eat'. Barbara Lierheimer spoke of a 'splendid meal'; Mair, by contrast, called the meal a 'feed' (*Gfress*), a word which in German alludes to the way animals eat food.[25]

So firmly was cannibalism associated with women that it was easy for the one man accused, Jörg Kürschnauer, to extricate himself. He had been interested in the drink at the sabbaths, not the food. As he said, 'the Devil doesn't like having men around, because they drink too much, and curse, and you can't do anything with them. The bath-keepers are always thirsty; and he could always rather have three women for one man.'[26] At the dance, 'one girl was prettier than the next', and the Devil used to put his leg over his wife even in the bath-house parlour, not just in bed. Kürschnauer himself sounds as if he might have stepped out of the pages of one of the Protestant Devil Books of the period, comic moral tracts that lampooned particular sins in the guise of their own patron devil. He behaves like a Drink Devil or a henpecked She-man. It did not save him from the flames, but it was a style of confession which had none of the brooding interiority of the female witches. Kürschnauer used comedy to preserve his psychological integrity. His confession is a perform-ance of venomous bravura, pouring out hatred against his wife who he said 'was worse than he' and whom the Council ought to imprison and interrogate. He named woman after woman as witches: the customers of his bath-house who lived around the square and whose gossiping had implicated him. Perhaps he was indeed someone who hated women. As a bath-keeper, he would have known a great deal about people's bodies and probably their secrets too. It is certainly noticeable how many women denounced him as a witch, not only just before his trial but consistently throughout the first wave of trials in the 1590s.

When in 1594 Maria Holl refused to confess despite sixty-two rounds of torture and was freed from prison, it seemed that her steadfastness had finally broken the cycle of witch-hunting in Nördlingen. One final event was needed, however, before the panic was finally over. In 1598, the town gravedigger was called in by the Council and interrogated on suspicion of having tampered with dead bodies. While in prison, he hanged himself. His wife Margaretha Minderlin fled the city, but she was soon captured, imprisoned and interro-gated. After some hesitation, she admitted that her husband had been digging up bodies in order to sell the winding sheets and the cushions from under the corpses' heads; she had bought wine with the proceeds. Gradually, as torture proceeded, her admissions became more grisly. Her husband had sold body parts, cutting off a finger and a foot. Finally, Minderlin confessed that she and her husband had dug up whole bodies of babies and had sold them to men, women and Jews. They got only a trifling amount for the corpses, usually just 6 *batzen* per body. She had known of the business for about a year, but her husband had been at it for a long time. Minderlin could give the name of each child they had exhumed, their parents and their personal circumstances. After all, it was her business to know the name and relatives of each corpse in the burial ground.

By the seventh interrogation, and after considerable torture, Minderlin's story began to sound more and more familiar. She admitted that she had been with the women who had been accused in the first wave of panic, and she con-fessed that she had eaten child's flesh with them. Only after this did she confess to having been seduced by the Devil, explaining that she had been despairing because of her bad marriage. Her husband was out getting drunk, and she went to her chamber to look after her children. Immediately the Devil appeared. The tempter rapidly grasped her plight and put it into words:

> ... she has a husband who is not interested in her and is in the tavern day and night, and if she would be his, she would get every good deed from him, he was the Big Devil.[27]

Later she had attended a banquet with many of the women who had since been executed as witches. The food was the body of a young child.

In subsequent interrogations, Minderlin returned to the story of the children sold to the Jews, and added that 'the children will certainly have been eaten'. With this last admission, she tied the story of the cannibalistic witches to the hoary myth of Jewish ritual murder: one was just a transmutation of the other.[28]

The Council responded in the usual way. It dug up the bodies of three of the children Minderlin claimed to have sold, but all were intact. In subsequent interrogations, Minderlin wavered, sometimes repeating her story, sometimes denying the exhumation of one corpse but admitting the sale of another. Her formal condemnation, which is brief and uninformative, makes no mention of the gruesome goings-on, for by that stage Minderlin had admitted to a seemingly endless list of vicious injuries she had caused to men, women, children and animals. Just as she had earlier blamed her dead husband for the evil doings in the cemetery, only to make his activities pale in significance compared to her own, so too did she take sole responsibility for her daughter's death, having previously laid it at her husband's door. Whether or not the Council believed the story about grave desecration we cannot know. Certainly no physical evidence was found to support her story. But as Minderlin herself said, the Devil is a villain who is master of illusion. The absence of physical evidence could not prove that the Devil had not, by means of some glamour, made it appear that the corpses had been exhumed and enable her really to sell them.

Minderlin was the ultimate witch, her evil far overshadowing that of her husband. From the outset the Council had suspected her of dealing with the Devil. It was alarmed by the black dog she had with her at the cemetery and which the civic officials had taken from her. Yet the Council was clearly in no mood for much more. It declined to prise from her further names of witches she might have seen at the diabolic feasts, contenting itself with those who had been executed already.

Minderlin's confession has a strangely ghostly quality. All the old witches who had died in the panics of 1589–94 appear before us one after another; all are gone. Maria Holl and the others who did not confess, however, do not appear. Minderlin seems to be recycling the elements of their confessions read out at their executions, weaving them into a single coherent narrative. The story thus also serves to exculpate Holl and to underline that Minderlin is indeed the last of the Nördlingen witches, for all the others had met their deaths.

By the time she confessed, Margaretha Minderlin seems to have self-consciously adopted the identity of the witch. This is what seems to underlie the dreamy, coherent quality of her narrative, quite unlike that of most witches, as if she in effect acted as the historian of the witch sect in Nördlingen, telling the tales of all of them one more time. By so doing she effectively ensured that the persecution would end with her, establishing social harmony in the town again. Her trial vindicated the magistrates whose credibility had been so dramatically undermined when Holl had not confessed. The story of the cannibalistic witches was unearthed and proved yet again before it was finally interred, just as the Nördlingen citizens managed to bury their own connections to the witches whose executions they witnessed, resuming their lives as if the witches had never been.

Many elements in the stories of witchcraft were closely connected with motherhood, from food, to lying-in, to birth itself. The woman who praised a child, gave it something to eat, or tried to heal a woman who had just given birth, might find herself accused of witchcraft. Catherine Aißlinger recounted how Katharina Keßler had given her a boiled hen and an egg for her childbed. But something stopped her from eating them, and as soon as she had received the gift, she had 'no peace'. Later it emerged that the hen 'had a hole under the breast like a penny, and it was quite clean'; and as it was explained to her, 'when the hen begins to rot, the woman will start to flow until the hen rots away'. Perhaps the spell was designed to rid her of the lochia; perhaps to bring back her periods. Or perhaps it threatened uncontrollable bleeding. In her testimony against Keßler, Aißlinger carefully left the meaning of all this – whether positive or negative – vague.[29] Barbara Stecher was accused of killing Jeronimus Neher's 'little boy': she had given him dried fruit to eat and the child 'became very ill and looked like a crucifix'. Aißlinger herself supposedly visited the four-year-old son of Tobias Scheber, and 'passing her hands over the little boy's head, she said "what a beautiful big-headed boy you have, he will be just like your father"', whereupon the child became ill.[30] These events triggered accusations against women when something went wrong and the child sickened. In the course of their interrogations, the accused witches began to transform these accusations into stories about how they caused harm to children by means of diabolic powder, finally supplying gruesome accounts of the digging up and eating of newborn children.

Birth is another key theme. The witches describe digging up the corpses, as if engaging in a second forcible delivery, pulling the child out of the earth with

SEBAST. RÖTTINGERVS I.V.D. COMES PALATINVS. SVEVICI AC FRANCICI EQVE
STRIS ORDINIS NEC NON REIPVB. NORDLINGIANÆ. ADVOCATVS.
In Silentio et Spe. ÆTAT. SVÆ. 71. OBIIT. NORDL. 16 MAII 1608.

20. Dr Sebastian
Röttinger.

metal implements just as midwives removed dead foetuses with hooks, and robbing it of its place in the fellowship of the Christian community in consecrated ground.[31] Several described 'whose' child it was, as if it were important to name those from whom they had stolen it. Some admitted promising their child to the Devil while they were pregnant.[32] Nearly all the women reported the presence of midwives at the scene of grave desecration. This was not because the midwives possessed special medical knowledge, but because both the women and their interrogators imagined the scene as a birth in reverse. They were exercised by the awesome power of she who gives birth to do the opposite, to take life; and worse, to rob the dead of bodily integrity and to steal souls for the Devil.[33]

Any exploration of the witch-hunters' psychology needs to consider the stories which the interrogators found so fascinating. As the judges heard the terrible stories of witchcraft told by women who had themselves been mothers, they confronted a shocking vision of the evil mother which stirred unconscious anxieties. The truth of the nightmare was apparently confirmed by each witch's appalling confession, unleashing a cycle of increasing violence. This may be why the witch so often was a woman who had herself given birth or who cared for children; and why the stories were so repetitive. Though the fantasy had to be vivid, studded with detail which was each witch's own, it also had a hackneyed familiarity. Each woman's fantasy – even if head-splitting or salve-smearing initially featured – was pressed in the end into the procrustean bed of the cannibalistic narrative.

It is impossible to know for certain what investment the interrogators might have had in these tales. To be sure, witch crazes monopolized judicial resources and occasioned enormous expenditure, requiring special guards and absorbing much of the time of the Council's two legal advisers, Dr Röttinger and Dr Graf. The witch cases fascinated more than these two men, however: almost all the members of the Council took part in at least one interrogation.[34]

Unlike most victims of the witch persecution, the Nördlingen witches included rich and powerful women, members of the town elite.[35] Four were widows of councillors, and one of those four the widow of a mayor; another was the daughter of a councillor. This must have lent a peculiar urgency to the images of maternal savagery. After all, these women were not outsiders but members of the interrogators' own social circle, women not safely distant from

21. Franceso Maria Guazzo, *Compendium maleficarum*, Milan 1626: woodcut illustration showing a child being roasted by two witches while in the background a pot of cannibalistic broth is being boiled.

their own kin. Some were even of higher status than those who interrogated them. The widow of a mayor who must have agreed to the witch trials became a victim of the witch panic shortly after his death.[36] Witch persecutions became superimposed on political division. It was no accident that Rebekka Lemp retaliated by locating the cannibalistic feast in the town hall itself.

The political elite of Nördlingen was tiny. At most, 20 to 25 men would have belonged to the group of councillors in a ten-year period; and these men had graduated through recognized political careers, in a system which made great use of co-option and almost none of popular participation.[37] A series of councils, large and small, represented the citizens, but true power was concentrated in the tiny Secret Council. It is likely that the men who participated in the trials bonded closely together, as they shared a special, dreadful intimacy with the witch. She was a woman they knew, a woman with whom they might have engaged emotionally, and towards whom they could well have felt envy. Envy, after all, is an emotion which relies on identification. These councillors inherited the political power of those who had gone before them, and it was the widows of some of these men whom they executed as witches. In 1589, shortly before the outbreak of the Nördlingen witch panic, two of the five members of the Secret Council (the real governing body of the town) were replaced. For the first time, Johannes Pferinger joined the Secret Council, and immediately he acted as mayor. It

22. Mayor Johannes Pferinger.

is possible this activated a number of tensions, unavoidably connected with the struggle of each new political generation to destroy its fathers and come into its own patriarchal inheritance.

This may be why the stories of the witches' cannibalism exercised such a fascination at this time. As Freud argues in *Totem and Taboo*, the practice of cannibalism can be a kind of intense identification, a type of primary love where attachment is guaranteed by literally incorporating a piece of the other. He suggests there is a cannibalistic component in the fierce love children bear their parents, wanting to consume and replace them utterly.[38] In Nördlingen, the new generation of political rulers set the seal on their regime by ridding the town of those who, they believed, were harming and killing the next generation. But to an extent, they may also have identified with the cannibalistic witches, who were exhuming the dead and assuming their power, just as the councillors were doing as they took up the reins of political authority. This might help us understand why so many of the alleged witches were so closely linked to their accusers, and came from the same political and administrative elite. The episode had the character of a short but intense crisis – thirty-three of the 'witches' were executed in two panics from around late 1589 to 1591; and late 1593 to early 1594. The need of the new elite to incorporate its past may also explain why the witches may appear to have been so rapidly forgotten, the witches' families and their accusers reabsorbed into the fabric of town life.

In Nördlingen's witch craze, psychic conflict of the deepest, most irrational kind merged with political factionalism. Paradoxically, this may be why witchcraft did not cause any lasting division within the town. Peter Lemp – widower of Rebekka Lemp who was burnt as a witch in 1590 – soon married the widow of the city clerk Paul Mair and received a wedding present from the Council. After her death he married the widow of a councillor who had been amongst those who condemned his first wife; and in 1596, he capped his political career by joining the Council himself. Dorothea Gundelfinger was executed in 1593, but both her son and her nephews eventually became mayors in the town; while the son of Katharina Keßler, a tanner's wife executed as a witch, rose to become a councillor.[39] The spectre of the cannibalistic mother gradually faded and the town never experienced a recurrence of witch-hunting. The terrors of witchcraft could, in the end, be kept within the family.

Chapter 4

Sex with the Devil

The first time, he, the Evil One, came to her about eight years ago; before her bed, dressed in black, with smooth trousers. She was a widow at that time, and he knocked on the shutter (since she intended to take a second husband at that time, she thought that it was the man whom she desired to marry, a thresher called Michael). He said to her that she should take him, he had 25 gulden, he was Michael Thresher, didn't she know him? So he slipped under the bedclothes to her and he had to do with her bodily. Everything about him was cold. She was badly shocked by this, and sensed that it was not right.

[He came again two days later but didn't sleep with her.] She lay with him in bed, but he only took off his coat. He had hard feet.

[He came a third time, and she opened the door for him again.] He said that she was his now, because she had lain with him. [She slept with him again.] He said he was called Little Feather (*Fäderle*). . . . [He said she was his.] He said he would not leave her her whole life long, she should have good things, but she didn't have many good days. . . . The third time, as he left her, he let out such a stink (begging your pardon), that she thought that she would die of this terrible stench in her chamber. It looked like a blue mist.[1]

This was the story told by Barbara Hohenberger, wife of Leonhard Hohenberger, when she was interrogated early in what were later to develop into the mass witch panics in Würzburg in 1590. A born story-teller, she used vivacious dialogue, telling detail and dramatic pace to convey a vivid sense of her emotional relationship with the Devil. This was not unusual: most women provided compelling accounts of their love affairs with the demon. Few insisted that they had never slept with the Devil at all – though it is important to remember that as with all elements of the witch fantasy, it remained possible to deny even the most standard parts of the story. Anna Stärr, a midwife accused of witchcraft, did not have sex with the Devil, because 'he said she was too old for it'; Affra Mertzler, by contrast, slept with the Devil yet insisted 'she had not completely denied God'.[2]

23. *The Devil as the Witch's Lover*, 1490, woodcut.

As such confessions were made as a result of torture or the threat of torture, they may not have been told as the flowing narrative they appear to be, but were extracted bit by bit, with stops and starts. We cannot know how Hohenberger's story sounded when she related it during interrogation, or to what extent her persecutors and the scribe gave it shape. Nor do we know when they replaced her words with euphemisms or turned her spoken phrases into sentences. What we have reads rather like the vivid stories that crowd the pages of a work like Nicolas Rémy's *Demonolatry*, mixtures of the preconceptions of the interrogators and the startling detail that seems to be drawn directly from peasant experience. Sex with the Devil was at once an axiom of demonological theory and a genuinely popular story with roots in local culture, everyday life and fairy tale.[3]

To Barbara Hohenberger, the Devil came in the guise of a person whom she knew and whom she had already imagined as a sexual partner. The story begins as a tale of everyday courtship, but suddenly starts to depart from the familiar as she senses that her lover is unnaturally cold. Yet Hohenberger establishes a relationship with this strange creature with hard feet, and he visits her not once but three times. She should, of course, have known his identity at once, and she supplies the clues that prove her guilty half-knowledge: the strange coldness, typical of the Devil, who does not have a human body; the hard feet, which hints that these are cloven animal hooves. Not only do the two have sex, but afterwards the Devil insists that she is now his; that is, the Devil maintains that by consenting to intercourse she has actually married him.

Here, Hohenberger drew on older understandings of marriage that were just beginning to come under assault with the Counter-Reformation. As her story has it, she was minded to marry. The man she wanted to marry appears, offering her the money which will make it possible for them to wed. Does she consent to his promise of marriage or is her assent implicit when she lets him under the bedclothes? If she had agreed to a promise of marriage, so traditional Catholic understandings of marriage would have had it, then the act of intercourse sealed the bargain, making the marriage indissoluble. At just this time, Bishop Echter in Würzburg was beginning to implement a new vision of marriage in line with the decrees of the Council of Trent, requiring banns to be read and a priest to be present if the marriage was to count as valid. Hohenberger's devil, however, tricks her into thinking she has already become the Devil's own and has entered into a marriage with him. Like all cautionary tales, it ends in disappointment. Though the Devil makes smooth promises to care for her, 'she didn't have many good days'. And the story ends with the Devil letting out a terrible fart, the stink of brimstone dirtying the aftermath of the lovemaking. Sex with the Devil, which began with courtship, is unmasked as degrading, filthy and anal.

Stories of this kind were at the heart of the witch craze. The witch was a human who had sex with the Devil. This was what made her 'his', sworn to harm all other Christians. As the demonologist Henri Boguet put it, mixing a low view of women with a high regard for the power of sex, 'The Devil uses them so because he knows that women love carnal pleasures, and he means to bind them to his allegiance by such agreeable provocations. Moreover, there is nothing which makes a woman more subject and loyal to a man than that he should abuse her body.'[4]

Intercourse with the Devil was the physical counterpart of the pact with him – and it was sex with the Devil which many accused witches talked about at length, rather than the pact which, according to demonological theory, actually made them Satan's own. After all, making a pact was an experience foreign to most of the accused, many of whom could not even sign their names. Sex with the Devil was the crucial admission for most of those accused of witchcraft. It was the first part of the diabolic narrative, the 'fall' which, like the first sexual lapse for a virgin, was believed to have set her on the path to damnation. But it was also a paradoxical component of the fantasy of witchcraft, for the kinds of stories to which it led were often different in character from the terrifying visions of old, cannibalistic witches. Under interrogation, women told tales about their seduction by the Devil which were gentle, even playful in nature, and which were studded with details apparently drawn from daily life.

It is striking how often the confessions of the accused witches did not quite accord with demonological theory. Because confessing to witchcraft nearly always meant supplying stories about copulation with the Devil, it forced women to tell convincing tales about sex, stories which would draw on individual detail in order to persuade the interrogators that the stories were true; and the more individual detail was supplied, the more the tales departed from the demonologically conventional. It is also evident that different localities followed different practices of recording, some leaving criminal records which include a very wide range of idiosyncratic stories about the Devil; others, accounts which are numbingly formulaic.

This was the case in sixteenth-century Marchtal, where the records of interrogation betray little of how confessions were arrived at, how or when torture was applied, or even what questions were put. During the witch-hunting panic of the 1580s and 1590s, the stories women told were virtually interchangeable. The Devil came dressed in black, wearing a black hat with a feather on it. His name was nearly always Federle, or Federlin – the little feather. The feather was a symbol of duplicity and trickery as well as being a jaunty decoration for the hats so many devils wore; and it could even refer to the penis.[5] The moral significance of the name was thus immediately clear: the Devil was the master of illusion and trickery, his phallic feather stood for his lubricious nature. But there were always the exceptions that proved the rule: one woman boasted a devil by the saintly name of Bonifazius (Boniface), while her sister Margaret had a devil called Pauli Fazius, the unconventional detail now repeated in garbled form. The Marchtal stories follow more or less the same pattern. The woman meets Federle dressed in black and she has intercourse with him. Usually she gives a list of two or three places where sex took place: a barn, her dwelling, the forest. She gives him her right hand, he offers her his left and she swears the diabolic pact. He says very little at all. Sometimes she notices his goat's feet, sometimes she notices his coldness. The richness of detail in the Marchtal confessions is reserved for the list of people, animals and children she harmed, and the precise ways in which she did so.[6]

The Marchtal confessions were unusually dry. When Ursula Bayer, for instance, recalled her seduction, she said only that her diabolic bridegroom had come thirty-five years before, wearing 'black clothes, with a black satin hat, black feather on it, into her house, and said, she should follow him, he would give her enough all the days of her life, upon which she converted, and gave him her right while he gave her his left hand', and forthwith, she forswore

God and the saints. The bulk of her interrogation, thirteen more pages of it, was taken up with listing the people and animals she had harmed.[7] The confessions from Marchtal reflect the particular constellation of circumstances in the territory ruled by the abbey, where the sixteenth-century interrogators do not seem to have been especially interested in the details of life with demons. Abbot Konrad Frei, under whose incumbency most of the trials took place, was a local from a prominent family in Munderkingen, just west along the Danube from Obermarchtal, and he had served at Kirchenbierlingen, the home of three of the victims of the witch craze. Interested in learning, he sent young monks off for training at Dillingen, the bulwark of the Counter-Reformation and a university which also boasted experts on demonology.[8] The trials, however, appear to have been presided over by local secular officials and judges. These men were drawn from the same communities as the witches or from similar villages and townlets in what was a very small territory. They shared the mental worlds from which the accused witches came, and they lacked the anthropological curiosity about their subjects shown by the interrogators at Würzburg.

Barbara Hohenberger's tale at Würzburg, by contrast, conveys the excitement of being wooed by the persistent lover who won't take no for an answer. Many women described the Devil as their ideal lover. For Maria Schöpperlin at Nördlingen, he was young, with 'not much beard, very good looking, and looked like her beau, who was a young cloth weaver'. In Eichstätt, one woman saw the Devil in the shape of a priest with whom she had had an affair, surely the epitome of glamour in this rural town surrounded by hills and dominated by glorious Counter-Reformation buildings with a new seminary to train clergy; another in the Würzburg region also saw the Devil as a 'young pastor'.[9] To Maria Marb in Nördlingen the demon was no mere citizen of a medium-sized town like her own but a nobleman, an imposing man on horseback. In a story that has the ring of fairy tale, he had first asked her where she was going, to which she answered that she had to beg. Immediately, the liberal aristocrat gave what was to her the vast sum of 50 thalers, with which she and her sister bought velvet from Nuremberg; she was lucky, for the Devil's gifts usually turned to dirt or leaves. The fabulous courtship continued, as she described it in fittingly courtly language: 'The noble one came into her mother's house after her mother's death, in the evening, desiring that she should do his will, which happened. Afterwards he desired that she should promise herself to him and be his, although her heart was heavy ....'[10] Most, however, located him in the same social group or slightly higher than that in which they would normally look for a marriage partner. Agnes Heylmann met the Devil as a young man in black clothes, white stockings and goat's feet, wearing a peasant collar.[11]

Usually the Devil is a young man, virile and sexually knowing, unburdened by the staid responsibilities of mature manhood. Hans Dülicken's wife met the

Devil when she was a young girl keeping geese at the local castle, and he came to her in the form of a shepherd's boy, speaking with a soft voice.[12] The women describe his clothing in loving detail. Often he wears trousers of satin or velvet. He sports a hat with a crest of feathers (*Federbusch*), a stylish adornment which hints at his potency as it sets off his attire. As a young man his clothes are figure-hugging and alluring, not the usual sombre black garments of men of authority. He might have stepped right out of the pages of the sixteenth-century Devil Books, which excoriate the excesses of young men's overly fashionable clothing. These women are skilled judges of dress, knowing what the feel and texture of the velvet will reveal of the social standing of its wearer. Which class of people were permitted to wear what clothes was prescribed by elaborate sumptuary ordinances, so that a people's status could be read from their garments – the heavy golden chains permitted merchants, the fur denied craftsfolk. When the sixteenth-century merchant Mathäus Schwarz wanted to create a monumental biography of himself, he chose to commission portraits of himself in over a hundred of the outfits he had worn during his life, from the racy doublets of his youth to the staid black cloaks of his mature years.[13] And in an age when many people had but one set of clothes, descriptions of a fugitive's clothing might be circulated in place of physical description.

Colour is always mentioned. The Devil's colour is black, and many of these demons did appear as 'black men', a designation which might refer to skin colour or to clothes. Occasionally he was dressed not in black, but in green, the colour of the huntsman. In the Würzburg trials, Barbara Schluchter's devil was 'a small man in green clothes' and Anna, known as the 'one-eyed locksmith's wife', 'saw him coming from far off, he had a green tunic, a high hat and a feather'. Often the Devil wore vivacious colour combinations: red clothes with a black hat, or as another woman described him, 'he was a beautiful young man with a black beard, red clothing, green stockings and black hat, with a red feather upon it'.[14]

The Devil promised love and marriage. He appeared to Waldburga Schmid in the form of Schnörrers Steffan, with whom she was in love, and who used to come courting to her window at nights. Waldburga had slept with Steffan and wanted to marry him, but her people would not allow her to wed him and often beat her, so that she said, 'If God would not help her to a husband, then the Devil should help her to one'. This was a sin, not only because she was acting in defiance of her parents' wishes, but because she had uttered a curse, invoking the Devil. When Steffan left the area, the Devil continued to visit her in Steffan's shape, kissing her and saying 'You know that I have always loved you'. Indeed, the Devil had helped her to a husband – himself – and she had turned from father and mother to cleave to him.[15] To Anna Grauch the Devil appeared in her parents' parlour at Gerolzhofen as an ordinary, tongue-tied suitor, and her parents fetched bread and wine as they would for a formal betrothal, where the ceremony of swearing a promise of marriage to each other was followed by a simple meal:

> afterwards they went with one another into her parlour, sat down at the table, father and mother sat there too and also ate, they had bread and wine, her mother fetched the wine, they sat at table for about half an hour ... the Evil One didn't say much but just kept repeating, 'she should have good things'.[16]

Like a simple peasant, this devil is not good with words, but he keeps saying the only thing that matters, the promise dear to the heart of every bride, that 'she should have good things'. For Anna Grauch and women like her, marriage held out the promise of security, of being able to become one of the solid matrons of village society instead of a rootless, dependent maid. Widows too faced the threat of the kind of poverty that would drive them out of village or town society. For the widow Barbara, later married to Leonhard Hohenberger, marriage was the answer to her prayers. A marriage would have solved her problems of debt and enabled her to escape from the impossible twin burdens of caring for her children while scraping a living as best she could.

The language the Devil used to bind his victims to him was borrowed from that of courtship. He promised 'that he will not leave her'; that 'she should be his', that 'if you will be my lover and give yourself to me and do what I command you and what I want, then I will give you enough to eat and drink, and I will not desert you'. These are the forms of words which women cited when they sued for breach of marriage promise, as abandoned women often did in the sixteenth and seventeenth centuries. The dialogue is supplied, the scene is set, just as it would have been in a court case. Often the demon gives the woman a token, frequently some money, symbolizing the stream of money he will supply as a husband. This too was the custom in promising marriage, where a suitor would give a token – a ring, a coin or even a ribbon – in earnest of marriage. The gift of such an item would then be cited when a woman sued to enforce the marriage.

In these stories, the Devil emerges as a real character. He is given his own dialogue. Sometimes he introduces himself straight out, like one demon who boldly announced that he was the Devil and that his name was Frank.[17] Anna Lang found the Devil in her kitchen while she was cooking, and he said to her 'Can't you cook something better than that?', to which she replied, 'What poor folk have, they must cook.'[18] He visits the accused witch not once but several times so that a relationship between the two of them develops. Sex with the Devil is not a one-night stand but a long-term relationship, the culmination of a passionate wooing. Barbara Herpolt recalled that

> [While she was a widow with small children] and worried about herself, he came to her ... in her chamber, like a servant man, a red face and a red

beret, smooth trousers and stockings, a hat with black and white feathers, and he spoke to her: Where are you going, Miss? and asked, Whether she had no husband?, and she answered, No. Upon which he said, she should take him. If she would follow him, he would help her, so that she should have sufficient all her life long. She said to him that he was too good looking for her, and asked him where he came from. He said that he would tell her later, and that he wanted to come to her that very day. She said to him: Bring me something good, and he said: Yes. That night he came to her in her chamber and said: Come here. I love you. Wanted to give her enough, she should be his, and do what he told her. Had sex with her. He had a cold member, and called himself *Spitz Hutlein* (pointy little hat).[19]

His name did not just refer to his headgear. The sense of longing and satisfaction in the rhythmic dialogue Herpolt supplied to her Würzburg interrogators is palpable – this is a lover who brings gifts. He is impatient for the loved one, he knows how to tease and how to speak the words of love. Although the Devil promises her material goods, it is not the desire for money which is her undoing. She and the other women who describe their relationships with the Devil dream of a lover who will provide economic security, pleasure and love. The scope of their ambitions was in one sense narrow. Few imagined fabled wealth or noble bearing. For the most part, they did not want to marry the fairytale prince. They wanted to be looked after, to be 'given enough', to be free of the worry of making ends meet and secure in the social position they had.

If the woman was already married, the Devil sometimes promised a trade-in for a better husband. Margaretha Schmid was tempted by her cousin, who invited her to her house and said, 'Cousin, since you have such an evil husband, I will give you another in his place', to which Schmid replied 'Yes, if she could give her a pious one, she would take him and be satisfied.'[20] The women shared the secret of the worthless husband, plotting together to be rid of him. Other women were tempted to adultery by the Devil. Margareta Limpart agreed to sex with him when he promised to give her 'good times', exclaiming 'if only she knew it were true', to which he responded with earnest promises and a thaler coin.[21] Their stories too follow the lines of the narratives of seduction and fall which are to be found time and again in court records of prostitutes and adulteresses. The women trade sex for money. Even so, they dream of a long-lasting affair, of a steady, reliable beau. Typically the Devil promised that 'she should not want her whole life long', a promise which he, like all callous seducers, had no intention of keeping.

The Devil had a knack of worming his way into the secrets of the unhappy wife's heart. In the village of Alleshausen in Marchtal, Margareta Moll was in desperation over the cruelty of her husband, Hans Hepp. She ran away from him to the nearby town of Biberach, planning to stay at her cousin's house. On the way, as she passed through a wood, a hare repeatedly ran across her path, and she was so troubled by this omen that 'she turned around again, back, and went home in all kinds of thoughts'. But when she arrived she found that her husband had thrown her bed and all the household goods that were hers into the garden. This, she said, probably made her fall into despair. Though the Church would never have sanctioned this kind of informal divorce, it did occasionally permit separations from 'bed and board'; while in popular culture, throwing the other spouse's goods out of the house was a recognized way of terminating the marriage, breaking the community of goods that bound the married couple together. In her misery, the Devil appeared to Margaretha in the barn where she was now living, he was dressed in black with an ash-coloured hat. He spoke sweet words to her, and promised that 'if she would do his will, he would teach her a way that her husband would never beat her again'. Indeed, perhaps the Devil fulfilled his bargain, for Margareta's brutal husband was executed in August 1586. He met a terrible death, broken on the wheel as a 'witch-man', murderer and fish-poacher.[22] Moll's is one of the fullest narratives of diabolic seduction to be found in the records from Marchtal, and its story of the strange behaviour of the hare and the journey through the forest draws on folk tale as well as on the conventions of diabolic seduction.

Things became more difficult when men were accused of witchcraft and began admitting to diabolic intercourse. This posed no problem for demonological theory, for the Devil could take on any human shape, male or female, in order to have intercourse with his victim. But when it came to making confessions, men's descriptions of sex with the Devil were frequently unorthodox and convoluted. Hans Holz described how he had been seduced into witchcraft by his sister in autumn in the cow stall. He had been drunk, and had not understood what he was doing when he promised to obey her and learn the trade. Shortly after, a pretty young girl appeared in the cow stall, dressed in white with a white apron and a hairband on her head. Black would of course have been a more conventional diabolic colour. He had sex with the white-clad girl on his sister's instruction. Sex with her was like that with any other woman, but cold. The girl's hand, however, was rough, hairy and chill, characteristics which suggested the true masculine nature of his paramour. Moreover, the Evil Spirit usually showed up when Holz was drunk.[23]

Men's stories about sex with the Devil frequently diverged from the path of faithful heterosexual union. Often, male witches said that the Devil had appeared in the shape of a particular woman they knew. Women sometimes said this too, but it was far more common amongst men. Stories of this kind fitted with the conventions of the Faust story, where the Devil brought Faust any woman on whom he set his fancy, even including Helen of Troy. More frequently, men confessed, like Faust, to having sex with a number of women, whereas most women had a sole diabolic lover. Conrad Schreyer from Marchtal, for instance, admitted to having intercourse with Margareta Haller, who had confessed to witchcraft. He had also had intercourse with a female devil dressed in black with a hat, called Jhenofher, a wonderfully exotic name that contrasts with humdrum Federle. In an interesting reversal of terms, he said that she had promised herself to him completely. Though this formulation satisfied male pride, it did not make demonological sense, since Conrad ought to have been promising himself to the Devil. Where a female witch like Hohenberger spoke of the Devil as someone who looked like the man she planned to marry, Schreyer's story retained diabolic intercourse with a devil in a female body as well as human intercourse with a witch. He went on to confess to committing sodomy with a red cow while standing on a milking stool.[24] Martin Getz also confessed in 1627 at Marchtal that he had committed bestiality on the urging of the Devil, who told him to 'ride the mare on which he was now sitting'. He was tempted by his neighbours' cows and the Devil advised him to visit them on Sunday afternoons, when he would not be caught – compounding his sin with profanation of the Sabbath. The Devil had met him again on his father's meadow and had asked him whether he still 'rode'. When he told him that he had given up the vice, the Devil tempted him once more, fatally as it transpired, for he was caught and executed. Getz maintained that the Devil had sheep's feet. As his interrogator noted, he surely meant goat's feet; but since there were no goats at Zell, he had probably never seen one, and so made a mistake.[25] This was not a story about diabolic intercourse but a confession to bestiality in which the Devil played the active role, guessing his desires and tempting him to indulge in 'riding'. Nor did Getz confess to any acts of malefice.

Some women, too, described their experience of diabolic sex in animal terms. The Devil is like a 'roaring lion', some said, drawing on the biblical description; Ursula Grön said 'she had to lay herself down on the floor in her house, he pushes you down like a dog. So it was, certainly the spirit doesn't deal with you subtly.' One woman recounted how sex with the Devil 'was as if a rooster hops on a hen, so fast did it come to an end'.[26] These were bestial, degrading acts of intercourse. Some described a terrifying sexual encounter with a being who was not human. Or as the woman fondles her lover, she suddenly notices that his flesh is not yielding: she 'touched him on his shame and his breasts and found that it was hard, and she said Lord protect us, what is this? and he disappeared'. Often the Devil is described as a creature with animal features: cat's paws, goat's feet, horse's hooves, even a snout like a pig.[27] Here women could draw on depictions of the Devil which they saw in their own parish churches, or in woodcuts, of a figure with animal attributes. Such images reflected the way in which Satan disrupted the order of the natural

24. Francesco Maria Guazzo, *Compendium maleficarum*, Milan 1626: woodcut illustration showing a witch giving the anal kiss to Satan.

world, mixing human and animal. Strange animal behaviour features in many of the confessions. The conjunction of human, animal and diabolic found its most terrifying expression in the stories of diabolic familiars which are so often also reported in English witchcraft confessions. These are animals who suck the witch's blood from teats, sometimes near her genitals, and are used by her to carry out errands of malevolence.[28] German confessions to witchcraft never mention familiar spirits, and are drawn from a repertoire of magical and demonological beliefs quite different from the English. Yet though the German confessions generally begin with accounts of sexual union which are shaped by the conventions of heterosexual courtship, they also occasionally suggest images of demons whose hybrid shape summons up visions of monstrous beings that are conjunctions of human and animal.

Often the Devil arrives when the woman is in despair. He appeared to Dilge Glaser in Basle when she was contemplating suicide, asking, 'Dilge, how come you are feeling so low, how can you behave like this?'; while he came to Kethe, the wife of Claus am Stein, as she was thinking 'that she was so poor and miserable. The Evil One said, he knew well, that she was poor and miserable, and did not have much for the best, if she could love him, he would give her something from time to time.'[29] The Devil seems to understand her plight and he offers a way out. His apparent sympathy, however, is a trap. He might tempt one to suicide, an act which many believed would exclude one forever from the community of fellow Christians. Suicide was held to be a crime, and those who committed it were punished by being buried in unconsecrated ground or even put into barrels and cast upon the water.

Such gruesome customs reflect a strong cultural hostility to feelings of depression. These were emotions which might expose one to the snares of the Devil. If one felt despair, one's very relationship to the community of Christians was at risk. One might be diabolically tempted to commit suicide, one might waver in one's loyalty to God and endanger one's immortal soul. Becoming a witch was akin to committing suicide, for not only did a witch face death, she had also taken the step of excluding herself from the community of Christians and allying herself with the Devil against God. Times of despair are evidently remembered – or related – by the women who confess to them as moments in which they were particularly vulnerable to sin, an apprehension which would have been shared by their interrogators.[30] Demonologists were well aware of the power of melancholy to expose women to temptation. In his elaborate categorization of the reasons why people become addicted to witch-craft, the Catholic demonologist Peter Binsfeld listed too much sorrow as the eighth cause, a condition 'which is often found amongst women'. He went on: 'For when women fall into revulsion, do not wish to work, or fall into sadness, their dispositions become distorted, and in particular, if no comfort, advice or help is present, the Devil sees this and in the form of a fictitious person, he offers help, advice and protection with miraculous trickery.'[31] The dangers of despair were a theme of popular literature too: in 1559, Martin Montanus's collection of diverting tales included one story of a widow with young children who fell into despair; immediately the Devil appeared, offering to marry her and solve her financial problems. She agreed, but the Devil then spent such a boisterous night with her that all the neighbours heard the noise. Intercourse was such torture that she realized – too late – that her husband must be the Devil; and eight days later she was found dead in her bed, 'ridden to death by the Devil'.[32]

Some stories of seduction by the Devil breathe romance; others are cynically realistic about power between men and women. The Devil, despite his 'smooth, smeared words',[33] is not a reliable lover. He does not provide for her, and good times do not follow. Even the pleasure of seduction is only a prelude to painful, unsatisfactory intercourse: the Devil is cold, she never feels pleasure with him, his penis is long and hard. As these women well knew, marriage does not guarantee a fairytale happy ending. Their picture of sexual exchange with men is bleak. Men do not give the material security they promise. The Devil is a heartless young male seducer who seems to understand the woman's despair but leaves her in the lurch. Anna Schinleder was canny enough to spend the money he gave her at once on drink; those who did not found to their cost that the money turned to leaf mould or to dung.

Sex and marriage were, at their most basic, about possession. At the heart of the bargain with the Devil lay the promise, made in marriage as in the diabolic pact, that 'you are mine'. Barbara Herpolt's demon said that 'she should be his, and do what he told her', linking the giving of oneself in marriage with the duty to obey. As women plundered the language of courtship and marriage to convey what the bond with the Devil was like, their picture of marriage became very grim. Marriage meant being owned by another, giving sex with the expectation of economic support. With the Devil it was often a one-sided bargain, in which women were the losers. A few insisted that copulation with demons was just like intercourse with their husbands. Barbara Dämeter had intercourse with the Devil in the form of her husband, and she did not realize it was a demon until she noticed that he often visited when her husband was away. But she rapidly added that it seemed to her that her husband's coition was better than the Devil's, and soon she was reporting that the Evil One's nature was cold and hard, and he had no male seed.[34] Here she may well have been responding to the prompting of her questioners, who also had no wish to encourage the worrying idea that the Devil might have ejaculated seed and therefore produced demonic offspring. More conventionally, Anna Melber, tried in 1617 during the Würzburg panics, said that 'her lover had practised indecency with her often, his male organ had come into her body, but she preferred her husband, for it was very cold and she had little joy of it, but it lasted about half an hour'.[35]

The theme of sexual ownership found its most complete and terrifying expression in the idea that women might be visited by their demons even while they were in prison, and might engage in intercourse with them. These nocturnal visits strengthened the women in their resistance to questioning and torture, for the Devil would admonish them to be brave and would promise – vainly, as ever – to save them. Lucia Vischer from Marchtal had sex with the Devil in prison, adding that the Devil had been there for two hours with her. Lena Greter's devil came to her at night in prison, and 'did his desire with her in a hideous fashion, so that it made her quite ill'.[36] One of the fullest accounts of diabolic intercourse offered by the witches of Marchtal was that of Anna Moll, who said that 'when the evil spirit had done the work of unchastity for long enough, she vomited, and so he had to leave her then'. Moll and her father Michel both confessed to committing incest with each other, so her revulsion towards diabolic intercourse may have mirrored her feelings about sex and its results in her life. When Anna harmed people, she did so by giving them eggs, smeared with salve. Eggs symbolize fertility, but these eggs were meant to harm and kill. This made psychological sense. Moll's whole family had been virtually rooted out by the witch panic. Her mother, uncle and grandmother had been executed for witchcraft seven years before, her aunt, three years ago; while her father perished with her in the flames in 1593. Incest features time and again in this family saga: Anna's uncle, the infamous Hans Hepp who had ended up being broken on the wheel as a witch man and murderer, had also confessed to committing incest with his sister-in-law, Anna's mother. In the case of the Molls, sex had led not to the increase and fecundity of the family but to its almost complete extinction – small wonder that Anna chose eggs to revenge herself on others.[37]

Indeed, the language of seduction and marriage sat uncomfortably with the diabolic fantasy, for which after all it was not designed. Although the *Malleus* and other works of demonology mentioned the possibility of marriage with the Devil they did not dwell on it. Nicolas Rémy, whose work is perhaps closer than that of any demonologist to the criminal cases he tried, noted that devils frequently contracted marriage to the women they seduced, and provided examples of diabolic weddings. However, in proper orthodox fashion, he pointed out that such marriages were not of course true sacramental marriages, but false illusions.[38]

In diabolic theory, there was no need for the Devil to promise marriage to a woman: a witch was his already, through the pact she made with him and through her bodily surrender. It was the conventions for talking about sex that shaped the witches' confessions, even when what they confessed did not quite fit diabolic theory. These conventions were clear. In sixteenth- and seventeenth-century Germany, women who found themselves abandoned by their lovers could go to court to attempt to force the men to marry them or at least pay them damages for loss of virginity and child support. When they testified in court about their sexual relations, the seducer's promise of marriage was always part of the story, except if either party was married already. There were good reasons for this. In the years before the Reformation, there was considerable ambiguity about what counted as a marriage.

If a man promised to marry a woman in the future, and then had sex with her, the marriage was fully binding according to canon law, regardless of whether a priest was present or where the promise took place. But a woman could only win a marriage suit and force her partner to marry her if there were two witnesses to the promise they had exchanged. Nearly always, the woman lacked two such witnesses, because the 'promises' were usually made just before intercourse. So familiar had this procedure become through years of the operation of church and marriage courts that women well knew they had no chance of winning a case if they lacked the requisite two witnesses, yet they still insisted that their lovers had promised to marry them.

After the Counter-Reformation had got under way, even the two witnesses would not have been sufficient to force the seducer into marriage, as the promise had to be made with the consent of parents and banns had to be read – yet this did not stop women maintaining that the apparently pointless promise of marriage had none the less been made. The promise simply had to be in the story because it guaranteed the woman's honour. So also, when women imagined being courted by the Devil, they pictured him promising to marry them; sex otherwise was inconceivable.[39]

To say that she had been seduced by the Devil also allowed the woman to claim that she was a victim. Presenting herself as a weak woman, she could claim her despair – or her concupiscence – had made her easy prey for the Devil. As in claims for compensation for childbed and child support, where the woman had to appear to be her seducer's victim to deserve economic support, so also these women presented themselves as gullible innocents and the Devil as the real agent. Instead of being powerful figures of maleficence, sworn to kill and injure all Christian souls, these women spoke as if they were victims in the age-old story of men's heartlessness towards women.

Often an intermediary ensured their undoing, an older woman, usually the mother. She is the so-called *Lehrmeisterin*, the mistress who, like the master of a trade, instructs her apprentices in the diabolic arts. In Eichstätt, Barbara Weis recalled how:

> Thereupon the Evil Spirit came to her for the first time in her mother's kitchen, when she had come there on her own from Spalt. He came in the form of a craftsman, dressed in black clothes, a feather on his hat, and with a cloven foot. He was also black. Her mother was present and desired that she should commit indecency with him, but for a long time she didn't want to do it, which however her mother insisted on, so she was forced. And she completed the act of bodily indecency with him, upon which her mother went out and laughed. He was utterly cold. Afterwards she had to deny God and give herself to the Devil.[40]

The mother's laughter is chilling, mocking the destruction of her daughter's soul. Margaret Schreyer said that

> about twenty years ago she went with old Scheidlerin in the woods of Gerolzhofen looking for pasture, and Scheidlerin began, if she would follow her, she would give her enough her whole life long, which she immediately promised her. Then a young man in red clothes and a black hat appeared, and her *Lehrmeisterin* began, she had taught someone something!, he said, she was right about him, whether she wanted to be his, which she promised him, giving him her hand, and he giving her a thaler, so that she could buy bread, she lay down, and was uncovered in the presence of her *Lehrmeisterin*.[41]

Here it is the old woman who makes the seductive promises on the Devil's behalf and who acts like the witnesses at a wedding, present while the couple bed down together. In the cases from Marchtal, a woman – mostly the accused witch's mother – is sometimes the Devil's go-between. She explains what the witch has to gain by joining with the Devil and is often present at the sexual scene. Ursula Bayer inducted Margretha Selg into the diabolic life, promising her a good time and smearing the white rod on which she rode to the Sabbath; Anna Moll was misled by her mother, Anna Hiert, executed as a witch some time before Moll confessed.[42] Like a procuress, she handed over the young woman to her seducer. This configuration of course again places the burden of guilt on women, this time older women. Just as the shadowy figure of the procuress got both seducer and prostitute off the hook – she was led astray by a heartless older woman; he was merely acting like a virile young man – so the *Lehrmeisterin* turns out to be the real villainess.

This variant of the story of diabolic seduction simply reflects the pervasive power of parental figures in early modern society. Parents – whether kings and queens or peasant men and women – devised marriage strategies for their children which would conserve property and advance family interests. The inclinations of the children were a secondary consideration. When an accused witch told a story about her seduction and marriage with the Devil it was natural that her parents, especially her mother, should figure in the tale. As in any craft, learning to become a witch necessitated training. Early modern society constantly elided relationships of parental authority with authority of any kind. The *Lehrmeisterin*, like the master who trained his apprentices, was a father figure in psychological if not biological terms. Witchcraft, moreover, travelled in the blood. It was widely believed that being a witch was bequeathed by parents to children.

The effect of the presence of the *Lehrmeisterin* is to invoke the figure of the old woman, raising the spectre of barrenness and death. Once intercourse is over, the fantasy becomes sombre: gone is the world of pleasant dalliance and in its place is a grim, diabolic realm of death and destruction. In the formulaic accounts of sex with the Devil which survive for Marchtal, the seduction scene is followed by revolting accounts of diabolic feasts and of harm caused to pregnant women, babies and young children. Anna Mayer saw the Devil dressed in black. His name was Federlin. On the advice of her diabolic bridegroom, she killed her own child in the womb by giving it a knock or pressing it hard. Anna Glenzinger had met the Devil eighteen years ago while walking home, and he asked 'why she walked thus, whether he should not go with her, and be her escort'. After this polite beginning, however, he made endless sexual demands on her. He gave her a potion which destroyed two children in her womb, and he had sex with her while she was pregnant, so that the unborn children would not come to baptism.[43]

In these cases from Marchtal, the formulas of the narratives create a repetitive pattern. Sex with the Devil results in the killing of children, their exhumation, cooking and eating. It even leads women to kill the fruit of their own wombs. The same is true for the confessions of witches from Nördlingen, where stories of diabolic seduction rapidly give way to darker tales about the cooking and eating of exhumed children. And in Würzburg too, the structure of the confessions moves from stories about seduction to catalogues of the blasphemies and vile deeds of witches.

Sex with the Devil was the opposite of the warm, fertile mingling of human procreation. As medical theory then had it, heat was essential for conception, and the friction of intercourse created the warmth which would release male and female seed, allowing them to join together. How far those accused of witchcraft understood the medical account of conception is unclear, but they would certainly have believed that heat played an important role. By contrast, nearly all witches concurred that the Devil's member was cold. As ever, as we have seen, there were exceptions: Affra, widow of Michel Mertzler, recounted how

> at that time he made love to her in her bed, his shame was very hot; he had cat's feet and a nature like another man, but she didn't see properly how he was equipped in every detail. Upon which she was asked 'Since according to her testimony her lover was formed in his nature like another man, why she had not become pregnant?'[44]

Her answer was matter-of-fact: she had not become pregnant, she said, because she had not got pregnant in the past twenty-six years. Generally, witches completely ruled out the idea that sex with the Devil could result in offspring. Instead, their vision was of a congress which was cold, joyless and had no fruit.

From the very beginnings of demonology, writers had worried about whether demons could father children. Such anxiety had a long pedigree: Jewish thinkers had worried that seed spilt during masturbation might be stolen by demons and used to father children.[45] Indeed, the question is raised near the start of the *Malleus*, in the third chapter, where a lengthy disquisition leads the author to conclude that it is possible for children to be born of diabolic intercourse, but that such children would not be the children of demons. According to the theory of demonic intercourse, an explosive mixture of theological knowledge and medical speculation, demons had no bodies. They could only take over corpses or use bodies made of condensed vapours. The number of demons was fixed, and demons could not increase their number by propagation. They could, however, turn themselves into succubi and in this form, steal human semen from males. As incubus devils, they could inject this semen into female partners. The semen, however, remained natural, human semen. Consequently the offspring were most assuredly the children of men, not devils.[46]

As demonologists were forced to consider, there were a number of difficulties with this theory of diabolic artificial insemination, and Rémy wrote witheringly about their intellectual inconsistencies. How could two entirely different species, human and spiritual, commingle he asked. How could the Devil get the seed to the recipient fast enough, and would it not lose the vital heat necessary for generation *en route*? In any case, since all those he had heard confess agreed that intercourse with the Devil was cold and painful, these women could not have released seed through orgasm, and neither could the male and female seeds have been hot enough to mingle. Diabolic intercourse, he argued, could simply not lead to conception. In so doing, Rémy was once again in close accord with what accused witches said in trial.

However, Rémy was also well aware of other currents of belief. He conceded that many thought the offspring conceived through diabolic intercourse from stolen male and female seed were children who 'in their infancy . . . cry day and night, and are heavy but emaciated, and yet can suck five nurses dry'. Here he was developing an observation made by his former teacher Jean Bodin, who had maintained that the children of such unions were called 'Vechselbelg' – he expressly employed the German term – or changelings, and that they 'were much heavier than other children, although they always remain thin, and could suck three nurses to death before they get even a bit fat'.[47] Bodin had thought these might be explained as the result of demons stealing human seed. When Johann Fischart, the translator of Rabelais into German, produced his expanded translation of Bodin's work, he could not resist interpolating a story of his own into Bodin's text. In Saxony near Halberstadt, a man had a changeling child, or as it was known, a *Kilkropf*, or *Kehlkopf*. This child had sucked its own mother and five other nurses dry, and it ate as much as any peasant or thresher. The unfortunate father was advised to take the child to Our Lady at Hockelstatt and weigh it, and so he 'carried the lovely garbage there in a basket'. When they came to a river, a demon was hiding in the water, calling 'Kilkropf, Kilkropf!', and to his amazement, the changeling, who had never spoken a word before, suddenly said 'Ho, Ho, Ha!' and then got into conversation with the Devil, explaining in perfect rhyming Saxon, 'I want to go to Our Lady in Hockelstatt, and be weighed, so that I will thrive' ('Ick will gen Hochstatt zur Lefen Frawen/ Vnd mick allda laten wigen/ dat ick mög etwa digen'). Horrified, the father threw the basket in the river, where the demons greeted the *Kilkropf* as one of their own, saying 'Ho, Ho, Ha!, and turning somersaults with him in the river.[48] The joke in this story, told by the Protestant Fischart, is at the expense of Catholic belief in Mary and at the idea of a changeling who can speak Saxon. As ever, Fischart seizes any chance to tell a good story, even though the tale distracts from Bodin's argument. The subject of changelings, with its mixture of fable, grotesque, tall tale and joke, is simply irresistible, summoning associations which refuse to fit neatly into demonological theory. Such children would have been human, according to conventional demonic theory, because they had arisen from male seed injected into witches; but the story implies that the *Kilkropf*, casually thrown to drown in the river, is actually demonic and not human.[49]

Creatures like changelings, Rémy claimed, could be explained naturalistically, as caused by defects in semen, the influence of the stars and moon, or malformation of the womb. There were also, he added, infants who cry and twist in a diabolic manner, but these could be explained as the effects of the mother's imagination. Witches who had frequent intercourse with the Devil were liable to be affected in this way, for

> if a woman receives a strong mental impression and dwells deeply upon it, either at the time of conception or some time during gestation, the image of that thought will generally be imprinted upon her child: if she fixedly concentrates upon some real or wished for object, the result is that her vital essences are affected by it, and its image is transfixed to and imprinted upon the child in her womb.

Indeed, the presence of a demon could also affect a woman's imagination so that, in rare cases, she gave birth to a monster. Rémy describes the 'horrid harsh hissing which such infants utter instead of wailing, their headlong gait and their manner of searching into hidden places'. As often happens in Rémy's writing, what appears to be a forthright rejection of a vile possibility – that there could be offspring of diabolic intercourse – ends up invoking in vivid detail the very horror he is ruling out of court. He goes on to explain that in some cases the Devil can enter the child's body soon after birth even without the mother's permission. He concludes that such children should not be baptized by the Church and deserve to be put to death – a licensing of infanticide which was of course completely counter to Catholic doctrine.

Rémy's view that demonic intercourse was sterile did not command universal assent amongst demonologists. Martin del Rio, for one, took Rémy to task, pointing out that two separate orders of being were not involved in generation through demonic intercourse, but only stolen human seed. It was of course no problem for the Devil to cover great distances at enormous speed, thereby retaining the warmth of the seed. The pain women attested to on intercourse proved nothing, for the Devil could also simulate warmth. For the most part, if the Devil did not disguise himself, his semen was cold; but if he wished to trick his partner, he simply ejaculated warm fluid. Generation in such cases, Del Rio reassuringly conceded, was exceedingly rare; and he ruled out altogether the possibility that incubi and succubi could generate children between them, using stolen seed. But his arguments seemed to allow that there might occasionally be offspring born of demonic intercourse, though not of demonic seed. These arguments were repeated by the Italian Francesco Maria Guazzo in his *Compendium maleficarum*. Guazzo was a systematizer, whose work is plodding plagiarism of existing works of demonology, with little spark of original argument. He repeated the by now familiar formula that while a child can be born of demonic intercourse, the father is not a demon but the man whose semen was stolen. It was in any case rare for demons to wish to engage in generation. And if the witch knew she was having intercourse with a demon, the semen would be cold.

Demonologists, like Del Rio, Binsfeld and Guazzo, were not prepared to concede that copulation with demons never produced offspring. Their solution was to argue that the offspring were human and had human parents. As Peter Binsfeld put it, such children were not the children of devils but resulted 'with the help of a human, by taking the seed from the man with shameful subterfuge, and even more shamefully they expel it while coupling with the women, but all according to the special ordinance of God, so that he who is thus conceived and born is not the Devil's child, but the child of the person from whom the seed was taken.'[50] It followed that the copulation did not produce beings who arose from true sexual commingling, as is the case with humans, but only seemed to do so through the Devil's trickery. The human and demonic orders remained comfortingly separate.

Guazzo, however, prefaced his account of the operations of incubi and succubi with a rather more disquieting story that was in circulation in the period and is even to be found in a Jewish version amongst the tales included in Glikl of Hameln's seventeenth-century autobiography. It tells of a woman criminal who was deported to a desert island where she was captured by a tribe of apes and forced to become the wife of one of them. She gave birth to several children and lived on the island for some time in this state of degradation. At last she was found by Portuguese sailors and escaped onto a ship. When her ape consort discovered she had fled, he took one of the children and drowned it in front of her, and then another; but she still would not leave the ship and return to her ape husband. When the ship arrived at port, the woman was condemned to be burnt as a sodomite. This tale is unsettling on several levels. It suggests the possibility that congress between humans and animals could result in offspring, and thus, by implication, suggests that there might be diabolic progeny. Apparently the story insists that the union between animal and human must end in death and destruction: because she has committed bestiality, even though under duress, the woman must be executed once the ship reaches human civilization again. But, Guazzo tells us, her sentence was commuted to life imprisonment, and whether the offspring are real human beings or not remains uncertain. Even after Guazzo has finished the chapter and moved on to provide his conventional demolition of the case for the existence of true diabolic progeny, the disturbing implications of the story may well have remained in the reader's mind.[51]

Demonologists tied themselves into knots over this issue because they were confronting contradictions that lay at the heart of the idea of the witch. On the one hand, most agreed that there could be no offspring who were a mixture of humans and demons, though some quoted the passage in Genesis about the sons of God lusting for the daughters of man and producing a race of giants. On the other, demonologists were drawn to discuss the phenomenon of 'Vechselbelg', or changelings, who seemed to be demonic children of some kind. Bodin uses the German term, and it is also evident that Rémy was dealing with vivid popular beliefs in Lorraine, an area that blended French and German traditions. Yet we should perhaps exercise some caution in describing these passages of demonology as straightforwardly reflecting popular belief, for it is noticeable that all authors use virtually the same words in describing *Wechselbälge*. All repeat the memorable formula that such infants sucked three (some even say five) nurses dry without getting fat. Indeed, Bodin himself seems to have lifted this description straight from Johannes Weyer, whose sceptical writings about witchcraft Bodin's book was intended to disprove. Changelings are one of the chestnuts of demonological writings, cropping up like the borrowed stories every demonologist told and embroidered yet again, and it may be that they reflect not so much popular belief as an abiding topos of demonological writing, an issue on which every demonologist had to take a position.

Demonologists, then, were at odds over the question of whether diabolic intercourse could produce children. All agreed that, as Balthasar Bekker trenchantly put it, 'there is not a Christian, be he Protestant or Papist, who believes that spirits are truly capable of engendering'.[52] But their very fascination with the idea of sex that resulted in no direct issue led them to speculate, to entertain the possibility that the Devil might pervert human fertility to his own ends. There, the speculation stopped. No demonologist proffered tales which illustrated such conceptions, or pursued the possibilities of the discovery of the true human father by the child engendered through demonic intercourse.

People in the sixteenth and seventeenth centuries did not make our more modern routine separation between sexual pleasure and reproduction. For them, sex was bound to generation. This did not mean that they did not seek to control their fertility in marriage, using the effects of lactation or taboos on sex to allow longer intervals between births, engaging in coitus interruptus and other forms of birth control or simply having sex less often towards the end of a woman's reproductive life.[53] But the reproduction of the next generation had first to be ensured, and this was a deeply held social value. In some of the historical writing about witchcraft in the early modern period, witches have been viewed as the ones who provided knowledge about abortifacients, as guardians of a tradition of female lore and self-help which could free women from the consequences of sexual relationships.

Such accounts rest on the belief that early modern people dreaded having too many children and desired the pleasures of extramarital sex without the burdens of offspring. They reflect a modern preoccupation with the origins of the science of birth control, and distort sixteenth- and seventeenth-century attitudes to fertility. Certainly, being pregnant was a shameful condition for the unmarried maid, who might commit infanticide, or might try herbal preparations to induce miscarriage. And there were women who worried about the dangers of childbed and feared the effects of repeated childbirth on their health. But consideration of these cases can lead us to miss one of the fundamental values of early modern European society. Fertility and its preservation were key social imperatives. Most of the magic that passed from mother to daughter or was sought from wise women or cunning men concerned fertility: how to cure male impotence, how to ensure the birth of healthy children. The need to have children could be a concern for royal houses, for whom a barren wife might mean the crumbling of a dynasty; as much as for peasant farmers, for whom the lack of heirs meant an uncertain future, without the hands necessary to work the land or to complete the marriage strategies essential for securing more land. Chance, war or disease might rob a couple of all their children, undoing their careful planning. In the late sixteenth and early seventeenth centuries, when tight controls on marriage meant that people had to wait to marry or might never be able to wed, the chance of being a fecund wife, honoured as a matron in town or village, was something to be desired. This was why women told stories of yearning for the marriage that would bring good times, pleasure and prosperity; and why neighbours, judges and even the accused women themselves feared barren old women as the source of death and annihilation.

Chapter 5
Sabbaths

Witches dined off gold and silver plate, they drank vast amounts of wine, they danced and made merry, and they fornicated with the Devil. They indulged in every imaginable pleasure, and would accept no limit to their gargantuan appetite for delight. They broke every rule. And they flew. Flight is the attribute most closely associated with witches, and it is the hag astride her broomstick or pitchfork, or riding backwards on a horned goat while her loose hair streams in the wind, who has planted herself in the Western imagination.

Flight also beggared belief, and it offered an easy target to sceptics. From the outset, it was the idea of flight that many of those who wrote about witches and demons found hardest to swallow. Time and again, demonologists recounted stories of hapless husbands whose diabolic wives went out to demonic dances leaving them alone in bed, or intrepid spouses who pursued their errant wives to their nightly revels. The demonologists worried away at these stories because they posed the problem of how flight was possible, and how a person could seem to be asleep when they were actually flying to sabbaths. Some argued that witches put a spell on their sleeping partners, or placed an object in the bed to fool them. Other demonologists responded by claiming that the witches' flight was not real, that it was illusory, or that it was merely a dream.

This, however, did not mean that witchcraft was not real. The Devil, as master of illusion, could easily hoodwink his victims into believing that they had flown, yet their allegiance to the Devil and the malevolence they did in his name was certainly no dream. Protestants in particular were inclined to believe that many of the witches' activities were imagined; but this did not always make them sceptical about witchcraft. Ironically, their theology may have made it easier for Protestants to entertain the wilder speculations about witches, since unlike orthodox Catholics, they did not have constantly to worry about which of the claims could be incorporated into church doctrine without stretching credibility too far: the tall tales were simply the Devil's tricks. The Protestant *Faust* of 1587 includes a fabulous airborne tour, as Faust flies over the towns of Europe on the back of his evil spirit Mephistopheles, who has handily transformed himself into a horse with wings. On a whim he

25. Francesco Maria Guazzo, *Compendium maleficarum*, Milan 1626: woodcut illustration showing the witch flying naked on a goat to the Sabbath.

flies off to look at Trier, with its wondrous palace made of bricks and its churches built of 'incredibly big stones held together with iron'. They fly on to Paris, Basle, Rome, Würzburg (where naturally Faust tries the wine), Cracow and even as far as Turkey, Mephistopheles helpfully providing tourist information *en route*. Much of this is lifted straight from Hartmut Schedel's *Book of Chronicles*, published in Nuremberg in 1493 and richly illustrated with woodcuts.[1]

In the huge Protestant collection, *Theatrum de veneficis*, compiled in Frankfurt in 1586 when the witch hunt was in full swing, Hermann Witekind's tract of 1585 contains a lengthy passage on flight, much of which *Faust* in turn pillaged. Witekind even incorporates a wonderful yarn about a kind of magic carpet: 'I myself heard from a magician, that together with others from N. in Saxony he flew more than a hundred miles on a coat to a wedding in Paris to which he had not been invited, but they quickly left when they noticed that people were murmuring in the room about what sort of guests these were and where they came from'.[2] Witekind, like many of the authors whose work was anthologized in *Theatrum de veneficis*, espoused a robust scepticism about the reality of flight and even doubted whether sex with the Devil really happened, while insisting that the pact with the Devil itself could be real; the Protestant demonologists Lambert Daneau and Johannes Gödelmann were firmly convinced of the reality of witchcraft, but thought that the Sabbath might be an illusion.[3]

By analysing witchcraft in this way, Protestants and sceptical Catholic demonologists were drawn into considering the nature of pleasure and of fantasy: Gödelmann even employs the words 'fantasy' and 'imagination' in his discussions. It may seem incredible that intellectuals could be sceptical about much of what witches supposedly did, could be interested in the power of imagination and ponder the mechanics of illusion, and still be firmly convinced of the reality of witchcraft. Yet they apparently found no difficulty in squaring this particular circle. This is why some of the boldest speculation about mental phenomena – the nature of dreams, the character of perception, the capacity of humans to be hoodwinked – came out of demonology, for these were questions with which demonologists were confronted from the outset. They were forced to consider the relation between soul and body, imagined and real harm – in short, psychology itself.

In doing so, convinced witch-hunters might find they shared intellectual preoccupations with radical sceptics. This was why, without any apparent sense of inconsistency, the editor of *Theatrum de veneficis* reprinted Johannes Weyer's sceptical preface about witchcraft in the same volume. Weyer, too, had developed the idea of diabolic illusion and considered how melancholy women were particularly prone to fall into delusions about the Devil; but in *De praestigiis daemonum* (1563) and *De lamiis* (1582) he had concluded that most of those accused of witchcraft were innocent. Demonologists who wrote after him took care to demolish his arguments, and Jean Bodin's famous *Démonomanie des sorciers* includes a lengthy rebuttal of *De praestigiis*. Yet as they engaged with Weyer's ideas, so their own thought was shaped by his.[4] Witch-hunting Protestants tended to argue that most of what witches and the Devil did was fantasy, but that the witches' ill will and apostasy were real and should be rooted out. To do so, these Protestants devised a theory of the imagination and fantasy to explain witchcraft. Even Catholic writers like Peter Binsfeld, very influential in southern Germany, occasionally had it both ways. Careful to argue that since good angels can travel from one place to another, so too can evil angels, he describes how those who suffer mishaps on flight 'sometimes fall from the trees, and break or mangle their limbs' – proof that flight is real. It is not the natural virtues of herbs, he insists, that cause people to fly, but the power of the Devil alone. Yet even he maintains that sometimes flight is fantasy.[5]

Indeed, witchcraft was bound to raise the question of belief, constantly forcing the demonologists to reconsider what was possible, because the tales of witches' doings were never the creation of demonologists alone. Information about what witches' confessed deeds to constantly fed back into works of demonology, and interrogators had to enlarge their view of what horrors witches might commit. This was a process of dialogue. Several authors on witchcraft appended trial records to their tracts, as if to set up in the pamphlet itself a dialogue between theory and evidence. Hermann Witekind, for one, concluded his disquisition on witchcraft with a trial transcript: what fascinated him was how an individual could come to confess things which could not be taken as literally true. At the same time, the vividness and immediacy of the confession added greatly to the treatise's readability. This was a tried and true formula, long exploited by writers on witchcraft then and now, who leavened their learned works with stories of the vile doings of individual witches.

After all, witchcraft confessions came out of a collision between the worlds of the interrogators and those they interrogated. These two cultures were never truly separate. For many a witch-hunter, tales of witches and night riding transported them back to their childhood and the stories of demons and hobgoblins told by the servants who brought them up. Nicolas Rémy, for one, refers to his own childhood as he muses about witches in Lorraine:

> This brings to mind the rumour which, in my childhood, was spread concerning certain hobgoblins which were said to be seen often dancing at night at the cross-roads, and were called '*La mequie Hennequin*', that is the Helequin family.[6]

For a learned judge like Rémy, at home in classical culture and skilled in Latin, encounters with witches summoned up half-remembered tales about creatures who did not fit into the neat categories of Christian demonology, memories drawn from his small-town infancy. And when those accused of being witches confessed to what they broadly knew about witchcraft they used their own idiom, talking not about complex Satanic rituals in which every detail of the Mass was inverted but about the local village festivities they knew. Under interrogation, every witch had to develop an account of her life with the Devil and her fellow witches. The outlines of her confession were predictable. To be a witch meant to confess to flying to the Sabbath, participating in diabolic sabbaths, and engaging in sex with the Devil. If an accused witch was not already familiar with the main ideas, having heard them from the public confessions of witches who had been executed before her, or knowing them from sermons, stories or print, the questions put to her ensured that she would cover the essential points. Yet nearly every witch made the story her own, conveying complex emotions or providing idiosyncratic detail.

To reach the Sabbath, the witch had to fly. The very idea of flight implies a transformation of perspective. When the witch flew, she looked down on village society. Not every witch could execute the imaginative feat of seeing the village, the fields and hills from the air, an exercise all the more difficult in the era before powered flight. Part of the exhilaration of this fantasy must have lain in the sensation of sovereignty over distance, an experience foreign to sixteenth- and seventeenth-century society, where to travel from one place to another required effort and labour – small wonder that the tailor's seven-league boots made such a compelling idea for fairy tale. Flight made travel effortless. But there is a further psychological dimension here. To imagine oneself flying requires the ability to dissociate oneself, and to see the world from the outside. This was a process of alienation which the experience of torture itself probably intensified, heightening the individual's own feeling of having become an outsider to the village. As we have seen, some forms of torture literally involved suspension, as the witch would be hung from the rack, her feet no longer touching the ground, and weights would be attached to her feet. Torture almost certainly also alienated the witch from her own body, as the accused had mentally to dissociate herself from her body in order to begin to cope with the pain.

The witch flew on a fork, a stick or most frequently a goat. Barbara Dämeter's diabolic goat had the convenient habit of letting her know when it was time to go to the dance: he would come and bleat outside her door.[7] For some witches, speed was the key sensation. Waldburga Schmid described how 'it was sometimes fast, sometimes slow; while she was travelling it didn't feel as if she were flying in the air but it seemed to her as if she were travelling on a cart'. Often, the sensation of flying is described in terms of riding.[8] Riding naturally had a sexual dimension. Most witches described how their diabolic lover accompanied them on the flight. Some gripped the mane of the goat to keep from falling off, or they held fast to their diabolic lover, sometimes riding in front of him, sometimes behind. Riding bareback with a lover on the most sexual of animals, the goat, or on a phallic rod, stick or fork, was a fantasy of sexual abandon. In images of the witches' flight, women are shown with their hair streaming out behind them, a sexual symbol which underlines the orgasmic nature of the ride. It was a motif which also drew upon stories of the wild horde, who rode in troops in the sky, and who were creatures neither fully human nor fully supernatural. In England, the motif of riding seems to have developed somewhat differently: there, the witch rides her victims, appearing to them often at night and causing them to sicken and become weak, as though she were able, in this sexually laden fashion, to steal their vitality.[9]

Once the witch arrived at the Sabbath, she had a long night of demonic revelry before her, beginning with the dance. Yet on the whole, witches did not confess to attending the morbid gatherings described by demonologists or depicted in Salvator Rosa's gruesome paintings of the witches' sabbaths, with elaborate rituals of humiliation before the Devil, infant flesh cooking in pots over the fire, old women drawing enchanted circles on the ground and wild, desolate scenery. Most of the dances described by witches were not like this.

Rough, even mundane assemblies, they have all the character of the church ale, the local festivals of eating, drinking and dancing organized by peasants, which were often held to help a fellow villager who needed money.[10] Waldburga Schmid described a dance with a devil who acted rather like a tipsy youth: 'each dancing round the other, pushing each other back and forth, the Devil knocks you around and bites as he comes'.[11] There was music too. Maria Gleichmann heard drums, a big fiddle and pipes, just the music she would have heard at the village dance; but she noticed that they only played 'cheeky boy' songs, songs which would have been packed with sexual innuendo and jokes against neighbours.[12]

One might expect the Sabbath to take place on a striking regional landmark, such as the infamous Venusberg or the Blocksberg in the Harz mountains, renowned in popular legend as the meeting ground for witches. By the last decades of the seventeenth century, the Protestant Eberhard Werner Happel's bumper five-volume collection of the most curious stories of the world could list the Blocksberg amongst the highest mountains on earth, noting in passing that it was common rumour that witches held their yearly gathering there on the eve of the first of May, Walpurgisnacht. Witchcraft had become a matter of fable and curiosity.[13]

But at the height of the witch craze, when accused witches described the dances, the sites they described were often tucked away locally, by the mill perhaps, a place associated with boundaries between the wild and the settled, and situated usually on an isolated area or at the edge of habitation; or in the woods. In Würzburg, each locality had its own witches' dance square, as it did in real life: just as villagers looked within their communities for the witch, so even in fantasy the witch never quite left home. One witch from Sulzheim said the dance took place in the village under the lime trees, while another witch from the same village placed it more eerily on the moor, by the witches' hedge. Witches did not promiscuously attend dances in other areas, a fact which may also reflect the way authorities administered the trials, which often proceeded village by village. Seventeenth-century witches from Obermarchtal held their dance at a macabre site, the gallows, where they knew their own executions would take place.[14] Sometimes a witch might shift the dance into the heart of town or village. Margaretha Schmid described a dance at Gerolzhofen which had been held at the fountain in the market 'where butter and cheese is sold'; while Anna Grauch said the Reyschofen witches held their dance at the town hall, right by her father's house; and in Michelau, they danced on the square in front of the church, almost certainly the place where the village dance was held.[15]

When demonologists described the sabbath feast and dance, they envisaged a host of devils giving obeisance to a grand Devil. The niceties of Satanic precedence do not seem to have greatly interested these village and small-town

26. Francesco Maria Guazzo, *Compendium maleficarum*, Milan 1626: woodcut illustration of witches dancing with devils while a musician in a tree plays a fiddle.

witches, who grounded their fantasies in the experience of the local dance.[16] Community life meant antagonism between rich and poor, young and old. Maria Gleichmann's description of the dance mirrored the hierarchies of village society. Each witch was given an appropriate diabolic partner, and she noted the colour of the outfit each wore. As she recounted, Claus Pfrimb 'was very jolly, for he is very rich, and feels contempt for the poor people, he speaks with no poor person, and he has great power in the gatherings, is contemptuous of the poor, thinks that everything should go according to his head, his lover was black, and dressed like a substantial burgher's wife'. Her vivid sociology of village society carried its own acid revenge: as she well knew, to name him as a participant at the dance was to call for his interrogation and execution. Margaretha Müller saw the youngest Stockle daughter at the dance. 'She is still young and jolly, she danced too and had a pretty young diabolic lover with a yellow outfit.' She saw the mayor's wife as well: 'she was quite big at the dance, she was in a good mood and had a gorgeous lover, also in yellow'. This was a bitterly envious fantasy: she herself, she noted dourly, had only a hideous black devil lover and she did not dance. Another witch from Würzburg attempted to turn the tables on her tormentors in the same way, saying that at the witches' dance she had seen Herr von Grafeneck, one of the chief interrogators of the witches, unmistakable in his cathedral canon's long coat.[17]

The gathering divided rich and poor, just as village society itself did: as Waldburga Schmid put it, 'at the feasts, the rich usually sit together and the poor don't count for much'. And it was a chance for gossip. 'You converse about all sorts of things, and people really lay into women's honour.' In real village life, witchcraft accusations often began in court cases, where women who had been called witches took their accusers to court, trying to regain their womanly 'honour'. In the circular logic that characterized witchcraft trials, to fail to prosecute someone who had insulted you as a witch was itself a strong sign of guilt; to take someone to court, however, was to set the first stone rolling in a case which might spin out of control.[18] Waldburga Schmid's description of how gossip operated at the Sabbath was uncannily like what happened in a trial itself. Those whom an accused witch named as having been present at a dance had their womanly 'honour' destroyed once and for all, since particular trust was placed in any denunciations a woman made when she faced imminent execution and would soon meet her Maker.

Dances punctuated social life in town and country. They were held at weddings, at the festivities after the end of the lying-in period following the birth of a child, in summer, and at church ales, and they defined who belonged to the community. In a town like Nuremberg, membership of the patriciate was determined by which families could legitimately be invited to the patrician dance. So important was attendance at such occasions to family pride that special exceptions to convent rules were made for nuns to join their families at the event. Yet dances could undermine as well as underline social boundaries. In villages, the musicians to whose music people danced were strangers, dubious travelling folk who did not belong to the local community and who were accounted dishonourable. Conrad Schreyer, who foolishly stopped to play for a witches' dance in a forest glade, was burnt with his fiddle hanging around his neck.[19]

Dancing meant a suspension of work, an interruption of the routine of town or village life. It took place in public areas, on flat ground; and this may explain why these witches did not report dances on mountain tops: they were thinking of village festivities rather than wild sabbaths in desolate surroundings. The etchings of Dürer or Hans Sebald Beham, which were produced for an urban market and presented earthy peasant pairs in a parade, remind us that dances were festivals of coupling. At the witches' dance, each witch appeared as part of a pair. Male or female, each witch had his or her own diabolic lover. Most witches described how the dance culminated in actual copulation between humans and devils, making the sexual dimension of the fantasy explicit. For dancing was also associated with pre-Christian ritual and with fertility cults. Dances were often held on St John's Day, 24 June, mid-summer. Fires were burnt and couples would jump over the fire, so as to ensure the fertility of the crops. The superficially Christian celebration barely disguised the heathen festival of the sun which it replaced.

This fact was not lost on demonologists. Sixteenth- and seventeenth-century authors could draw on a doughty tradition of moralizing about dance as part of a general campaign against superstition. Dances had long been the target of Protestant and Catholic divines, who lamented the sexual display and riotousness they occasioned:

> Dear friend, why does the world dance, old and young? To satisfy and fulfil the lust and pricking of the flesh, and to serve one another according to the flesh, to satiate the eyes (if not worse) on other people wickedly.[20]

The author Melchior Ambach, a Protestant preacher, advocated banning all but the most honourable dances outright, since (he averred) dancing invariably leads to indiscipline, fighting, adultery and murder. A fellow preacher Cyriakus Spangenberg told how, in 1203, when the local priest had sunk so low as to play the fiddle for his parishioners' dance, God had struck with a thunderbolt, severing the hand that held the bow, and killing another twenty-four of the godless revellers outright.[21] Not all Protestants were as vehemently opposed to dance as Ambach or Spangenberg. None the less, for pious Protestants, dances were potential occasions for sin, and as such, already opened the door for the Devil. Johannes Praetorius's collection of stories about witches published in 1669 condemns the disgusting foreign dances where people 'touch each other on the shameful places', in language that could have been borrowed from sixteenth-century Protestant divines, and goes on to blame magicians for bringing these dances from Italy to France. Not only did they lead to sin, but to murder and miscarriages, a point which had been made by Jean Bodin long before. Bodin had condemned the 'whirling dance' of the witches, which made 'people wild and raging, and women to miscarry'. As these writers saw it, such dancing was a kind of anti-fertility rite.[22] The Catholic judge and witch persecutor Nicolas Rémy averred that 'we know well enough from experience that this passion for dancing is nearly always the begetter of sin among men'. In an extraordinary passage, he informs the reader that witches wear masks, and goes on to condemn those who 'run masked about the streets in their Carnivals of pleasure'. In one fell swoop, he linked disguise, Carnival and pleasure with the demonic. Indeed, Catholics and Protestants alike could share Rémy's disgust at the excesses of Carnival, and side with Lent. The metaphor finds literal visual expression in Peter Brueghel the Elder's famous *Battle between Lent and Carnival*, where a gaunt, drably dressed Lent riding on a cart pulled by a monk and a nun chases away a fat Carnival, who is riding on a wine barrel and brandishing a roasting spit skewering a pig's head, sausages and chicken.[23]

Sensations of movement, music, light and colour were the predominant themes of the witches' description of the dance. By contrast, Nicolas Rémy insisted that the witches' dances caused 'weariness and fatigue and the greatest distress'.[24] By the time the Augsburg Protestant Bernhard Albrecht composed his treatise on magic in 1628, the diabolic dance had become the opposite of a festival of pairing. The witches danced in the round, back to back, in order that none should see the faces of the others and thereby betray them. The dancers sing 'Har har, Devil, Devil, jump here, jump there, hop here, hop there, play here, play there' and 'lift their hands and brooms high to demonstrate their great delight, and to show that they are willing and inclined to serve the Devil'. Albrecht's sensationalist reporting and his rather plodding rhythmic repetitions aim, at least, to recreate the atmosphere of the dance for his reader.[25] Praetorius's much later collection describes a witch dance involving strange, disgusting and repellent gestures, where the witches turn their backs on each other and join their hands together in a circle, 'throwing their heads around as if they were crazy or foolish people'.[26] He lifted this account of the Sabbath from another earlier author, and his version of the abandoned dance owes a good deal to the idea of St Vitus's dance, a dancing mania which eventually tires the dancers so much that they injure themselves or even fall down dead. What started as a dance, and was condemned as part of the campaign against sinful dancing, had now become a frenzy which was being confused with a type of mental illness, a sign of madness and possession.[27]

The possibilities inherent in the myth of the diabolic Sabbath led the demonologists to describe a world of devils that turned the hierarchy of the Church upside-down, standing Christian rituals on their head. The witches were bent double, candles in their anus, and in place of the kiss of peace in the Mass, they had to kiss the Devil's anus. When Francesco Guazzo penned his description of the dance, culled in large part from Rémy, he added that the witches always danced to the left, the sinister side. By the time Pierre de Lancre, poet of the Sabbath, published his vivid evocation of the sights and sounds of the Sabbath in 1612, every detail carried a freight of religious and moral detail – the bread was made of black millet, the hearts of children who had died before baptism were ritually presented to Satan and the whole Sabbath was like a gruesome fair, full of vile wares each clamouring for the hapless visitors' attention.[28] In De Lancre's hands, the Sabbath is a satire on the world of the market. Exchange has run riot, no longer commerce that leads to prosperity but a murderous clamour that betokens disorder and death. So important was it that the reader should miss no detail of this extraordinary diabolic universe that the edition of 1613 was furnished with an elaborate illustration, where every detail of the Sabbath was labelled and explained.

Along with the dance came a grand feast, the two virtually indistinguishable in the confessions of many witches. Some described the food and drink or the

27. Jan Ziarnko, *Description et figure du Sabbat des Sorcièrs*, copper etching from Pierre de Lancre's *Tableau de l'inconstance des mauvais anges et demons*, Paris 1613: this extraordinary image is printed as a large-format fold-out page in the volume. Each dreadful scene is marked with a letter, and below (not reproduced here) is an alphabetical key explaining exactly what that letter depicts, so the reader is left in no doubt of the precise details of the Sabbath.

banqueting tables; others, the magnificent silver plate and cutlery. One Augsburg fable told of a diabolic banquet held in a corner of the town: the table was laid with silver, but the revellers had vanished. Diabolic feast and town banquet might blur into each other: one substantial citizen's wife from Nördlingen recalled a wedding feast where she had been socially slighted. The Devil came to her table and said her husband had been made to sit at a low table with those of menial status. Furious, she called on the Devil to avenge her, and flew off on a goat to Heilbronn, where she attacked the abbot in his chambers, pressing down on him, smearing him with her diabolic salve, and making him seriously ill. Now, under interrogation, she was anxious that the matter be kept a secret, for if it were to come out, her husband would lose his job: the abbot was his boss.[29]

Demonological theory, however, adhered to rigid formulas about such meals, relentlessly drawing out their theological significance: neither salt nor bread was to be had there, because these items were Christian and therefore intolerable to the Devil. Though there was food aplenty, it did not satisfy. Time and again, demonologists and interrogators tried to corral the glorious profusion of detail into schemes that fitted their religious concerns, presenting the Sabbath as a systematic inversion of central religious mysteries. So, in the Würzburg, Eichstätt and Nördlingen trials we meet a peculiar variant, that of the diabolic baptism. This motif seems to reiterate many of the themes of witch confession – witches' misuse of the Host, their pact with the Devil, their abuse of the sacrament of marriage – by adding yet another sin against the sacrament. Its prominence reflects the concerns of the Counter-Reformation strongholds of Würzburg and Eichstätt, eager to re-Catholicize the masses. But they had no monopoly on it. Reports of diabolic baptism are also to be found in Protestant Nördlingen, reflecting Lutheranism's equally didactic insistence on the role of the two sacraments, communion and baptism.

Yet again, however, the fantasy of witchcraft resisted the attempts of the authorities to systematize. Soon, diabolic baptism became further elaborated, with baptisms occurring a magical three times, just as intercourse with the Devil also often took place on three occasions. So, for example, Barbara Dämeter was baptized by the Devil first in her kitchen, but was unable to understand the words he used: at least this saved her from providing a liturgical parody for her interrogators. On the third baptism she promised herself to him, body and soul, exactly the words which a woman normally used when she married the Devil or entered into a pact with him. Margaretha Müller went to the street to get water from the fountain. When she got home, she found the Evil One there, and he took water out of the pitcher with his hands and shook it over her, baptizing her in the Devil's name. She too provided accounts of three baptisms, locating one at a brook and describing another that happened while she was out grazing the animals.[30]

Maria Marb from Protestant Nördlingen gave a grisly description of her diabolic baptism. The water with which she was baptized was like blue water or brimstone, and it was the water in which dead children had been cooked. Her hands and feet were put in the water and with four midwives in attendance, together with two devils, she fell at the feet of the Devil, praying to him.[31] In these descriptions, baptism has been stolen from the Church and is carried out by the arch-enemy of God. Yet baptisms were not the sole prerogative of the priest. They could be carried out by midwives in emergencies outside the church, a practice about which the Church was becoming increasingly uneasy. The practice

28. Francesco Maria Guazzo, *Compendium maleficarum*, Milan 1626: woodcut illustration, sabbath scenes.

continued, part of the seepage between the religious and secular worlds. The Counter-Reformation insisted on the power of sacramentals, sacred objects in everyday life made holy by the blessing of the Church. Holy water was one of these; so the witches were committing a further blasphemy against the Church and its liturgy. Baptism was also a rite of naming. As a sign of the relationship of fealty, the Devil usually told the newly recruited witch his name; and might give the witch a special diabolic name in return. All this made theological sense. Yet the names themselves were often associated with excrement and could be very funny. We meet devils rejoicing in the names of Caterpillar, Dog's Caspar and Hens' Dirt, and women who were called Witch Beast, Devil's Stink or, in a pun on child-minder, Child's Fool.[32]

Diabolic baptism rapidly acquired a set of elaborations that went far beyond its original religious significance. The idea of the magical triple baptism resembled the threefold diabolic intercourse; and the motif of shaking water over the witch may echo the idea of sex with the Devil. The doctrinal elements that were so important to the clerics collapsed into the fundamental structure of the witch fantasy as the women developed their stories in collaboration with their interrogators, and theology began to accord with psychological necessity. This was a two-way traffic for, as we have seen, what accused witches said in interrogation also found its way back into the work of demonologists, modifying and extending the intellectual tradition. In many cases, works of demonology were written not before their authors had been involved in a witch hunt, but after the experience, as they sought to come to terms with what they had heard and seen and pass on their knowledge. As a result, witches' confessions were not just the product of demonologists' fantasies – indeed, one might say that works of demonology were also the product of the witches' fantasies.

The complexity of the relationship between elite and popular culture is evident in the fate of one remarkable motif, the idea that witches flew into cellars, a detail which is not often found in the work of demonologists. David Meder mentions it in a fairly late tract of 1615, describing how witches steal wine from cellars, corn from barns and 'milk from the udders of cows and sheep (and so also the butter and cheese, which could be made thereof)'. These were all ways, he argued, in which witches sinned against the commandment 'Thou shalt not steal.'[33] Yet flying into cellars had become such an accepted part of the repertoire of witch activities that in Würzburg, interrogations mention it along with weather-making, flying, pact-making and harming, giving it its own subheading in the witches' confessions. Stories about cellars

29. Francesco Maria Guazzo, *Compendium maleficarum*, Milan 1626: woodcut illustration, diabolic baptism.

repeat some of the themes of witch confessions but give them a distinctive character. Whereas the dance and flight occurred outside and convey a feeling of space, the cellar meetings took place within confined spaces below ground. Ursula Götz described how she and her co-witches had fetched wine from the local tavern-keeper's cellar, 'always taking the best' and drinking out of wooden tankards; her alleged confederate Anna Traub said they had each taken a tankard with them to drink on the flight home.[34] Nearly always the cellars belonged to a rich or important person in the village. In Nördlingen, Barbara Stecher, a woman who made a living collecting rags, said she had drunk wine from the cellar of the paymaster's wife at a diabolic gathering. This confirmed that her wealthy hostess, who lived in a big house on the Wine Market Square and had been executed just a month before, was indeed a witch. Stealing wine from the cellars of people like her was an attack on those who had more than their fair share of the good things in life.[35]

Stealing wine was also a folk memory. Raiding the lord's cellar and drinking his best wine had long been a ritual of rebellion, often one with disastrous consequences. During the Peasants' War of 1524–26, peasant armies were diverted from their military aims by the prospect that they could break into cellars and get the wine – once drunk, they were easy prey for the soldiers of the authorities. It was redolent, too, of images of Cockaigne or Schlaraffenland, the mythical land of plenty where no one needed to labour and no one suffered want. In sixteenth-century pictures of this mythical place, roasted pigs offer themselves to the lucky inhabitants, forks sticking out ready for eating; while wine flows from fountains like water. One woman who confessed to hosting feasts in her cellar said, in an image that inverted Christ's miracle at Cana, 'the Evil Enemy put wine in the cellar into her barrels, so that when she let wine out, he renewed it, and she always had enough wine and bread, and the more she took wine out of the barrel, the more wine he made for her'. To be a substantial citizen was to own a cellar full of wine; to have stores was to be free of the threat of starvation in bad times, the fate of so many people in the insecure economy of the sixteenth and seventeenth centuries. Raiding the cellar meant breaking the peasant law of prudence, enjoying the moment of excess – all the sweeter for its being one's neighbour's stock rather than one's own.

People made strong symbolic connections between humans and their dwellings. They equated the intactness of the house with the unsullied honour of its occupants. Consequently, to publicly dishonour a person one scribbled rude graffiti on their door; to cross the threshold uninvited was to issue a challenge. A young man might break the windows of a woman's house, throwing stones to indicate that she was no virgin but sexually 'open'; or assault the honour of a householder by taking off the roof of his dwelling. Animals and humans were normally housed under one roof. Psychologically, the cellar may have represented the lower part of the body, the guts and sexual parts. The

30. The King of Schlaraffenlandt, *c.* 1650, copper etching.

fantasy of flying into the cellar involves stealing fluids from powerful people. Such thefts, like stealing a man's potency or drying up a nursing mother's milk, were connected to seed and fertility.[36]

From sabbath dance to cellar feasts, the stories witches told were highly ritualized. Vast questionnaires were devised to catch every nuance and detail of the tale, as if the completeness of a confession might guarantee its truth. No morsel of information about the conspiratorial activities of witches was too inconsequential for the witch-finder. So for example, in the case of Barbara Kurzhals from Reichertshofen in Bavaria in 1629, a full clean confession survives, each topos of the witchcraft confession carefully numbered and with her answers noted down in exhaustive logical sequence, point for point. She provides no fewer than twelve separate items of information about flying into cellars, chambers and stables, all of which are systematically numbered. Of course this monument to bureaucratic exactitude can have had little to do with the hesitations, applications of torture, denials and partial concessions which characterized the actual process of interrogation.[37]

Drafting these kinds of clean-copy full confessions is itself testimony to their hearers' investment in this kind of tale and their need to 'fix' the bizarre and horrifying detail into an orderly sequence which repeated broadly the same scenarios from witch to witch. Pleasure and horror had to be pinned down. Sixteenth- and seventeenth-century culture was obsessed with the subject. Both Catholics and Protestants were convinced that pleasurable sensory experience could be deeply sinful. Clerics of all persuasions tried to curb popular culture, discipline sexuality into marriage and combat drunkenness and idleness. The same deep suspicion of pleasure seems to be evident in demonology.

And yet this literature is equally strongly fascinated by pleasure and horror. The works of demonology are mesmerised by language. Words become pleasurable in themselves, the stories and the language as important as the content. In the Devil Books, there is much use of alliteration, rhythm, long sentences and extravagant hyperbole, as is appropriate for a genre which provides didactic entertainment. But such techniques are also evident in a work like Pierre de Lancre's *Tableau de l'inconstance des mauvais anges et demons*,[38] where the language is strikingly physical, and rhythm and repetition are used to build towards endlessly postponed climaxes in impossibly long sentences. Nor is De Lancre afraid to dwell on horrific and unpleasant details. In Boguet's compendium on demonology, it is rather the headlong rush of appealing example and story which provides the excitement. Nicolas Rémy says in the foreword to his work that he felt the need to give his preoccupation with the witches' sabbath some form in art. Poetry suggested itself to the judge in his leisure hours, since witchcraft 'seemed to me to be a subject not unsuitable for verses, which it was my pleasure to make during my vacations'.[39] Rémy's *Demonolatry* was published in Latin at Lyons; but German editions soon followed with a German translation appearing in 1598.[40]

It was not only in literature that witchcraft became part of the culture of entertainment. Popular woodcuts and pamphlet accounts of trials also circulated, the stereotypical sensationalist images, providing a sequential narrative which 'fixed' the terrors of the witch story in visual form. Such images were often literally interchangeable from one pamphlet to the next as printers used old blocks to illustrate new horror stories. So, for instance, the pamphlet account of the trial and death of the lying-in maid Anna Ebeler from Augsburg, who killed young babies by witchcraft, recounts her terrible deeds and awful end in word and image. All the key scenes from the witch fantasy are there, numbered with reference to their verbal description: meeting the Devil, the pact, sex with the Devil, flight, sabbath, dance and harm caused to children. The pamphlets did much to codify the themes of the witchcraft confession by organizing them visually. And the same block could be used for more than one trial. We know, for instance, that several of the scenes featuring Anna Ebeler were recycled in pamphlets dealing with the trials of other witches. The pamphlets belonged to the literature of entertainment, teasing the reader with dreadful and shocking events: the same printers also produced accounts of bloodcurdling murders and miraculous births for a mass market.[41]

Demonology had it both ways. On the one hand, demonologists set out the awful facts of the conspiracy of witches; on the other, many of those who wrote about demons held that much of what witches did was imaginary, not real. Their scepticism allowed them to entertain the wildest stories about witches, while invoking the horrors of witchcraft permitted them to indulge their taste for elaborate language. In fact, writing like this formed the bridge to the picaresque novel of the seventeenth century. Eberhard Happel, for one, crammed his magnificent five-volume *Größte Denkwürdigkeiten der Welt* (*Greatest Curiosities of the World*) (1683–91) with anecdotes and popular stories, many of them featuring witchcraft and the supernatural. It is impossible to divide fact from fiction in his jaw-dropping tales. Happel belongs to the tradition of the German baroque writers like Grimmelshausen, yet he is also heir to the style evident in so much demonology, piling one incredible tale on another.

· · ·

The motifs of the witch craze were anything but original. Flight, cannibalism, sexual orgies: all had long featured in the accusations made against heretics from at least the fourteenth century. In the fifteenth and sixteenth centuries, Waldensian heretics were believed to engage in dancing and sexual orgies after the sermon.[42] Jews had been accused of stealing hosts and maltreating them until they bled, and of kidnapping children and killing them to use their blood in religious rituals or even eating them.[43] All these foul rituals served to bind the members of the sect together, and explained why the whole group, not just individuals, were guilty and must be rooted out. The myth of witchcraft simply took these myths and applied them to the latest of the Devil's brood: witches. The fantasies of witchcraft, it might be argued, were no more than the usual mud flung at all those perceived as religious deviants, not the animating force behind the hunt.

But this would be to misconceive the nature of fantasy. The motifs of witchcraft were indeed familiar, but the fact that they were already known gave them added force, organizing fears and myths that were half forgotten. The myth of Jewish ritual murder had been directed against all Jews, male and female; Cathars of both sexes were believed to have flown to secret assemblies and offered dead flesh to Satan. When these fantasies were applied to women as the chief agents of Satan, the myth took on a different character. The Devil's male aspects became more prominent, and his personality as seducer of the witch was now seamlessly related to his role in the myth. Flight became more closely linked to sexual abandon as women, the more sensual sex, were imagined to ride on the most lecherous of animals, the goat; and cannibalism was even more dreadful because women, who bring new life into the world, were the ones digging up and cooking dead infants. The myth became tied to the capacities of the female body, to women's ability to enjoy limitless sexual pleasure, and to the experience of birth. This meant the psychological anxieties touched by stories about witches went far deeper. They were connected to fundamental fears about separation from and longing for the mother, about birth and death; and they could not be so safely projected on to a group of outsiders like Jews or heretics. They were about women in one's own community, even in one's own family. These women, vipers in the bosom of honourable society, were in league together, and the membership of their sect might encompass such unlikely conspirators as pious, God-fearing women, clerics or children. At the same time, the stories could be very firmly fixed in everyday life, as women described the clothes the Devil wore, his gait and even where they had met him. It also meant that particular motifs in the myth began to take on a life of their own.

One such was the *schmiermachen*, the salve-making. A sinister meeting, it took place not outside in nature, but indoors, usually in a parlour or kitchen, and in many interrogations it was more important than the Sabbath or dance. While the dance featured witches and their male lovers, the salve-making was notable for the near total absence of men. Indeed, the Devil often waited outside, while the salve was pounded or boiled by a gathering of women gossips supervised by a senior witch, who was often a midwife. Once made, it was used to rub on oven forks so that witches could fly on them, and to cause harm; or the cooking-water was used to whip up storms. And the ingredients were gruesome: the pulverized bones and fat from exhumed infants.

The idea of the salve-maker put into one terrifying image everything people most feared about women. The witch cooks, but what she boils or bakes is human flesh; she is responsible for reproduction but she steals and murders the products of conception, robbing them even of salvation; she disturbs heaven, whipping up storms to destroy the crops.[44] The gathering for *schmiermachen* was not strictly essential to the witch myth. Indeed, given the diabolic Sabbath and the vow of fealty to the Devil it was not even necessary, just as the motif of flying into cellars was superfluous. Yet imaginatively and emotionally it was key. The gory celebration bound the witches together: their individual malice derived from their secret rituals. A women-only affair, it placed women and the harm they directed against children at the centre of the story; while their obeisance to the Devil, which technically explained their malign power, faded into the background. There was a deep psychological truth in this, because it meant that women were the agents of death.

The terrible irony of the confessions themselves is that they were supplied by tortured women who were made to talk about sensual pleasure. During the interrogation, the pleasure the women first described was transformed into its opposite. The dance, instead of being an occasion for celebrating coupling and fertility, became instead a spectacle of humiliation: the women are too old, not able to dance but forced to cluster at the edges watching; their lovers are hideous. The poor are not welcome at the dance and count for little. In Gerolzhofen, older women recount how they were forced to act as human candle-holders, lighting the dancing of the young ones with a candle stuck in their anus, their heads upside-down, a motif which one witch bowdlerized to holding 'the candle with her hand on her back'.[45] This is an inversion of the holy candles of the church held by altar servers. But applied to women, it tells a tale of anal sex and humiliating mock-rape while others dance and couple. Her lighted anus is a parody of the custom in southern Germany where young girls on the cusp of womanhood put lighted pots outside their doors, as if to advertise their sexual ripeness.[46] Fire in the genitals suggests sexual hunger, from which the old woman witch was believed to suffer. For her, sex could only be topsy turvy, part of the world turned upside-down, leading not to fertility but humiliation.

So too, in the trial itself, the victim was subjected to extreme physical torture until he or she cracked, giving up their – as their interrogators saw it – diabolically inspired resistance and resigning their allegiance to the fellowship of devil-worshippers. Pain was used to produce stories about pleasure. This was a sadistic cycle in which the extremities of pain were what made it possible for the accused witch to describe the loss of physical control that intense pleasure can occasion: the sensation of flight or the abandonment of dance. Yet within the fantasy, the outcome was always the same. Pleasure turned to disappointment and loss. The enjoyable seduction of the witch by the Devil was followed by painful intercourse, sometimes even a rape; the coin the Devil gave the witch in earnest of marriage turned to leaves or dung; the banquet that was served on silver plates did not satisfy, leaving the revellers hungry; or it turned out to be a vile cannibalistic meal. The dance was wild and the music harsh and raucous, and many witches described themselves as humiliated spectators, forced to realize that the Devil preferred younger, prettier or richer women. Nor would he keep his promise to rescue her from prison: as Susanna Mair tartly remarked, he had not bothered to rescue her because 'she was just too old for the Evil One, he has plenty of young ones'.[47]

Witchcraft confessions gave voice to a mistrust of pleasure which went far beyond the moral asceticism of the Reformation and Counter-Reformation. Witches abandoned themselves to sensual enjoyment, flying, drinking, eating, dancing and having sex; to celebrations that draw one human being to another. In the stories they told, the conviviality and the joy of human exchange that ought to lead to fecundity was always perverted into death and disease. This is a fundamental fear of libidinal energies, as if too much pleasure might destroy society itself. Such fantasies fitted a society in which marriage really did have to be delayed and individual wishes forced to fit the requirements of inheritance, where resources had to be husbanded and life itself could be threatened by too much – or too little – fertility. As the Sabbath aped communal festivities – dances, feasts and assemblies – so it also transformed the individual witches, each with her own diabolic lover, into a secret community sworn to harm all Christians. This is why uncontrolled sex and enjoyment meant an assault on charity, love and social fellowship; and why the confessions of witches are so often sprinkled with casual hostility towards old age. The witch's sexuality was fundamentally envious. It stole the fertility and pleasure which rightfully belonged to others.

31. Female witches eating together. Woodcut from Ulrich
Molitor, *De lamiis et pythonicis mulieribus*, Basle, 1495.

Part Three

Womanhood

In a case from early sixteenth-century Basle that has the ring of folk tale, three witches sat together under a peach tree in spring. They considered what they wanted to eat. The first wanted all the cherries that there would be that year as a compote; the second wanted all the birds that would hatch that year, and the third, all the wine that would be grown. These were women with gargantuan appetites, hungry for luxury food: cherries, little birds and wine. Sitting together under the peach tree they plotted how to steal this wonderful food, eat it all themselves – and destroy spring with its promise of rebirth and plenty. And then they attacked a woman in childbed, taking the milk from her breasts, killing the baby, and nearly killing her too, 'out of envy'. The witch was a woman who wanted it all for herself, and who envied others. If she could cause a mother's milk to dry up she could do the same to cows, or make the butter fail to churn. She represented the destruction of fertility itself.[1]

Chapter Six
Fertility

When Magdalena Winder was lying in after having given birth, a strange man appeared. Casting aside the protective hangings around her bed, he said 'she should promise herself to him, and be his, he would not leave her'. No sooner had she promised, than he 'committed indecency with her, he kept his clothes on'.[1]

Magdalena was sure this was the Devil. Sexual relations were completely prohibited during the six weeks of lying in, before the new mother had been churched. Ignoring the taboo, her Satanic lover did not even bother to undress. Alone in the curtained bed, prey to the evil influences that surrounded new mothers and babies, Magdalena had been ravished by Satan and had become a witch, excluded for ever from the community of good Christians.

The terrors, anxieties and dependence that childbed brought lay at the heart of the witch craze. Women like Magdalena Winder thought they had seen the Devil during lying in, and when they were interrogated for witchcraft, they recalled the guilt and misery they had felt. As they well knew, the Devil preys on those who despair. More often, however, new mothers directed their fears outwards, accusing others of harming them and their baby by witchcraft. Frequently they named women they knew, who had visited during the lying-in period or before the birth. Sometimes it was the lying-in maid, the new mother's intimate, who brought her the nourishing soups thought to be required to turn blood into milk for the baby, and who cared for both in the six-week period. If mother or child failed to thrive, she, or another elderly woman connected with the care of the child, was the most likely person to be accused. It was dangerous to cross the lying-in maid, since she could retaliate in occult ways, causing the baby to suffer from cramps and spasms, or to break out in terrible pustules. It was dangerous to behave churlishly to any visitor during the lying-in period, to fail to greet or give a responding gift to any woman who called to wish the new mother well. She might dry up the mother's milk in revenge. Where accusations of witchcraft were under way, women who had given birth might be asked whether anything untoward had happened during birth or lying in, and witnesses and judges alike took such

32. Jonas Arnold (active in Ulm and Augsburg), *The Lying-In Room*, seventeenth century, ink pen. This was probably intended as a design to be used on an ornamental vessel.

suspicions seriously. In witness statements before a court, they found a way of speaking about the harrowing and wordless experiences after birth when mother or baby fails to thrive.

Madalena Mincker of Nördlingen described how her child was harmed 'while it was in swaddling bands'. An old woman, Margretha Knorz, had come to visit her while she was in childbed without being invited, and had stayed until she bore the child. She had brought her wine, apples and milk, but they had a disagreement about money, and Knorz told the young mother she would rue this. Just three weeks of her lying in had passed when the child sickened, eventually becoming 'quite lame and crippled in hands and feet'.[2]

Time and again, stories about old women who harmed mothers and infants were told during witch trials. In Marchtal, they were still current as late as the mid-eighteenth century, when Catharina Schmid's neighbours described how she had visited Francisca Cadus, complimenting the mother on her beautiful baby. Shortly after, the child sickened and died miserably.[3] Like the wicked stepmother in the tale of Snow White, old women confessed to giving children titbits, especially apples: the children died in terrible agony. In 1588, Margaretha Menz was said to have touched a child after having smeared her hand with her salve: 'in five days it would neither suck nor eat nor cry and it lay just as it was put'. The child's frantic mother described how 'the witch' had often visited, 'and sometimes she brought apples, and she was not pleased that they got the child blessed'. Menz eventually confessed to killing or harming no fewer than twenty-three children and one unborn child, only one of whom made a complete recovery. She could give their names, ages and dates of death and often some circumstantial detail as well.[4]

It was not only village women who worried about fertility. Fears about witches could easily take root in a society which placed strict controls on marriage and fertility. The problem of how to ensure reproduction, while at the same time limit population, was a preoccupation of early modern governments. In Germany, the fifteenth and early sixteenth centuries had seen the culmination of a period of economic and demographic expansion, as the massive population losses resulting from the fourteenth-century Black Death were gradually overcome. By the mid-sixteenth century, however, economic growth was slowing and population appeared to exceed resources. Poor people seemed to be flooding the cities and towns, begging in great numbers and threatening to overwhelm systems of poor relief and charity, while authorities, town councils and territorial governments alike expressed anxiety about the tide of poor and idle. They worried above all about marriage, especially about those marrying before they could support themselves. In line with these concerns, both Catholic and Protestant governments began to develop laws forbidding such marriages.

Marriage became a tool of government policy, one of the few ways open to governments for limiting immigration and the numbers of improvident poor. In Catholic Bavaria, an ordinance of 1553 forthrightly condemned what it termed 'irresponsible marriages', castigating those who married without parental permission, and banning marriage between servants outright.[5] Less drastic steps were taken in Würzburg, where an ordinance of 1583 forbade so-called 'corner marriages' (marriages undertaken secretly and without a priest), and, in line with the decrees of the Council of Trent, ordered that all marriages must take place in front of a priest, with witnesses, and after banns had been read.[6] These innovations counted on community pressure rather than law to forestall imprudent marriages. In Bavaria, however, ordinances throughout the sixteenth century went on to create a legal apparatus preventing couples from marrying unless they had enough resources to form a self-sufficient household, thereby contravening the authority of the Church in such sacramental matters.[7]

Throughout Western Europe, this sort of legislation about marriage and family had been pioneered in the towns as civic fathers, from London to Lyons, struggled to establish new systems of poor relief. In Protestant Augsburg, the Council condemned the 'forward marriages' of young folk who wed before they were in a position to support themselves, and complained about the increasing numbers of the indigent and workshy. The Council did more than wring its hands: it prevented non-local couples without assets from settling in the town and forced others to provide guarantors so they would not become a burden on poor relief. These measures endured when the town became bi-confessional, and were applied to Catholics and Protestants alike. In Lutheran Nördlingen, parties to a marriage were supposed to have sufficient financial resources and a similar policy of preventing the marriages of outsiders with insufficient capital was followed.[8] This hard-nosed policy could cause misery and humiliation. In 1587, the Nördlingen Council saw fit to delay the marriage of one citizen to a non-local woman 'because he has not produced sufficient documentation concerning his bride's property'; in 1601 the marriage of a Nördlingen widow to a non-local weaver was summarily halted even after the banns had been read 'because he is a dirt-poor journeyman'.[9]

Guilds and trade associations all over Germany were also exercising increasingly harsh controls by insisting that only those who were independent masters with their own workshops might marry. Guildsmen held that journeymen, who worked in the workshops of others, should be counted dishonourable if they took wives before becoming masters. As the population increased, and craft masters attempted to choke off competition, guilds and trade associations tried to restrict the numbers of workshops. Masters feared the competition that yet another fully qualified independent craftsman would bring to established traders, and many trades closed their doors, allowing entry only to masters' sons, sons-in-law, or those lucky journeymen who married a master's widow; and continuing to exclude altogether those 'dishonourable' men born out of wedlock. Thus in towns, both trades and town councils pursued protectionist policies for different motives but with similar ends. Both tried to realize their aims by restricting marriage and penalizing illegitimacy; both made marriage the key instrument of population control.[10]

Even where such laws and regulations did not exist, community pressures and economic realities were enough to force the poor to postpone marriage or forgo it altogether. These pressures acted with particular force on women, who often delayed marriage until their mid or late twenties. Later marriage had a very significant effect on overall reproduction, because the most fertile years of a woman's reproductive potential were lost: where this has been studied, as by Schofield and Wrigley for England, it has been found that late marriage resulted on average roughly in one child fewer for every two years of delayed marriage.[11]

Fluctuations in the age of marriage amongst women responded not only to the longer-term economic cycles, but also to short-term harvest crises. Women postponed marriage, waiting for better years to wed, when they had managed to set more by for the crucial dowry they needed to supply a household, or when the couple had come into an inheritance. Malnutrition brought on by dearth depressed fertility and increased infant mortality. Even in towns, economic status could be directly correlated with numbers of children: in Augsburg before the devastation of the Thirty Years War, we know that the families of poor day labourers numbered on average 1.36 children, while those of the rich goldsmiths' trade averaged 2.25.[12] And there were many bad years: the late sixteenth century saw the phenomenon of the 'little ice age' lasting into 1630, of unusually cold, wet years. A series of years in which spring was late, winter cold and autumn and summer wet would play havoc with harvests; and just such sequences occurred in Germany in 1560–74, 1583–89 and

1623–28.[13] One bad year might be managed. Two in a row brought misery and famine. The return on agriculture was always on a knife edge, with yields often ranging between little more than 1 to 3 and 1 to 6 on grain sown.[14] In town and countryside alike, marriage and fertility were privileges, and not everyone could afford to marry or have children. It also meant that the communities of the sixteenth and seventeenth centuries walked a demographic tightrope: they had to ensure that population numbers did not exceed resources, but they had to safeguard the fecundity of those women who did marry, in order to secure future generations. This was why the idea of the envious death-dealing witch, attacking mothers, children and babies, could gain such a powerful hold on people's imaginations.

At Würzburg during a massive witch persecution which caused the deaths of over a thousand people, women who were interrogated were routinely asked, after they had supplied their name, age and place of birth, to give their reproductive histories. Sabina Pforinger, interrogated on 14 September 1626, had borne eight children of whom four still lived; the others had died of fits, 'when they were very little'. Anna Stärr answered the questions on 11 April 1603. Of her seven children, only two were still living; the others had died of pox and measles. Married twice, she had had seven stillbirths, all of whom were buried in the churchyard. She realized the significance of the interroga-tors' inquiries, and added that she had heard that if you went barefoot the Devil would come. Her assertion that she hadn't gone barefoot in fourteen years is unlikely to have persuaded the authorities of her innocence.[15]

The Würzburg authorities were not unusual in asking for these details, nor in attaching significance to them. A woman whose own babies had died might be a victim of witchcraft, or she might herself be a witch, in league with the Devil to murder infants. The catalogues of miscarriages, stillbirths and untimely deaths made grim listening, with the litany of suffering evoking the link between death and children at the very outset of each trial. Whether or not these particular infants turned out to be the victims of a witch – their mother perhaps – it was as if the alleged witch's testimony could only be understood in the context of the sufferings of children.

These reproductive histories were not in themselves so unusual. After all, half of all babies died before they reached the age of one. But these mothers could recall exactly how many pregnancies they had had and they knew the outcomes and precise details of each death, even if they had happened as long as half a century before. Children's lives were fragile and no one could be sure, no matter how many live births they had, whether they would secure a line of descendants. Like the weather and the harvest, human fertility was precarious, the transmission of the line uncertain.

In this world of conservative demographic policies, where chastity and marital virtue were cherished as religious values, the treatment of women who became pregnant outside marriage was harsh: they were punished, exiled and shamed for their sin. Even young women who were pregnant by the time they stood at the church door to wed might be subject to dishonouring rituals, forced to wear a mock wreath of straw in place of an honourable bridal garland; or to sport a wreath suggestively open at the back. As the century continued, women were starting to bear the sole brunt of the punishments for illegitimacy. Increasingly they found it harder successfully to sue their seducers for breach of marriage promise or for child support, as authorities began to blame them for unchastity.[16] Women who committed infanticide, unable to marry their seducer and facing shame and loss of position and livelihood, were treated with unparalleled harshness. The Carolina of 1532 made the death penalty mandatory for such offences.[17] In Augsburg, Frankfurt, Nuremberg, Württemberg and a host of other towns and regions, a stark rise in executions for infanticide ran from the late sixteenth to the late seventeenth centuries, coinciding with the period of the witchcraft persecutions.[18]

On the whole, these strict measures seem to have worked. Illegitimacy rates sank in the late sixteenth century, remaining at very low levels of 1 to 2 per cent and rising only in periods of extreme economic and social dislocation during the Thirty Years War (1618–48).[19] Then soldiers who had no ties to local communities left women dishonoured and pregnant. Fertility was confined on the whole to marriage, and a rising group within the population – perhaps 10–20 per cent – postponed or even resigned the chance of having children.[20] The bitter economic years from the late sixteenth century to the end of the seventeenth century were accompanied by slowing population growth. In Nördlingen, for instance, the years of the witch hunt lasted from 1589 to 1594, during the hard decades of the 1580s and 1590s when people across Europe were experiencing crisis.[21] It took place against a backdrop of declining fertility in the town: Nördlingen's population had been growing rapidly, from over 5,000 in 1459 to somewhere between 7,000 and 11,000 in the second half of the sixteenth century, but then numbers of births began to decline.[22] These grim decades saw trials in Marchtal too, part of the first mass panics in the German south-west, when hundreds were executed. Such outbreaks were repeated elsewhere in the 1580s and 1590s in Germany and beyond, in Lorraine, the Low Countries, Switzerland and Scotland, which also faced dearth and famine.[23] Even worse in terms of numbers of executions was the period from 1610 to 1630, years which saw the high point of the persecutions in Würzburg. This was the time of the disaster of the Thirty Years War. Famine, dearth and plague endangered fertility and there were even rumours of cannibalism. In Germany as a whole, by 1650, the population was only at about the level of 1520.[24]

When recovery came after the Thirty Years War it was patchy. Fears about fertility did not evaporate. Instead, they seemed to change character slightly, even becoming more apocalyptic, and still capable of nourishing witch hunts. In Augsburg, for instance, though the years after the war were ones of solid and rapid demographic growth, brought about in part by migration to the city, numbers of baptisms never returned to anything like their pre-war levels.[25] Augsburg had not been touched by the witch-hunting panics of the late sixteenth and early seventeenth centuries, even though there had been extensive trials in the surrounding rural lands, and its witch trials did not really get going until after the devastation of the war.[26] This was the pattern in a number of towns and cities across Germany: in towns like Esslingen, Rothenburg or Nuremberg, which had seen little or no witch-hunting during the panic years, a series of dramatic trials for witchcraft were held after 1650.[27]

Throughout the sixteenth and seventeenth centuries, communities wrestled with the twin problems of controlling population numbers while ensuring demographic continuity. Authorities attempted to restrict imprudent marriages, and gave more power to parents to pursue family strategies by controlling the marriages of their offspring. But they could not really measure the consequences of their policies because they lacked accurate statistical information, and regulating marriages remained at best a blunt instrument of population control. At the same time, they repeatedly faced demographic disaster, caused by wars, pestilence and dearth. Everyone knew how easily the best-laid plans of king or villager might go awry as children died in infancy or a wife proved barren, leaving no one to succeed to a kingdom or a property. Protecting fertility was as vital as limiting population.

It was not until the close of the eighteenth century, perhaps even the end of the nineteenth century, that this conservative demographic regime finally gave way.[28] By then, the witch craze had long since definitively ended. But it had coexisted, between the sixteenth century and the first half of the eighteenth century, with a demographic system which shaped the most intimate decisions of men and women. Material goods, land, sexuality, social status and reproduction were bound together in a tight nexus.

In demography, natural fertility and human decisions come together. These human choices range from the attempts of law-makers to control their subject populations through to the timing a particular couple may decide for marriage. Not all of these decisions are conscious, and not all are made in the knowledge of their wider impact. An individual couple who, for instance, postponed marriage for a few years may not have calculated that this might give them one child less; a servant-woman still single at thirty-five may yet have hoped for the lucky marriage that would make her a respected matron.

Demographic regimes belong to the slow tides of history, where change is barely perceptible to those living through them. Except at times of extreme disturbance, such as during the Thirty Years War, governments could not observe demographic change.[29] Here, Augsburg was an exception with a reliable statistical base. From the late fifteenth century onwards, churches had registered numbers of weddings, baptisms and funerals and council officials aggregated the figures each year, so it probably was possible for contemporaries to gain some sense of population growth in the town as a whole. But for the most part, figures for births, marriages and deaths were not centrally collected. When clergy first began, in the late sixteenth and seventeenth centuries, to keep baptismal, wedding and later death registers, their entries were used for certifying an individual's life course, not for providing authorities with accurate demographic statistics that might link numbers of weddings to projected numbers of births. As a result, fecundity was mysterious, its operations apparently part of nature. It was also believed to be subject to supernatural forces, some of them evil.

It is no accident that it was only in 1741, as the witch craze was on its very last legs, that the Prussian field-preacher Johann Peter Süssmilch (1707–67) wrote his *Divine Order in the Transformation of the Human Race, through Birth, Death and the Reproduction of the Same.*[30] This was one of the first attempts to penetrate the secrets of human generation of a whole society, linking statistics to arrive at a scientific, rationalist account of fertility as the outcome of the interplay of individual decisions to marry with economic resources for the population. Süssmilch tried to explain why it was that population growth was not continuous, and why it was subject to checks and reverses. His work prefigured that of another clergyman, the Englishman Robert Malthus, whose account of the role dearth plays in population control still remains the best description we have of the operation of the strictures of early modern demography.[31] Their rationalism could only come out of a world no longer in thrall to an occult view of fertility as imperilled by the forces of supernatural evil beyond human control.

Süssmilch's concerns were in many ways the same as the concerns of those who hunted witches, but he offered a scientific account of the operations of fertility. He too saw fertility as under threat. But unlike witch-hunters, he did not believe the answer was to root out the sect of witches. People could only marry when there were farms enough for them. It was the duty of the ruler to overcome any obstacles to procreation. Amongst these obstacles, like a good Protestant, he included clerical and monastic celibacy, whoredom, loose living and a love of luxury.

Ironically, Süssmilch put his finger on all the issues which had animated the witch hunt in the first place, from the inexplicable deaths of infants to delayed marriage and breast-feeding. Late marriage, he argued, was a principal cause of low population, for those who married at the age of thirty or older would bring four or five children fewer into the world. Prolonged breast-feeding, especially in rural areas, he averred, also endangered fertility, and should be stopped; but he was equally scathing about wet-nursing, one of the chief causes of weakening of the population because women became pregnant too soon, before they had recovered from the last birth.[32] Unequal marriages between women aged forty and over and young men (and old men with young women, though here he did not give ages) should be banned outright because of their deleterious effects on reproduction. His account of the brakes on reproduction, therefore, was entirely naturalistic and moralistic, and it built on statistics. The machinations of old women witches had no place in it. Sexual disease inhibited procreation, not old enchantresses who tied knots in string to cause impotence. So too, Süssmilch devoted attention to childhood illnesses, proving statistically that most children died within the first year of life. He lamented the fate of the 'unfortunate children ... who perish when they are still at the breast, either through stifling by the wet-nurse or by the mothers, or in some other way'.[33] Where earlier generations had so often blamed witches for childhood deaths, Süssmilch blamed illness and maternal neglect. Süssmilch grasped some of the central connections that lay behind the witch hunt, but he reorganized them in his attempt to identify the barriers to population growth. He was right, however, about the importance of the demographic regime, even though he inhabited a very different intellectual world.

The system of late marriage that depressed fertility had psychological consequences, and its legacies were both physical and emotional. Not surprisingly, fertile, fecund married matrons could be envied by their fellows. In turn, they might be watchful for the attacks of jealousy that they believed must surely shadow their good fortune, suspicious of older women who could no longer have children. Fertility itself, a resource that was tenuous, might be thought to be prey to magical, evil attacks in both the natural and the human world.[34] After all, as people saw it in the sixteenth and seventeenth centuries, the natural world was related by a series of correspondences to the human world, and one was a microcosm of the other. The same social imperatives that led contemporaries to pour resources into celebrating the childbeds of respectable women could also sow dissension amongst women, generating suspicion and hatred at the same time as they created networks of obligation.

Indeed, the rise in prosecutions and executions of women for infanticide offers ironic testimony to the strength of the culture of mothers in early modern Europe. Married matrons reported infanticidal mothers, and their accounts commanded respect and credence. They supplied the damning testimony that sent their unmarried, infanticidal counterparts to their death, squeezing the breasts or feeling the stomachs of single women they suspected of illegitimate pregnancy. Their willingness to testify – as well as the new legislative framework established in the mid-sixteenth century which prescribed death for infanticide – was what largely accounted for the dramatic rise in prosecutions.[35]

· · ·

We might expect Catholics and Protestants to have adopted radically different attitudes towards witchcraft, since they proposed such divergent ideals for women. Catholics venerated Mary; Protestants denied that she could intercede for sinners with her Son and held that she was a model of humility for both sexes to emulate. Catholics continued to allow the possibility of a monastic life for women; Protestants argued that the simple prayers of a mother who washed her infant's nappies would reach heaven before the devotional exercises of a nun. Anti-clerical Reformation polemic hinted that both monks and priests were 'secret or public whorers' because it was so difficult for humans to overcome their natural sexual natures. Catholic reforms imposed stricter enclosure on nuns, removing them from all contact with the world outside the convent walls and attempting to safeguard their sexual purity. But they did not obliterate their public role – in Counter-Reformation Munich, for example, the nuns of the Pütrich convent staged a public veneration of relics which they had acquired from the catacombs in Rome.[36] The prayers of nuns continued to offer an important spiritual resource to the communities in which they worked.

Catholic demonologists elevated Mary as the perfect woman, but saw the nature of ordinary women in Eve. Eve, after all, was the first to succumb to Satan's wiles. Here they built on an older, pre-Reformation, tradition. In the *Malleus*, first published in 1486, Heinrich Kramer includes passages execrating women, decrying their carnal nature, their voices, their slippery tongues and their gait, posture and habit, 'in which is vanity of vanities', concluding the section with the infamous passage, 'All witchcraft comes from carnal lust, which is in women insatiable. See *Proverbs* XXX: "There are three things that are never satisfied, yea, a fourth thing which says not, It is enough; that is, the mouth of the womb. Wherefore for the sake of fulfilling their lusts they consort even with devils"'.[37]

Kramer belonged to the Dominican order who were keen advocates of the cult of the Virgin; at about the same time that Kramer was engaged in witch hunts, his fellow member of the order and Prior of the Cologne house Jakob Sprenger was propagating the Rosary.[38] In the sixteenth century, the Jesuit Peter Canisius was a proponent of the cult of Mary and supported – if with some circumspection – the exorcism of women possessed by the Devil, while the demonologist Martin del Rio also authored treatises honouring Mary.[39] The connection between Marian devotion and passionate witch-hunting was not merely fortuitous. These men's view of women was profoundly split, their castigation of earthly Eves and their lauding of heavenly Mary but two sides of the same coin. Mary is alone of all her sex.[40]

For Catholics, Mary played a particular role in the fight of good against evil. She could physically liberate people caught in the snares of the Devil and her aid could be invoked to help those possessed by demons. Indeed, the Counter-

Reformation in southern Germany progressed in part through a series of dramatic exorcisms as men and women spoke in strange voices, rolled on the floor and exhibited terrible physical suffering. In the 1560s, several women servants in Augsburg became possessed. They worked for the Fuggers, one of the richest families in Europe, who were standard-bearers of Catholicism in a town that was then largely Protestant. Peter Canisius, who was trying to consolidate the Catholic Reformation in the town, tried to moderate the excessive fervour of the Fugger women and their supporters. When they were successfully exorcized at Altötting, having invoked the Virgin's aid, their liberation was powerful testimony of Mary's power. Their story was soon put to the service of confessional polemic, because it demonstrated that Catholics were right to venerate Mary.[41]

Del Rio's work featured tales which demonstrate how devotion to Mary and obsession with demons might combine. He told of one young man who had used love magic against the woman he lusted after with the direct assistance of the Devil. The young man confessed his heinous sin to a priest at the shrine of Mary of Loretto, and the priest imposed a series of strict penances, offering to say Mass himself on the young man's account. For three days, the youth was admonished to practise penance by 'abstaining from food, wearing a hair shirt, and whipping himself while imploring the aid of the Blessed Virgin'.[42] While the sinful man was engaged in prayer, prostrated in front of the Virgin and repeating from memory, 'Show that you are a mother. Let him who was born for us and acknowledges himself to be your son receive my prayers through you', the miracle took place. Mary herself gave the sinner back the dreadful pact he had signed with the Devil, thereby releasing him from the demon's power. This miracle underscores a string of the key points of Catholic orthodoxy which Protestants were so keen to assault: the efficacy of the sacrament of confession, the immense power of the priest who was able to free from sin, and the power of Mary's maternal mercy which brings about liberation from the Devil.

Equally clear is the place of sexuality in this drama. The sinner's concupiscence is his undoing. This looks at first sight more like an even-handed critique of male behaviour than the usual alignment of women with lust, so often the staple of demonology. But Del Rio's story actually works the hackneyed tropes of female lubricity and guilt, for it was, after all, the beauty of the woman the young man desired which enslaved him in the first place. Moreover, as the author had explained earlier in the book, the Devil cannot 'bend the will of anyone to love a person he does not want to love'.[43] Del Rio is careful not to blame the woman in this case for seducing the man: that was, after all, the work of the Devil himself. The miracle is, however, structured around a neat image of the double nature of woman. On the one hand there is the base, sexual wanton, whose nature is to be easily swayed to lust; on the other there is the glorious mother Mary, who can plead with her Son to save the sinner.

Such radically polarized views of the feminine cast women as either Madonnas or whores. Del Rio can certainly not be convicted of overt misogyny. Men and women alike are prey to diabolic temptation, and he retails stories about men's fall into the Devil's snares just as he relates tales about women. There are no passages in Del Rio expressing the kind of vitriolic, physical revulsion from women to be found in the *Malleus*. To this extent, it is certainly correct to say that demonologists were not particularly misogynist; and that it is a distortion to assume they all evince the kind of crass woman-hating that can be found on every other page of the *Malleus*.[44] But they held ambivalent attitudes to women which proved to be just as dangerous. Here Marian devotion played a key role. The idealization of woman that Mary embodied allowed her devotees to nourish a vision of feminine perfection to which ordinary women could by definition never approximate. No ordinary woman could be both virgin and mother. In Mary, her devotees could honour the ideal of maternity, mercy, female authority and chastity as womanly virtues, while the elements of femininity about which they felt ambivalent – lust, beauty, ordinary motherhood, even attachment to others – could be allocated to the common run of earthly women and treated as sinful.

Hence the link among Catholic clerical witch-hunters between Marian devotion and witch persecution. Bishop Julius Echter, for instance, insisted that the inmates of his hospital recite three Hail Marys daily and established a Rosary brotherhood there in the Virgin's honour – hospital inmates were encouraged to wear their rosaries outside the hospital 'as often as possible publicly in their hands or on their belt'. He established Marian sodalities throughout the diocese, and was himself a member of the academic sodality to which the bishop, the town clergy and the entire university belonged. Atop the corner tower of his castle he had placed a golden image of the Mother of God.[45]

Though Protestants did not dispense with Mary, and even left some Marian festivals and images intact, they insisted that she was a woman like any other.[46] They apparently held a far less polarized view of femininity, developing instead a single model of the virtuous womanly life that was meant to apply to all women without exception. A woman's destiny was to become a wife and bear children, enduring the subjection to her husband which God had ordained. In giving birth, she was pleasing God, whose divine plan it was that women should have children. Such a vision of female destiny did not leave much room for women who, for whatever reason, did not marry or have children. As the pious spinster Margaretha Blarer, sister of the Protestant preacher Ambrosius Blarer, remarked when the reformer Martin Bucer chided her with being 'masterless', 'Those who have Christ for a master are not masterless'.[47]

Protestantism removed the realm of male and female saints wholesale, the Queen of Heaven along with them. It insisted that salvation came from God's free gift alone and not through intercession to members of the heavenly host.

It is hard to imagine two more superficially divergent views of the nature of woman. Why, then, did both confessions hunt witches with ferocity, to the extent of borrowing liberally from each other's tracts and treatises? It is difficult to provide a satisfactory resolution of this paradox. For Catholic priests and monks, forbidden to marry, the feminine was liable to remain alien, the subject both of propagandist idealization and equally passionate denigration. Denigration was most likely to be touched off by issues to do with sexuality, because the presence of women constituted a genuine threat to the vision of a new, reinvigorated, celibate clergy, who were to be the foot-soldiers of the Counter-Reformation. After all, barely a generation before, in some parts of Catholic Bavaria, clerical concubinage was not only common but was even welcomed by some communities who felt that this would protect their own womenfolk from the attentions of lascivious priests.[48] Clerical attitudes to women were certainly an ingredient of many witchcraft persecutions. In areas ruled by prince-bishops, many of the personnel who interrogated the accused were either clerics themselves or else had worked in ecclesiastical institutions with a strongly clerical ethos. Julius Echter inaugurated his reign in Würzburg by banishing all female relatives from his court, and he also dedicated himself to abolishing clerical concubinage in the diocese and clamping down on what he held to be lax convents full of libertine nuns.[49]

It is less clear how far such clerical attitudes influenced those villagers and townsfolk who denounced women as witches. Nor do we know to what extent, if at all, they affected how women accused of being witches perceived themselves. Revulsion towards their own sexuality does not seem to be a feature of most Catholic women's confessions to witchcraft. Instead, they recount lively stories of their seduction by the Devil which are strikingly candid about the pleasures of sexual dalliance. One woman even saw the Devil in the shape of a comely parish priest. Her tale may bear witness to the effort of sexual repression that a morally pure priesthood demanded, on the part of parishioner as well as priest, but it hardly amounts to an excoriation of female sensuality. Like Protestant women, Catholic women's stories do not neatly fit the polarized thinking about female nature that characterizes so much of Marian devotion.

Despite their ostensible differences, there were deeper commonalities in Protestant and Catholic attitudes to women. Protestants, like Catholics, believed that women were naturally lustful. According to Protestants, a nun's vocation was a contradiction in terms, for women could never escape their sensual nature by taking a vow of celibacy. In both Protestant and Catholic communities in the seventeenth century, women were increasingly being burdened with the greater share of blame for sexual misdemeanours and punished more severely. Catholics venerated Mary's maternity; Protestants idealized the so-called 'house-mother', the good peasant or burgher wife who raised her brood and ran the household. Both confessions tended to propose a vision of motherhood and motherly virtues which could make it hard to accommodate the normal failures of real mothers. One propounded a religious icon of motherhood, the other proposed a secular version which could be just as stifling. Both placed immense cultural emphasis on mother-hood. Idealizations of this strength and tenacity are likely to breed their own monsters.

What motherhood meant was not just a creation of theologians. Religious ideals had to make sense of the realities of generation, marriage and mother-hood. Indeed, it may be that the consequences of the demographic regime of sixteenth- and seventeenth-century society, whether Catholic or Protestant, counted for more than the apparent differences between the confessions.[50]

So while, when faced with demographic realities, both Catholic and Protestant authorities became drawn into shaming women for illegitimacy and into regulating marriage, they did so from very different understandings of what marriage was. For Catholics, it was one of the seven sacraments and therefore fell under the jurisdiction of the Church. Protestants, by contrast, thought marriage primarily a matter for civil authorities, a view which opened the door for secular authorities to legislate on matters relating to marriage, and allowed parents to prevent marriages of which they disapproved. In both Catholic and Protestant communities, marriage was the great social divider. On ritual occasions, women would be separated into those who were married and those who were not. At weddings, there were different tables for unmar-ried girls and for matrons. At festivals, special dances might be danced by girls, while others were reserved for married women. Even village sociability was determined by marital status, so that married women spun and gossiped together, while unmarried maidens had their own separate spinning groups. All this was reflected in witchcraft confessions. Dancing figured prominently in the stories Catholic and Protestant witches told about the Sabbath; and at witches' banquets, married women sat apart from girls. And it was at social gatherings like spinning bees that people might while away the time with tales of the Devil.[51]

Just as Protestants and Catholics took different views of Mary, so they took different positions on the question of the fate of unbaptized children, a funda-mental imaginative theme of witchcraft fantasies. But here too, despite the apparent differences, the underlying concerns they faced were the same, and this accounts for how myths about witches who fed on exhumed baby flesh were as potent in the witch craze in Lutheran Nördlingen as they were in Catholic Würzburg. Traditionally, midwives had carried out emergency baptisms of endangered children, baptizing even a limb so that the child might at least get to heaven. Protestants attempted to restrict midwife baptism, because they often suspected midwives of being unreliable crypto-Catholics, ready to give in to the emotional needs of women in childbirth and inclined to Catholic 'superstition'. The babies who had undergone this emergency baptism still had to have a baptismal celebration in church, to confirm the rite the midwife had carried out. But what should happen to the bodies of children who died before baptism could be administered? The official Lutheran view sought to contain the cluster of superstitious beliefs that held that unbaptized babies would become revenants and haunt their relations. However, precisely because of such fears, separate burial of such children in a separate part of the churchyard was hard to abolish in practice, and did not disappear, for example, in staunchly Protestant Ulm until 1699.[52]

For all their differences, Protestants and Catholics also shared a culture which celebrated pregnancy and childbirth. Images of pregnant women and mothers breast-feeding abounded in sixteenth- and seventeenth-century Europe. In the religious domain one might think of the depictions of the Annunciation, or the greeting of Mary and Elizabeth, both pregnant. The genre of the Birth of the Virgin, popular before the Reformation in German as in Italian art, even used apparently 'realistic' detail from contemporary birthing chambers to depict a woman – St Anne, the mother of Mary – who is just recovering after giving birth. Such paintings showed the lying-in maid, as well as the midwife and even the tools of her trade. They also hinted at the complex dynamics between the two women and their employer, the new mother. Behind the midwife and lying-in maid looms the bed where St Anne lies. Here she will be confined for the first weeks of the lying-in period, as she rests and regains her strength. Only by degrees will she be able to leave the bed and re-enter the household, and only after purification will she be permitted to leave the house on business like ordinary women. These were intimate images, closely documenting physical experience: men were ordinarily excluded from birthing chambers altogether. Like the new father, the viewer is permitted a glimpse of a physical process which has just concluded, and in which he cannot take part. This is a realm reserved for women, but we are reminded of its reality by the bowl for the afterbirth, and the washing of the baby. It could also be a place of dread, the scene where so many witchcraft accusations were formed, as mother or baby failed to thrive, and the midwife or lying-in maid seemed to parents and friends to be not a comforting professional but a death-dealing harpy.

The visual culture of sixteenth- and seventeenth-century Europe was explicit, too, in its depictions of women suckling babies. Paintings of the Murder of the Innocents show hordes of mothers, many of them with exposed breasts, their babies being ripped from their arms – horrific images whose

33. Jacob Lucius, *Christ Blessing the Children.*

power partly derives from the way they present beautiful, maternal bodies at
the mercy of cruel soldiers. In paintings of the biblical Flood, mothers with
suckling children appear in the foreground: the child being ripped from the
breast is the most evocative image of disaster the painter can depict. Images of
Jesus welcoming the children, an iconography which found favour in
Lutheran churches after the Reformation, gave scope for painters to represent
women whose bodies also mark them out as mothers, together with their children. In one such woodcut by Jacob Lucius, Jesus is surrounded by nursing
mothers and hordes of children, while a lying-in maid holds out an infant –
probably stillborn – on a cushion to be blessed.[53]

The suckling of infants, always a subject in Western art because of its
importance in Marian iconography, was not restricted to images of the Virgin
and can be found in classical contexts too. One striking painting by Tintoretto
shows the young Hercules being placed at Juno's breast by his father Jupiter,
who wished to make his offspring immortal. Hercules's mother was mortal, so
Jupiter wanted guilefully to use the Queen of Heaven as a wet-nurse to make
his illegitimate son a god. The milk spurts upwards to form the Milky Way, the
baby reaches for the breast, and around the edges of the painting, putti spin in
a disorientating movement, conveying the primal dependence, confusion and
abandonment of the infant whose need for a woman's milk is overwhelming.

34. Jacopo
Tintoretto,
*The Origin of
the Milky
Way, c.* 1575.

35. Peter Paul
Rubens, *The
Drunken
Silenus.*

36. Hans Springinklee, *Women's Bath*, c. 1518, based on Dürer's drawing.

Tintoretto's depiction of this mythic scene is a breathtaking image, which captures the pleasures of nursing and the terrors of weaning in one. The painting ended up in the collection of the Emperor Rudolf II, who was fascinated by magic and the arts, and who suffered from melancholy, a disease which contemporaries linked both to creativity and to witchcraft. So also, in Rubens's *The Drunken Silenus*, an inebriated satyress is sprawled across the bottom left of the picture, a child sucking at each of her swollen blue-veined breasts. The milk runs down one infant's chubby cheek and the satyress fondles the penis of a child. This is an image of fecundity, sleepy excess and satisfaction rolled into one.[54]

The fertile female body – the theme of so many witch trials – was also an obsession of many sixteenth- and seventeenth-century artists. Albrecht Dürer's famous early sixteenth-century drawing of the *Women's Bath* was one of the first non-religious, non-classical images of naked women and it shows a set of nude women of varied shapes and ages. The genre soon found

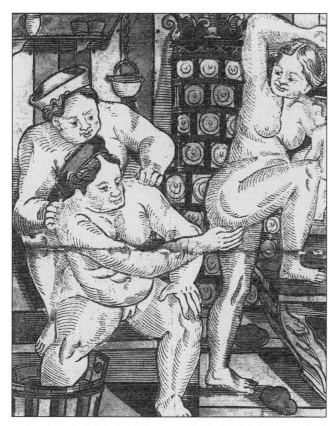

37. *The Bath House, c.* 1626, poor-quality woodcut: this image was confiscated as pornographic and so ended up in the collection of court exhibits in Augsburg. It brings together the conventions of images of witches made famous by Baldung Grien with the well-known motifs of the 'Women's Bath'.

imitators.[55] Images of the woman's bath by painters such as Hans Bock or Hans Springinklee show large-hipped women with big bellies and full breasts, proudly pregnant, scattered amongst a range of women of different ages, shapes and sizes. After all, married women in early modern Europe were on average pregnant every other year, so people expected women's bodies to be constantly filling out and contracting. Whether it led to the birth of a child or not, 'breeding' was a continual phase, filling most of their child-bearing years. Women's clothes emphasized the breasts and then fell in full folds over the stomach, to suit the changing shape of mature women – and so artfully did they conceal the woman's shape that some managed to carry an illegitimate pregnancy to full term without being discovered.[56]

Happiness, plenty, offspring and the plenitude of the mature woman's fertile body went together. Albrecht Dürer's Fortune is a wide-hipped woman with the full stomach of mature womanhood. Her hair is bound, as was the hair of all married women, indicating that she is a respectable matron. Interestingly, Urs Graf drew a parody of this famous image, his Fortune a prostitute with an obscenely lifted swirling skirt. She retains bound hair under

38. Albrecht Dürer,
Nemesis, c. 1501–2.

39. (*facing page*)
Urs Graf, *Fortune
as a Prostitute,
c.* 1518–20.

her courtesan's extravagant hat, and a devil who has appropriated Dürer's
Fortune's wings sits on the vessel she holds.[57] Fortune, Graf is saying, is a
whore. His satire underlines the dominance of Dürer's image: prosperity is a
fecund matron and it is she whose virile body bestrides the world.

The work of Peter Paul Rubens in the seventeenth century breathes a similar
fascination with voluptuousness, and his paintings are crammed with flesh, as in
his extraordinary *Last Judgement*, where the bodies of the saved surge up
towards Christ as the bodies of the damned are pulled downwards. The left side
of the picture is dominated by naked women of child-bearing age who have
clambered out of their graves, one still clutching her winding sheet. The full-
bodied woman on whom the light falls is balanced by another beauty on the
other side of the painting, hauled off to hell by a demon. Sexual female flesh is

not shown as something sinful, inevitably damned; on the contrary, these bodies are saved as well as damned in their fleshliness. This remarkable image was intended for the High Altar of the Jesuit church in Neuburg on the Danube in 1616; but by 1653 it had been removed because of its 'offensive nudities'. It is one of a series of images of the Last Judgment probably commissioned for the newly reconverted Counter-Reformation churches of Pfalz-Neuburg. But although the Catholic convert Duke Wolfgang Wilhelm of Pfalz-Neuburg sponsored Rubens, they were images even vanguard Counter-Reformation Catholics found hard to stomach. They represented a fleshliness that was at once of its time and yet had the power to shock. Rubens's women may seem ugly to us. The modern viewer, reared on a very different aesthetic, finds it difficult to understand why he should have painted these gross female forms with their overpoweringly fleshy tones.

40. Peter
Paul Rubens,
*Great Last
Judgement*,
1615–16.

His vision of female loveliness – the voluptuous, wide-hipped and heavily
bosomed woman – was an ideal of the beautiful woman as fecund and fertile.[58]

   This was also the aesthetic which underpinned the witch hunt. Fecundity
and fertility were blessings in early modern Europe; barrenness a curse.
Women, rich and poor alike, sought cures for sterility at shrines. If the man
was not impotent, a fruitless marriage, it was believed, was caused by the
woman's infertility. Peasants had their fields and animals blessed to ensure
their fruitfulness – and to protect crops and beasts against witchcraft and the
Devil. The same magical thinking was applied analogously to humans, beasts
and the soil – all could be blessed to protect their fertility from harmful attack.
Nor was the idea that fertility in humans and nature was interconnected
restricted to rural imagery. A woodcut by Melchior Lorck of 1565 makes the
same point, as it shows a wide-hipped nude female figure whose breasts spout

41. Melchior Lorck,
Allegory of Nature, 1565.

milk while animals lie in pairs at her feet. Behind her we can see an ideal city. As the rhyme beneath the picture explains, the earth is 'fruitful with all its strength, gives oil, wine, milk, cider and good juice'. Feeding all living things just like a mother, the earth 'nourishes her children with tender feminine breasts. Like a pregnant woman who bears children when her time has come, so also nature brings forth and nourishes everything at the right time'.[59] The pious Christian should observe this and give thanks to God. Fruitfulness in the human and the natural world were allied, and, as in this image, one could stand for the other. The analogy, of course, disguised as much as it revealed, for while one could glory in the abundance of the natural world, in the human world fertility also had to be regulated.

The other side of the controlled demographic regime of early modern Europe was that those who enjoyed the privilege of marriage bore the burden of ensuring the fertility of the whole society. Prayers for fertility abounded in Lutheran collections of prayers and in private devotional literature while in

Catholic regions women often undertook pilgrimages to seek help for problems in pregnancy and in conceiving.[60] For early modern Europeans, a woman's body was markedly different depending on what phase of the life cycle she was in: the small breasts and taut stomach of the woman who has yet to experience pregnancy; the wide hips and fuller stomach of the woman in her child-bearing years; and the shrivelled breasts and sagging stomach of the woman whose fertile years are past. With their obsessive focus on breasts and stomachs, early modern German artists seem almost to reduce women to their position in the reproductive hierarchy. As Luther put it, child-bearing was women's calling. 'Let them bear children to death; they are created for that' is one of the reformer's less charming and more memorable remarks about womankind.[61] Its misogyny reads less harshly when we remember that Luther was here arguing against the idea that women giving birth were under the power of the Devil, and was claiming that giving birth was a work as worthy of salvation as the prayers of a nun. 'Calling' is the term Luther applies to the office of the pastor, and to any profession, trade or craft a man might undertake, consecrating all such labour. Luther was therefore claiming that child-bearing was a physical function endowed with God's blessing. It could lay claim to the dignity of labour in just the way a man's craft might.[62]

In advancing such a view, Luther was giving religious sanction to what had long been a secular value. Pregnant convicted criminals could not be executed. There was a generally accepted consensus that their whims should be obeyed, that they should be protected and that they should be given good food. Care had to be taken of the pregnant woman, for if she were exposed to sights of death or of physical deformity, her child might be born dead, pale or deformed; and if she were to weep excessively during pregnancy the baby would suffer from colic.[63] The provisions of poor laws often stipulate larger rations of food for pregnant women. Once her child was born, the new mother had to observe the six weeks of lying in, refraining from work and eating special foods.[64] On the other hand, the unmarried servant stood to lose her place once her belly showed, and she had to sue the father to receive the maintenance she needed and have her childbed expenses paid.

Childbed, celebrated and protected as a special time of life, marked by a series of festivals, drinking, present-giving and even dancing, was also a time of dread and anxiety, when evil powers were at work and witches might attack. Children were believed to be especially at risk during the first forty days. In Württemberg it was a popular custom to keep a bible or salted bread in the child's bedding, to shut the windows and keep a candle burning all night by the infant's bed. Excrement was even rubbed on the infant's forehead to protect it against jealousy and magic.[65] All the festivities protecting and honouring women's fertility were paralleled by rites to ensure the fertility of the soil and the animals. The rituals of the Christian year from Easter onwards

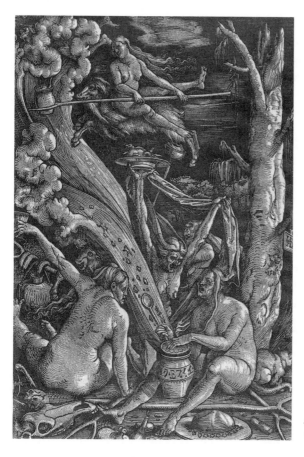

42. Hans Baldung Grien,
Witches' Sabbath, 1510.

formed part of a grand fertility cycle, with fires on St John's Day in mid-summer to promote fertility and to drive away witches. Remnants of Easter fires would be spread on the fields to promote crops and preserve them from witchcraft.[66] Both human and natural fertility needed magical and spiritual protection, for both were subject to jealous attack.

These preoccupations about fertility, women's bodies and the fragility of infancy lay at the heart of the witch craze in Germany, and it was in German art that the image of the witch found its fullest exploration. We owe to a German artist what is probably the first mass-produced single-leaf woodcut dedicated to witchcraft, Hans Baldung Grien's extraordinary image of the *Witches' Sabbath* (1510), which uses the new light and shadow technique of chiaroscuro woodcut devised only two years before.[67] German artists developed the idea of contrasting the bodies of women of different ages and linked this to witchcraft, a subject to which Baldung returned time and again, and which he explored in a range of media, including paintings and printed images for a large audience.[68] The chiaroscuro woodcut print of 1510 shows a group of witches of different ages, sitting around a pot and brewing up a storm. We see an attractive woman from the back, and her rounded buttocks are matched with the half-hidden front view of a woman in her prime. Their bodies are contrasted with the sagging, pointed breasts of the old hag, as if in ironic commentary on the bodies of the younger women. Behind her the viewer can just make out the pointed breast of another old hag; once again, the artist is playing with the effects of viewing women's bodies from different vantage points. The gnarled, rotting tree on the right echoes the decaying flesh of the old crone.[69] Above them a young woman rides backwards on a goat, her hair flying. All the women have loose hair, clearly connoting sexual licentiousness. Baldung played with the same repertoire of visual elements in etchings and sketches intended for a smaller audience. In these we see naked women of different ages, cats, pitchforks, and witches with flying hair. In one, a woman holds a rosary aloft, but it is a mock rosary, composed of dice and the skull of a foetus (ill. 43). This conjunction of a woman of child-bearing age, the little hand of the chubby child pressing into her upper arm, with the skull of the foetus, is deeply shocking. Such themes were echoed remarkably closely in many trials of witches.

It is tempting to interpret such images as the visual counterpart of the early modern European witch hunt. But this would be misleading. After all, the images date from the first two decades of the sixteenth century, a period before the real beginnings of the witch craze – though there was a serious persecution of witches between 1515 and 1535 in the bishopric of Strasbourg, the area surrounding Baldung's home town. Through his family connections to lawyers and judges, Baldung would have been well acquainted with the circles of men who were involved in carrying out such trials.[70] The use of nudity and the range of allusions in the images indicate that these are very far from being realistic pictures of witches. Sometimes the erotic suggestion teases by its ambiguity: in *Witch and Demon* (1514) (ill. 44), is the dragon licking the beautiful young witch's vagina or is her vaginal flow streaming into his mouth? What do we make of the possibly self-pleasuring hand of the witch in the *New Year's Sheet* (1514) (ill. 43)? Both these were pen and ink drawings, destined for an individual recipient, not aimed at a mass market. We know that *New Year's Sheet* was intended as a New Year's greeting card for a cleric – a double-edged joke, for the card teases the cleric with what he cannot licitly enjoy while at the same time representing it as diabolic.[71] A time of role reversals and licence, when a mock bishop was elected, New Year was also the moment when the cleric should renew his vows of celibacy.[72]

None the less, these images do point to some of the central imaginative connections at the heart of the witch craze. In joining the erotic and the demonic, Baldung was teasing his viewer in the same way that demonologists and apol-

43. Hans Baldung Grien,
*Three Witches (New Year's
Sheet)*, 1514.

ogists for the witch hunt occasionally teased their readers. Jokes about lewd women and suggestions of female nakedness were part of the currency of writings on witchcraft too, hidden though they often are in reams of scholarly argument. Part of the appeal of the writings of demonology derived from their exploitation of shared sexual jokes and titillating invocation of the bodies of women. Jean Bodin, for one, was not above employing salacious detail, describing in his *Démonomanie des sorciers* (along with the *Republic*, the only one of his works to be published in French) how 'in a convent there was a dog people said was a demon, which lifted up the dresses of the nuns to abuse them. It was no demon, in my opinion, but a normal dog'; while in the Protestant Johannes Praetorius's compendious *Witch, Magic and Ghost Stories from the Blocksberg* of 1669 we read of lesbian witches in Africa who lure the respectable wives who take their fancy; of Lilith and the Jewish spirits that grow on menstrual blood, enjoy sex with young men and stalk the chambers of women in childbirth.[73]

44. Hans Baldung Grien,
Witch and Demon, 1514.

The pictures of witches by artists like Baldung Grien exploited a very particular kind of erotic imagery, which drew its charge from contrasting
women's bodies at different ages. This might be viewed as a kind of moralistic commentary on the transience of beauty. Or it might be interpreted as
a misogynist attack on women, presented as in league with each other
against men. True, the witches in Dürer's tiny *Witch Flying Backwards on a
Goat* (ill. 46) or Baldung's *Witches' Sabbath* (1510) (ill. 45) appropriate the
phallus as they grasp the pitchfork. They skewer sausages, then as now a
potent symbol for the penis, and roast them; their fellowship constitutes an
all-female world in league with an animalistic Devil. But interpretations of
such imagery as expressions of sexual hostility between men and women, or
as excoriation of female sexuality, miss a simple but crucial dimension.
Images of this kind drew on established codes for age and sexuality, and
only made sense within a distinctive way of understanding the female body
and its ageing processes.

45. Hans Baldung Grien,
The Witches' Sabbath,
1514.

'The Ages of Man' from which these witchcraft images borrowed was a popular subject for woodcuts, etchings and paintings. Frequently used in calendars, it had a very wide currency, and people might describe their own experience of growing old in its terms. It allowed artists to contrast the silhouettes of older and younger men and women, showing how individuals grow into maturity and then decline. Each 'age' also represents a social status, a position in society. For men, marriage (usually placed in the decade of the thirties in such images) is allied with coming of age, running a workshop and household. 'Ages of Man' series were commonly divided into two matching halves. On one side, women were presented decade by decade, sometimes going up in a series of steps, while men matched them for each age on the other. Yet there is an interesting difference between the sexes. In the case of men, age is associated with authority, and decline sets in from the age of sixty. For men, fifty is the high point of life, but the fifty-year-old woman is a grandmother, no longer an authority in her own family. In Jost Amman's version of the subject,

46. Albrecht Dürer,
*Witch Flying
Backwards on a Goat,*
c. 1500

47a–d. (*facing page*)
Jost Amman, *The Ages
of Man,* ages 40 and
70 for both men and
women.

the forty-year-old woman is a mistress-matron (*Herrin-Matron*) who brings
up the children and bears the burdens of governing a household, while her
husband is like a lion, at the height of his powers; but at seventy she is greedy
and can never be satisfied, while her husband suffers from envy (ill. 47a–d). In
another such series, which takes the ages up to the full century, the eighty-
year-old woman is wretched and cold; the man no longer wise; at ninety, he is
'the figure of mockery for children', though he still retains a posture of authority, while she is portrayed as 'a picture of suffering', shrivelled and hideous,
with an attentive girl at her side.[74] This was, of course, an allegorical depiction
of ageing. But it was not accidental that the iconography of witchcraft drew so
heavily on the imagery of the ages of women: both were concerned with the

female life cycle, and fears about witches were always closely tied to anxieties about fertility.

In sixteenth- and seventeenth-century Europe, women's daily lives – even their shapes – were crucially affected by the position they occupied in the demographic structure. Economic status was linked to reproductive status, often quite literally, for old women were prominent amongst the poor. How reproduction is organized within a given society has immense physical and psychological consequences. In early modern Europe, for the entire period between marriage and the cessation of natural fertility, a married woman who was fertile would be subject to the hormonal fluctuations that accompany pregnancy, birth, lactation and recovery for the duration of her matronhood.

Her physical shape would undergo the constant ebbs and flows that attend pregnancy and birth.

Early modern people understood the emotions as deeply connected with the body. Even into the eighteenth century, their thinking was dominated by the humoral system of medicine, the idea that the body was governed by four fluids, or humours. This supplied not only an understanding of the body, but tools of psychological assessment as well. The choleric individual, whose constitution was dominated by yellow fluid, was given to anger as well as being physically hotter; the melancholic was governed by an excess of black bile, predisposing him or her to certain diseases as well as to melancholy, which might cause mental illness or might confer special gifts of creativity. The old woman was dried out, lacking fluid yet prone to the attacks of melancholy which might allow the Devil to seduce her.[75]

These physical and emotional realities combined with cultural beliefs to feed a distinctive set of fantasies about women, in which old women were imagined to be cannibalistic, murderous witches in league with the Devil. Society aimed to regulate and control sexuality within marriage, to harness and to protect fertility. But these women were believed to be engaged in promiscuous sex with their handsome diabolic lovers at all hours of the day and night. Their sexual congress was barren and, consumed with envy, they attacked the property and fertility of others. Fantasies like these fully reflected the demographic regime of early modern Europe. That regime did not, of course, determine them, nor did demography cause the witch craze. The system of delayed marriage and controlled fertility outlasted the era of belief in witches. The witch hunt could not have taken place without the legal and administrative structures to run it, or without the inflamed religious situation that bred witch-hunters convinced they were fighting Satan. Fantasies, moreover, are not clockwork responses to reality but products of the imagination, growing through the interplay of reality and experience, and latching on to material buried in the unconscious. They do not spring fully armed from our heads to surprise us, though they certainly catch us unawares. Physical realities may make certain kinds of fantasy more likely and more persuasive in particular societies at particular times. It was the fears surrounding procreation, motherhood, fecundity and age that formed the potent brew from which stories about witches were made.

Metaphysical fears about fertility, prosperity and prospects for the future became relentlessly literal once they were transposed into the humdrum idiom of village life, as we saw in the case of Ursula Götz, who confessed to killing eighty-eight cows, horses and pigs as well as maiming and murdering men, women and children. Animals embodied wealth and survival. The line of fat cows the rich peasant was able to drive through the village was the most vivid representation of his economic well-being. For him, milk flowed, and his herd was fertile. He had manure, protein and capital. The widow's poverty could be read from her thin-flanked, single cow that gave milk too poor to make butter. What more frightening example of disorder in the natural world could there be than the cow who gave blood instead of milk, the red liquid signifying illness and death instead of life? Cows were a frequent target of the witch's malice. As givers of milk, and closely linked with their owners, they could easily stand for things to do with maternity and nourishing liquids: in Franconia, witches were known as 'milk thieves'.[76] This made their owners likely to fear, and therefore to interpret, their illnesses as the assaults of witches.

Ursula Götz's story is the classic tale of the witch, the old woman who heartlessly murders little children, babies and pregnant women. Her vindictiveness spreads out into an attack on sheep, cows and horses, into destroying the livelihoods of those to whom she has taken a dislike. She robs men of their virility; she spoils the butter. Her homely malevolence assumes cosmic dimensions as she whips up storms or calls down hail to blight her neighbours' crops. She glories in destruction. She threatens motherhood itself, for she destroys all that nurtures and leads to growth and warmth: the crops, cows, milk, the animals, babies and children. She turns motherhood upside-down, for in the diabolic world, sex leads not to generation but to death. Instead of giving birth the witch makes women miscarry and babies die; instead of feeding children she poisons them; she does not heal with salves but uses diabolic powder to bring about illness and shrivelling; she turns cows' milk to blood; she makes horses go lame and fall down dead; she causes fruit and crops to be ruined instead of nourishing her charges. She is the deadly enemy of Christendom, sworn to attack fertility and growth in the natural and human world alike; but she is also the woman next door.

Chapter Seven

Crones

The cruelty shown to older women is one of the more disturbing aspects of early-modern German culture. Demonologists were careful to underline that anyone, male or female, young or old, could fall prey to the wiles of Satan, but they were also well aware that witches were predominantly older women. When the opponents of witch-hunting grappled with the problem, even they could not keep the tone of disdain for old women out of their writing. For the Dutch sceptic Johannes Weyer, writing in the 1560s against the witch trials, most of those accused were only pathetic, melancholic, hallucinating old women, whose age and sex made them a prey to diabolic fancies; while the Englishman Reginald Scot wrote that many 'are women which be commonly old, lame, bleare-eied, pale, fowle and full of wrinkles'.[1]

Menopausal and post-menopausal women were disproportionately represented amongst the victims of the witch craze – and their over-representation is the more striking when we recall how rare women over fifty must have been in the population as a whole. In the cases of witches from the Würzburg trials, we know the ages of only 255 of those who were executed, and around a quarter of those were men. Of the 190 women, fully 140 of them were over forty. Even more strikingly, 112 of them had already passed their fiftieth year and were clearly post-menopausal.[2] The same phenomenon emerges elsewhere. In Nördlingen during the witch panics of 1589–98, thirty-four women and one man died. Again, older women were strongly over-represented. Five gave their age as fifty or over and we know that another four were at least fifty at the time of trial. Eleven had married at least fifteen years before being arrested for witchcraft, so they were probably at least forty or older, and a further six had adult children at the time of the trial. All except the two unmarried women had had children. In Nördlingen, therefore, the pattern is clear: witches were women who were no longer fertile. They were menopausal or post-menopausal, and they had been mothers.[3]

In Obermarchtal, where the documentation is fragmentary, we can say much less. There were around fifty-five probable victims of the witch craze in the sixteenth and seventeenth centuries in the course of two panics, one in the late 1580s, the second in the 1620s. Three of the victims were men. We cannot establish the ages of the women with any accuracy, but we do know that twenty-six of them were married or had given birth to children. For most of the victims we have little more than a name and the barest information; but the broad trend is evident. In Obermarchtal, too, witches were on the whole women who had given birth and had been married.[4] Indications in the record strongly suggest that many of these women were also infertile, menopausal or post-menopausal.[5]

In Augsburg, finally, where there was no witch hunt as such, but only a series of isolated or small chain-reaction cases which nearly all took place after 1650, patterns are more difficult to discern. Of seventeen victims, one was a man. Nine were women over forty, and seven were under forty. However, four of those seven were connected with an older woman executed as a witch, and one was actually a woman who confessed to committing infanticide on the Devil's urging.[6] In two cases, we know for sure that the victims had children; three more were lying-in maids, one was a former midwife and another cared for children.

Evidence from these places confirms a general pattern: older women were strongly over-represented amongst the victims of the witch craze and nearly all of them had undergone the experience of motherhood. They were people who might be thought likely to envy young mothers in the prime of life, and so to wish to harm fecundity. Older and less secure financially, they were likely to want to strengthen their ties to society through caring for children. And often, this was what led to their undoing.

For early modern Germany more widely, it is difficult generally to be certain about the ages of those accused of witchcraft – the records are fragmentary, people often did not know their ages exactly, and many authorities did not bother to ask or record such information systematically. But in the Saar region, we know that 35 per cent of those women accused of witchcraft were in the 40–45 age group, while fully half of the total were aged over 50. That is, nearly 85 per cent of the total were 40 or over.[7] This is likely to be a typical pattern. In Lippe too, the largest age group was the 50–60-year-olds; and nearly all the victims of the witch hunt were older women.[8] Trials for witchcraft were thus very often directed against a group of the population who hardly ever got caught up in other criminal trials. Many were women who would have looked old, women over fifty whose bodies would have showed the physical alterations that attend the hormonal changes of menopause: facial hair, bent posture resulting from thinned bones, wrinkled skin. Women from the age of forty on, the end of the normal reproductive span in early modern Germany, form the bulk of those accused of witchcraft. What made a woman a plausible witch was intrinsically related to the ending of fertility rather than to the visible onset of old age. This connection is even clearer when we keep in mind that most of these women had borne children.

48. Hans Bock, *The Bath at Leuk*, 1597.

Why were so many witches old women? Hatred of old women was pervasive in German art, literature, medicine and popular culture. Many of the
images of pregnant and mature women examined in the previous chapter also
display old women, their shrivelled bodies an ironic commentary on the transience of the fecund women's full figures. In Hans Bock's *The Bath at Leuk*, the
strong, erect full body of the noble woman with her gold chain and wonderful
red hat is placed next to a bent, sagging elderly woman who is unadorned. In
the *Fountain of Youth*, the ultimate fantasy and a common sixteenth-century
subject, depicted in woodcut by artists such as Hans Sebald Beham, Lucas
Cranach shows us a medley of female forms, the old hags entering the healing
water to emerge with plump rounded limbs and glorious golden hair, tripping
across into the alluring tents where noble lovers await them. As Cranach well
knew, youth, fecundity and plenty were allied in reality too, for old women
were often exposed to poverty and want.[9]

While both sexes were regarded as suffering from the ravages of age, women's
social status was tied far more closely to their reproductive capacity. The
'Women's Bath' had its male counterpart but it was a paler imitation. Hans
Bock's painting of the men's bath, for instance, does not have the power of his
depictions of women. It has less of an erotic charge and lacks the sheer ruthless-
ness of his portrayal of older women's ugliness and failing reproductive powers.[10]

Such imagery drew on common understandings of the ageing process and
were mirrored in medical beliefs about ageing, based on humoral medicine,

49. Hans Sebald Beham, *The Fountain of Youth*, *c*. 1530: this woodcut image makes a similar point to Cranach's painting.

50. (*below*) Buryam Walda, *Rejuvenation Furnace*, 1594: in this version of the same idea, old women are dropped into the furnace and emerge youthful below.

which also played an important part in the witch hunt.[11] In a demographic regime in which, once a woman was married, fertility broadly followed the natural human rhythm, it was usually the beginnings of menopause that brought a halt to conception.Women were believed to be moister and colder than men; but as women's bodies aged, so they became drier. This, however, only made their lusts more powerful, because they craved moisture. Since they were no longer menstruating, they were thought to be incapable of ridding their bodies of impurities. One writer even cautioned against marrying an old widow, as such women had concentrated impurities in their bodies, evidenced by their poisonous breath. Marriage to such a woman could lead to an early death.[12]

The contrast between old and young, men and women was also a subject for barbed comedy. Pictures of unequal couples were another favourite genre image, the lecherous old man with his nubile young wife, her hand safely on his purse; or the hideous old woman decked out like a young girl with her youthful husband beside her.[13] These caricatures mock the disjuncture between age and sexual appetite. In imagery like this, both sexes are equally the target of satire; but the direction of the barbs is interestingly different. The old man is rendered foolish by his sexual desire: age ought to confer wisdom, but his lust overwhelms his reason. In contrast, the old woman shocks because her ravaged face and aged body combine with her limitless sexual desire. Mutton dressed as lamb, the old woman with her sunken toothless face is both a fearful and a comic figure. It is the young man who must fear the sexual greed of the old woman since her dry body hungers after his male seed. But because she cannot conceive children, her sexuality is terrifying: desire that does not lead to fertility.

Above all, it was in images of witches that the motif of the old, post-menopausal woman was developed. Baldung Grien's versions of the old witch are so familiar – to us as to his sixteenth-century viewers – as to have the character of cliché. Indeed, the witch varies little among sixteenth-century artists, her wild hair, muscly arms, prominent nose and sagging breasts making her instantly recognizable whoever the artist. In Dürer's tiny image of *The Witch* (ill. 46), we see her riding backwards on a goat, her hair flying outwards; she dominates the canvas of Jacob Cornelisz van Oostsanen's *Saul and the Witch of Endor* (ill. 52). She peers through the window at the *Bewitched Groom* (Baldung Grien, 1544), holding her torch aloft, her hair flying out and her naked breasts sagging; she raises her arms high from behind the cauldron at the very heart of his woodcut *Witches' Sabbath* of 1510 (ill. 42). In Grien's corpus, images of older women in such subjects as the *Ages of Women* or *Death and Women* closely resemble his images of witches, as if any older woman could be a witch.[14] Her age is represented not by a stiff gait or bent posture; on the contrary, many of these witches boast strong, muscled legs and their stance

Wie ein altes Weyb/bulet vmb eins Jünglings Leyb.

51.Wolfgang Strauch, *Ill-Assorted Couple: Old Woman and Young Man*, 1570.

is upright and defiant. Rather, it is the loss of her reproductive functions to which the artist pitilessly draws attention.[15] At the same time, the practically universal attribute of the flying hair carries an unmistakable message. These, the images point out *ad nauseam*, are old women who are sexually hungry but cannot give birth to children.

The motif received perhaps its most vivid representation in a drawing of Niklaus Manuel Deutsch (ill. 53). Here an old woman is shown stripped bare, with prominent, drooping breasts, their knotty shrivelling clearly detailed, the nipples pointing downward. Light falls on her stomach, her womb which is no longer fertile. Her hideous, billowing, snake-like hair is matched by the light falling on her vulva. She stands in a sexually provocative pose.[16] What arouses the viewer's revulsion is not the woman's age but the conjunction of sexual rapacity and an infertile body. This is what suggests to the viewer that she may be a witch.

Such old witches are figures of horror. Almost all images of witches contain at least one such old woman – indeed, her identity can even be the visual clue

52. Jacob Cornelisz van Oostsanen, *Saul and the Witch of Endor.*

that resolves the ambiguity in the rest of the image. Rarely depicted realisti-
cally, the witches act as a hideous counterpoint to the images of voluptuous
women. The artist has stripped these women naked for the viewer, just as the
executioner would have done to search a woman for a witch's mark, so that
the signs of age are visible, not just indirectly in the wrinkled face, bent back,
or stooping gait that would have identified a woman as old in early modern
Germany. Early sixteenth-century depictions of witches in 'high' art are not
individualized, and their repetitive quality dehumanizes their subject. These
are images of fantasy.

By contrast, there were also images of older women, such as that of Dürer's
mother or of Rembrandt's mother, which are fully characterized, sympathetic
representations. Yet even apparently sympathetic images of old women might
occasionally slide into visual associations with more disturbing images drawn
from witchcraft depictions. Hans Baldung Grien's *Study of an Old Woman* is
also known as *The Hag* or *The Witch* (ill. 54). Here we see what appears to be
a life drawing of an old woman, with a fine, compassionate portrayal of her
face. But her left breast is revealed to us, showing the shrunken, wrinkled skin
of a woman who can no longer suckle a child. The drawing resembles other
representations of old witches in Baldung Grien's *oeuvre*, and though this
woman's hair is chastely covered, the exposure of her breast hints at her sexuality. Whether or not she is to be identified as a witch, the visual similarity with

53. Niklaus Manuel Deutsch, *Old Woman.*

54. Hans Baldung Grien, *Study of an Old Woman,* c. 1535, also known as *The Hag* or *The Witch.*

his other representations of witches is unmistakable.[17] In so many of these images, it is the figure of the old witch who is the most repellent and terrifying. She carries the weight of the moral message. Indeed, when artists came to depict the allegorical figure of Invidia, envy, they showed her as a thin hag. Envy and the witch were virtually interchangeable.[18]

Those accused of witchcraft most certainly did not look like Baldung's harpies. And yet, on to the figures of village and neighbourhood women were projected the terrors associated with the figure of the witch. They gave expression to a hatred of older women's bodies which was a rich seam of early modern culture. This revulsion undoubtedly played a role in the witch craze, even though not all of its victims were old women. These images insist that women of all ages can be witches, and their witch-like qualities are related to their connection with the old woman, most terrifying witch of all. Because women's bodies inevitably age, all crones were potential old witches. Such images circle around the same preoccupations like moths around a candle: birth, sex, fertility, destruction and death.

These visual realizations had their literary counterparts. In Johann Fischart's *Flöh Hatz, Weiber Tratz (Flea-Hunt, Women's Gossip)*, which appeared in full version in 1577, as the major witch hunts were about to get under way, the poet imagines the world from the perspective of the flea. Fleas, it was believed, preferred the bodies of women. Fischart's poem is a sadistically tinged erotic exploration of naked female bodies as he describes the journeys of the fleas and the women's futile struggle against them. Like the artists of the earlier sixteenth century, and in particular Baldung Grien, a fellow inhabitant of Strasbourg, Fischart uses the ploy of contrasting bodies of women of different ages, lingering over the bodies of old women with particular fascination. One old dame sits like death and wears a huge fur, poking out of it like 'a tortoise out of her house'. When she burns the fleas in the fire, they get their revenge by raising sparks and embers and 'set alight the old cavern of the old bottle [*Fläschen*, a word referring to the old woman which can also mean vagina], together with the hole from which the stinking breath crawled'. Fischart is making fun here of the old woman's sexual heat, her foul smell, hinting that she is incontinent, and mixing up mouth, anus and vagina as if they are one interchangeable hole.[19] This is the same kind of repellent description of the hideous old woman into which even the most beautiful young woman will eventually be transformed as we find in the visual images of witches, and it plays a similar role in the eroticism of the poem as it does in the images. The old woman of Fischart's poem is not a witch; but it is worth noting that Fischart was not only the translator and re-worker of Rabelais's works, the *Geschichtklitterung* for which he is most famous. He was also the translator of Jean Bodin's work of demonology, a vivid and powerful polemic against witchcraft crammed with the sort of fantastic tale and detail from which Fischart drew so much inspiration. Both are products of a single imaginative universe.

Examples of this style of writing about older women could be multiplied, and they can be found in seventeenth-century works too. In Grimmelshausen's *Simplicissimus*, the great picaresque German novel about the Thirty Years War published in 1669, our hero finds himself in a French brothel where an old woman introduces him to three beautiful young French women with breasts like alabaster. When the hag asks him which is most beautiful, he replies that he can see no choice amongst them. She proceeds to misinterpret him on purpose as meaning that she is more beautiful than any of the damsels on offer. Revealing her hideous charms, 'the old woman began to laugh, so that one could see all four teeth that were still in her gob'. Full of lust, she tricks him into spending the night with her and she turns out to be an alarmingly passionate lover, tearing off his clothes, 'and out of sheer desire just about biting off his lips'. The only German she knows is 'Come closer to me, my heart!' which she enunciates with a strong French accent. The old woman's violent lust, her execrable German, the mock Judgment of Paris scene, are exploited for their comic potential. Her hideous body is contrasted with the beautiful alabaster breasts of the young women on whom Simplicissimus has missed out – but she is, it transpires, an expert lover and Simplicissmus spends a week with her.[20]

Grimmelshausen's most famous creation is Mother Courage, the tough old woman whose fictional autobiography describes how she ruthlessly makes – and loses – her fortune out of the Thirty Years War. She stands for the complete moral and material devastation of war. Mother Courage is no witch. But in one chapter she purchases a familiar, an animal who is a diabolic spirit. It brings her lots of money, for where other traders sold a single barrel of wine, she got through three or four; when a customer had once tasted her food or drink, he had to come a second time; and if she set eyes on someone and wished to enjoy him, he immediately was willing, honouring her as a goddess.[21] Later in the novel, having sold the spirit in the nick of time to avoid damnation, she meets (in a knowing reference to Grimmelshausen's other work) Simplicissimus. He is dressed as a nobleman and the indefatigable Courage woos him: 'he came, according to my wish, sailing with a full wind into the dangerous port of my insatiable desires, and I treated him as Circe did the errant Ulysses'.[22] Courage acknowledges that she has 'only the seventeenth part of my previous beauty' by then and is delighted to read in Simplicissimus's memoirs that he held her to be 'smooth-haired': 'I helped myself with all sorts of paint and make-up, of which he licked off not little, but a great amount.'[23] The two cheat each other, and in revenge she tricks him into thinking that the son to which her maid has just given birth is actually his, the fruit of her forty-year-old womb. This is a delicious revenge since she gets the idiot Simplicissimus to believe 'the infertile one had given birth'.[24]

Mother Courage is a whore. Full of sexual disease – as she advises the reader in her postscript – she enters one liaison and marriage after another, to satisfy her lust and avarice. She is a perversion of Dürer's figure of Fortune, a mature woman whose moral degradation symbolizes the fickleness of fate in war. Grimmelshausen's description of her does not exploit physical disgust to the same extent that a writer like Fischart did. Much of it is shorthand. But then, by the time he wrote, not much was needed to invoke the cultural tradition to which he was heir, the representation of the figure of the witch as an infertile, lubricious and avaricious old woman. Despite the continuities, however, Grimmelshausen's was a secular idiom, and though he repeatedly refers to the Devil, his use of the diabolic is only for comic and moral effect.

Stories and images of old women had a way of imprinting themselves on the imagination. They could even structure how people viewed the world around them. In Augsburg in 1694, witnesses described how an old woman called Ursula Grön would stand 'blood-naked' at her window, with loose hair. Some even saw the fork beside her on which she rode to the witches' sabbath. It is as if one of Hans Baldung Grien's witches had stepped straight off the canvas. And there were stories about her to match: she would take young men to her chamber, show them her bed and say it was a shame such a clean bed was not shared; or she would raise her skirt up over her head, flaunting her genitals. One witness saw her pay young students to go with her, a reversal of the normal direction of trade in prostitution that the witness seems to have found deeply disturbing.[25]

Ursula Grön was aged about eighty when she was brought before the Augsburg Council and accused of witchcraft. Despite her age, she was imprisoned, and in the course of the third interrogation she was subjected to torture with the 'bock', the fifth and most serious degree of torture, which involved being tied to the bench and whipped. This extreme physical brutality against an elderly woman was nothing new to Grön. In the period before her incarceration she had been whipped out of a graveyard, had been beaten with a stick by a young student until the blood ran and the stick broke in two, and had stones thrown at her by young children on the street. Even when she was taken to interrogation, so she complained, the civic guards were rough with her. One drew his dagger and laid it on her breast. Grön's very presence seemed to elicit physical violence. So inured to such treatment had she become that while there is anger in her account of it, there is no surprise. Nor is there any defensiveness in her persecutors' description of their attacks. As one witness put it, 'she deserved to be burnt alive'.[26]

Ursula Grön was accused of injuring young children. Her entire household did not want her to live there because, another witness said, 'there are many children and pregnant women'.[27] In their accounts, witnesses focused on exactly what had happened to their children's bodies, their descriptions of the injuries mirroring the weapons which had been used against Grön. So one witness described how a child had '*kugel*', balls or bullets, in its body, lumps which swelled up hard, and which had emerged shortly after he and some other children had thrown stones at Grön. Another child seemed to have arrows darting around inside its body, and 'the poor thing ... was like a cannonball when it lay in bed'.[28] Taking down the record of the allegations, the scribe noted that 'the place of the swelling is rock hard, as one felt for oneself': touching the child's body and feeling for oneself had become part of the process of ascertaining proof.[29] Witnesses recounted how Grön had offered children apples and pieces of bread,[30] but these turned out to be poisoned. As Grön herself said under interrogation, 'people don't like old women to give children things'.[31]

People believed that Grön attacked their fertility. One witness described how she invaded her bedchamber at night, and lunged at her sexual parts. Another woman remembered how, when she married for the second time, Grön kept on walking around the bridal wagon – clearly she was up to no good.[32] Another female witness remembered how, eighteen years before, Grön had begged for a sausage at her engagement party. As she explained, Grön was her enemy because her sister had rejected Grön's son's advances. Even without this tricky background, engagement parties could be fraught events. Around the time he married, a man usually came of age as a master of his craft and took out citizenship in the town. Celebrated in front of his fellow masters, engagements were rites of passage to sexual, economic and political maturity – and of course they were just the moment when a witch might choose to attack. The more Grön talked about sausages, the more those assembled feared an assault on the bridegroom's potency. And sure enough, the worst happened: when the couple celebrated the wedding 'and went to bed, he wasn't up to it'.[33]

Grön begged. She asked for wood and food – yet she was also able to dispense money to those whom she favoured or give apples and bread to children. Something of the unsettling character of her begging can be caught in her own demand to the Council, at the end of her first and second interrogations. She complained that she received only bread and water in the evening, and she demanded a half pound of meat and a good drink of beer in the evening because of her age. The theory of nourishment on which the Council would have relied implied the opposite: precisely because she was so old, she should have needed less food. Grön's self-confident demand for more meat has nothing of the humility that might be expected of a woman at the mercy of the Council. Such a red-blooded demand for meat in one so old was fearsome, just like her sexual appetite.

Grön was even said to have attacked the dead. The gravedigger told how she habitually sat on the grave of her dead son, and heaped bones of other dead people around it. When the time came for the bones to be transferred to the charnel house she had refused to move from her son's grave and they had to eject her from the graveyard by force. Who knew what harm she was causing to the dead by stealing their bones and possibly taking them out of the grave-yard? Grön unwisely tried to refute this imputation by arguing that chemists made use of ground-up bones in preparing medicines. This only strengthened the impression that she had indeed been stealing human bones, and suggested she knew how to pound bones to make witches' salve. Worse was to follow. It was said she had committed incest with her illegitimate son, who had also died some years before. This tale must have been told many times, for it turns up at third hand in several of the witnesses' stories. Small wonder it was a story no one forgot. It provided further proof of her unnatural lust, while rein-forcing the image of her as a mother who consumes her offspring sexually and whose children die.[34]

This was a baroque fantasy, and it made sense in relation to sets of cultural fears about old women which poured out in a host of contexts, from medical treatises to woodcuts to paintings of high art. She was known, witnesses said, as the Miau woman, a nickname that aligns her with cats, long associated with witchcraft. In the words of one male witness, her body was like alabaster.[35] The comparison conveys both the fascination and the horror of this woman's elderly body, not shrivelled with age but preserved by magic (so he believed), taunting and haunting him at the window. What the witnesses saw was of course formed by their own sexual desires and terrors. They saw an image that was culturally recognizable, familiar to them through what they already knew about witches. Her sexuality was lethal, and yet her body was beautiful, coloured with the cold alabaster whiteness of death.

Prejudices against older women were deep rooted and long lived. In 1617, a generation after the major witch panics in Marchtal, when villagers of Saulgart were asked whom they suspected of witchcraft, Conradt Weggeman told how his little daughter Catharina had been bewitched and had gradually faded away. She had lain ill for fourteen days and blessings had not helped. Whom did he suspect? An old woman from Oberwachingen who went begging, and who had been in the parlour in his house shortly before his daughter sickened. And recently two cows of his had died within a week, and he had heard cats making loud screams at the time, so he thought it was witchcraft. He had no suspicions except of his neighbour, though he could say nothing specific about her behaviour.[36]

So widespread was the assumption that witches were old women that even women who confessed to the crime of witchcraft frequently mentioned seeing old women at diabolic gatherings. Some said they had been seduced into witchcraft by an old woman, who had introduced them to the Devil and had watched while he debauched them. Like a master of a craft, the old woman teaches the younger the secrets of the diabolic trade. Hans Dülicken's wife recounted how, forty-seven years before when she was only ten, she had been working at the castle driving geese. The bailiff's wife had been her undoing, seducing her into witchcraft and giving her a root which she could use to fly to the Sabbath.[37]

These women were like procuresses, looking for young bodies to supply the appetites of their diabolic masters. As such they resembled a species of perverted mother, turning their charges over to a life of Satanic corruption instead of arranging a respectable marriage. So tight were the imaginative links between witchcraft, harm to babies, and childbed that shadowy midwives sometimes stalk these tales. In Nördlingen in the 1580s, several accused witches spoke of seeing a midwife at their gatherings as they dug up the corpses of infants who had died.

Such trials exemplify the fascinated hatred that a witch could arouse. The result was violence, frequently and systematically directed against old women's bodies. Executioners experimented to come up with forms of torture that could be applied to the elderly. They believed their old bodies were inured to pain, but they knew that they might die if subjected to the rack. This kind of vicious aggression may also help to explain one of the features of the witch hunt which regularly emerges, the persecution of mother–daughter pairs. This pattern had been long established in Marchtal where, in the sixteenth- and seventeenth-century trials, no fewer than five mother–daughter pairs met their deaths. In one case the connections were very tight: Barbara Miller, her two daughters and their aunt were executed. The tendency persisted into the eighteenth century, when four of the seven trials between 1746 and 1757 concerned mother–daughter pairs.[38] It is apparent from these well-documented cases from the eighteenth century that part of what provided the dynamic of the trial was the link between mother and daughter. In Nördlingen, we know of one such mother, executed at the age of seventy with her two fifty-year-old daughters.[39]

Trials of mothers and daughters substantiated the conviction common amongst demonologists that witches passed on their secret arts to their children, and amongst the population at large that witchcraft travelled in the blood. But there is also a deeper psychological imperative at work, related to the power of the myth of witchcraft. If witchcraft truly was inherited then we might expect sisters, sons and aunts to be as commonly cited as victims; but although they certainly are named, they do not emerge with the chilling regularity of mother–daughter pairs. In part, the naming of a daughter by a mother or vice versa resulted from the pressures of interrogation and the kinds of questions put by the interrogators. Canny questioners were able to exploit the ambivalence or even the intensity that might be inherent in the relationship between mother and daughter in order to make one betray the other, giving away intimate secrets or details.

But more than tactical shrewdness was at work in these interrogations. The questioners were more probing because they expected there to be a connection between mother and daughter and were fascinated by this. The relationship condensed the fears of the trial, magnifying the anxieties about fertility, for it made its audience speculate about two wombs: one of the mother that had given birth to the daughter. Normally – strange as it seems to use such a term in connection with witch-hunting – a witch panic worked by mobilizing anxieties about fertility and motherhood and projecting these terrors outward on to other people. Such fears usually stuck to a particular kind of figure, a woman who could no longer bear children but who had been a mother herself, or who had some kind of caring role in relation to young children. Older women thus served as the lightning conductors for fears that had their origin in the mother–child relationship itself.

By contrast, in trials of mothers and daughters, the maternal relationship itself came under scrutiny. The witch and her daughter were unmasked as a pair of evil mothers, the elder seducing the younger and corrupting her into diabolic vice, the younger repeating – or about to repeat – her mother's heinous perversion of the function of procreation. She too would adhere to Satan's sect, sharing her mother's lover, engaging in sterile demonic intercourse, and killing and harming Christians. In cases like these, the trials did not protect the mother herself by blaming someone else for illness and disease. Rather, they intensified the focus on the mother–daughter relationship itself, casting the pair as evil mother figures linked by blood and maternity. They thus served to make the themes of motherhood, age and wombs even more important in the fantasies that surrounded witches and fuelled the trials.

Hatred of older women had an enduring afterlife, even as the witch craze seemed to be nearing its end. We can witness its slow transformation as we return to the tiny territory of Marchtal, with which we opened this book, and to an inhabitant of the villages of Seekirch and Alleshausen up on the high moorlands, the eighteenth-century poet Sebastian Sailer. He wrote the first works of literature in Swabian, pioneering the transcription of dialect. A Premonstratensian monk from the abbey at Marchtal, he also worked as a priest and had his own rural parish. A gifted preacher, he knew how to communicate with ordinary people and understood the importance of story and parable in moving the heart. He was famous for his plays, written for an elite audience, which treat religious subjects by transposing them into the idiom of Swabian daily life. In his verse play *The Creation*, first performed in 1744 at the nearby monastery of Schüssenried, also a Premonstratensian foundation, God the Father checks the calendar just like a peasant to see when is the best time to sow the first seeds. Eve grumbles about her housework, including making *Spätzle* (noodles), that prized speciality of the Swabian kitchen.[40] Sailer's dramas are populated with all the stock figures of village life: the simple

55. Sebastian Sailer.

mayor, who wants nothing but an easy life, the apparently stupid but cunning peasant farmer, the boisterous village youths, all painted with gentle sympathetic humour. Attacked at the time for its apparent irreverence, and never published during his lifetime, Sailer's work circulated in manuscript.

But an undated poem titled 'Mourning Song for an Old Woman'[41] presents a different side of the rural idyll. It too is composed in Swabian dialect, and it plunders the conventions of love poetry to comic effect, enumerating not the beautiful features of the beloved, but her utter hideousness in every bodily part. The poem is a supposed lament for her, and the imaginary speaker is her newly widowed husband.

Aged eighty, she is lame and ugly. She has a large goitre on her neck, a nose 'like the chimney on Blasius's house' which she seldom wipes, and big round eyes like the night owl, so scary that they frighten away all other creatures.[42] She has long white fingernails, with which she has scratched him many a time. But it is as he writes about her mouth that the old, familiar fantasies about elderly women make their full appearance: her 'gob' has 'eight corners', looks

like that of an old nag, and she growls as if possessed. When she opens her
mouth

Everyone runs away and screams
'Oh no! She's going to gobble me up!'

We are reminded of the witch in the 'Hansel and Gretel' story who fattens the
children in order to eat them. There is a sexual innuendo here as well: the
poem's narrator married the woman when she was already old and lame, and
old women's lubricity was a common trope. Indeed, as he says, she loves
dancing, 'though she is about as graceful as a gyrating cow'. In long tradition,
the woman with the wide open mouth stands for the woman with the wide
open vagina; and Sailer expects his readers to be amused by the woman's
sexual predatoriness.

The rest of the poem goes on to describe how she pours brandy down her
throat and fouls the bed, and how her bedchamber stinks so much that it can
never be cleaned. She has a 'weather hole' from which 'it rained right into the
bed': she is incontinent. The 'weather hole' trumpets and thunders everywhere
like a horse in its stall, and blows out behind like a trumpet blast; the 'powder'
in her room from 'the old pepper mill' can never be got rid of. Here Sailer is
drawing on the well-established genre of the man of excess, the coarse
Rabelaisian figure whose physical functions are not held in check by any of the
normal bonds of civilized politeness. He drinks until he vomits, and urinates
and defecates in his own bed. This is a style of writing which dates back to at
least the sixteenth century when Fischart provided his lengthy and even more
grotesque elaborations of Rabelais's writings; and when moralists warning of
the dangers of alcohol painted its effects in vivid physical terms, describing
vomiting and defecation in graphic detail. Such writing reached its peak in the
mid-sixteenth century, with Friedrich Dedekind's stories of Grobian, the disgusting boor whose behaviour breaks every rule of civilized manners with
gusto. In this genre it is usually men who engage in these revolting displays –
but by the third edition of his work Dedekind had invented a female variant
of the character, Grobiana, whose exploits rival those of Grobian. Dedekind
wrote in Latin, but German versions of Grobian were still being prepared in
the seventeenth century. Sailer's eighteenth-century poem, knowingly popu-
list, is clearly plundering the conventions of this kind of writing.[43]

Throughout the poem, it is her lack of cleanliness – her inability to wipe her
nose, her use of cooking spoons to clean her monstrously large ears – and her
disgustingly filthy nether regions which are used to excite the reader's amused
revulsion. This is the distaste of an educated class, which can mark itself off
from peasant grime with its clean white shirts, ruffs and handkerchiefs. But
there is much more at work here. Repeatedly, Sailer plays with all the clichés
of witch accusation. The woman has a 'weather hole', though it is used to

pollute her own bed rather than whip up tempests; she snores so loudly that one would think a storm was coming. He concentrates on her anality, another theme from the witch hunt: a woman suspected of witchcraft might be detected by using a special smoke which would force a true witch to defecate foully. Just such a technique was tried out on a witch at Alleshausen not long before Sailer wrote.[44] Sailer also insinuates that the old woman is full of obscene lechery, like a witch. She has a 'powder', but it is the powder of her own dirt, not a diabolic substance. She growls like one 'possessed'.

Yet Sailer is not directly suggesting that this woman is a witch. She is, rather, a freak of nature and a figure of fun. As it happens, Sebastian Sailer had been working as a junior assistant priest at Seekirch, the parish to which Alleshausen was attached, during the years 1745–47 when a late and particularly nasty witch hunt took place.[45] It is conceivable that his role was more significant than the junior nature of the post suggests: Father Milo Stecher, technically the incumbent priest in 1746–47, was seriously ill and died in 1747.[46] The role of the local clergy in that trial was complicated, and the accused witch's daughter certainly believed that the parish priest supported her mother.

Sailer was no witch-hunter, though as late as 1771 he was prepared to argue that the trials in Marchtal had been justified. Interestingly enough, he also passionately defended the institution of childbed, which came under attack in the eighteenth century as peasants tried to encourage their wives to go back to work as soon as possible. Lying in, he insisted in the parishes for which he was responsible, must last for four weeks at least. The same man who defended the rights of new mothers and insisted that the period after birth was special could also fully understand his parishioners' fear of witches. For the most part, Sailer, as an enlightened cleric, saw the popular culture of the villages around the Federsee as an object of curiosity, a village way of life for which he felt affection and which, as an intellectual, he could chronicle for the entertainment of others. But he shared with his parishioners a cruel, mocking contempt for old women, albeit in predominantly secular rather than demonological guise.

Witchcraft was born in part out of the antagonisms between women who had given birth and who were experiencing the disorientation that follows childbirth; women whose young children died; and women who could no longer bear children. There was a powerful cultural current of hatred of elderly women in early modern Europe, an antagonism which was sometimes shared by women as well as men. What fascinated painters, poets and printmakers was the process of physical decay in women as the no longer fecund body shrivelled and became hideous. Time and again, the themes of the witch trials turned on birth, fertility and the dangerous wishes of old women, even when old women were not its only victims. Not everywhere in Europe were witches hunted. But attitudes of this sort, shared by opponents and enthusiasts of the witch craze alike, formed part of the currency of early modern societies. And they were not prejudices that could be rationalized; they were linked to sets of fantasies which clustered around the human body itself. In particular, these fantasies concerned mothers and wombs. Deep-rooted, inchoate fears of this kind found expression not only in the patterns of accusation, but in what the witches confessed to doing – having sterile sex with the Devil, and eating the flesh of dead babies. It was not until the eighteenth century that these fantasies gradually began to shift focus.

Part Four
The Witch

Chapter Eight
Family Revenge

By the middle of the seventeenth century the heyday of the great mass witch persecutions was over, and by the century's end the image of the death-dealing old crone-witch was gradually loosening its grip on the popular imagination. But this did not mean witches were no longer persecuted: now, ironically enough, individual interrogations of suspected witches – when they took place – became more thorough, more detailed, and more systematic. Where before, a mere dozen pages of records and a few weeks might have sufficed to condemn a witch, now fifty or even several hundred pages, and trials lasting many months, were not uncommon. The resulting mountain of documents allows us to explore the hatreds, grudges, hopes and longings of individuals who themselves for the most part could barely write and have left no other trace. Many of them, too, were witches of a different kind: young women, youths and even children.

Suspicions of witchcraft had never been aimed solely at old women, as we have seen. Men, even rich and powerful men, could be accused; and around a quarter of the victims of the witch hunt across Europe were male, though in many areas of southern Germany this proportion was smaller. The protean nature of witchcraft – you never knew what tricks the Devil might get up to next, or whom he might recruit – made the myth hard to refute and helped to generate new targets: in Bamberg, the former mayor was executed for witchcraft, in Würzburg, clergy and hospital inmates.[1] Children and youths had also occasionally suffered the death penalty for witchcraft: in Augsburg, one young girl had been executed with her mother in 1625; in Würzburg, several children were executed between 1627 and 1629. But in the final years of the witch persecutions, as interrogations began to focus more clearly on the motives, life histories and individual psychology of accused witches, attention increasingly shifted away from the old woman as witch, and over to youths and children. Their miseries and lurid imaginings now became the stuff of witchcraft interrogations.[2]

In Augsburg, the cases of child witchcraft form part of the more sombre early history of what is often taken to be the enlightened, secular, progressive interest in children as separate from parents, and in their imaginative worlds.

One historian, aptly summarizing current views of this transition in the history of childhood, argues that 'the key to these changes is the long-term secularization of attitudes to childhood and children'.[3] As J.H. Plumb described this development in relation to England, there is but one shadow in this optimistic, light-filled picture of eighteenth-century attitudes towards children, and that is the increasingly repressive interest in masturbation.[4] There were certainly many developments which led to a new interest in children and an understanding of childhood as a separate state; but in Germany, these cannot simply be attributed to secularization. Children were crucial to the Pietist project, a movement about to reach its height in bi-confessional Augsburg with the arrival of the charismatic preacher Samuel Urlsperger in 1723. It had been around the newly established 'Poor Children's House' that early Augsburg Protestant Pietist devotional activity had first centred at the turn of the century;[5] while Catholic Jesuit pedagogy, with its use of theatre and exploitation of popular culture, had long operated with a shrewd sense of how to communicate with children and the unlettered.[6]

Just how bitter such cases could be, and how intense the family legacies of cruelty and suspicion, is evident in the case of a young girl named Juditha Wagner, who was accused of witchcraft in in 1689. Her story began nearly two decades earlier, in 1670, when the widower Tobias Wagner, a master carpenter aged seventy, took a wife. He married a woman less than half his age, Margaretha Keberle from Ravensburg. This was a good match for her, a servant girl nearly thirty years old with a bad reputation: she must have just about given up hope of marriage. And she almost failed to secure the match. Tobias's children vehemently disapproved of the marriage: after all, Keberle was around their age and was likely to have children whose claims would eat into their share of their father's estate. Tobias's son Esaias had married only the year before, and had probably become a master carpenter himself about the same time. Perhaps this gave him the confidence to flex his muscles and attempt to make his father see reason. Esaias put it to his father in the following terms: 'Just as we children have not brought shame on you, so he [sic] should not do so either to them, and not take one who has been every nailer's apprentice's whore.'[7] He and his sister found their father a wife they felt to be eminently more suitable, Maria Durst, a comfortably off sausage-maker's widow. Significantly, she was aged forty-three, so she was also much less likely to have children.

The engagement party for Durst was in full swing when Margaretha Keberle appeared, saying that though Durst might have her arms around Wagner now, she did not have him yet. And so it proved. The sausage-maker's widow had not been told about the old carpenter's debts. When she found out (through Margaretha's intermediaries), she pulled out of the wedding, opting instead for comfortable retirement in St Jakob's foundation for elderly folk of good

56. Simon Grimm, *Pilgrimage to Holy Cross Church Augsburg* (detail), *c.* 1680, copper etching. Holy Cross was a double church, Catholic and Protestant. The Catholic church housed a miraculous bleeding host.

57. *The Interior of Holy Cross Church.* The Protestant church was rebuilt by international Protestant donations after the Thirty Year's War.

name. Margaretha and Tobias were duly married in the Protestant church of
the Holy Cross.

Wagner's children, Philippina and Esaias Johannes, were not reconciled to
their father's choice. Philippina began to call her 'my father's witch', so
Margaretha banned her from the house; and in 1671, Tobias and Margaretha
summoned Esaias, Philippina and her husband before the mayor to force them
to stop bad-mouthing Margaretha. Life in the households of father and son continued in parallel: a year or so after the wedding, Margaretha did indeed give
birth to a daughter, while in 1670, the year of the wedding, Esaias and his wife
had a baby girl too, named Juditha, on whose fate our story centres. Four years
later, in 1674, Esaias's wife gave birth to their next child, a son, Juditha's little
brother.[8] Relations between the two households had apparently improved to the
extent that Margaretha Keberle was asked to act as her lying-in maid.

During the lying-in period, however, Margaretha entertained the convales-
cent mother with a fateful story. She told how a young mother in Ulm had
been harmed by evil witchcraft, so that she could no longer pass water, had
swollen up and died miserably. That night Esaias's wife had a terrible dream,
and the very next day, she suffered the same fate. Within the year, she was
dead. Esaias was certain that Margaretha had bewitched his wife, putting
something in her soup and doing strange things to her bed. He never let her
cross his threshold again, and treated her as his enemy.

A year after his wife died, Esaias took a second wife, Rosina Esslinger. She
came from a well-established local tailor's family. They married in July, and
eleven months later their first child was born: they named him Esaias Johannes
after his father.[9] Juditha was now aged seven. In the same year the family
moved house, to just a few streets away from where they had been living, but
in a different parish, that of the former Franciscan church.[10] Juditha was no
longer welcome in the new house, and was soon living with her stepmother's
brother and mother, the Esslingers. There, Juditha's step-grandmother sickened and died, and within twelve months, her son Abraham the tailor,
Juditha's step-uncle, followed her to the grave. It was thought he had been
struck with the same illness as his mother. No one, however, considered the
deaths suspicious at the time.

Though her father was still alive, and would certainly have been in a position to support his daughter financially, Juditha was now shipped off to the
orphanage, far away on the other side of town. The teacher at the orphanage
later described her as a taciturn girl who rarely spoke and would barely give an
answer if asked a question. She was slow at learning. Others described her as
stupid and childish. Her uncle thought her simple, and described how, when
she was aged nineteen and old enough to know better, she had been so taken
with a cheap ring his little son had found that she begged him for it, showing
a childish delight in the bauble when the lad gave it to her.[11]

Eventually, Juditha left the orphanage, returning to her father's house to live. At around this time she began to tell incredible stories, first to her half-siblings, and then to her father and stepmother. Juditha confessed that she was a witch. It was she who had killed her step-grandmother Esslinger and her step-uncle, using a powder the Devil had given her. She had killed her little half-brother and half-sister, murdering baby Abraham when he was only five weeks old and putting diabolic powder in baby Sara's pap. And she had killed six children in the orphanage. She had flown out using a salve the Devil had given her, and at the witches' dance she had seen many fellow witches from Augsburg. Her father was naturally eager to know whether his hated stepmother Margaretha had been amongst the witches; Juditha confirmed that she had indeed been there. She had seen her going behind the meat market in Augsburg quite clearly and 'her spirit' had spoken to the grandmother's spirit.[12]

Two officials from the Council arrived at Juditha's father's house to arrest her, and Juditha, as they noted, 'willingly' followed them to prison, 'where she herself demanded to be brought'.[13] Soon her interrogation commenced, and during its course Juditha again confessed that she was a witch. When she was just six years old, the Devil had pricked her hand and guided her writing as she signed herself to him in blood for fourteen years. But the fourteen years had now expired. Four weeks ago, he had appeared to her at one in the morning, while she was in bed, telling her to sign once more 'or he would tear her to pieces'; she signed, but only in ink; and he let her off a quarter-year. A fortnight ago he had come again at night in the form of a boy, trying to get her to sign again, but she refused. Juditha told the story freely, and her interrogators gradually just let her talk, discarding the questions that had been formulated in advance.[14]

Juditha had grown up with stories of witches, and in the orphanage too, rumours of witchcraft were rife. At least in theory, the orphanage operated as a kind of household, the 'orphan father' pledged to care for the children's spiritual welfare, his wife the orphan mother obliged to interest herself closely in the children's doings. (The extent to which it could ever feel like home was of course limited: at this time there were over sixty children in the orphanage, which hardly gave much scope for close bonds between the orphanage parents and the children.)[15] In the orphanage Juditha had met 'the Fleck girl' who, she said, had taught the children witchcraft for payment. This girl was almost certainly one of the daughters of Maria Fleck whose execution for witchcraft had been hideously botched – the chief executioner's hand slipped when he attempted to execute her and he had sawn her head off on the ground.[16] Another orphanage boy kept a wand the Devil had given him under his bed,[17] and when Juditha said she had seduced a young boy into witchcraft but could not be sure of his name, stories about devils and strange goings-on came tumbling out as soon as the Council summoned the suspect boys and their masters for questioning.[18]

But it was not just the special circumstances of this orphanage that fostered such a climate of fear, housing, as it happened, children of executed witches; nor was this the monopoly of one confession. Augsburg was a bi-confessional town, Lutheran and Catholic; and both religions were exercised by the power of the Devil. On the surface, the two religious communities had learned to live peacefully enough together by the late seventeenth century; Holy Cross was a double church, where the Lutheran adjoined the Catholic church. But they were still two separate worlds. People married according to religion and few converted. You could guess a person's religion from their Christian name.[19] Hell-fire religion was still popular. The Capuchin friar Marcus de Aviano was making well-attended preaching tours, visiting the city in 1680, 1681 and 1684, healing and driving out devils. A contemporary chronicle includes a copper etching of him, which bears the legend 'Through whom God's hand performed miracles, all infirmities, yea Devils had to yield to him through his laying on of hands and making the sign of the cross'.[20] Dramatic exorcisms had been a feature of the Counter-Reformation in Augsburg from its very beginnings, when the famous Jesuit Peter Canisius himself expelled devils from a servant woman of the Fuggers, as we saw earlier, and many Protestants had converted.[21] Priests who could command devils were imbued with awesome powers, and printed images of such miracle-workers were still circulating amongst Catholics in the late seventeenth century.

Though Protestantism might seem hostile to what it termed papist magic and superstition, and though developments in Protestantism towards a more interior form of religion might seem to leave less room for a real external Devil, Lutheran understandings of evil provided equally fertile soil for fears of witchcraft. Lutherans felt themselves to be embattled: theirs was a religion with a history of persecution. In Augsburg, they commemorated the terrible days of the Thirty Years War, when Protestant services had been banned and the city suffered a siege in which many starved to death. On the fiftieth anniversary of this catastrophe, memorial services were held in all the Protestant churches, and at Anna Juditha's church the children were given special pictures and a Peace Festival bun so they would never forget. Anna Juditha would have been aged just eleven. In the glory days of the Reformation in the sixteenth century, Protestants had greatly outnumbered Catholics: but now they could read the story of their declining numbers in the official published tables of Catholic and Protestant births, marriages and deaths published each year. Around the beginning of the eighteenth century they ceased to be in the majority for the first time, and never regained numerical superiority, even after the influx of Protestant refugees from Salzburg in 1731.[22]

Lutheranism was also a religion that retained a powerful sense of the ongoing activity of the Devil in the world. Just twenty years before, in 1661, the Protestant Church had publicly prayed for some boys who had been given money by the Devil: through the power of collective prayer, the boys were

58. The Capuchin friar Marcus de Aviano (1631–99) preaches repentance to the Augsburg populace, *c.* 1681, unsigned copper etching.

freed from the Devil's clutches.[23] In Juditha's own church, the pastor Georg Riß had no compunction about saying the local midwife was a witch, and he flatly refused to baptize any children she brought to the altar. The Pietist minister Gottlieb Spitzel was convinced of the power of the Devil, and in his hands, spiritualizing religion did not mean magicking the Devil away – quite the reverse. Though preoccupied with the internal state of the individual and convinced of mankind's sinfulness, he was also certain that innocent individuals could be possessed by devils and could harm others. When Spitzel published his dramatic *The Power of Darkness Broken* in 1687 he devoted chapters to the magical arts, summarizing the cases of several witches who had been executed in Augsburg. Christoph Ehinger, another Pietist and pastor at the Holy Spirit hospital, published his *Daemonologia* in Augsburg in 1681; his interest in demonology had been greatly strengthened by his own dealings with a parishioner of his, a shoemaker who was being plagued by the Devil.[24] Throughout the 1670s and 1680s the Augsburg clergy had found themselves embroiled in the sensational case of Regina Schiller, a woman who said she had signed a pact with the Devil and who sought solace from both Catholic and Protestant clergy. She was eventually hauled before the Council, and banished in 1673 – though she soon returned. Her case monopolized the attention

59. Pastor Georg Phillipp Riß, Holy Cross Church, who thought the local midwife was a witch.

of Gottlieb Spitzel for some time, and was addressed by the whole Protestant synod of ministers.[25] Spitzel tried and failed to exorcize her, and had to suffer the indignity of being the butt of comic songs about the episode. In 1682, after a criminal interrogation, she was finally banished from town forever by the Council and led out of town in public.[26]

Schiller's case saw Church and town Council finally working hand in hand, and this established a fateful pattern, the synod pursuing a case initially, and handing it over to the Council for criminal trial; the Council commending those whom it freed after interrogation to the spiritual care of the Church. This co-operation could sometimes work not to remove witchcraft from the criminal arena altogether and turn it over to spiritual remedies, but to produce new witch trials. As late as 1696, Euphrosina Offinger appeared before the synod of the Church in a case which clearly went back many years. She had admitted to Herr Spitzel that she had had intercourse with the Devil, but later, before the synod of ministers, she said that Spitzel had forced her to confess that she was a witch: 'she had to say it, Herr Spitzel would not leave off'.

Offinger was a grown woman in her early thirties, but she appeared before the synod with her mother. She had been tempted by the Devil to commit suicide. She had also – so the ministers alleged – engaged in fraud, feigning illness caused by the Devil in the hope of getting money. Her relationship with Spitzel, who had died six years before, was clearly complicated: she had switched confessor to Senior Müller, because Spitzel asked her things at confession 'of which she was ashamed'.

Offinger may have been a godless manipulator and fraud, as the ministers believed, or she may have been the victim of Spitzel's belligerent obsession with young people, especially girls, whom he thought he could save from the Devil. But though the Church summoned witnesses and questioned her on several occasions, the matter did not rest there. The ministers passed the protocols of the case to the Council's legal advisers, and in 1697 the Secret Council, which directed criminal interrogations, determined that she should

M. GOTTLIEB SPITZEL. 146
Pfarer und Senior beÿ St Iacob, in Augspurg.
Anno.1690.

60. Pastor Gottlieb Spitzel.

be punished with three days' imprisonment on a bread and water diet. Offinger was lucky to escape the rigours of a criminal trial.[27]

Like several young women in this period, Offinger nearly came to see herself as the clergy saw her, as a creature of the Devil; Juditha was convinced she was a witch. Though she was twenty, all agreed that she was childish, and the Council thought her so short of stature that it demanded documentary proof of her age when she came for interrogation. Stunted, probably poorly nourished, untrained in any craft, a slow learner who needed the Devil to guide her signature,[28] Juditha was more of an adolescent than an adult, and this was reflected in her fantasies about the Devil.

The chief confession, to which she endlessly returned, was that she had murdered her half-brother and half-sister, Sara and Abraham. On leave from the orphanage on a Friday, she had made a *Heimsuchung* or 'visitation' on her new mother and father, as she put it, a word used both by Juditha and her stepmother. The word can mean 'visit' but may also be used in connection with something malign, such as an illness or chastisement from God.

Food had been ordered for Juditha – sausage, beer and dumplings from the baker's. Her stepmother Rosina described what happened next. While Rosina went to the bedroom to comfort the other crying child, Juditha was left alone with baby Sara in the parlour. No sooner was Rosina out of the room than little Sara began to scream piteously, and her mother rushed back. Rosina gave her the breast, but was unable to feed her. Immediately afterwards, Juditha returned to the orphanage. By the Monday baby Sara had passed a strange stool, and soon after, she was dead: she died 'with laughing mouth', as her mother put it. So it had been with Abraham two years before; he had taken five weeks to die but had been the picture of health at eight days old. Now Juditha revealed exactly what had happened to baby Sara all those years ago.While she had been alone with the baby in the parlour she had seized the chance to feed her devil's powder, red and black, mixed into her pap.[29]

Juditha, exiled from the family home and allowed only to visit, had not only seen her mother replaced by a stepmother, her 'new mother' as she called her, but had seen herself supplanted by new babies. We do not know what had happened to her natural brother, whose birth had led to their mother's death; four years younger than Juditha, he is not mentioned in the documents. Little seems to have remained from her mother. When she moved out of the house it was to the Esslingers, Rosina's relations, not to her mother's kin that she went. During the trial, no relatives from her mother's side testified for or against her.[30] In confessing that she had murdered her half-siblings, Juditha was picking up the stories of witches and childbed with which she had grown up. Childbed and its aftermath were often the context for witchcraft allegations when something went wrong for mother or child, and an older woman

61. Karl Remshard, *Schwedenmauer with Schwedenstiege* with the Untere Graben, *c.* 1720: the Protestant orphanage is on the right.

might well find herself accused of being the witch who had wished them harm. But Juditha cast herself, not an old woman, in the role of the witch.

Juditha's half-siblings, Sara and Abraham, had been named after the Esslingers, the stepmother's side of the family. They bore the names of Juditha's step-grandmother and step-uncle, who had taken her in when her own family did not want her.[31] Chance – or perhaps it was over-determination – thus gave the supposed killings a compelling logic. All those she had attacked were connected with her stepmother Esslinger and her children, even down to having the same names. And soon Juditha was confessing that she had smeared her diabolic salve on her stepmother's shirt and 'on the place where she lay in the bed', causing her great pain – the location clearly indicating that this was a sexual assault.[32] Stepmother Rosina and her husband Esaias, in their turn, confessed that she had indeed suffered severe pain, so severe that she had been unable to sit. All this had happened after Rosina had given birth to her last child and her menses had failed to resume. Rosina had taken all this to be natural; now she was not so sure.

Juditha also claimed that she had killed six children in the orphanage. The new orphanage father was asked to check the records, and he consulted the orphanage doctor, who remembered that a number of children had died of a strange disease he had been unable to identify.[33] It is highly unlikely that Juditha had actually killed anyone. No accusations, either against her or anyone else, had been made at the time and all the deaths had been considered natural. The deaths had not resembled each other, the lists of names of supposed victims could not be made to match and the symptoms were all different. It is difficult to see in any case how Juditha could have come by an effective poison. She lacked the financial resources, and was held to be slow-witted, hardly the prototype of the cunning thief who would have known what to look for in an apothecary's.

Where had Juditha got the materials for such a story? Since each witch's story was read out publicly at her execution, and often circulated soon after in broadsheet form as entertainment, the stories of Augsburg witches were common currency.[34] Juditha spoke of a witches' table spread with food in a corner of Augsburg, a detail she had surely copied from a story which had been circulating since the 1640s of a mysterious table found in a summer-house, where witches had supposedly held a banquet.[35] Many of the details in Juditha's confessions seem to have been lifted from the confessions of earlier witches, in particular a group of three executed in 1685, when she was fifteen years old. This band included Maria Fleck, whose children Juditha knew from the orphanage. Under questioning, Juditha repeated the bizarre so-called witches' prayer she had learned: 'White patch, blue patch, brown patch, green patch, you had to leave out the black because the devil could not endure it.' This prayer, she later said, had been taught her by the comforter paid by the Council to keep her company and care for her spiritual state while she was in prison. It had figured in Maria Fleck's interrogation too, and most likely this was how it had ended up being recited by the comforter and then by Juditha.[36] Similarly, it was well known that Maria had seduced into witchcraft a four-year-old boy named Caspar Mayer; Juditha too confessed that she had perverted a young boy at the orphanage into witchcraft. Fleck had taken the boy to the Devil's dance; Juditha said she had been taken to the dance by an old woman when she was four. The details of Mayer's case would have been seared into many Augsburgers' memories, because the Council had publicly decreed that the nine-year-old Caspar Mayer must watch the execution of the three witches in 1685 as a terrible warning – they could not have foreseen how horribly the execution would go wrong, with Fleck hacked to death on the ground.[37]

In the bricolage of stories Juditha told, there was a profusion of mothers, stepmothers and grandmothers. After her own mother's death Juditha had, as she said, become close to a woman called Felicitas Christele, a distant relation who had spent time in the house during her mother's lifetime and who, her stepmother claimed, had poisoned the girl against her. As Rosina put it, Christele 'misled' her, so that Juditha 'let all the love that she had previously borne her, the witness, disappear, so that she thus came to the orphan house',[38] a telling admission, for it suggested that the stepmother had in fact shipped Juditha off to the orphanage.

Christele had given her powdered sugar to eat, sweets and treats in a house where there did not seem to be much affection left over for Juditha. She picked her up from school and brought her home. And it was Christele whom Juditha now identified as the woman who had led her into witchcraft. Christele had kept a 'little man' in a drawer, presumably a mandrake, and it could magically make money grow. One put coins under it, and found more later. She had flown out to the witches' dance with Christele, who, together with the Devil, had encouraged her to kill her little brother and sister. The only person in Juditha's life who seems to have been connected with her mother, Christele took her place in the girl's affections. But in the unstable moralism so characteristic of witchcraft belief, Juditha now invested Christele with evil, claiming that the woman who had shown her kindness was actually a witch leading her to damnation. In the emotional poles of her confession, if her stepmother were a good mother, then Christele must be a witch and so too must Juditha herself.

Felicitas Christele was safely dead by the time Juditha made her allegations. She was a likely candidate for the role of witch, an older woman who had coaxed Juditha with special treats of food, who hung about the Wagner household, dabbled in magic and was involved in caring for Juditha. In blaming an older woman for her fall into witchcraft, Juditha shared the mentality of those around her, who expected that it would have been just such an older woman who was the sinister witch behind her.

Her feelings about her father, however, could not be so readily deflected on to someone else by means of a story about witchcraft, and they played a major emotional part in the course of the trial. Juditha never confessed to harming her father, and seems to have wished desperately to please him. Fathers – the 'iron father' who ran the prison and whom Juditha asked for a knife and fork with which to kill herself; the 'orphanage fathers' who governed the children; the pastors who heard her confessions; the 'city fathers' who were her judges – appear, like her real father, as figures who were as remote as they were powerful.

It was no accident that Juditha dated her seduction to fourteen years before, the year of her father's remarriage. It seems likely that once her half-siblings and step-relatives had died, Juditha felt overwhelming guilt, as if her own seething hatred and rage had been literally murderous; as if, by wishing them dead, she had killed them. The brooding piety of late seventeenth-century Pietist Lutheranism, with its emphasis on discerning one's innermost secret sins and emotions, would have strengthened such a view. Contemporary thought patterns also fostered this multiplication of parental images, encouraging people like Juditha to write their familial relations into cosmic dramas, because all relations of authority were conceived as inherently paternal and maternal in character. In this way, the patriarchal values of society could become ingrained in people's minds and souls.

Seventeenth-century patriarchalism, however, had none of the folksy closeness that the rhetoric of fatherhood carried when it had been deployed by the

Council in the first half of the sixteenth century. Then, the councillors and office-holders were drawn in large part from the ranks of guildsmen, and shared with people like Juditha the experience of life in a household workshop. But under the revised constitution imposed by Charles V in the wake of the city's defeat in the War of the Schmalkaldic League in 1548, the members of the Small Council and those who held significant posts in the city government were almost exclusively patricians or members of the *Mehrer*, the extended patriciate who intermarried and socialized with the patriciate. They were a class apart. Dwelling in fine urban palaces, they knew little of crowded craft life. They wore luxurious clothes with fine white collars and cuffs; they owned heavy jewellery and plate. Juditha was pathetically grateful for the gift of even a cheap ring. If they were 'fathers' to a girl like Juditha, they were distant embodiments of power, not intimates who shared her life.

Throughout her trial, Juditha tried to draw her interrogators into her own mental world, unconsciously trying to make them participate in it. During her second interrogation, her face underwent dreadful contortions as she 'twisted her mouth hideously three times and pulled her mouth together with her teeth, and changed colour variously'. When asked why, the scribe noted that 'she said, the Devil rages so loudly and shockingly outside in front of this door, and would not have that she should confess any more, which he often did outside upstairs, and stokes the fire; and today when she was taken to the place of questioning, the Devil said to her that she should confess nothing, even if they should use great force, or he would tear her to pieces'.[39] In her third interrogation, she addressed her interrogators directly, telling them that the Devil was standing right there by the heater and forbidding her to confess anything.[40]

It was not so much that Juditha was what we might call an attention-seeking adolescent, the explanation often offered for many similar cases of witchcraft accusation and possession.[41] Rather, what made the case possible was her interrogators' willingness to see cosmic significance in Juditha's stories. They were after all the fathers of the city, charged with caring for its salvation, conscious of the divinely sanctioned task of administering justice. Through Juditha they were engaged in their struggle with the Devil. Witchcraft was more than a language for expressing what could not otherwise be said. It created a symbolic world in which those conflicts could be lived, and where others could be drawn in to act in a religious drama.[42]

Juditha's Devil had little individual character. More of a prop than a main character in her story, we do not even know what clothes he wore, and he made no apparent effort to seduce her; after all, he had carried her round since she was a child. It is not so much the Devil's relationship with her as Juditha herself and her own mental state which is the focus of her account. This is evident in Juditha's remarkable, deeply idiosyncratic accounts of diabolic intercourse.

She had never committed indecency with the Devil. When it was said to her, why then did Abraham Esslinger find her lying naked on the cutting-out board, she said and asked You Lords won't do anything to me will you, and when she was told, she should confess the truth, she confessed, that at that time the Devil came in the form of a little whore boy to her, touched her with his slippery on her (if you will excuse the expression) shameful parts or bull [= flask or sheath], as she called it, tickled her, lay on her and put black wool into her (excuse me) bull, so that for some time, until she pulled it out, could not pass water any more, this gave her pleasure, but when she wanted to pull the wool out again, the Devil wanted to beat her. She had not hurt anyone though.[43]

This account, and the variations on it she later offered, have none of the assurance or conventional plot of the stories told by older women about sex with the Devil. Juditha seems even to have been uncertain of what words to use to grasp her experience, plumping for the word 'bull' for her vagina, which seems to have been novel to the scribe, for he explicitly notes the term she used after giving his translation. 'Bull' can also mean flask or sheath, and its metaphorical significance is plain. But why should the Devil have put black wool in her flask, and why should she have been unable to urinate until she removed it?

Juditha's sexual fantasy seems to bear a surprising resemblance to the story of her mother's death, a story which we know only because her father related it to the mayor during the trial. He had evidently told it several times at the mayor's office in an effort to have his stepmother Margaretha imprisoned. Juditha's mother, so Esaias said, 'had been most badly harmed by evil people and they had caused, that she could not pass (excuse me) water, and thus had to perish miserably'.[44] What Juditha herself reported is a fantasy of sexual intercourse which seems to have little relation to sexual experience. Instead it resembles the crude fantasies which many children share about how babies are made, and which concentrate on the mother's body and its contents.[45] In early modern understandings of the body, what the woman had to do in giving birth was to open her body, to let it flow, not seal it.[46] By contrast, childbirth had sealed up Juditha's mother's body. She was now unable to let the flows out of her body as was crucial, according to humoral theory, to the body's health, and so she had swollen up and died. All this had been caused by her stepmother's malign story-telling. Juditha's story, gradually normalized somewhat as she repeated it under interrogation, represented intercourse as leading to a plug of wool being put into her body, which stopped her urinating. In her story, Juditha was in the same position as her mother on that fateful night sixteen years before.

Juditha's story about the Devil corresponds to what we know of her emotional life. A motherless child, she put herself in her mother's position in her sexual fantasy, but it was a fantasy about death, about lifeless black wool, about animals and not humans. Her world had collapsed when her mother died, and she had become part of the Devil's brood. She dated her contract with the Devil to the time of her father's remarriage and her confession that she had killed six children in the orphanage was, in the patriarchal grand 'household' of the orphanage, the nearest thing to six further 'siblings'. And she had attacked her stepmother, and the fertility of her union with Juditha's father. Mothers, fathers and siblings were fixed slots in her story, into which the various characters who passed through her life were all made to fit.

Juditha's story is most unlikely to have been true in reality, although those around her thought it credible. It is certainly likely that Juditha had wished them all to die, and when they did perish, felt that she had brought about their deaths. In Protestant understandings of witchcraft, this was exactly what the Devil did, tempting his victim into making evil wishes and then, by means of illusion, making it appear as if the wish had worked, even though it had not been the real cause of death. Some held the wish alone sufficient to justify execution, if a pact with the Devil had been made. In living out her story of witchcraft, Juditha, like all those who accused others of witchcraft, explained illness through relationships between people, and saw the incidents of daily life as part of a cosmic moral drama between God and the Devil. By accusing herself of witchcraft, she committed suicide by proxy. Just as a case of witchcraft could be resolved by executing the witch, purifying the community, and offering the witch the chance of salvation and return in death to the fellowship of Christians, so Juditha secured her chance of going to heaven by having herself put to death.

In May 1690, Juditha was executed with the sword and her body was thrown on the fire and burnt to ashes, the 'merciful', honourable death for which Juditha had begged. She was accompanied to the place of execution by Gottfried Zäh and Andreas Harder, deacons of the Franciscan church, who offered her spiritual comfort as she faced death.[47] Jacob Schmid, eventually fingered as the boy Juditha had seduced into witchcraft, had been released but had confessed enough to add plausibility to Juditha's confession; Christele was dead. It might seem that all the loose ends of Juditha's case had been tied up.

One issue, however, remained outstanding. Juditha had died confirming the truth of her confessions, including the confession that her step-grandmother was a witch. As early as 8 November, shortly after Juditha's first interrogation, the mayor had been ordered by the Council to instigate secret inquiries about Margaretha Wagner. But Mayor Gottfried Amman did not do so, for whatever reason; and his successor Adrian Imhof did not actually carry out the order until Juditha's main interrogations had long been finished. No further action was taken against Margaretha, even though shortly before she died, Juditha confirmed having seen her at the witches' dance.[48]

But Margaretha was not to remain lucky for long. In November 1694, Margaretha Wagner's stepdaughter Philippina Fischer, Esaias Wagner's sister, appeared before the mayor Christoph Sigmund Amman, demanding that Margaretha Wagner be imprisoned as a witch, for she had been infamous as such for over thirty years. Margaretha did not seem unduly disconcerted by this accusation, as the scribe noted, and confidently asserted that the accusations all arose from envy; she had been cited to appear at the mayor's before, and nothing had been proven. However, when Amman insisted that she would have to be put in the cells this time, she got angry. Amman ordered her house to be searched for salves and poisons and passed the matter over to the Council.[49]

Margaretha was another classic witch. There had been rumours for a long time; some said she had been thought a witch even before she came to Augsburg. In her early fifties when she was interrogated, she was an older, post-menopausal woman who had a reputation for promiscuity, an outsider who had married into the town. She was poor, lived in lodgings that were described as 'very mean', and supported herself by all manner of expedients, most often by buying and selling second-hand goods, work that depended on having a shrewd eye for objects and their value, and knowing perhaps more than was healthy about people's needs and circumstances.[50] She had worked as a lying-in maid at least once, a job which exposed women to suspicions of witchcraft, and by this time she was a widow, with no husband who might have offered some protection against witchcraft accusations, and only one unmarried daughter aged twenty-three. In short, the omens were bad.

The miscellany of crimes of which she was accused was also standard. She had allegedly killed her fourteen-year-old stepson, and caused another child to die. She had made a child swell up terribly after some clothes of his had come into her possession, she had given an apple to a young boy who had then sickened, she had made two other young brothers ill after giving them food, and she had killed a child aged eight. That child had died screaming 'Oh Mother, the Wagner woman, the Wagner woman!'

This was not all. Philippina, Margaretha's stepdaughter, testified that Margaretha had bewitched her former lover, a journeyman carpenter, causing his arm to wither when he deserted her. Pointedly, she hinted that Margaretha's daughter, born during her marriage to Tobias, was actually the fruit of an illegitimate liaison: at seventy, Tobias had been too old to father a child. This insinuation attacked the daughter's right to a share in the family inheritance, an issue that had probably figured in Philippina and Esaias's opposition to the marriage in the first place. And there were other stories about harming old women and mothers. When Margaretha entered Susanna Vaigeler's house, the finches twittered. Susanna's mother thought this a sure sign, and Margaretha was duly accused of killing poultry by witchcraft.[51]

The two most vivid accusations concerned childbed. The first tale about how Juditha's mother died when she was lying in had been rehearsed in public several times, raised with the Protestant mayor over twenty years before, and repeated at Juditha's trial. Esaias now gave more details. Margaretha had given Juditha's mother a soup with a kind of big lump in it. She had conjured up giant lice which, however, did not bite. The whole lying-in room was 'unsicher', unsafe, and she would not let him into the chamber even after the birth. Three times Esaias had begged her to heal his wife, but she had responded, 'I cannot help you, I have done nothing to you' – a sure sign that she was responsible for the illness. Repeating the request a magical three times was meant to compel the witch to do one's bidding; so if the victim recovered this proved the witch had caused the illness. On the other hand, if the suspected witch did not help, then (in the inexorable double-think of witchcraft accusation) her refusal demonstrated that she wished the victim harm.[52]

The other story concerned Margaretha Gauss, who came in person to testify against Margaretha. Her pains had come upon her very suddenly, and she had sent her husband to fetch the midwife and any experienced woman he could lay his hands on. Again, Margaretha Wagner had stepped in as lying-in maid. When the child was born, she, not the midwife, took it in her arms to wash it and brought it to the new mother in bed. And then, when her husband had left the house for the first time since the birth to invite people to act as godparents, Margaretha Wagner had blessed him 'as if he were standing among pure devils'. (That she had spoken a blessing when he left the house was probably not in itself unusual, for the new mother and the birthing chamber were believed to be especially vulnerable to the assaults of the Devil.) The poor man had stood stock still and his feet had begun to tremble. His mouth had become contorted and he had lost the power of speech for ten days. Wagner had also taken the afterbirth to dispose of it at the Upper Saw Mill. While it was being removed, a cat passed over the unbaptized baby twice, and Margaretha Gauss, the new mother, suffered pains in her body. When she was breast-feeding the child, Margaretha Wagner persuaded her to buy a fur coat – selling second-hand goods was after all her trade, and this was a good business opportunity. But when she put the fur coat on, the baby at once refused to drink, and then she developed an abscess which would not heal. Margaretha Gauss banned Margaretha Wagner from the house.[53]

Despite what she claimed were her initial misgivings, the new mother had trusted Margaretha Wagner enough to continue to rely on her help and even to buy clothes from her. In her defence Margaretha insisted that, so far from banning her from the house, they had asked her in for a meal; indeed, she lent the new mother the clothes she had worn to her post-natal purification.

Allegations about devils and supernatural goings-on in lying-in chambers, breast-feeding that went wrong, harm to new mothers and infants – these were all the familiar fears. The witch had no sympathy, and her body was hard and dried out, lacking the flow of fluids that was the mark of the healthy, fecund woman. As Margaretha herself said during her interrogation, her heart was so 'betrübt' or clouded that she found herself unable to move her mouth in crying. The inability of her body to act with Christian sympathy, to show emotion and to flow was, as she well knew, yet another indication that she was a witch.[54]

The allegations against Margaretha seemed to have almost nothing to do with the trial of Juditha. After all, they had taken shape many years before. After Juditha's mother's death, there is every reason to think that the two households no longer had any dealings with each other. Yet there is one feature which parallels Juditha's case and seems to reflect the narrow constellation of forces, the endless doubling of characters and situations that mark Juditha's tale. One of the most bitter allegations Philippina Fischer brought against her stepmother was that she had killed her brother, aged fourteen. He had become infested with lice crawling in and out of his body. So full of holes was he that his body looked like a honeycomb. Only careful bathing could save him, and when he left Margaretha's house for the pilgrim's house to recuperate he was lame, hunchbacked and ill. He had finally ended up in the orphanage where, Philippina added tellingly, he had been killed by none other than Juditha Wagner.[55]

In one fell swoop, Philippina linked the two cases: Margaretha's stepmaternal neglect had just about killed her brother, and Juditha had finished him off. Margaretha countered the charge, alleging that the child was well while he was in her house, and that the illnesses had started only later. It was Philippina who had neglected the child, not she.[56]

There is no Wagner child on the many lists of possible orphanage victims of Juditha's revenge that were compiled during her trial. Philippina was making a novel connection, and doing so without any support from the actual evidence of the trial. In her eyes, however, it all made sense, for everything, all their misfortunes, were the result of the machinations of evil witches.

Yet there was a genuine structural connection between the cases, the same combination of circumstances as in Juditha's miserable childhood. A child whose mother has died becomes superfluous in a new household where there are young children from the new partner, and ends up – whether through sickness, 'loss of love', or some other cause – in the orphanage. In Juditha's case the legacy was a witchcraft allegation directed against herself; in this case, the charges were eventually to be directed against the stepmother.

But Margaretha was used to fighting her corner. After all, she had twenty-five years to prepare for a witchcraft trial, and she had successfully countered allegations at least twice before. She marshalled her defences, and they were impressive. She virtually ordered the Council to question a certain Caspar

Reuschlin and his sister Maria Durst, her erstwhile rival for Tobias Wagner's affections, whom she called by the familiar name 'Marilen'. She must have been very confident that they would testify in her favour. Reuschlin, the sexton of Holy Cross, who had acted as Margaretha's intermediary all those years ago when she got Durst to give up Tobias, duly appeared, as did Maria Durst, to testify on Margaretha's behalf. Their behaviour suggests that Margaretha knew how to create lasting bonds of loyalty – or how to call in favours when needed.[57] Under interrogation, Margaretha named several individuals who, she said, should be summoned and asked about her character. Among them were Marx and Euphroisa Mehrer, substantial patrons who testified strongly in her support.[58] And, cunningly pre-empting her rival's accusations, Margaretha recalled that during her pregnancy, Philippina Fischer had gone about saying she would give birth to a devil who would rip people apart as soon as it was born. This was just Philippina's malicious gossip, as she could prove through the testimony of Jacobina Bucher, who had officiated.

Even so, Margaretha's behaviour once in prison was anything but calm. When confronted with Philippina Fischer, her rage knew no bounds. The two women started abusing each other, Fischer repeating her assertion that Wagner was promiscuous, Wagner insulting Fischer as 'a Jewish and Christian whore'. When Fischer first entered the room, Wagner greeted her with 'She the Fischer woman brings her into all this misfortune, her tongue will yet rot in her mouth' – just the kind of threat that could well be interpreted as a witch's curse. Wagner went on to threaten her that she would go mad, to which Fischer retorted that if this were to happen, she would know whom to blame, that is, she would have proved that Wagner was a witch.[59] When Esaias reproached her to her face with sending a plague of lice during his wife's childbed, she replied that if she had been able to conjure such a thing, she would of course have made sure they bit him, adding pointedly that if she were a witch then he was a witch before her – an allusion to the fact that since witchcraft travelled in the blood, his daughter's execution as a witch might cast a cloud of suspicion over him too. Her contradictory replies show how difficult it was to steer a course through the morass of witchcraft beliefs: in one breath, Margaretha professed disbelief, trying to use humour in her defence; in the next, she tried to turn suspicion back on her opponent. The more she responded to her assailants in anger, the more she appeared to curse them; and the more likely it was – since they knew they were attacking her – that they might really suffer the torments with which she threatened them. Yet had she not mustered the full force of her verbal aggression to defend herself, she might well have caved in like Juditha, begging their forgiveness and courting execution.

By this point, there seemed to be enough evidence against Margaretha to justify further interrogation under torture, even though she had withstood the confrontation with the witnesses. Despite the threat, Margaretha did not lose heart, saying 'even if there were as many devils against her as tiles on the roofs of all Augsburg, she would not desert her Jesus'. Torture was applied: she was placed on the bench for half an hour, but she trembled so violently that the executioner feared she would fall into a fit. He advised against further torture, and this brought her case to an effective standstill. The Council decided to release her on a sworn oath, and it freed her on 22 January under oath that she leave the town and return to her 'homeland' of Kaufbeuren – this after having lived twenty-five years in Augsburg.[60]

Margaretha never confessed that she was a witch. She never colluded with her interrogators, and gave little of her inner world away: perhaps it was her intemperate anger that saved her life. This means that we do not have the same kind of insight into her as we do in the case of Juditha. She avoided the kind of psychological disintegration that characterizes the testimony of so many convicted witches, perhaps because at the point of torture she collapsed physically. But though she escaped, she was not declared innocent and she did not go unpunished. A woman in her mid-fifties, exiled on suspicion of being a witch, her prospects for a new start elsewhere would have been slim indeed.

It is hard to know what to make of Esaias Wagner, who played a key role in witchcraft accusations against both his daughter and his stepmother. A master carpenter, he was comfortably off with his own workshop and paid a regular 19 Kreuzer tax throughout the period: his father, by contrast, had been encumbered with debts and his widow Margaretha lived in mean accommodation by the time the case against Juditha was heard. Esaias died in 1704, aged sixty-four.[61] Was he a bloodthirsty bully? He seems to have had at least some qualms about accusing his stepmother, saying that 'he did not wish to wash his hands in his stepmother's blood'.[62] All the same, he had told the story of his wife's death to the mayor when he was called as a witness in 1690, and fully supported his sister's allegations in 1694.

His role in his daughter's trial was even more ambiguous. When Juditha revoked her confessions in her third interrogation, she blamed her father. She said that she was not a witch: her father had coached her in what to say. Esaias, summoned and questioned on the point on the morning of 24 December 1689, vehemently denied that he had ever put his daughter up to it. If she 'had not herself told him, his children and then Mr Beckh [*sic*], that the spirit would not let her pray, he would have known nothing about it'. He wished it were not so, but then 'why had she told him in such detail about the signing to the Devil, and everything else, if she were honest and not a witch, he would like to know'.[63] Juditha maintained her denials, contradictory as they were, for four days after her interrogation. But when she was confronted with her father, her resistance collapsed completely. This interrogation took place in the afternoon of Christmas Eve, a time when Juditha might have expected to be at home with her father and family. She did indeed meet her father, who came not to take her home, but as her accuser. He repeated the statements he had made that same morning. Weeping, Juditha took back all her accusations against him. She affirmed, 'she just was a witch'.

This capitulation sealed her fate. Juditha must have known she would not be released for the festivity and would be remaining in custody in her cell. We know she feared the dark: at her first interrogation, she had begged to be allowed to remain 'in this parlour where she now is, and not be put in a dark one, for the temptations were too great for her'.[64] Her half-siblings, her father and her stepmother would be celebrating the birth of the infant Jesus without her. In her own Lutheran parish church, that of the Franciscans, the dour interior was dominated by one image, that of the infant Jesus holding the orb of the world. Made in 1632, it stood above the pulpit, reminding the faithful that Christ the Saviour was God made flesh as a baby.[65] Once again, Juditha could not share in the joy surrounding the birth of a child, just as – so she now believed – she had turned the joy of new birth to grief when she killed her baby half-siblings a decade ago. She concluded this part of her interrogation by saying she would rather die than live, following this with a full confession of all the diabolic misdeeds that might be expected of a witch – sex with the Devil, the diabolic kiss front and back, finally adding 'she would happily die under the hangman's hand, rather than come out again, for otherwise she would fall into her old evil life'.[66]

This was the lowest point of Juditha's confession, for to die by the hangman's hand was to suffer the most ignominious form of death – in all her other statements, she begged to escape such a fate. It is surely significant that all this followed the encounter with her father on Christmas Eve. Indeed, Esaias's own attitude to his daughter seems to have hardened in the course of the case, perhaps because he felt himself to be under attack when Juditha blamed him for making her say she was a witch.

In this way, the bureaucratic punctiliousness of the trial procedure itself – interrogation of the suspect followed by questioning of the witnesses on the relevant points, and then repeated questioning of the suspect on the basis of the revised information – allowed witness and suspect to communicate with each other. This not only helped to make the testimonies of witnesses and suspect converge. It strengthened the conviction, on everyone's part, that by revisiting incidents in the past they could gain understanding of what had really been going on, what diabolic powers had been at work.[67] It also, of course, amplified the destructive dynamic in relationships like that between Juditha and her father. Esaias started to mention strange sounds he had heard in the house years before, which could well, he now thought, have been Satanic. He too was beginning to think his daughter had been a witch from when she was just a little girl, even before her mother died – earlier, of course, than Juditha said herself.[68] This left very little time in her short life when she had been his Christian daughter.

Esaias's relationship with his daughter was clearly difficult. He described her as 'halsstärrig', stiff-necked, meaning that she did not easily submit to those in authority. He said she was 'verstockt', blocked, a word which carries connotations of stubbornness and, within the system of humoral medicine, may mean that the individual is cut off, not open to the world. Other witnesses concurred that she was disobedient. Esaias had punished her for small thefts; indeed, Juditha had got her guardians and her uncle to intervene because he was disciplining her too severely.

Whether wittingly or not, Esaias had actively testified against his daughter and so had contributed to her death. Perhaps, as he saw it, he was merely doing his civic and godly duty in handing over to judgment a woman who had long ago been seduced into witchcraft. When, five years later, he confronted Margaretha Wagner, his conviction that he was surrounded by witchcraft seemed to have deepened still further. He accused Margaretha not only of killing his wife and bewitching him with lice, but of killing his father, her husband, too. He said his daughter Juditha had visited her often, and had told him so.

Margaretha rejected this allegation, saying she had never spoken a word with Juditha in her life and accused him of failing to care for his daughter. To this, Esaias cried 'it hurt him enough, that she had seduced his daughter'.[69] Here, of course, Esaias, like his sister, and like so many of those involved in the witch craze, was rewriting history. Five years ago he had blamed Christele for seducing his daughter into witchcraft – now Christele and Margaretha seem to have turned into one evil stepmother. It is conceivable that repressed feelings of guilt about his daughter led him, in the kind of thinking that characterizes witchcraft accusations, to blame Margaretha for his daughter's end. Instead of having actively brought about his daughter's trial and death, he could now regard himself as the innocent victim of malevolent old women.

Chapter Nine

Godless Children

Witchcraft, we might say, was always in the nursery, indeed, in the nursing bond itself, in the sense that it was nourished by infantile fantasies and fears about mothers. But in the final stages of the witch panic, the death of the old woman as a credible witch led to a brief moment in which the fears and fantasies of children themselves – the psychic source of the witch terror among adults – emerged in pretty much unmediated form. Before witchcraft was finally consigned to the nursery, it paradoxically helped to give birth to an ambivalent fascination with children, their games and their fantasies.

Just twelve years after the execution of Juditha Wagner, in 1702, another adolescent girl, Regina Groninger, was facing criminal interrogation in Augsburg. Like Juditha, she had also gone about claiming to be a witch. The case was shaping up to end in yet another execution, when, in her third interrogation, she began to laugh.[1] The more the allegations about sex with the Devil and causing harm to others were put to her, the more she giggled, and insisted that the whole affair was caused by gossip. Regina's laughter probably saved her life. As the Council eventually determined, she was to be taken away from her stepmother, who was maltreating her, and transferred to the care of a relative. This was doubtless just what was needed, and Regina does not emerge in the records of the town again.[2]

Regina's case forms part of the growing disenchantment with the Devil, and is an example of a diabolic story which did not really work. Her original story, repeated at school and in the neighbourhood, concerned a black man who visited her at night. Regina herself was chary of describing her visitor as the Devil, but those around her had no such compunction. Her account of her relations with the 'Black Man', repeated at her criminal trial, mixed sexual and excremental themes:

> He 'comes to her nearly daily, lies on her whole body, and thus presses on her in such a way that her (if you will excuse the expression) shit goes out of her body'; he 'put something pointed like a spindle in the front part of her body . . ., from which she felt great pains, but she did not feel that any-

62. Detail from Wolfgang Kilian, *A bird's-eye view map of Augsburg*, showing the area where Regina lived. Copper etching on 9 plates, 1626.

thing was left behind in her body, and when he had to do with her thus, it lasted a quarter of an hour'.[3]

Her description of the Devil was equally striking, and unlike that of a conventional witch narrative:

Finally his form was not like that of a human, the head was black and as round as a cannonball, on which there was neither face, eyes nor nose nor anything else to be seen, as well he had quite dried out thin arms, and claws which were quite pointed, had feet like a goat, but otherwise walked like a human.[4]

This description has the quality of a child's drawing, and it bears no relation to the smooth-talking, luxuriously dressed Devil of most witchcraft confessions.[5]

To her family, Regina confessed that she had harmed and killed others. She had put mouse poison on her natural brother's dummy, causing his death. At one family prayer session, she told how the black man had instructed her to do it; and had also ordered her to put mouse poison in the soup to kill her stepmother. But this was not the behaviour which had initially alarmed her stepmother; and these extreme confessions of malevolence emerged only later on.

The case began because something else was causing her family concern: Regina collected and ate her own excrement. When her stepmother upbraided her, she resorted to picking up excrement from the pavement and taking it to school to eat, spread on bread. She also ate her own fleas and lice. Regina's behaviour frightened her schoolmates and she was asked to leave, and Regina and her mother were summoned before the synod of Protestant clergy headed by Superintendent Miller for questioning.[6]

Like Juditha's tale, Regina's story concerned parents, a stepmother who seemed, as Regina first described her, to be virtuous and God-fearing unlike her natural mother, but who emerged by the end of the case as someone who treated her badly; and a father who was largely absent from the dramas between Regina and her stepmother. Regina, the Council and the clergy all knew that when a father failed, another paternal authority had to intervene. Her behaviour therefore set her on course to be either punished or shown mercy by the synod and the councillors. This was a role these men played not only in their public office, but also in their private lives. All town councillors were supposed to be married heads of households; and all Protestant clergy were also supposed to have wives, presiding over an ordered domestic congregation of children and servants. But in this case, the collusion between the interrogators and the suspect was limited. Although the Council's scribe, at least, appears to have been disconcerted by Regina's sudden outburst of laughter, and to have inclined to interpret it as yet another instance of diabolically inspired immodest behaviour,[7] the Council ultimately determined that Regina was not a witch. It, too, refused to pursue the fantasy of witchcraft any further, and freed Regina.

Regina was attempting to find symbols for a morass of feelings connected with her relations to her parents, herself, and what may have been an actual traumatic sexual experience of some kind.[8] But it was also a symbolization which did not quite work within the demonological paradigm, and suggests that belief in witchcraft no longer explained evil satisfactorily. She offered only a skeletal narrative, her Devil as rudimentary as her stick-figure description of him. Her interrogators, both in the Church and Council, were doubtful enough of her story to be unsure whether it was genuine or her behaviour merely pathological. Groninger reduced the complex mythical superstructure of diabolism to excrement itself. As she recounted it, a black man was forcing excrement out of her body and making her eat it. This was a pretty unvarnished communication of some of the underlying psychological themes of demonology. Regina did not express her rage against all Christians by stroking diabolic salve on her enemies; instead, she dirtied her bed in retaliation against

63. Superintendent Dr Georg Miller, who chaired the inquiry.

64. Magister Christoph Raimond Schiflin, who questioned Regina.

her cruel stepmother. There was no black devil's powder, made of the ground-up flesh and bones of unbaptized children, only mouse poison which her natural mother had bought and hidden behind the stove.

Regina was not the last person in Augsburg to be accused of witchcraft, and her case did not challenge belief in witchcraft itself. In the short term, cases of witchcraft amongst adolescents – of which there were many more than were ever tried – strengthened belief in witchcraft. What the authorities heard as they began to try cases which did not fit the witchcraft formulas were stories about deeply unhappy children. Gradually, fears about witchcraft began to open up the subject of childhood itself.

Twenty years later, in 1723, a new scandal broke: a group of children had been seduced by the Devil and were committing acts of malefice in the city. An old woman, a seamstress, had led them astray. They had put glass splinters, teeth and diabolic powder in their parents' beds, they fought one another, they committed indecencies with each other, and they frequented diabolic sabbaths.

The allegations spread. One after another, worried parents appeared before the Council, begging it to imprison their own evil children, to 'take them into its judgmental justice' as one Franz Ludwig put it, asking the Council to remove his thirteen-year-old son into custody.[9] Otherwise, so he feared, the child's brother and sister would be 'infected'. In all, around twenty children, aged between six and sixteen, were taken into custody; most aged around ten or under, well below the age of puberty. The first children, held in tiny dark cells, were assigned comforters to pray with and visit them, but they were often kept in solitary confinement. Four of the children, one aged as young as seven, formally begged the Council to be allowed to die, just as Juditha had done over thirty years before.[10] It was not until a full year had elapsed that they were transferred from what all agreed was manifestly unsuitable accommodation into a hospital which, as was pointed out, had more warmth, cleanliness and light. At the height of the panic, around twenty children were held there, and four guards and three attendants had to be employed in supervising them. And it was not until 1729, a full six years later, that the last of these children were finally freed, having cost the city the vast sum of 6,675 gulden, 4 kreuzer and 4 heller in accommodation and attendance expenses alone.[11]

This case raised fears of witchcraft in a new form: now they concerned children, who began to be seen as the source of evil that threatened the whole community.[12] It took place very late indeed, a good quarter-century after executions for witchcraft in the region had ceased. Germany was on the cusp of the Enlightenment. Augsburg was a major town, not a rural backwater. Home of Pietism, it was a centre of publishing, and a town which, though its golden age was over by the eighteenth century, still remained one of the major centres of the Holy Roman Empire, as famed for its goldsmiths, instrument-makers and clockmakers as for its libraries, historians and natural scientists. It was the last place one might have expected to see an outbreak of witch persecution.[13]

Regina Groninger and Juditha Wagner had both been Lutherans; the godless children were Catholics.[14] Catholics, too, felt their religion was under assault by the forces of the Devil and his agents, the Lutherans. Every now and again, one confession would attack its rivals from the pulpit, not always with such dramatic results as in 1696 when a Protestant preacher who had 'blasphemed' against the scapular and the Virgin Mary was (so Catholics alleged) carried off in mid-sermon by the Devil in the form of a bear. Religious difference could still lead to bloodshed, as it did in 1718, when several people died in the course of a riot during a Catholic Corpus Christi procession. Periodically, the city was gripped by a kind of exorcism mania, with Catholics trying to display the superiority of their confession through the effectiveness of the exorcizing priest, or Protestants (usually vainly) attempting to free their own sufferers from the snares of the Devil. Catholic children learned in their catechisms that 'Lutheran doctrine is a pestilence and death to true believers' and were told in this connection the story of the Catholic boys of Alexandria who hated the Arian heretics so much that when the ball with which they were playing was touched by one of the heretics' donkeys they cast their plaything in the fire.[15]

Lutherans and Catholics adopted different stances towards these diabolic children. For Protestants, the whole affair might be viewed as a plot by the

Catholic clergy to stage yet another dramatic set of exorcisms, and one contemporary Protestant chronicler certainly thought it possible that the Catholic
clergy had put the children up to it, threatening them and forcing them to
make all kinds of false confessions.[16] Throughout the case, the memorials of
advice by the Protestant jurisconsult Christoph Friedrich Weng (whose compilation of records of the case forms the chief source) persistently pointed out
the contradictions in the children's testimony, and he could barely contain his
scorn for the 'nonsense' to which the children confessed.[17] Protestant and
Catholic councillors could not agree on what to do with the children or how
to punish them, Protestants stressing the expense the whole affair was causing
the city and insisting that advice be sought from a bi-confessional law faculty
while Catholics wanted to get to the bottom of the matter by confronting the
witnesses, taking yet more children into custody, and interrogating all the suspects. Because the only agreement they could reach was to continue
questioning the children and witnesses, the affair multiplied into a larger and
larger tangle of stories and counter-accusations, each interrogation generating
yet more loose ends.[18]

Yet this was no simple battle between rational Protestants, sceptical of the
Devil's power on the one hand, and superstitious Catholics on the other. Neither
Weng nor the anonymous Protestant chronicler can be taken to represent all
Lutheran opinion. Pietist Lutheranism, a movement only beginning to gather
strength in the town, might fervently believe in witches: Gottlieb Spitzel, the fore-
most Pietist, whom we encountered before, trying to exorcize young girls, had
congratulated the Augsburg Council on its godly deed of burning three witches
in 1685, and thought that scepticism about the power of the Devil led to atheism.[19]

Occasionally, the town's jurist advisers united across the confessional divide
in the advice they offered in the affair of the godless children; although the
sceptical attitude of Weng would not have been shared, for example, by the
Lutherans who denounced Regina Groninger as a child witch just twenty years
before, and Weng sometimes found himself in a minority among his colleagues.[20] Moreover, Weng himself was persuaded that the children were evil,
and he thought the parents who reported them were led by desperation and by
what he termed 'the instigation of the spirit of murder', a formulation which
came close to saying they were led by the Devil. Once again, the tradition
within Protestant demonology of arguing that the Devil might do his work
through illusion meant that it was not enough to prove that the children suffered from fantasies or delusions. This did not show that the Devil was not
involved or that witchcraft was not afoot.[21]

The children's parents denounced their own offspring, commending their
sons and daughters to what the Augsburg city fathers called their 'official
keeping', as if it were a place of sanctuary, although it meant their incarceration in prison cells for long periods of time. Contemporaries too found this

shocking, and one Protestant chronicler remarked how much gossip there had been about the astounding spectacle of parents 'denounc[ing] their own bodily tender children to the government, and giving them over even to capital punishment'. And the children were not vagabonds or paupers: they came from established middling craft families, from cattle-butchers, brandy sellers, brewers and innkeepers; their parents were mostly citizens, some with substantial means.[22]

Several key themes emerged in the course of the witchcraft epidemic – and parents themselves explicitly used the medical metaphor, fearing that the infants' siblings would be 'infected'. Time and again, the children were described as having put 'diabolic powder' and other strange objects, including powder 'which looked like mouse dung or linseeds', in their parents' beds to cause their parents sickness and pain.[23] The children also engaged in group activities, cutting each other's fingers in a kind of blood brotherhood ritual which drew on the traditions of demonological theory. The blood was used (with the Devil's aid) to sign a pact and to enter the new recruit's name into a big Devil's Book. The children fought with one another and engaged in rough games, in particular, as many agreed, on the stairs behind St Jakob's, a Protestant church. At the witches' sabbath, and sometimes in the town – on the haymaking floor of the father of one of the girls, on balconies, and behind the church – they engaged in what their accusers termed 'indecency'. Trousers were dropped, shirts raised, skirts lifted, and the children 'kissed the shameful parts'.

These episodes of sexual exhibitionism allegedly also involved genital inter-course. One boy aged ten was accused of violating his sister aged sixteen months, his parents claiming to have witnessed palpable '*signa pollutionis*' on the young boy's shirt – an allegation which the Protestant jurist dismissed as a physiological impossibility. Throughout the case, children, parents and com-mentators alike referred to their initiation into the group as a 'seduction', naming those who had first 'seduced' them and whom they had in turn 'seduced'. Whether this word was their own or whether it was suggested to them we cannot now disentangle: like all witch fantasies, it was a heady com-posite of the questions asked, the witness statements, and the accused's admissions.

Anal themes played an important part, just as they had in the case of Regina Groninger. The children were able to produce plagues of 'lice and mice', mobile dirt or excrement, which polluted the household. Diabolic powder is a highly symbolic substance, which synthesizes the key elements of the myth of witchcraft. It was believed to be the product of the flesh and bone of unbap-tized infants, exhumed from the ground by old women in terrifying ceremonies where the Devil was in attendance, often hovering outside the graveyard since he was unable to tread consecrated ground. The infant flesh would be cooked by the women to join the meat on offer at diabolic sabbath feasts. The powders or salves were manufactured from the leftover bones; the cooking water used to raise storms. In criminal interrogations witches referred to powder or salves only by colour, as 'black', 'grey' or 'red'; and the substance exhibits only the uniform texture of salve or powder, betraying no visual or tactile hint of its horrific origins.

But here, symbolic processes seem to have gone into reverse, and the diabolic powder emerges shorn of mystery, revealed as glass splinters, teeth, bones, threads, nutshells, wholegrains and hair, all kinds of 'filth', as the Council termed it; or looking like 'mouse dung' or goat droppings.[24] This places it far closer to the preoccupations of early childhood. The children said almost nothing about how the Devil's salve was made and did not mention feasts of unbaptized child-flesh. It is as if the latent content of the witchcraft fantasy had been stripped of its mythic overlay to reveal the crudest primary structure of infant psychology underneath. The children seemed to be using bodily products, excrement-like material and sharp cutting objects as harmful substances with which to attack God and injure their parents.

In particular, they attacked their parents' sexual relationship, sometimes the father's potency, sometimes the mother's fertility. Maria Steingruber suffered from the attacks of witches while in childbed, and discovered this was caused by her stepson. Franz Joseph Kuttler bewitched his parents' bed and his mother stated that her husband had lost his strength as a result. Time and again parents, especially fathers, reported the progress of their maladies to the Council as strange objects appeared in their beds. Weng conscientiously investigated and confirmed the presence of strange substances in one of these cases, finding 'straw, dirt and uncleanliness'. But he offered a class-bound, naturalistic explanation: these things 'occur in all the bedclothes of poor people, who do not always keep their bedding clean'. In the Betz family, anal attacks, the parental relationship and the fertility of the marriage were woven into a tightly symbolized story that ultimately led to the dissolution of the household. Evil stuff was found in the bed. The children's mother suffered during pregnancy 'as if pure knives were inside her', the father endured terrible toothache and, as his wife noticed, could no longer carry the armchair, the whole family lived 'like cat and dog', and the children put powder in the beer (which doubtless did not help matters). The powder looked like mouse excrement. When it was removed from the bed, peace returned between the parents. But shortly after, when the father found a further packet of material in the bed, he begged the Council to take his other two 'incorrigible' children into custody.[25]

In many, but not all, of these cases, the parental union was a step-union, just the conjunction of circumstances which had played such a fateful role in the cases of Juditha Wagner and Regina Groninger.[26] Common though step-relationships were in seventeenth- and eighteenth-century Germany, they could bring a snake-pit of antagonisms with them all the same. A parent's own feelings about remarriage and the loss of the previous spouse may unconsciously have made them more likely to expect and thus to believe that their children were using witchcraft to retaliate; and in the self-fulfilling nature of witchcraft, they often truly sickened or their relationships went awry.

The children also seem to have engaged a good deal in cutting and biting – the odd tooth in the parental bed, the cutting of fingers – an interesting detail, since normally the Devil required only pricking to draw blood for signature. They emerged, too, in one sacrilegious version of what we might call a 'doctors and nurses' game. On Good Friday, one child played Jesus on the cross while his girl counterpart was pierced with Mary's seven daggers of sorrow. Again, complex mythical structures were being reduced to physical processes in the children's play. Mary's seven swords of sorrow become real cutting implements, piercing the little girl's body; Christ's wounded body becomes part of a sadistic cutting game. The parents reported that the game had left real marks on the children's bodies: a lump 'about the size of a pea' was seen on the boy's hand, while 'seven yellow dimples' circled the region of the little girl's heart.[27] In other circumstances these physical signs might have been taken as evidence of the children's sanctity, stigmata which proved their election by God. Here, however, they were treated as evidence of evil.

A similar literalism is evident in the children's behaviour at the witches' sabbath, where they allegedly tortured hosts. This, too, was pretty normal activity at a sabbath. But the children prosaically put the hosts into a dyer's press. They were playing with the metaphysical image of Christ in the wine-press, giving out his blood for all Christians, a subject popular in woodcuts, but they improvised with whatever machinery lay to hand about the house, pressing the Host until the blood ran out. Religious mysteries were reduced to household tasks, as the children played with sacred objects.[28]

Witchcraft by its very nature involves attacks on other Christians; but usually the harm caused is of an indirect kind and requires the agency of the Devil. It rests on a set of beliefs about his power. A witch might stroke or touch her victim, or sprinkle diabolic powder on the food of the individual she wishes to harm, but it is not her physical action which directly causes the malady. Rather the diabolic powder or the force granted her by the Devil magically brings about suffering, withering, illness or pain in her prey. By contrast, here, the themes of blood, biting and cutting are so direct as to be barely disguised.[29]

The sexual themes of the witch craze, too, had undergone a transformation. Sexual themes, mixed with anal preoccupations, emerged in the children's play. So David Kopf, in one such game, reputedly dropped his trousers and raised his shirt, while his companion 'let herself be beaten with a little stick on her bare behind'. One boy located the witches' sabbath at the Sow Market, thus linking it to pigs, blood, filth and possibly by implication to Jews (*Judensau*); and there, too, the children 'committed indecency'. One girl said the Devil tickled her in her lower body.[30] These were the same kinds of themes that had emerged in the trials of Regina Groninger and Juditha Wagner, and they had little to do with conventional accounts that adult witches gave of being seduced by a male Devil. Because many of the children were even younger, the understanding of sexuality that coloured their confessions was infantile in character, concerned as much with anal as with genital sensation.

The anxious parents became convinced that the Devil was attacking their children physically. One father who denounced his young stepdaughter Theresia Fleiner as one of the godless children described how she awoke in bed, screaming 'Father, father!' As he rushed to her bed, she cried that the Devil was blowing into her mouth and ears – a kind of inversion of baptismal exorcism, where the Devil is blown out through the mouth and ears. He groped for the candle, and saw her covered in blood, 'blood shooting from her nose, mouth and ears'. The Devil kissed her at night, the father reported, and touched her all over her body, except for her heart. This little girl died not long after. It seemed that her hair was being pulled out by the Devil, as at least one witness confirmed.[31]

The spectacle of the suffering girl was utterly terrifying; yet the Council – and perhaps the parents – held that the source of evil was the girl herself, who had an insatiable appetite. The Council advised that the mother should moderate the child's food intake. She did. As the child minder reported, the child was 'fed the leftover soup scraps for the dog' and sometimes given nothing at all. Convinced the child had been starved to death, the child-minder eventually accused the mother, who had allegedly told her 'she had never not given her food for more than a day, yet she still didn't perish'. In this case, it seems very likely that the mother was so disturbed by her daughter's behaviour that she actually starved her to death.[32]

The case of the godless children raised the issue of parental responsibility. The Protestant jurists saw the matter in straightforward terms: these children of artisan families were the parents' responsibility, and if they insisted on handing them over to the Council, they should be made to foot the bill for their care. The parents, however, strenuously insisted that they ought not to pay, the poorer parents pleading poverty, the richer claiming that they had already spent money on the children. Implicitly they regarded the city as responsible for the children.

Throughout Europe in this period, as new workhouses and orphanages were being established, the question of parental responsibility was a vexed subject. Inmates of these institutions might include not only vagrants and poor families but children whose families could not afford to keep them or even, by the late eighteenth century, children of middle-class or aristocratic families whose parents could no longer control them. In demanding that the Council deal with their incorrigible offspring, the Augsburg parents – like their children – were taking metaphor literally. From the Reformation on, in Augsburg (as elsewhere) the Council had developed an elaborate system of fatherly control over its citizens, intervening in marital disputes, punishing its citizens for sexual lapses, and instructing them in their moral duties in endless proclamations. Now these parents were insisting that the Council, who in well-worn rhetoric described itself as its citizens' father, should actually take over the paternal role of punishing children.[33]

The debate about parental duty went to the heart of the nature of obedience in general. Whipping and beating were themes which recurred in the children's description of their activities, sometimes apparently sexualized, as in the case of the little girl who, in the games of sexual exhibitionism which had occurred behind the church, was whipped on her bare bottom; while David Kopf said that as part of the sexual games, each of the children had to give the others a hiding in turn. Discipline and authority were troubled matters in early eighteenth-century Augsburg. In 1726, during the course of the case, there was a dramatic demonstration of the hollowness of natural authority when the Augsburg journeymen cobblers staged a revolt against their masters and decamped to the neighbouring small town of Friedberg while their masters looked on, powerless. The Protestant jurist was convinced that the way to deal with the godless children was to give them a sound whipping, and an elaborate schedule of beatings was drawn up, the worst children to be beaten twice weekly with fifteen strokes for four weeks in the workhouse, the youngest or least delinquent only once a week with ten strokes. Yet the affair of the godless children also showed what happened when parents were simply left to exert power through corporal punishment. One parent sliced off his son's finger in the course of punishing him; and a teacher of the same boy burnt him with a rag during an attempt to make him confess to his diabolic activities. This was certainly not felt to be appropriate chastisement. At the same time, the very description of the children as 'incorrigible' expressed the conviction of parents, teachers and masters that these children could not be 'corrected' through punishment. The Council itself eventually agreed, after having taken the children into custody and subjecting them to corporal punishent, that some of them were indeed 'incorrigible'. The benefits of corporal punishment became even less clear as the case began to reach its end, and David Kopf, whose initial confessions had sparked the whole affair, claimed that he had only made these confessions because he had endured such terrible beatings from priests and then at the Catholic workhouse.[34]

The witch hunt as it operated in the sixteenth and seventeenth centuries had offered a clear way of dealing with evil, by locating the source of evil in an old woman. In this case, just as in the cases of Juditha Wagner and Regina Groninger, there *was* such a figure who might have been blamed. Nearly all the children accused a woman they called 'the seamstress' of having seduced them. She certainly fitted the part: she was an older woman who was not the children's mother but who fulfilled a maternal role, who knew the children and played a part in their imaginative worlds.

But the councillors had learned to be sceptical about such allegations, and though the needlewoman was incarcerated for a full twenty weeks, she was not interrogated until she herself demanded to be put through the rigours of a criminal interrogation, convinced she had already been tacitly condemned by the Council. During these five months the web of children's accusations against her had grown, with more and more children being taken into custody until there were no fewer than eleven willing to testify against her. Just a generation before, the needlewoman – a non-citizen, non-native, poor, lame, old and dependent for her work on the comfortable craftspeople who now denounced her – would almost certainly have been tried as a witch. She was even reported to have been seen with an 'oven fork', presumably the vehicle on which she rode to the Sabbath; while other children said they had seen her wearing 'a Jewess's wimple'. Not all the parents accused her; and something of the crisis in witch belief can be detected in the response of her neighbours. They petitioned the Council, refusing to pay for her imprisonment and asking for her to be expelled from town, since she had neither residence rights nor citizenship. But they studiously forbore to accuse her of sorcery or witchcraft, arguing instead that 'although they did not suspect her of witchcraft and perhaps had no seduction to fear, nevertheless general opinion was against her'. Other parents were making their children avoid the neighbourhood or removing their children from the school.[35]

The Council had shown the same scepticism when it came to the case of another of the children, Theresia Fleiner, whose nurse eventually accused the girl's mother of starving her to death. Early on, the girl herself had, like so many of the children, accused an old woman of seducing her into the Devil's power: she did not know her name, but she came from Friedberg, a small town not far from Augsburg. There was, of course, another woman who might well have been accused of witchcraft in this case, the girl's nurse; and since Theresia had died, there was every reason for the mother to cast about for a likely witch. The child-minder was summoned to corroborate the father's testimony that strange matters were afoot, and she was questioned. Whether or not she sensed that she was in danger of being accused, she responded with a very effective counter-attack, accusing the mother of having caused the child's death. Again the Council was reluctant to act, and the child-minder's accusation precipitated a complete stalemate. When the mother insisted that she was only doing what the Council had advised in moderating the child's food intake, the Council determined that the two parents 'had purged themselves by oath' that they had not brought about the child's death, and closed the case against the two women without further ado.[36]

But if there was no witch, at least as far as the Council was concerned, then the focus of attention necessarily shifted: why were the children devising such stories and such 'evil imaginings'? Under the old symbolic economy of the witch hunt, hunting a witch enabled people to identify with the victims of the witch's malice: mothers, children and babies in particular. Passionately sympathizing with the plight of those who were apparently harmed by witches, the councillors and accusers felt entitled to turn their violent anger against the witch. Their unbounded identification with the witch's innocent young victims left little room for recognizing children in this context as separate individual beings. But once the old woman was no longer the source of all evil, the child was no longer an innocent.

In the case of the godless children, parents found their children's behaviour intolerable and were unable to dismiss it as childish play. The children's world of fantasy with its unmediated aggression was disturbing to parents because it forced them to encounter childish emotions – hatred of a new partner, fascination with sexuality – in situations where parents were implicated. Their attitudes throughout the case indicate that they felt a sense of helplessness in the face of their children's behaviour, an impotence which led them finally to resign their parental responsibilities altogether, taking the Council's own rhetoric about its paternal role towards its citizens at its word. Something seems to have gone seriously awry in these parents' relationships with their children, making them unable to deal with childish aggression. Instead, they seemed to enter into their children's imaginative world, becoming ill from the dirty objects in their beds, beating their children to excess, viewing the children's activities as diabolic, and in one case starving them to death to drive out the Devil. Their participation in the fantasy suggests that the children may have been expressing some of the parents' own unacknowledged confusions, ambivalences and hostilities. Parents saw their own dilemmas in their children without recognizing them as such, and reacted by becoming unable to care for their children.

Instead of tending their poor bewitched children's ailments, as they might have done when witches were old women and children were innocent, parents began instead to inspect their children's bodies to discover the signs of witchcraft. A nine-year-old girl was found to be covered in bruises she received when the Devil beat her. Other parents found diabolic marks on their children's sexual parts, or, like the parents of the children who played the Jesus and Mary game, discovered tell-tale scars. One mother claimed that she had seen 'with her own eyes two small brown marks on her daughter's genitals; and that she was formed like a woman who had lived in marriage for some years'. At first she had been reluctant to have her child inspected because she could not believe that children of this age – her daughter was about nine years old at the time – could have sex but had submitted to the orders of her confessor that the child should be investigated. These examinations were just like the physical inspection that a witch had to submit to at the hands of the executioner; but now parents were scrutinizing their children. Later, on the Council's orders, the girl underwent an inspection by midwives to see whether she had indeed been debauched by the Devil. She was found to be a virgin, but the girl herself testified that 'the sign had been pressed into her by the Evil One, but it hadn't hurt her. He reached with his hands or claws inside her body, and this gave her pleasure, and he committed indecency with her.' It was noted that 'she was not to be questioned further about the corruption of the body in order not to give her ideas'. She and another girl who also claimed to have had diabolic intercourse and to have been 'tickled' in the lower part of her body by the Devil were inspected by a surgeon and vicar, who found nothing 'contrary to nature'.[37]

This interest in children's bodies was not new: a similar lively interest in the physical symptoms of child victims of witchcraft was evident throughout the seventeenth century. But when the physical examination had 'disproved' their claims to be the Devil's paramours, the children immediately produced elaborate stories about how the Devil had stamped them with his mark. The progress of the case now forced parents and authorities to ponder the nature of the fantasies which the children insisted so vigorously were true.

Gradually, the authorities became interested not only in children's bodies and their fantasies but in masturbation. The prison warders reported that Juliane Trichtler and Anna Regina Gruber were committing indecency with each other by means of a sheet. By the time Gruber was interrogated, she had converted this into a partially diabolic narrative, confessing that she had 'committed indecency ... with the Devil as well, and both of them already had committed this indecency while in irons'. She blamed the Devil and the seamstress as the ones who had led her astray. Gruber was considered 'incorrigible', and was reported to be corrupting another girl. Consequently, the Council's deputies recommended that she should be separated from the other children, removed from the hospital and returned to solitary confinement in the irons. Joseph Betz and Franz Anthoni Ludwig were found to 'have been milking themselves, and committing indecency'; or as Ludwig put it, 'pressing one another like the dogs, when they are on heat'. It was recommended that these 'indisciplined incorrigible children', boys and girls, 'were to be separated, beaten painfully with rods, and put on a fourteen-day diet of bread and water every other day'. After deliberations in the Council the beating of Gruber was suspended; but the 'worst' children were still to be separated from the others and, if there was no room in the hospital, to be returned to the prison.[38]

The Council was also worried about the sleeping patterns of the children in the hospital. At first, the deputies thought they should not be allowed to sleep during the night, because this was when the Devil was most likely to attack them and take them out on flights while they slept; instead, they should sleep during the day. However, after council elections had been held, the incoming councillors argued that their sleep patterns should not be inverted in this way, because 'the children become very fatigued in body and spirit as a result, and are strengthened in their fantasies'.[39]

By April 1726 the warders were reporting that almost all of the children showed improvement and could be let out of custody altogether. But amongst those who were still being pestered by the Devil were all those accused of masturbation.[40] The boundaries between fact and fantasy were becoming ever harder to draw. It was reported that many of the children were still flying to sabbaths, but when three of the girls were reported to have told stories about flying to a 'beautiful green square' at night at table while the warder watched, it was thought they were only confessing to these 'foolish and absurd things' in order to cast doubt on all their other confessions, in particular their admission that they had harmed the warder by means of a diabolic powder. But the diabolic powder had been acquired on a visit to a sabbath. Even when they had supposedly recovered, some children still spoke of flying to sabbaths, of flying naked, and of sabbaths full of naked people – yet the warders knew they remained in the room, and indeed the whole point of keeping them awake at night was to prevent them flying to sabbaths. How, then, could one distinguish between real reports of the sabbath and stories?[41]

The Council now received from the warders regular reports on the children's masturbatory activities and their alleged night flights. Ludwig, Steingruber, Gruber and Fischer, all guilty of masturbation, remained the last of the evil children, 'persisting in their old wicked life'. Once again, the Council thought that reducing their food intake would dampen their sexual desires, and the Council's deputies advised that they should be 'brought to recovery by putting them on a diet of such poor food that they hardly have enough to live'. But by then the advice of the legal faculty of Heidelberg had arrived, assuring the Council that 'not all the acts and pleasures of these unfortunate people consist in reality, but often in illusions, fantasies and dreams'. As had been suggested by other Augsburg officials before, healing them was a matter of 'by degrees gradually drawing their imaginations and fantasies from their minds, and leading them by contrast to a true fear of God'.[42]

This was the course finally settled upon by the Council: a combination of beatings for godlessness, incarceration in the hospital and later at home, and detailed spiritual supervision. Finally the children were released, and in line with its responsibility of care, the Council appointed spiritual advisers, admonished the parents to raise their children in a God-fearing fashion with regular attendance at Mass, and provided certificates that the children were 'witch free' so that they could gain positions as apprentices.[43]

The interest in these particular children in Augsburg stemmed from a conviction of childish evil, not of innocence. Concern with their masturbation was intrinsic to the preoccupation with children and fantasy. This interest is often taken to be a late eighteenth-century development in Germany: the literary debate in German on masturbation did not fully unfold until the 1780s, when it linked the themes of childhood, excess and imagination.[44] There were of course earlier eighteenth-century publications against onanism: the English *Onania* in the first decade of the eighteenth century, published in German in 1736, the even more famous French work of Samuel Tissot in 1758, and of his German counterpart Georg Sarganeck, who in 1740 wrote the first major publication in German on masturbation.[45]

But strictures against masturbation were not unknown before the eighteenth century. There had been some discussion of the 'dumb sin' amongst Calvinist and Pietiest writers, an issue that occasionally arose in connection with witchcraft. Demonologists warned that the Devil might steal the seed of those who practised the sin, to use when he took on incubus form in sexual relations with witches.[46] Because the sin of witchcraft so often involved sexual sin – witches had intercourse with the Devil – the subject inherently highlighted the connection between the imagination and sexuality, the issue which also lay at the heart of the eighteenth-century concern about masturbation.

And yet there is an important difference in emphasis between the condemnation of masturbation within demonology and the later discussions which moved beyond the demonological framework. A writer like Johann Ellinger argued that those guilty of the 'dumb sin' supplied the Devil with seed: but though he moralized about the wickedness of masturbation, he was more interested in the role semen plays in the diabolic economy of seed collection and distribution. Or the Augsburg Pietist Gottlieb Spitzel could warn in 1687 that 'as soon as the Whoredom-Devil has crept inside ... the Evil One often disguises himself in the shape of the desired person and appears before them, inciting them to unseemly things, and makes them one of his fellows through damnable intercourse (*Unzucht*)'.[47] Here, the individual's fixation on the desired person allows the Devil to appear through illusion; but the relationship is real (and, we might note, heterosexual), as are the diabolic consequences. The 'fantasy' is just a tool of the Devil by which he tricks us into committing real sin. Spitzel was still in the grip of the witch hunt.

By contrast, Georg Sarganeck in the 1740s could speak straightforwardly of 'imagination' and 'fantasy' as what lay behind masturbation. In this kind of writing, the prime focus of concern is the behaviour of the individual, their fantasies and the nature of their sexuality, rather than the activities of the Devil. Even for those who no longer believed in witchcraft, the Devil could remain the ultimate source of wicked fantasy, but it was the mental world and the physical actions of the sinner that increasingly commanded attention. In their last phase of crisis and dissolution, witchcraft beliefs provided a major stimulus for an interest in fantasy and the world of the child, just as throughout their history they had provided a forum for an interest in the imagination and in sexual pleasure.

In Augsburg, it was not just the councillors and the jurists whose growing scepticism about witchcraft led them to develop the case against the children in new directions. Catholic parents continued to deploy the old-established remedies against the diabolic, blessing their children, using protective scapulars, and even in one case lacing their children's food with St Philip's water to ward off the Devil. But these did not work. When parents failed to get the seamstress executed, a deed fervent believers in witchcraft would have expected to end their troubles, they were faced with having to deal with their 'incorrigible children'. After all, no witch had been executed in Augsburg since 1699; and even a case of 1701, brought by powerful merchant parents, had ended with the acquittal of the witch.[48] The involvement of large numbers of children and the focus on the content of their fantasies took the material of the witch fantasy into new realms – the objects in the parents' beds, the sexual games of childhood – and confronted the parents with the problems of raising children, dilemmas which could not credibly be blamed on the witch.

Some parents became convinced that their children were no longer infected with witchcraft: for instance, Johannes Wilhelm Kuttler tried to get the Council to let his son Franz Joseph out of custody and requested a certificate to show that his son was 'witch free'. The boy had been told he could not take up a prestigious apprenticeship with a clockmaker in nearby Friedberg because of the witchcraft allegation. Convinced his son was no witch, Kuttler apparently said, 'he knew from experience, that such children often confess more than is true because of their incomprehension'.[49] By April 1725, some parents were petitioning to be allowed to take their children back as cured: this time the Council refused. And when the other parents were finally told that they had to take their children back again, they had to live with children who had lost their families for some of the key years of their growing up; and who had finally come to learn – or persuade the Council they accepted – that their troubles were caused not by a witch but by their own 'evil imaginings and fantasies'.[50]

The parents and step-parents of the diabolic children were unable to merge themselves with the suffering victims of witchcraft by blaming a mother figure and securing her execution. In any case, they were confronting children whose behaviour they found intolerable, and with whom they simply could not cope. Parents, step-parents and children confronted the sexual games of infancy – the hostility to parents expressed through putting excrement in their beds, the oral and anal sadism – and both sides, adults and children, seem to have felt the attacks were real, whether caused by the 'diabolic' children themselves or a witch. But the old symbolic structure of witchcraft was starting to crumble, which was partly why the material of this case was so poorly symbolized, the latent content of the fantasies – sex and excrement – barely disguised at all. The elaborate demonological science which had converted such powerful hatred of the mother into mythic form, taking it out of the realm of real motherly relations and translating it into the language of witches, sabbaths and diabolic hierarchies, was losing credibility. And when the children drew on the repertoire of witch beliefs they formed their own childish versions, telling of devils who came down the chimney on a donkey, who told them not to obey their parents, and who instructed them to drop their trousers and kiss each other's shameful parts. What had always been the source of all witchcraft fantasies – the fears and obsessions which spring from childhood – emerged in more direct, and therefore more troubling fashion.

When attention shifted away from the mother figure and on to the child, it brought with it a new interest in children's imaginative worlds, and in play. As belief in witchcraft crumbled, the boundary between the realm of fantasy and the realm of reality had to be redrawn. Play is often about the intersection of these two worlds.[51] What went on in children's heads – what they imagined as they played, what fantasies surrounded their sexual games – became an object of parental concern. The transition was only partial, for at the same time as the Protestant jurisconsult Weng was convinced he was dealing with childish imaginings – none the less wicked for that – other parents were equally passionately persuaded of the Devil's real activity, their children's diabolic activity, or the mysterious seamstress's guilt. The children's 'fantasies' on the whole accorded with what was culturally known about the Devil and witchcraft,[52] and so they could not be dismissed out of hand. But in the end, parents, too, had to accept that the 'witch' would not be executed, and had to learn to live with their godless children.

Chapter Ten
A Witch in the Age of Enlightenment

On a summer day in 1745, Catharina Schmid, aged seventy-four, was facing her eleventh interrogation in prison. She was suspected of witchcraft. Torture was about to be applied, and this, her interrogators were sure, would make her confess. Catharina came from the small Catholic village of Alleshausen on the edge of the Federsee lake on a high plateau in what is now Württemberg, in south-western Germany. She had herself set in motion the legal process which now brought her to this pass. Insulted in public as a witch, she had, like many accused witches before her, brought her defamers to court to demand an apology and to restore her good name. This was a high-risk strategy – but Schmid had little choice. If she had let the matter lie, her inaction would itself have been a sure sign that she was indeed a witch. As it was, Schmid and her accusers had made the day-long journey from the lakeside village of Alleshausen down to the headquarters of the territory, the monastery court at the hamlet of Obermarchtal, the new onion-shaped towers of its remodelled baroque abbey church rising above the fields. Once there, the court inquiries rapidly changed character, as, with the support of the village headman, her fellow villagers testified at length that Schmid was a witch and had harmed them, their animals and loved ones.

There were two key charges against Schmid: that she had caused a young girl to become possessed and that she had killed the wife and children of Caspar Strom. As the trial proceeded, however, a range of villagers recited a litany of miscellaneous misfortunes for which they held her responsible, from the deaths of children to the mysterious reappearance of some lost spinning yarn. Caspar Strom was the most bitter witness against her. His young wife Magdalena had been turned mad by her, six of their children had died in terrible circumstances, six of Caspar's children from his first marriage had died after losing their wits and becoming rabid, and he himself had temporarily lost his mind, gambling away his farmstead in a drunken stupor. Meanwhile Georg Holl's girl lay ill, suffering from possession. Schmid had given her shredded dumplings to eat six years before, and she saw visions of the old woman during her fits. The visions proved that Schmid had most likely caused the possession by summoning the Devil to torment the girl. Both Caspar Strom and Georg Holl had publicly called Catharina Schmid a witch, and these insults had precipitated the trial.[1]

Like her parents before her, Catharina had lived almost her entire life in Alleshausen, a village which contained around seventy farms and had a population of perhaps 500 souls.[2] Catharina's father was born in Uttenweiler, the next village, and had been forester and castle servant; her mother ended her days there, just outside the monastery's jurisdiction. She too was rumoured to have been a witch, and it was said that her sister had been hounded out of neighbouring Betzenweiler as a witch as well. It was a flat, brooding landscape, steeped in history (see Map, ill. 7). Remnants of the wooden neolithic villages built out over the lake on stilts, evidence of settlement stretching far back in time, were dotted in the water, and villagers knew how to avoid their stumps as they rowed around the lake. Fishing and agriculture dominated the economy and poaching from the fish farms was a time-honoured crime. The climate was harsh, storms were frequent and rheumatism and pneumonia common, as its nineteenth-century historian dourly noted.[3] Then as now, the traveller arriving at the edge of the lake at Ahlen can see from one village to another, and watch the stormclouds mass in a corner of the lake and then skid across from shore to shore. Eventually, Catharina Schmid would admit that she had once summoned the stormclouds to leave the lake and go to another village instead.

Catharina's life had been marked by just about every kind of tragedy that could befall a woman in the eighteenth century. Her first husband, a carpenter from Alleshausen, had died in a fire just four weeks after they were married. The blaze had been started by her new stepson Johann, and his carelessness caused the loss of the house and all the furniture as well as the death of his father.[4] After this disaster, Catharina lived six and a half years as a widow before meeting Peter Dornhauser, a weaver from Switzerland, whom she married. He was an outsider to the village. With him she had three children. But five years after they married, his wife of twenty years before made the journey from Switzerland and appeared at Alleshausen, accusing him of bigamy.

Dornhauser fled, making for the town of Biberach on the advice of the clergy. The small compass of the world of the lakeside villages is betrayed in even the priests' assumption that Biberach would be Dornhauser's safest bet. It was there that villagers from throughout the territory went for legal advice, visited apothecaries, travelled to market or even summoned a hangman. It was a bi-confessional town, where Protestants formed the majority of the population and Lutherans and Catholics took turns using the town's parish church. An imperial city, subject directly to the Emperor, it had its own laws and jurisdiction. Biberach could hardly have been more different from the village world of Alleshausen. But it was not far enough for Dornhauser to make a new start. He travelled on to Hungary, wanting Catharina to follow.

Instead, Catharina chose to stay in Alleshausen. There, she was a dishonoured woman, now with two surviving children whose legitimacy was in doubt. For the next thirty-five years, Catharina eked out an existence in the village, hardly ever, as she proudly remarked, resorting to begging. Born and bred around the Federsee though she was, the villagers still called her 'the Swiss woman' because of her marriage to Dornhauser. Somehow she kept what remained of the family together, her son in school and – after the first few difficult years – herself in more or less regular work as a farm servant. But it can never have been easy. Not surprisingly, her son Niclas married out, leaving the Federsee area to start a new life. He too died young, aged only twenty-five. Catharina Schmid was left in Alleshausen with her daughter Maria, and no close male relative. Meanwhile, Maria developed a discharge in her face and her nose shrank. With the help of a barber-surgeon and by means of prayer, the girl recovered, but she was left disfigured and, as her mother put it with brutal realism, she was 'unsightly'.[5] For the now bastard daughter of the deserted wife there was to be no chance of marriage, no escape from a life of serving and working for others; no escape, either, from her mother.

After many weeks of questioning, frequent use of blessings and blessed objects and nine sessions of interrogation had produced no result, permission was sought to apply torture. The court consulted Johann Sättelin, a university-trained jurist in Biberach, whose legal memorial on the question concluded that there was insufficient evidence against the defendant to justify the use of torture.[6] Since Schmid had not confessed to being a witch, the case reached deadlock. But events at Marchtal proceeded beyond legal control. Accusations had mounted, and witnesses had been making the journey from Alleshausen to Obermarchtal to testify against Schmid, some of them repeatedly. They blamed her for a string of misfortunes.

Catharina Schmid had her own explanations for the ills of her fellow villagers, and she had no qualms about parading her neighbours' dirty linen in court. She gave short shrift to Caspar Strom, one of her chief antagonists, who had alleged she had killed his wife and children. Strom, she said, had hit hard times because of his incessant drinking, his failure to work as hard as his father had done, and his poor husbandry. In his cups he swore at his wife and family. He had even cursed the entire monastery of Marchtal, calling on lightning to strike it to the ground – and she repeated his exact words to the court. The whole year round he never went to church or on procession. His wife was sickly before she even came to Alleshausen and had married too young: the brood of stepchildren was simply too much for her. Catharina judged that Caspar's madness was feigned, a ruse to make sure he didn't lose the farm to the man he had sold it to while drunk. And Caspar was a wife-beater. His first wife had carried 'blue marks to her grave from the beatings from her husband' – and after all, who should be better placed to know than she, a servant in the house at the time? Her own nephew, Jerg Schmid, she said, had only himself to blame for his sickly animals. He had overtired his horse, and 'if a man doesn't do his business himself, and gets his boy to do it, then this is what happens, and afterwards they blame the witches'. Besides, Jerg was a man with a grudge. He desperately wanted to join the religious brotherhood of their parish church and carry the banner in procession, but had never been chosen. In a rage, he had come home and called on thunder to strike him if he ever went on their procession again – and the same winter, two of his cows sickened and died. This, she implied, was not witchcraft but God's just punishment for his swearing.[7]

At seventy-four, Catharina Schmid was old, twice the age of many of the established members of the village who were testifying against her. Her matronly advice, one suspects, may not always have been welcome. Both Jerg Schmid and Caspar Strom had new wives, a full generation younger than their husbands. Bringing two freshly baked 'cross cakes' to Magdalena, the new wife of Caspar Strom, Schmid told her 'there are two cakes for you, you too should be able to bake cakes like these' – not, perhaps, well-chosen counsel to a woman who had become a wife at an unusually young age and had a clutch of eight stepchildren from her husband's previous marriage to care for.[8] It was scarcely calculated to make the new wife feel confident of her place amongst the village matrons. The day after this visit, or 'visitation' as the young woman termed it, she fell ill. Schmid knew how to needle where it hurt, and she had a psychological shrewdness born of years of working in other people's houses. Another newly married wife had told Schmid of her pleasure that her stepson had married into the village, so that he would still be on hand, able to help when her husband died. Schmid had replied that things might be going well now, but the worm would turn on her husband's death when the question of who was to inherit arose. Schmid was, of course, proved right. The husband died and the family duly fell out over the inheritance. This only convinced the young woman that Schmid must be a witch with a malign talent for second sight.[9]

Catharina Schmid was tough. Her interrogators described her as 'hard-necked', even to her face: how dare she be so hard-necked and persist in denying the truth; she was engaging in 'almost unheard of stiffneckedness'.[10] Twelve sessions of interrogation did not break her, and when her questioners resorted – with doubtful legality, for they lacked the approval of their legal adviser – to torture, she withstood three rounds of increasing severity, cracking only in the fourth. In all, she was made to answer 608 questions,[11] and her interrogation lasted from July 1745 until February of the following year.

Severe torture was used on her. When admonishing her to confess and showing her the instruments of torture had no effect, they tortured her with thumbscrews. As the scribe noted, her thumbs were pressed together for seven minutes until they were only the width of a knife, yet she did not react. Following this, they employed the legscrews, equipment which caused excruciating pain to the legs; and then the bench for seven minutes. Thumbscrews alone were enough to cause many witches to confess and legscrews usually sufficed in more difficult cases. Two days later, torture resumed and the diabolic mark (probably a mole, but it was believed the Devil left a secret mark on those who made a compact with him) on her left thigh was cut out by the executioner. No mention is made of any anaesthetic. She was then put on the bench and whipped for ten to eleven minutes – an act which, they recorded, pained their consciences to carry out on one so elderly. Schmid's apparent indifference to these tortures confirmed the executioners in their opinion that such endurance was possible only with the Devil's help. They were certain that she knew some supernatural way of causing the cords tying her to the bench to loosen, enabling her somehow to wriggle free of the blows of the whip. The executioners then poured vinegar on the weals on her back but even this, the scribe recorded, caused no reaction on Schmid's part.

Throughout, Schmid insisted on her innocence, repeating that she was 'as pure of this sin as a child in its mother's body', or 'as innocent as the Dear God on the cross', language which was carefully chosen, for young children were especially exposed to harm from the witch, who was an enemy of God. She steadfastly maintained her faith in divine, if not in earthly justice, warning her judges that those who judged her would themselves face a heavenly court; and declared that she would endure torture 'so that she might come to the crown of martyrdom sooner, and her innocence would yet emerge after her death'. Tied to the bench and threatened with forty strokes, she commended her innocence to the wounds of Christ. When she insisted that her sufferings were not the result of her own stiff-necked Satanic resistance to the power of the court, but were saintly martyrdom, she must have infuriated the court as much as she strengthened her own endurance.[12]

Catharina Schmid could not endure torture indefinitely. By November, eight months after she first left Alleshausen, her interrogators had found a method which produced the desired results. The upper part of her body was stripped and she was put on a chair, bound crosswise hand and foot to the legs of the chair and whipped in such a way that she could not loosen the cords.[13] In this humiliating posture, and after so long in custody, seven strokes were enough to get her to confess. True, this method did involve a repeated application of torture where only a single use was permitted, but Sättelin, the now-compliant Catholic jurist from Biberach, turned in a memorandum duly justifying the procedure on the grounds that, in this exceptional case, supernatural forces had interfered with the application of torture and its illegal repetition could therefore be defended. The argument was made, interestingly enough, with frequent supporting references to the century-old works of the Protestant jurist Benedikt Carpzov, an example of how witch phobia could make bedfellows of confessional enemies. Broken, Catharina Schmid now confessed that she had indeed met the Devil, had been seduced by him, had been forced to travel to Satanic revels, and had harmed children, adults, cattle, horses and crops. Over the following months her interrogators methodically continued their questioning, attempting with limited success to gain a full confession from her to all the misdeeds of which she had been accused.

News that Catharina Schmid had finally confessed soon spread to Alleshausen, as her nephew Joseph Schmid, another of her bitter accusers, made the journey back to the Federsee, carousing with friends along the route. Meanwhile, back in the village, Catharina Schmid's daughter Maria, living in her cousin's house as a servant, turned first to Hans Jörg Gaugler, then to Jerg Schmid's wife (another of Catharina's accusers) and finally to Jörg Traub, begging them to give her mouse poison, even entreating Traub to buy it for her in Biberach. Maria went to the bed she had shared with her mother in her cousin's house and there she hid the tiny quantities of mouse poison she had painstakingly scrounged from her fellow villagers. She took nearly all of it, but it was not enough to kill her, just sufficient to cause her to vomit foully. Attempted suicide, except if one was insane, was a criminal act in early modern Germany. Her cousin no longer wished to have her in his house; and Maria had nowhere else to go. She was questioned on the spot by the local village officials and bundled off to Oberarchtal forthwith. Once in prison with her mother, and knowing what her mother had confessed, Maria too was soon confessing that she was a witch, seduced into the Devil's power by her depraved mother.[14]

In 1746 Catharina Schmid and her daughter were publicly executed, Catharina strangled before burning and sacks of gunpowder tied around her neck, because she was so *hartnäckig* ('stubborn').[15] Maria suffered the milder, honourable punishment, bending her neck to the executioner's sword, since, meek to the last, she had not been obstinate like her mother, but had confessed fully without the need for any torture. As the jurist Sättelin advised, this punishment should ensure that she would not fall into despair and so suffer damnation[16] – the fate of those who attempted to commit suicide.

What is remarkable about the story of Catharina Schmid is not its outlines – they were thoroughly familiar – but its date. Her trial took place in 1745, a good century after the mass witch burnings and 120 years since the last known witch from Alleshausen had been tried. As the conduct of the case reveals, even in the eighteenth century torture was being applied to elderly women in a manner which violated all the rules, and it was still believed that if a woman could resist pain, it only proved that she was a witch with diabolic powers. This was the period of the dramas of Lessing and the early philosophy of Kant, the beginnings of the German Enlightenment, a time when torture was being denounced and a new understanding of human psychology was developing. The hackneyed stories which circulated around Catharina Schmid were tales out of joint, transported into an Enlightenment world where witches and devils supposedly no longer existed, banished by the light of reason.

But in rural Marchtal, as in some other pockets of Catholic south Germany, the violent, nightmare world of witch-hunting seemed to be thriving.[17] The Marchtalers were no strangers to hunting witches, as we have seen. In Catharina's own village of Alleshausen with its adjoining hamlet of Seekirch, thirteen individuals were executed in the late sixteenth century, six from one family alone. In the tiny village of Reitlingendorf eight witches had been executed. In Obermarchtal where the monastery stood, another eight individuals were condemned. A generation later, witch-hunting resumed, when in 1627 three women were executed for witchcraft, all of them from Obermarchtal itself. We have no record of further persecutions until that of the mid-eighteenth century in which Catharina Schmid died; but that outbreak was astonishingly severe. Six women perished in the flames in 1747 and a seventh died of injuries sustained in prison. All were from Alleshausen. The last cases about which we know in the territory come from 1756 and 1757. This time at least, the accused witches managed to persuade their persecutors of their innocence.

Between the sixteenth and eighteenth centuries, it seems, the targets of the witch craze had not shifted. Catharina Schmid was, like so many of those accused in the sixteenth century, an elderly woman. Four of the eighteenth-century cases involved mothers and daughters who were both accused of witchcraft: in the sixteenth century at Marchtal, five pairs of mothers and daughters perished in the flames. Throughout Germany, the largest group of suspects, whether in the sixteenth, seventeenth or eighteenth century, were elderly women. The sixteenth-century panic had caught some less usual suspects in its wake, including several men, but they were hardly straightforward witches: one was a highwayman, and witchcraft was simply added to his crimes for good measure; another, out for a country ramble, had somehow ended up playing the fiddle at a witches' sabbath; a third's involvement in the sect of witches emerged during his trial for incest with his daughter.

In the sixteenth century, it was the image of the death-dealing hag that fuelled the trials. These were witches who killed animals, infants and children and disrupted the weather. Anna Lepp caused the storm on the Federsee lake that had led to one villager's death. She had harmed a child of her own in the womb and when it was born, she attacked it further so that it died in ten weeks. She and her companions had so damaged a woman who had just given birth and was lying in that she died. Indeed, as the formal statement of con-demnation put it, 'it would be impossible to relate all the other harm she had caused to people, children, animals, livestock and horses'.

Familiar, too, are the themes of the sixteenth-century trials, the poison apples, the titbits offered to children. Like Catharina 150 years later, these women were neighbours or relatives of their accusers. The accusations testify to how well they knew the children, and how concerned they were in caring for them, trusted to feed and cuddle them or even take them to church for baptism. Margaretha Menz touched a one-year-old child, having first smeared her hand with diabolic salve: 'in five days it would neither suck nor eat nor cry and it lay just as it was put. She, the witch, had often visited, and sometimes brought apples, and she was not pleased that they got the child blessed.' Julianne Laub confessed to killing a child she had 'loved' and had taken in her arms. These women were able to attack, so it was believed, precisely because they were trusted neighbours who came into the house. Women whose des-peration to find acceptance in village communities led them to care, give food and bake for others, children in particular, were often then the ones who were exposed to suspicions of witchcraft. Like the witch in 'Hansel and Gretel', they charmed children only to trap them, cook and eat them. This was a pervasive myth, lasting long into the nineteenth century. In what looks like a virtual re-run of Julianne Laub's case, Catharina Schmid was said to have visited a young mother, saying she had heard 'what a beautiful child she had brought into the world!' She carried the baby about in her arms and kissed it. Six days later the child had sickened, its mouth turning red, two terrible blisters appearing on its tongue and then on its cheek, and it had finally perished miserably.[18] Another charge mirrored the case of Ursula Götz, executed in 1627 (with which this book began), where a woman was accused of harming the niece for whom she acted as carer. Catharina, too, was accused of killing the son of her nephew Joseph Schmid, in whose house she had been living. She had been heard to say that they should starve the child so as to put it out of its misery. Not long after, the boy had died after eating a piece of fruit she had given him.[19]

Just as Catharina Schmid confessed to killing nine horses and two calves, so the witches of 150 years before were accused of killing animals. The same places recur in the testimonies of witnesses: the cow stalls and stables where the witches were seen to lurk and where they had no reason to be; on the open street, where a witch might curse a horse that crossed her path or stroke one of a line of oxen, causing it to drop down dead. Witches might fly into barns and cow stalls, killing the animals or striking them with disease. Agathe Hageler chillingly described how a witch might take leave of her companions after an evening sewing together, only to disappear into the night, flying off to open the cow-stall doors. They 'rode the beasts' at night, a terrifying term which has a sexual resonance, for to ride a cow was to commit sodomy. Ursula

Motz described one such diabolic ride. The Devil appeared on a white horse, and 'they visibly rode quite wildly together under the cloak of night to Bierlingen'; she thought that all the horses in the district were running together with them, and that all would perish. Few witches could approach the wholesale malevolence of Ursula Götz, who killed 88 animals including 35 horses. Envy, so it was believed, was what drove these women on – envy of their neighbours' comfortable, well-stocked barns and dairies, and their fine, healthy children with their pretty red cheeks. By comparison with these death-dealing animal riders and storm-summoners, Catharina Schmid's attacks on animals look rather tame.

The uncanny, too, is as palpable in the eighteenth-century accounts of witchcraft as it was in those of the sixteenth or seventeenth century. In 1627, a boy who had worked in the smithy where Ursula Götz lived described how a strange black dog had appeared when he was putting hay down for the horses. When he turned round, nothing was there, though he searched in the manger for anything untoward. Eerie tales circulated around Catharina Schmid too. And yet there is an interesting difference. The strangeness of these eighteenth-century tales stems from what they reveal of people's hidden thoughts and feelings rather than from what they intimate about devils. One woman came to court to recount how, while Catharina was in prison in Marchtal, she and her friend were discussing the discomfort they felt at Schmid's imprisonment. 'If only the whole thing would come to an end ... whether Schmid be guilty or innocent, it simply must, you couldn't even sleep quietly any more,' the two women had been saying to each other. At that very moment, Catharina's daughter appeared, bearing a message from her mother: Catharina Schmid sends you her greetings, and says: 'Just sleep quietly again at night, the matter will come to rest.' 'Sleep quietly' – those had been their exact words! How could the witch have guessed? And what did she mean by the ominous phrase 'the matter will come to rest'? Did 'rest' mean 'death', and if so, whose? Had the witch known, then, that the two women had just wanted the case over and done with, put to rest, regardless of whether Schmid was innocent or not, regardless of whether it ended in her death?[20]

Indeed, though Catharina's trial seemed to be a fossilized version of those earlier witch panics, it was also of its time. The records of the sixteenth-century panics are skimpy, as if the scribe begrudged these women's stories time and ink. Sometimes they do not even merit their own list of charges, and their names are simply added over someone else's. Rarely are their accusers' statements recorded, and we get barely an inkling of these women's characters. By contrast, the eighteenth-century records positively ooze with emotion. Every minor village character has his or her day in court, telling riveting stories of their encounters with Schmid, voicing their fears and anguish, or recounting in detail the agonizing deaths of their loved ones. And though animals figure in the eighteenth-century trials, their role is not as important as it was in the earlier cases. People, their loves, tiffs and jealousies, form the stuff of these testimonies. Animals, the weather and the economy play a secondary role. The eighteenth century may not have witnessed the advent of the Age of Reason in Marchtal, but the Age of Sentiment had certainly dawned.[21]

Just how difficult it had become by the eighteenth century to convict a witch is evident from the length of the proceedings. Witnesses had to be recalled repeatedly and made to amplify their testimony so as to mention the chief points properly; the witch could not be made to confess. Even when the executioners arrived at a method that produced confessions, she still could not be made to supply the admissions which would at least fit the crimes for which there was any evidence. Lacking the expertise of a previous generation, executioners and judges alike had to rediscover how to try a witch and how to make her talk. Where it took perhaps six weeks – less in times of large panics – to convict a witch in the seventeenth century, the Marchtal court needed a full ten months to conclude Schmid's interrogation and did not actually execute her until a year later.

Those peasant communities were no longer the idealized villages which a poet like the eighteenth-century Marchtal monk Sebastian Sailer was evoking. Across south-west Germany, small village elites had crystallized, made up of the half-dozen or so leading families and bound to one another by marriage and kinship.[22] These people monopolized the political and judicial offices. It is apparent that Schmid had fallen foul of them, and her bitter complaint that the whole thing was cooked up by the local legal official Joseph Cadus and Caspar Strom in the village tavern has the ring of truth, even if it was not the whole truth. The Cadus family was a key player in the local judiciary, and Strom seems to have had substantial assets. Some of those whom she was accused of harming were officials who tried her. There was a growing sense of social distance between those who belonged to that elite, and those, like Schmid, who did not. These tensions too formed part of the background of the case. Again, this was not in itself new: social tensions figured in the trials of the sixteenth century. The Moll family who belonged to the village poor and criminal underworld lost six members in the witch panic.

Catharina Schmid was by age, repute and character an archetypal witch, and yet her interrogation lacks dynamism. Her trial was indeed a petrified relic, washed up on the shores of what was elsewhere the dawning Age of Enlightenment. Her confession, when it came, was unpersuasive and singularly lacking in detail. All was cliché, despite the punctiliousness of the court's record-keeping: the name of her demon Caspar, a common name for the Devil (and as it happened, the name of her chief accuser too), his appearance as a 'hunter' dressed in green (as so many devils were), and his almost bored seduction of her. Bothering only to reply 'Hey, here I am' when she asked who was there, and wasting no time in banter when he engaged in the requisite intercourse with her, 'Caspar' is almost entirely without character. He is not used as an imaginative figure through which Catharina might have recounted her life story or conveyed the bitter emotions of being rumoured a witch in a village society from which there was no escape.

By contrast, witch confessions in the 'golden age' of witch persecution were dramatic narratives, even if those from Marchtal lack the length and detail that characterize interrogation records from Würzburg, Nördlingen or Augsburg. Such confessions depended on the collusive combustion of interest between interrogator and accused witch. Women described what the Devil wore, how he beat down their resistance with blandishments and sweet talk, how he visited again and again, knocking at their doors or suddenly appearing in their bedchambers. They spoke of banquets of infant flesh. Anna Lepp from sixteenth-century Marchtal told how she and her mother had dug up three children and stewed them in her house. No emotionality coloured Catharina's laconic account of life with the Devil, though she talked at length and with passion about those who accused her or whom she had supposedly injured. Even motherhood does not emerge here as a powerful imaginative theme: there are no gruesome stories of cannibalistic meals of infant flesh, no elaborate stories about Catharina's own childbed. It is as if we have here the husk of a witchcraft fantasy, no less deadly for that. Both the detail and the sentiments so richly expressed in the testimony belonged to those ranged against her.

Like the flat countryside in which it lay, Alleshausen's religious landscape was brooding and inward looking. Alleshausen had no parish church of its own. The parish church was at Seekirch, the next village, just a short walk away along the well-trodden raised path beside the lake. It had its own statue of a *pietà*, which the locals venerated. Believed to be ages old, it appears in reality to have been of fifteenth-century manufacture. A single parish priest was responsible for both villages, and he could call on the services of an assistant. Usually, the clergy were monks from the abbey at Marchtal, the Premonstratensians who ruled the tiny territory. Little changed between the sixteenth and the eighteenth century. There was, however, one novelty: a village school for seven- to fourteen-year-olds which was open in the summer months. It was run by the sexton, who was church caretaker, liturgical assistant and teacher by turns. Nicholas Paul, the incumbent, had been there since 1736 and he stayed until 1773, dinning the basics of reading into the heads of two generations of village children. Catharina Schmid's son Niclas attended class too.[23] One witness said that as a pupil, Niclas knew how to conjure plagues of mice, every schoolboy's dream.

Educators, secular rulers, priests – from the sixteenth to the eighteenth century, all were men of the Church, all familiar with the ways of the order. Rulers, however, were not always treated with respect. Seekirchers still grumbled about the grandiosity of Abbot Johannes Haberkalt, who set out to build a country house in the village in 1516 and forced the villagers to hew the stone for it. The house was called Burgberg (castle mount) but local wags christened it Fluchberg (curse mount).[24] Generations later they were still grumbling at the imposition and today not a trace of the edifice remains. During the Peasants' War of 1524–26, when much of south-west Germany rose against the lords, inspired by Reformation doctrine and the conviction that all men were brothers, the Marchtalers too rebelled against their lords. They joined the Seegau and Allgäu peasants, plundering the abbey.[25] And in 1610 the peasants revolted again, complaining about the numbers of soldiers in the region and refusing to be sent to war as soldiers themselves. Those involved included members of the village court and substantial citizens.[26] By the eighteenth century, however, such displays of doctrinal or political disobedience were long past.

The abbey was the biggest landowner, gradually increasing its landowner-ship by purchasing land from indebted peasants. By the eighteenth century, it had renamed the plots of land it leased to its peasants after saints. Each lease-holder enjoyed the patronage and protection of the saint after whom his land was named. The monastery registers read like calendars of saints, the flat, dull, marshy land transformed by the monks into a holy topography. The order now saw itself as the guardian of these rural souls, sending its own members on stints as vicars to the scattered parishes. There some of them kept rural reg-isters, recording the baptisms, weddings and funerals of their flocks and writing down incidents of note. They were rooted, however, in the monastery and its familiar intellectual world. These were men who had friends amongst the Jesuits, who corresponded with monks in Augsburg, or at the monastery of Wengen near Ulm, or even visited Vienna. Some of them participated in a conservative republic of letters between the orders. They went to religious theatre performances by the monks at nearby Bad Schussenried. Obermarchtal was hardly a vibrant intellectual powerhouse – the monastery's own library was pitiful, and the monks' horizons did not stretch far beyond the Federsee – but it was distant enough from the world the peasants inhabited.[27]

Across the lake, at Bad Buchau, another territory began; ruled by an abbot, it was another of the handful of territories in Swabia ruled by a monastery and subject directly to the Emperor himself. This was a geography of parcelled ter-ritories, of tiny communities run by ecclesiastical institutions who were law, church, ruler and major landowner. Relics of an older system of lordship, dwarfed by the new princely territories with their trained bureaucracies, they would be swept away by the aftermath of the Napoleonic Wars at the start of the nineteenth century. Meanwhile, these territories were connected only remotely to the wider world through the monastic orders of which their rulers were a part. Yet this wider frame of reference did not override local allegiance. Of the fifteen abbots of the monastery at Marchtal between 1538 and 1768, thirteen were from the region, from Munderkingen, Buchau, Biberach, Steinhausen and even from the villages of the monastery itself.

Alleshausen and the monastery lands were strikingly different from the town of Biberach, less than a day's journey away. Another world, it was no redoubt of Catholicism. A bi-confessional town since Charles V reimposed toleration of Catholicism in 1548, its main church of St Martin was shared by Catholics and Protestants, one of very few such churches in Germany. In the wake of the Reformation, a thoroughgoing cleansing of the church had taken place, and every reminder of the richly ornamented parish church with its murals, altars to the saints, and statues was removed. We possess a moving description from the pen of the broken-hearted Catholic priest Von Pflummern of the world that was lost.[28] Protestants were the majority of the town's population. Sections of the church were reserved for the Catholic cult and the two confessions took turns using the building – but this could hardly allow space for the unfolding of a baroque Counter-Reformation visual piety of the kind to be seen in Marchtal's new monastery church or soon to arise in the astounding Zwiefalten, the chief church of yet another of these tiny nearby monastery principalities. By contrast, the Capuchin order in Biberach, which supplied Father Theobald to exorcize Catharina Schmid, and undertook preaching in the city parish church, was a Counter-Reformation foundation and was not wealthy. Its first church had been completed in 1618, just outside the city walls. It was destroyed in the Thirty Years War, and a new church was completed outside the town in 1661, a building which was simply not in the league of the vivid, uplifting architecture of the major monastic baroque churches in the region. By the eighteenth century Biberach boasted two theatre groups, one Catholic, one Protestant, and under the poet Christoph Martin Wieland *The Tempest* was performed in 1761, the first performance of a Shakespeare play in Germany – and of course, one in which magic plays a powerful part. In 1768 a society of music lovers was founded, and in the later eighteenth century, several famous actors and actresses began their careers in Biberach.[29] Such urban sophistication, small-town scale though it might be, was a long way from the secure Catholic world of the monastery villages, where an eighteenth-century Marchtal cleric could induce a Protestant convert to Catholicism to literally spit out the poison of Lutheran teaching she had ingested in her former life. And yet the cases of witchcraft reveal the interconnections of town and country: the jurist Sättelin whose advice played its part in the conduct of Catharina's case came from Biberach, as did the Capuchin friar who undertook the exorcisms. And it was from Biberach that Catharina's daughter desperately tried to procure her mouse poison. Historically, it had been Biberach which supplied the executioners for the territory, and Biberach's hangmen had carried out the burnings of all the witches convicted in the sixteenth and seventeenth centuries.

There is something brooding and oppressive about the magical and religious world of the eighteenth-century Federsee as it emerges in the trial of Catharina Schmid; and here, too, we see continuities with the sixteenth century as well as something distinctive. Every action is drenched in religious significance, every eventuality has its propitiatory or protective ritual. Animals are blessed to protect them against evil magic, prayers must be said at night to protect the household. This was not in itself new. In the sixteenth century, villagers told how they had taken animals to get them blessed when they feared witchcraft, and witches repeatedly said that they could not harm people or animals who had been blessed; indeed, such homilies on the power of blessing might even be read out at their execution, and what better way of getting the message across than from the witch herself? Catharina too, once broken, informed her interrogators that her curses only had effect 'if the goods of the house have not been properly blessed'.[30] Benign spiritual measures of this kind were not an alternative to aggressive witch-hunting. They were merely two sides of the same coin. For if a child or animal sickened, blessings were sought from the suspected witch. If she said a charm to help the sick person and they recovered, this might demonstrate that she was a pious woman with the gift of healing – or it might prove that she had caused the ill in the first place. Should she refuse aid, this might simply confirm her malevolent intent. And while taking the victim to a priest for diagnosis might seem to pre-empt a witch trial, it was often the priest or medical expert who opined that the cause of the malady was 'evil wishing', thus licensing the sufferer to seek out the person whose hostile wishes were to blame. All this was familiar. It was not that the Catholic Church lacked an arsenal of religious methods for dealing with evil: on the contrary, those remedies had always been hopelessly imbricated in the logic of witchcraft.

And yet there is something qualitatively different in the role religion played in the eighteenth-century case. All the actors in the drama leaned heavily on religious ritual to protect themselves: Catharina's fellow villagers crossed and blessed themselves against her, her interrogators showered her in blessed water and exorcisms, and forced her to eat blessed food. Even they feared the power of a witch. As the trial continued, the authorities' use of ritual became even more elaborate, approximating to a kind of body magic: they put blessed objects into her soup and sewed amulets into her clothes.[31] A specialist priest, the Capuchin Father Theobald from Biberach, was summoned to administer blessings and exorcisms to her at weekly intervals, just before interrogation sessions. The authorities used ecclesiastical magic aggressively, as if it were another weapon in their arsenal to bludgeon Schmid into confession. Schmid for her part used religion in almost mirror fashion. During torture, and at every shocking allegation, she called repeatedly on the Virgin Mary and on Jesus, as if they and not the Devil might be invoked in the torture chamber, and she threatened her persecutors with divine judgment. She and her daughter paid for Masses to be said for them in their parish church at Seekirch, a pointedly public insistence on divine protection.[32] She attempted to turn the tables on her questioners, reciting her pious deeds and invoking religious names to protect herself just as her fellow villagers and interrogators did against her.

By the eighteenth century, the rich symbolism of the witch hunt had become ossified. It had become a precarious system of hollow binary oppositions, of good and evil, black and white, in which there was little distinction between magical and religious thinking – just a fight to the death to determine which way around good and evil should be read.[33]

Even the way the witnesses framed their statements shows the same magical thinking. By going to Marchtal to testify, each one was engaging in a course of action which might result in Catharina Schmid's death. They were injuring her and attacking her honour; and they therefore had good reason to fear she might retaliate if she was a witch. On the other hand, if she was innocent, they had God's divine punishment to fear, as Schmid was not slow to remind them. This too was a dilemma faced by accusers in the sixteenth and seventeenth centuries. They commonly resorted to the ploy of describing in detail how their animals or loved ones had died. The description was always carefully framed to make it clear that the illness must have been supernaturally caused, and the witness would conclude with the ominous phrase 'whether it was witchcraft or not, he could not say'. The hearer, of course, was meant to conclude that it most certainly was witchcraft. In the eighteenth century the interrogators took pains to soothe the witnesses, telling them that 'God will not punish those who tell the truth' when they showed reluctance to repeat in court the stories that would seal Catharina's fate.[34] By this time, no one in the village could remember testifying against a witch, nor could they even remember such stories from their parents. The precautions witnesses took assumed an elaborate, even magical character. Jerg Schmid, her nephew and one of the most important witnesses against Catharina, had to swear an oath over a crucifix and two burning candles when he came to make a second statement, a ritual which might be understood as protection from the witch's power, or as straightforward intimidation of the witness. Jerg began by begging Catharina not to blame him and insisted he was sorry that he had to testify.[35] In response to these contradictory pressures, some witnesses adopted tortuous strategies. They prefaced their statements by saying that Schmid might be innocent, they reported the stories of the woes of others and whom they had suspected but carefully added that they had not suspected Catharina themselves, or they 'forgot' crucial details, and had to reappear before the court to retell their stories in full.[36]

Catharina herself was extremely devout. The forms her piety took mark her out as a child of the Counter-Reformation and its years of indoctrinating its village flocks. Its legacy is evident in her detailed knowledge of her faith and her elaborate devotional practices. During her very first interrogation, Catharina gave a long list of the pilgrimages she had undertaken to holy sites within the upper Swabian region, nestling low in the Danube valley, or near Biberach or up beyond the lake; even as far afield as Einsiedeln in Switzerland. Each had its own organized pilgrimages, its own miraculous images, and in the eighteenth century many were rebuilt in grand rococo style. The eighteenth century was the high point of pilgrimage in south-west Germany, with new devotions springing up throughout the region and old ones being reanimated. Sometimes whole villages, sometimes small groups, would process together. Close to Alleshausen was the pilgrimage church of Steinhausen which had been rebuilt in the early 1730s by the brothers Dominkus and Johann Baptist Zimmermann. They were responsible for some of the most famous of the southern German rococo churches, like the Wieskirche in Steingaden (1745–54). In Steinhausen, 'the most beautiful village church in the world' took shape, a Marian masterpiece which Catharina, devoted to the Virign, would have known well.[37]

By contrast, the interrogations of the sixteenth century reveal almost nothing about religious practices, though the local priests, the sexton and his wife emerge as village characters. In the late sixteenth century, pilgrimages were just beginning to be revived as the Counter-Reformation won territory back from the Protestants and grew in confidence: they did not play the role in religious life which they had assumed by the eighteenth century. Popular Catholicism at village level was a creation of the seventeenth and eighteenth centuries, not of the sixteenth.

As all her neighbours agreed, Catharina Schmid was conspicuously pious. She wore a scapular on which she had sewn Our Lady of Einsiedeln and of Landshut. She carried an Agnus Dei, a St Monica belt and a rosary. On her thumb was tattooed the mark of the cross, as if in inversion of the Devil's mark she eventually admitted had been stamped on her ankle. She had joined the Franciscans as a lay sister, and she prayed more assiduously than her accusers, as they too admitted. Everyone knew of her devotions, and of the religious charms and blessed remedies she used to help and heal. In other circumstances, she might perhaps have been considered a holy woman, a *beata*. All these were public forms of worship, part of the tradition of south-west German village Catholicism. But Catharina also practised the new forms of private devotion, which were just beginning to be propagated by the eighteenth-century Church as Catholicism began its transformation into a religion of individual, not just collective salvation. Every night before going to bed she prayed sitting on a stool by the bed, exhorting her sleepy daughter to do the same.[38]

The impact of the Counter-Reformation insistence on the importance of confession has left its imprint on the case too. At its heart lay what Catharina had supposedly confessed to travelling preachers when they visited the area. One of Catharina's own nephews, her closest living relative aside from her daughter, maintained that Catharina herself had confided in him that she had confessed to these visiting confessors that she was a witch, and that she had received absolution from them. This Catharina hotly denied. The issue here was the secrecy of the confessional, one of the innovations of the Counter-Reformation. It seems that these missionaries were offering amnesty to former witches, allowing them to confess in the privacy of the confessional box. What was intended to be the secrecy of the confessional became the subject first of rumour and then of judicial inquisition, and Catharina finally admitted to gaining absolution for taking an evil charm from some vagrant women; she claimed she had thrown it away. The sacrament of confession was intended to heal enmity and allow the peaceful fellowship of the Mass. But here it was being used to provide ammunition for village hostilities. Just how canny villagers might seek to get around the secrecy of the confessional is evident in one villager's admission that 'when he did have a suspicion [about witchcraft], and something evil happened in the village again, he mentioned it in confession'.[39] This tactic allowed him to gain absolution for his enmity and feelings of suspicion towards others in a Christian fashion, while at the same time ensuring that the priest knew that evil was afoot and knew who was suspected of causing it. Double messages like this put the parish priest in the firing line. He knew who was suspected; he was bound to provide spiritual remedies for affliction; his task was to preserve God's peace. Small wonder that parish clergy found it hard to steer a course, and small wonder that they faced competition from clergy outside the parish boundaries, less constrained by community pressures than they were.

Indeed, Catharina's case gives us more of a sense of the complexities of the Church's role and of the confused attitude of the clergy in the eighteenth century. In the sixteenth century, the battle against Protestantism in nearby Württemberg and the restoration of Catholicism dominated the concerns of the Church; but by the eighteenth century in Catholic south-west Germany, this battle had been won. What emerged was a distinctive and highly local form of Catholicism. Whereas in large territories like Würzburg or even smaller ones like Eichstätt, the Jesuits were the shock troops of the Counter-Reformation, in south-west German villages like those in the region of Marchtal, it was the Capuchins, a Counter-Reformation reformed version of the Franciscans, who held sway amongst the peasants. Much less intellectual in orientation than the Jesuits, they were closely allied to popular piety and supported pilgrimage, benedictions and popular religious practice even to the extent of advocating what others held to be superstitions. The Capuchins played a key role on the margins of Catharina's story. They advised Peter Ströbele of Brasenberg to get incense to help cure the fever of his ten-year-old son: he was told that if he lit it, the guilty person who had caused the illness would not be able to bear the smoke. He tried it out when Schmid visited while having a smoke of tobacco: she did not remain 'for longer than five Our Fathers'.[40]

Lorenz Engler, a man of substantial means and innkeeper at Alleshausen, suspected that witchcraft had turned him mad. On his pastor's advice, he turned to the Francisans for help, who gave him a paper with an indulgence which he was to nail to the house and the cow stall. But according to Engler, they also counselled him to give about three handfuls of salt in a piece of his bread to the person he suspected of having caused him to fall into madness. Engler, understandably reluctant to do this himself, got someone in his household to give the items to Schmid, and he promptly recovered his health.[41] Engler may of course have been trying to make it look as if his superstitious practices had the stamp of Franciscan approval. But the Franciscans clearly took his worries seriously, and their counter-blessings could all too easily become part of witch-hunting itself.

By contrast, local clergy from the order and the area did attempt to curb such waves of suspicion. Catharina Schmid's daughter Maria was convinced that the priest at Seekirch, their parish church, was admonishing the villagers not to persecute her mother – she was sure that his sermons last summer against witchcraft 'happened only to the end that one should have no evil suspicion of her and her mother', and she had cried afterwards.[42] This local priest had also encouraged the possessed girl Maria Glanzing to seek aid from the Franciscans and had persuaded another parishioner not to suspect his wife of witchcraft. Together with his vicar, the pastor had attempted to urge Schmid to tolerate the insults that she was a witch, and not to bring a case: good advice, as it transpired.

Harder to determine is the attitude of the Premonstratensian monastery in Marchtal as a whole. Though some of the clergy they had installed apparently attempted to quell the witch panic, the order itself presided over the trial, and the questions drawn up by its administrators and posed by its officials, senior official Rettig, chancellery administrator Dilger, the secretary and the scribe, were vigorously partisan: How dare she be so stubborn and not confess? 'The accused is already seventy-four years old and will die soon of natural causes anyhow, so she should rather confess her misdeeds, repent and save her soul.'[43] Pastor Theobald of the Capuchin order even visited Alleshausen in liaison with the legal adviser Johann Sättelin. He recorded the terrible state of affairs there in a letter, the contents of which were read to Catharina.[44] It is hard to see how the case could have proceeded without the connivance of the monastery.[45] As late as 1771, Sebastian Sailer, Swabian poet and monk at the monastery, was still defending the justice of the trials, long after witchcraft trials had ceased to be acceptable in intellectual circles, and after the last witch was executed on German soil.[46] At the very least, as the major landowner, the supreme legal authority and the superintendent of the administration, it was extremely well placed to put pressure on the peasants not to proceed with the case. The eighteenth-century monastery may have been strongly rooted in popular piety and responsive to local initiative, but it also shared the obverse of that piety: a watchful suspicion of those it held to be of the Devil.

Nowhere was the clash between the old and the new more apparent than in the issue of possession, which emerged as an important background issue in Schmid's case. At one level, possession and witchcraft had long been connected. Waves of possession often preceded witch hunts, raising the emotional temperature and predisposing people to see the hand of Satan at work. When a person became possessed, trembling and rolling in fits or speaking in tongues, this was because the Devil inhabited his or her body, though against his or her will. In witchcraft, by contrast, the witch intentionally made a pact with the Devil and went on to harm others. But the two could become linked if the possessed person accused a witch of causing her possession. And this was precisely what happened to Catharina Schmid when, at the outset, the maid of Georg Holl alleged that Schmid had caused her to become possessed. As Holl and his wife described it, the poor girl had suddenly sickened after her periods had ceased and she lay in bed groaning. She trembled in her whole body, and beat her hand vigorously on the bed, saying, 'Now I know where my misfortunes come from that I have to endure so much pain this winter' and she called on St Tiberius to help her.[47] All this might almost have happened in the sixteenth century.

And yet the details of the case were drawn from the heart of what was distinctive about eighteenth-century south German Catholicism. It was no accident that the girl said that St Tiberius had appeared to her, telling her that Schmid was the author of her ills. Tiberius was one of the new brand of historically attested saints, one of the catacomb martyrs discovered during the Counter-Reformation, and his bones had been brought to Marchtal from Rome in 1625.[48] Cults like his were being introduced between 1650 and 1750 throughout south-west Germany. At around the time of Catharina's trial, the monastery was introducing a special St Tiberius blessing in the territory. Under the tenure of the current abbot, an altar had been built to house his relics. In promoting the cult of St Tiberius, in teaching their villagers about him, and in linking the cult to the bones owned by the monastery, the Church was creating a piety that linked devotion to local identity. It was devotion that rested on the foundations of knowledge and on relics that were attested, and, in a monastic territory which had only rudimentary forms of government, it helped villagers in the scattered hamlets feel they belonged to an identifiable political unit (see Map, ill. 7). The Church's success is apparent in how much both Schmid and the Glanzing girl knew about Tiberius, even though they lived in Alleshausen, some distance from the monastery itself. Schmid was scathing about the idea that Tiberius could have visited the girl and told her who was causing her fits: she insisted that the priests had said 'Tiberius would not have come up from Marchtal and given her this idea'.[49]

Local saints were key to local eighteenth-century religious culture and to the monastery's means of anchoring its political authority. Catharina was certainly devoted to St Tiberius, whom she credited with her daughter's recovery from the sore on her nose. Asked by her interrogators whom she meant by Tiberius, she replied, 'Him on the altar down under in the church' – the altar in the monastery church. Schmid was adamant that what the Glanzing girl heard was an evil spirit, not St Tiberius. Her insistence struck the interrogators as suspicious. As they reminded her in their next question, St Tiberius's water was good to use against evil people and sorcery, 'and just about every child on the streets knows this'. Catharina, they implied, was maliciously denying that the girl could have been visited by the saint, when this would have chimed perfectly with his role as protector against witches. Schmid might think she had a monopoly on Tiberius, she might think she knew her saints; but, her interrogators made plain, the diocese's patron saint was to be used by them.

Indeed, possession itself, which seems to hark back to the age of the witch hunt, can also be seen to stand on the cusp of the Enlightenment. In outline, Maria's possession appeared to follow the classic course. The girl herself was adamant that her possession had been caused by another person, and in blaming Catharina she was doing what many possessed people had done before her: identifying an old woman who apparently had all the characteristics of a witch. (Although, towards the end of the case, when Schmid still persisted in denying that she had caused her suffering, the girl instead blamed Catharina's daughter Maria, who promptly confessed.) Just as cases of possession so often did in the sixteenth century, the case began to involve those beyond the village. The local priest encouraged her to seek aid from the Franciscans, and this she did, spending some weeks with them. As a result the girl was only able to testify against Schmid in person at quite a late stage in the case, when she returned. The Franciscans had attempted to cure her by means of exorcism, and they apparently invested time and energy in caring for this village girl. It is unclear whether or not they shared the girl's conviction that her possession was caused by another person, or whether they held her to be truly possessed. All this might have happened in the sixteenth century, and yet the appeal to religious specialists like exorcists and confessors for help in healing was also part of an eighteenth-century vogue for the medical market, for practitioners who could help with particular illnesses through supernatural or natural means.

The golden age of exorcism was not over. Just a generation later, in the 1760s and 1770s, the exorcist Johann Joseph Gassner was creating a furore in southern Swabia as he healed people using dramatic exorcisms. His approach was essentially different from the classic understanding of possession. He believed that any illness might potentially be caused by the Devil and by demonic possession. So far as their symptoms were concerned, naturally and supernaturally caused diseases might be indistinguishable from each other. In this, he parted company with the orthodox view of the Catholic Church since 1614. Then the *Rituale Romanum* had defined possession very narrowly, limiting proper cases to those where the possessed person spoke in foreign tongues, had the ability to discover secrets or discern events which happened far away, had unnatural strength, or showed many similar such signs.[50] This rigorous definition would probably have excluded Maria Glanzing, and it was designed to curb the excesses of the exorcism mania that had characterized the early years of the Counter-Reformation. How far it gained acceptance is another matter – the *Rituale Romanum* took some time to penetrate into southern Germany and it is evident that exorcism there was far from extinct. As his fame spread, Gassner found himself exorcizing and healing literally thousands of people whose ills he diagnosed as caused by possession, during his tours of southern Germany. Even more shockingly, he developed ways of teaching individuals to confine the unseen forces to a particular afflicted body part and then exorcize it themselves. Eventually, the church authorities began to move against Gassner, and he was finally condemned by Pius VI in 1776. But though this marked the end of Gassner's career, it did not put a stop to the crowds of those seeking cures. One year after Gassner toured the area north of Lake Constance, Franz Anton Mesmer travelled the same region curing people using what he described as his 'magnetic' powers. The techniques of the two healers were similar, but Mesmer's cures employed the unseen force of animal magnetism, and forcefully rejected religious formulas. Indeed, Mesmer explained Gassner's therapies as in reality a form of magnetism, dismissing the religious dimension as superstition.

The advent of Mesmer marks a significant moment in the history of psychiatry, and in understandings of the relationship between mind and body. Mesmer proved a seminal influence on the great nineteenth-century French medical doctor of the insane, Charcot, who also experimented with the techniques of mesmerism and hypnosis. In terms of their longer-term legacies, then, exorcisms can be seen not only as throwbacks to the past but as therapies that pointed the way forward. In a sense this is not surprising. When Franciscan monks attempted to cure girls like Glanzing, they took them in, cared for them and became involved in their life stories, their symptoms and their spiritual health. Just as Freud was later to do, they developed a therapeutic relationship with the girl. They started from the presumption that emotional, spiritual and physical states were interconnected; and they attached significance to the contortions and sufferings that the victims underwent. Charcot, too, was convinced of the connection between mental illness and physical states. He was fascinated by the strange postures and grimaces his patients suffered while in the state of trance induced by hypnosis, and we have photographs of his key hysterics in their contorted poses. Freud in turn learned from Charcot and though he broke from him, Freud's experience at the Salpêtrière was to be a crucial influence on his gradual move towards exploring the inner states of his patients.[51] Psychoanalysis, we might say, has a pedigree that goes back, through a convoluted history, to the phenomenon of exorcism in the late eighteenth century.

In Marchtal, witchcraft in the sixteenth century was concerned with harm to people, children and animals. It concerned prosperity and fertility. Eighteenth-century witchcraft had much less to do with animals or the economy. Instead it focused on the emotional relations between people and the trials gave villagers a platform from which to talk at length about their griefs and hopes. The sixteenth-century court officials of Alleshausen were locals, men who shared their village's values and concerns, and they saw little point in noting down the fantastic stories of witches or recording the full details of the interrogation. They lacked curiosity about their fellow villagers because that world was their own.

The heightened emotionality, the sensibility and elaborate language of the eighteenth-century trials mark a radical shift, suggesting a concern with the individual, and with the analysis of motivation. In this regard the witchcraft trials of eighteenth-century Marchtal do come from the age of Kant and Lessing. They are part of contemporary speculation about psychology and character, which was eventually to cut free from its imprisonment in the language of the diabolic, losing its religious dimension in the process. The science of demonology had always been a science of psychology, for witch-hunting required the interrogator to probe the witch's motivations and gain her trust in order to provide an account of her life history and her deepest truths. But by the eighteenth century, the drama of witchcraft had become less cosmic. Instead, in the rare cases when it emerged, it assumed the character of an interior struggle, where the truth of private confession played a key role, and where the issues at stake concerned people's emotional relations to each other.

The final dimension in which Schmid's trial both compulsively repeated sixteenth-century themes and yet was unmistakably of its time was its sexual aspect. As had always been customary in such cases, the executioners had to wash the body of the suspect before torture and report on any diabolic marks.

In Schmid's case, they were then entrusted to undertake a second investigation, this time reporting not, as they had the first time, on the diabolic marks decently evident, but on her sexual parts. This too would not have been unusual in the sixteenth or seventeenth century. Another executioner from Bach, known to be skilled in matters of witchcraft, was called in to assist.[52] The three men noted that 'the, pardon the expression, shameful part was quite too great, too fatty and too swollen up for a 74 year old tough and thin woman, as if she had congress with a male person every day and night'.[53] Here was a woman past child-bearing age, who according to humoral theories of medicine should have been dried out, but who was sexual, lubricious, and equipped with organs which were well used. The executioners' descriptions convey the horror they felt – and the vivid detail they supplied in their report doubtless evoked revulsion in the minds of their hearers. In their view it was clear with whom Schmid was having intercourse: the Devil. This was classic witch fantasy. Time and again, it had been menopausal and post-menopausal women who were the targets of the witch-hunters. It was elderly women's infertile but sexual bodies which seem to have excited their persecutors' horror, fascination and disgust.

What was less usual was the course the case then took. The dynamic which shaped Schmid's interrogation was the relationship between mother and daughter itself. Most of the substance of Maria's interrogation concerned what she and her mother did in their shared bed. Maria described how her mother slept with a bolster down the middle of the bed, because her mother said she would not even let her husband so close. In response to detailed questioning, Maria described exactly what prayers her mother said before joining her in bed, how much later she came to bed, and where she kept her blessed amulets during the night. Repeatedly the questioning circled back to the scene of the two women in bed, the interrogators trying, at one point, to figure out whether both women could have fitted their diabolic lovers into the bed at once: did the bed hold four or three? So were there two diabolic lovers, one each; or did one Devil satisfy both women in different shapes? Or did he just lie first with one, then the other? Catharina was asked too about the bed and the two women's nocturnal rituals. What concerned the interrogators was how precisely diabolic sex had been possible; but the effect of such questioning was to concentrate the imagination of the hearers on the bed that held mother and daughter.

This relationship was what the interrogators finally exploited to push Schmid into enough of a confession to satisfy their needs; and it was the symbiotic relationship between the mother and daughter that overshadowed the final part of the trial. Even after she had admitted she was a witch, Catharina continued to insist on her innocence of just about every specific case of malevolence of which she was accused, vehemently defending her daughter, who she maintained knew nothing of her mother's diabolic double life. In January

1746, the interrogators brought Catharina to breaking point once again, this time pursuing a new line of questioning. They now probed in detail her daughter's illness and the visit of the barber–surgeon. Prefacing their remarks with a delicacy they had not shown when questioning her about sex with Caspar, her devil, they said 'One is ashamed to put such matters before a seventy-four-year-old woman, the defendant should confess whether she never committed the sin of the flesh with the barber-surgeon.' Catharina emphatically repudiated such a suggestion, exclaiming, 'Lord protect us! Sinning with the barber-surgeon, that would be quite something!'[54] But her interrogators insisted there were witnesses and finally named her daughter, bringing her into the room in person to repeat the allegations.

It was surely significant that the crucial incident concerned the aftermath of Maria's disfiguring illness, and her treatment by the barber-surgeon (who, Catharina averred, had not cured her daughter at all: St Tiberius, patron saint of the diocese and scourge of witches, had helped her). Unable to pay the barber the sum he demanded, Maria said, Catharina had tried to meet his bill with some cloth and some cash given to her by the court official. But, her daughter continued, she had also paid him with sex. When Maria had remonstrated with her mother, she had replied, 'Foolish girl, I owe the man much too much, I must shift so that I settle with him.' In front of her mother, Maria repeated the allegation: 'her mother had lifted up her petticoat and shirt, but the barber had opened his trousers and let them fall.' In confirmation of her story, Maria added a new detail. Next day, the barber had said to her 'her mother had such a shockingly large navel'.[55]

This was a pointed sexual insult. The barber, a man whose business it was to know about bodies, was disparaging the body of a woman he had just enjoyed; and he made his remark to her daughter, who was the fruit of that body. The words humiliated Maria as well as Catharina, casually letting her know for certain that he had had intercourse with her mother. In repeating the words, Catharina's daughter was effectively doing what the barber had done, uncovering her mother's nakedness and her shockingly large navel to the interrogators, just as the executioners had stripped her mother in their search for the Devil's marks. There was something riveting and appalling in the detail itself, the navel. This is why Maria mentions it; the unforgettable insult guaranteed that her story was true. The shockingly large navel might seem like an insinuation that this old woman had a large, slack vagina. But the revulsion actually communicated in the words the scribe and judges heard is revulsion from a woman who had a shocking hole in her stomach, where her womb should be. The navel was commonly held to be the place where a woman's seed was made: from there it went to the womb, where it would mix with the man's seed at conception. The barber, then, had sex with an old woman, whose womb could not bear children, and who had a monstrous hole in the wrong place.

Linking sex with stories about witchcraft was not novel: in Marchtal in the sixteenth century, one series of witchcraft allegations involving a single family had become merged with accusations of incest, and a violent robber and rapist from the same family had also confessed to witchcraft. But in those cases, almost nothing was said about incest itself, and the woman who admitted to incest with her father did not blame him. The 'real' episode of incest and the fantastic story of witchcraft with all its salacious seduction stories remained carefully separated from each other. By the eighteenth century, sex itself, as much as witchcraft, seems to be what propelled the progress of the case and began to provide an underlying explanation for behaviour, even while the idiom of the case remained that of witchcraft. And it was the dynamic of the relationship between mother and daughter, not witch and devil, that provided the psychological nub of the case. In this sense, too, witchcraft had become a family drama rather than a cosmic battle between good and evil. It thus pointed the way towards the beginnings of the science of psychology, even in conservative rural Swabia, as well as marking the return of the most vicious features of rigid Catholicism.

...

At her next and final interrogation alone before her condemnation, Catharina began by insisting on her daughter's innocence, but she soon capitulated. 'What her daughter said and for which she would pay with her life, she did not wish to alter any more. She would like to be able to take her girl with her to heaven, if her daughter confessed a lot she would not fight against it.'[56] Stubborn even in defeat, Catharina was insisting that she was bound for heaven, not for hell, and that her daughter's sufferings too would redound to the glory of God – and, by implication, to the eternal condemnation of her questioners. To her interrogators, this was impious nonsense, yet more diabolically inspired ravings of the 'stiff-necked woman' who would not bow her head to those set in authority over her.

It was also a vision of mother and daughter united forever, finally free of the village of Alleshausen. This was what the interrogation in fact finally accomplished. By the concluding interrogations, Catharina was complaining that she could no longer hear the questions that 'the lords' were putting to her. The court permitted Maria to attend her mother's interrogation, repeating the questions directly into her ear, for Maria was the only person Catharina could now understand. Mother and daughter stood side by side, two witches whispering their story in the interrogation chamber. There could hardly have been a more potent image of the symbiosis of the mother–daughter relationship, excluding every other human being and leading to death – or, to those who cared to see, a more moving testimony to the strength of maternal love.[57]

Epilogue

Any parent who reads 'Hansel and Gretel' aloud at bedtime knows what a disturbing story it is. Its climax comes when Gretel shoves an elderly woman into her own oven and burns her to death. Famed as the most German of all the fairy tales, it is also the cruellest of the Grimms' stories. The house of gingerbread, the witch who wants to fatten Hansel and gobble him up, the children left alone to die in the forest – all this is hardly soothing material for children about to go to sleep. And there is something particularly unsettling about the bone Hansel sticks out through the bars of his cage to trick the witch into thinking that he is not fattened yet: why should plump fingers prove the child is fat? And how can one forget the witch's obsessive feeling of the bone, slavering at the prospect of cooked child-flesh?

It was hard not to be reminded of the story of Hansel and Gretel at every turn as I worked on this book. The fairy tale is about a stepmother who abandons her children to die because times are hard, and a cannibalistic witch who builds a fantastic house of bread and cake to lure children to her lair. The witch sounds just like the old women who complimented children on their fine ruddy cheeks or gave them apples and titbits, only to watch them sicken and die. There is a creepy eroticism in the story about food, fattening and being eaten which recalls the oral and sexual sensuality in witches' confessions.

There are telling differences, though. During witch persecutions, it was legal authorities, not the witches' victims, who had old women burnt to death. They did so on the basis of accusations brought by their neighbours, even their kin. Here, the story carries a good deal of psychological truth. Gretel thinks she will be eaten by the witch, but in fact the child is the one who kills the old lady. The fairy tale mirrors the realities of witchcraft accusations in which those who feared the witch's power actually brought about her death. Eating babies was exactly what witches were believed to do, though in the story it is living rather than dead children who the witch wants to cook. And although the story we know today starts with a wicked stepmother, the original which the Grimm brothers collected was actually about a mother. The fairy tale, so it seems, puts its finger on precisely what the witch craze was about: mothers.

And yet this quintessentially German tale, which seems to reflect the witch-hunting mentality with such uncanny accuracy, may actually have been French in origin. When, in the early nineteenth century, the brothers Jakob and Wilhelm Grimm began gathering German fairy tales from oral informants, they drew on their own social circle as well. The original 'Hansel and Gretel' was almost certainly collected not from a peasant woman or servant, but from the urban sophisticated household of an apothecary, the Wild family. Dortchen Wild later married Wilhelm Grimm, and her mother was descended from Huguenot refugees. Certainly, the family knew the existing published fairy-tale collections very well and, like the brothers Grimm, were fascinated by the genre. 'Hansel and Gretel' owes more than a little to the French tale of Thumbling, which appeared in Charles Perrault's much earlier collection of 1697, where the royal children trick the ogre who plans to eat them into killing his own children by mistake. In Madame d'Aulnoy's 'Finette Cendron', published in her collection of the same year, the princess-heroine encounters a cannibalistic ogre couple. The husband appears with a whole basketful of children; but the resourceful Princess Finette chops off the head of the ogress and shoves the male ogre in an oven. A tale which ranges widely, it captures the petty jealousies of the court as Finette's sisters try to exclude her from the reward she has earned – it breathes the air of Versailles rather than the fug of the peasant fireside.[1]

'Hansel and Gretel' has no obvious German antecedents: when an oral version was collected, it was a reworked version of the published text. In the story of *Das Erdkühlein* from the Alsatian Martin Montanus's collection of tales from 1559, two children are cast out by an evil stepmother and leave pebbles to find their way back through the woods; the rest of his story, however, bears no relation to 'Hansel and Gretel'.[2] Yet whatever the history of the version we know today, 'Hansel and Gretel' certainly drew on old European-wide motifs connected with cannibalism. The story of the Greek god Kronos, who devours his own children, had entered European culture merged with that of his Roman counterpart Saturn, who was associated with the planet and with agriculture; and he appears in sixteenth- and seventeenth-century woodcuts as a terrifying figure consuming his offspring. Cannibalistic giants who feed on children featured in popular culture too. In Nuremberg, we know that carnival floats regularly included a giant fool eating children and little fools; while pictures of child-eating ogres were being used to scare children in the sixteenth century, circulating as cheap woodcuts. A male version of such an ogre even looks down at us today from a sixteenth-century pillar in a square in the Swiss city of Berne (ill. 66).[3] And the gingerbread house, which is not found in fairy tales before the nineteenth century, has its counterpart in the images of Schlaraffenland, the land of plenty where everything is edible.[4]

65. Berne monster:
Kindlifresser, c. 1545.

Fairy tales cross the genres of print and oral culture, learned and illiterate, and they circulated across Europe from the sixteenth century, beginning with collections like that of Martin Montanus and the tales of Giambattista Basile from the middle of the seventeenth century written in Neapolitan dialect. The nineteenth-century collections of fairy tales all owe a debt to Basile and to the seventeenth-century printed French versions of Charles Perrault and Madame d'Aulnoy. No one nation can claim a monopoly on the motifs out of which 'Hansel and Gretel' was born.[5]

The same is true of the idea of the witch. Demonology itself, after all, is a similar mixture of learned treatise, fable, oral tradition and the confessions of witches. Often, the stories that seem to be taken from the people turn out to be old chestnuts of demonology, classic exempla that every demonologist was forced by the existing literature to discuss. Like the fairy tale, demonology was the product of a republic of letters encompassing Italian, English, Spanish and especially German and French authors, and it was transmitted in Latin as well as in vernacular languages. We cannot now tease out the pure oral original tale from

66. Hans Weiditz,
Childscarer, c. 1520.

the literary accretions; and indeed, such a search would be misguided, because fairy tales, like demonologies, are nourished by the culture in which they grow.

The emergence of stories like 'Hansel and Gretel' as part of a new literature for children in the nineteenth century, building on the eighteenth-century children's didactic and moral tales, measures just how far we have travelled from the world of the witches. Earlier collections of fairy tales had not been designed for children, and Jakob Grimm, for one, remained uncomfortable with the change, wanting to preserve the relics of an oral culture in scholarly form. It was in 1810 that the Grimm brothers began collecting their fairy tales from oral informants, and the first volume of the tales appeared in 1812.[6] Gradually, as the brothers collected yet more tales, the character of the collection changed. Under the inspiration of the younger brother, Wilhelm, the volumes of the *Children's and Household Tales* became transformed into stories explicitly designed for children, and in 1825, Ludwig Emil Grimm provided illustrations for a small volume of selected texts: 'Hansel and Gretel' was included.[7] The modern fairy tale was born. Even the classic fairy tale style was an invention. Over time, Wilhelm learned how to craft that spare, archaic language, the repetitions and unforgettable details which make the stories such a delight to read aloud. 'Hansel and Gretel' as we know it today is the product of the nineteenth-century German middle class. The Grimms knew their market. The liberal bourgeoisie of the time lived in houses with separate nurseries, and they bought the toys and books to fit them out, creating an entire domain for children.

What happened when the audience became explicitly children, and nineteenth-century children at that, affected the meanings of the stories too. The themes of a story like 'Hansel and Gretel' are certainly those of the witch hunt, but now their terrors concern the more intimate familial tensions of mothers and stepmothers, and the witch has become a figure to stalk the imaginations of children. The Grimms worked and reworked the story in succeeding editions in line with the taste of their times. In early versions, the children are deserted by both their father and their mother; but this was too much for the German middle classes of the nineteenth century, with their reverence for the paterfamilias. Instead, the children were abandoned by their mother, soon toned down by the Grimms to their 'stepmother'.[8] The nature of the anxieties to which the stories of witches spoke had shifted too: middle-class German families did not face starvation and dearth on a regular basis and they no longer knew what it was like to be utterly dependent for their livelihood on the vagaries of the weather, unable to predict it with any accuracy.

The demographic regime that had underpinned belief in witchcraft gradually vanished. The iron grip of population control relaxed. This took a long time. In Germany, the freedom to marry regardless of one's social and economic status only became established in 1868–70, and well into the late nineteenth century people still delayed marriage. But by degrees the demographic regime changed character, and urbanization spread.[9] The household changed too. The mistress of the house was no longer everywhere a powerful figure lording it over a houseful of servants, journeymen and labourers. The middle-class matron became a feminine presence whose domestic domain was separate from that of her husband. By the last quarter of the eighteenth century, lying in ceased to be observed, and with it, the customs that once surrounded childbed withered. The moral codes of the Reformation and Counter-Reformation years, which punished fornication and adultery, forbade swearing and regulated dress, had fallen into disuse. They became matters of convention and education, not of law and politics. With their disappearance went the attempt to create a godly community and to rid the world of witches. The baroque imagination, which had made witches fearsome and required their actual death, had finally faded away.

'Hansel and Gretel' begins with the children being lost in the forest, and it is there that they discover the witch. The forest is a brooding presence in the story, a source of mystery and foreboding; and yet it is through the encounter with the forest that the children can overcome evil, win the treasure and master their fate. This, too, is of its times: the German love affair with the mystic forest was a creation of the Romantic era, part of the wholesale redis-covery of the sixteenth century. Artists like Caspar David Friedrich were fascinated by its melancholic isolation and its irrationality. They found in Dürer and Altdorfer the dark, twisted pines which could convey the menace of the Tacitean Teutonic Forest, cradle of the original martial German people. Sixteenth-century thinkers had also linked the original Germans with the forest through their reading of Tacitus, and they were fascinated by the idea of the Wild Man, the uncivilized, hairy creature who roams the woods. To place the witch in the forest, as 'Hansel and Gretel' does, was therefore to put her at the heart of the landscape of German identity.

All this would have been incomprehensible to people of the sixteenth and seventeenth centuries, for whom the forest was a place of savagery and danger.[10] They had viewed melancholy as the Devil's gateway, the chance for the Devil to trick the unwary into bargaining their soul away. In the nine-teenth century, religious passions no longer reached the pitch of intensity of the Reformation and Counter-Reformation, and politics was not a moral crusade driven by religious zeal. Instead, by the middle and end of the century, politics was fuelled by the imperatives of nationalism, the clamour of class and the need for an accommodation between the forces of conservatism and liber-alism.

Indeed, the Grimms' collection was part of the creation of a self-consciously 'German' culture, as, fired by the idea of a mythic past, artists and intellectuals tried to forge a new German nation on the ruins of the Holy Roman Empire. Fairy tales played an important part in shaping a Germanic culture which had to be at once new and authentic: Johann Karl August Musäus and Ludwig Tieck had also published such volumes in the late eighteenth century, and the Grimms themselves were part of the circle around the Romantic poets Clemens Brentano and Annette von Droste-Huelshoff. At first, their *Children's and Household Tales* was outsold by another collection, that of Ludwig Bechstein. Indeed, the Grimms' tales became famous partly by being incorporated in Heinrich Dittmar's readers for schoolchildren, and finally tri-umphed when, in the 1870s, they were chosen to become part of the new Prussian school curriculum.[11] So, far from being an authentic production of an autonomous Germanic culture of the people, their place in a new German culture for children was very carefully cultivated.[12]

The Grimms were of their time in their fascination with fairies, witches and the epoch before the Enlightenment. In 1808, the year after the Grimm brothers first began collecting fairy tales, Johann Wolfgang von Goethe pub-lished his *Faust* Part One. Like the Grimms, Goethe was returning to the

Germany of the sixteenth and seventeenth centuries for his artistic inspiration, and to the world of the witch hunt. Goethe's *Faust* became the classic German drama, the towering tragic epic which expresses the human condition in the modern world. It created modern German literature as we know it. But it does not celebrate the irrational and the magical as the fairy stories did. Literature for adults, it dramatizes a post-Enlightenment vision of the fundamental ambiguity of good and evil themselves.

Known in oral tradition, the story of the Lutheran theologian who makes a bargain with the Devil to obtain knowledge and power was first printed in German in 1587. It appeared in Frankfurt, where there was a lively market in books about the Devil. In 1586, the Frankfurt printer Nicolaus Basse brought out a bumper collection of demonological works, and a year later, Sigmund Feyerabend reissued a hefty *Theatre of Devils*, a fat compendium of republished moral tracts, each lampooning a particular sin and its devil. In its pages we encounter the Trousers Devil, who is shocked by the popular fashion for wide Turkish trousers, the She-man Devil, who is a poor henpecked husband, the Wine Devil, and so on. The original Faust, then, emerged from a lively literary tradition where demonology and moral tract met the literature of entertainment.[13] One and the same writer could pen works of both sorts. Johann Fischart, the immensely productive poet of Strasbourg, translated Rabelais into German, producing a gargantuan German epic several times the length of the French original, and turned his hand to Bodin's *Démonomanie*. The sixteenth-century Faust bears more than a passing resemblance to the devils of the Devil Books. He is guilty of the deadly sins: he gourmandizes, satisfies his carnal lusts with any woman who takes his fancy (supplied courtesy of the Devil) and he blasphemes against God. A student at Wittenberg, Luther's own university, he is a terrible warning against intellectual arrogance, against lovers of learning who sell their souls to the Devil.

The story of Faust also owes a good deal to the genre of writing about fools, and to the tradition of comic stories about the Devil, where peasants outwit Satan. Faust sells a pair of fine horses to a horse trader (a byword for duplicity then as now), and warns him never to ride them through water. Of course the new owner cannot resist trying this at the first opportunity – only to find himself sitting on two bales of straw. Furious, he rushes off to complain, and, finding Faust asleep, takes him by the leg. To his horror, the limb comes off in his hand and the terrified horse trader flees the scene, thinking he will be accused of murder. Faust meets a peasant one night in town driving a cart laden with animal fodder. He falls into mock negotiation with the peasant, asking what he will take to let him eat his fill. The peasant, playing along with the whim of the drunken, well-heeled townsman, agrees a price – only to gape with astonishment when Faust opens his mouth and consumes half the load.[14] These motifs all derive from earlier comic literature about crafty peasants: the difference is that Faust, the urban sophisticate, is craftier still. But Faust is also Everyman. He knows that he must fulfil his bargain and that the Devil will come for his soul. Terrified of his own end, he begs his beloved student companions to eat and drink with him one last time, and then sends them off to bed, knowing he must face the Devil on his own. He stands for all of us, for, as good Lutherans knew, we must each work out our salvation alone.

Goethe's drama is a creation of the dawning Romantic era. It breathes an entirely different ethos from the sixteenth-century work. *Faust* Part One is a tragedy, though one which retains echoes of the hybrid mixture of burlesque and seriousness which characterizes the sixteenth-century original. A major theme is the tragic unfolding of the relationship between Faust and Gretchen. A creation of Goethe's imagination, Gretchen has no counterpart in the *Faust* of 1587.[15] She is an image of innocent womanhood destroyed by her love for Faust. He callously seduces and then abandons Gretchen, who kills her baby, the fruit of their union. Her crime drives her into suicidal dementia, and only then does Faust begin to realize the full extent of his corruption of her. And it is her constant love for him despite all his faults which will eventually secure his redemption.

None of this would have made sense to a sixteenth-century audience. For them, passionate love could have no moral value and was more likely to be a disease caused by an enchantress's spell. They would have spared no tears for Gretchen, but would have regarded her as a child-killer whose dreadful crime merited death. It was not until the eighteenth century that pamphlets began to sympathize with the plight of the seduced and abandoned infanticidal mother. Instead, the middle of the sixteenth century saw the beginnings of a wave of executions for infanticide which reached its peak in the late seventeenth century. Goethe's *Faust* comes out of this new Enlightenment sensitivity to such women. Indeed, he himself had worked as a jurist in Frankfurt and followed the case of one such woman closely, the maid Susanna Margaretha Brandt, accused in 1771.[16]

Goethe also understood evil differently, seeing it as a profoundly ambiguous category. Mephistopheles is not so much an emissary of Satan as a being whose psychological acumen makes him seem almost an emanation of Faust's own personality. Where the 1587 original has Faust make a pact with the Devil, Goethe's Faust enters a bet with Mephistopheles. The wager is not about Faust giving up his soul in exchange for something the Devil offers, but about him surrendering life when he feels it is no longer of worth to him. Of course the dramatic power of this bargain lies in part in the way it turns the screw on the moral certainties of the sixteenth century: suicide was a sin which brought damnation, and the Devil would tempt those who suffered from melancholy to kill themselves in order to gain their soul.

When Goethe turns to witches, his creations lack the menace of Mephistopheles. Faust himself is unimpressed by the old witch who gives him the rejuvenating potion: she seems to him to speak rhyming nonsense, and though her enchantments work, the spells are comically naïve rather than ominous. Mephistopheles masterminds the action, providing a running commentary on the preparation of the liquid, and the witch is little more than his prop. The creatures Faust meets on his way up the Brocken to the Walpurgisnacht witches' sabbath are vehicles for Goethe's satirical talents: each one represents a politician or intellectual, and we now need a scholarly apparatus to identify them.

The original *Faust*, too, had almost nothing to say about witches. It also had little to say about women, who appear as no more than the phantasms supplied by the Devil to feed Faust's lust. Goethe's Gretchen embodies innocence and youth; the sixteenth and seventeenth centuries valued fertility. The culture of the German baroque was fascinated by the wheel of human fortune, the cycle of birth, ageing and death. It knew well the toll child-bearing took on women's bodies and its artists were pitiless in depicting its effects. Their women could not be youthful sources of redemption as they were for Goethe; the fount of evil, they believed, lay in Eve's physicality, the inheritance of all her daughters.

This preoccupation with the stories of the past was part of a wider cult of a lost golden age. In 1854, the elder of the Grimm brothers Jakob, published Volume 1 of his monumental project, the first proper historical dictionary of the German language.[17] The sixteenth century played a key role for the Grimms, because it was the German of Martin Luther that had created a national language. To compile a dictionary was to provide a national history of German culture that would set it apart from the Latinate tradition. This was why the Grimms were drawn to the period before the Enlightenment, and why their tales seem to recreate the world of the witch hunt. They wanted a culture that would be self-consciously distinct from the French and from the era of Napoleon; that would evoke the original Teutonic nature of the German people through a Romantic recuperation of myth.

Goethe was drawn to the materials of Faust throughout his creative life, and there is no single message that his drama conveys. He confronts us with a hero whose passionate striving is his undoing, but also his salvation. This is why that struggle was personified by a man. Gretchen embodies simplicity, and her femininity resides in her innocence. She lacks utterly Faust's driving intellectual ambition, and in that contrast lies the key to the tragic dynamic between them. Once she is corrupted by Faust, she loses her mind, descending into madness. In the era of the witch craze, the question of the nature of evil had circled around witches, old women and the terrors of childbed. Women's bodies dramatized the struggle between good and evil. Milk that did not flow, blasted crops, poisoned children – all were the signs that the Devil was at work in the world. This cosmic battle between the hosts of God and the Devil did not speak to the preoccupations of post-Enlightenment intellectuals.

But as men like Goethe or the Grimms evoked the lost world of the six-teenth and seventeenth centuries, the figure of the witch underwent a transformation. She was banished to the world of the nursery, where her tale became a nightmare version of the private core of the mother–child relation-ship, the primitive elements of hatred, cruelty, consuming love and abandonment that we find it hard to speak about otherwise. This is why the tale of Hansel and Gretel remains so disturbing and so popular. Meanwhile, the themes that the witch had once dramatized – the nature of evil, the threat to the future of generation itself, the possibility of salvation – could no longer be embodied by a woman. Instead, witchcraft, which had been a fusion of learned and popular culture, divided into the low tradition of Mother Goose and the high cultural heroism of Faust. This was also a sexual parting of the ways. As women became idealized, and as witchcraft retreated to the nursery, the emotions that surround motherhood became the territory of individual psychology rather than public threats to Christendom. The grand questions of good and evil, fate and destiny, were scripted for dramas in which men were the heroes. No longer a death-dealing harpy, the old woman was finally cut down to size, reduced to a bogey for frightening children.

Notes

Abbreviations

SAN   Staatsarchiv Nürnberg
SAS   Staatsarchiv Sigmaringen
SAW   Staatsarchiv Würzburg
SSBAugs   Staats- und Stadtbibliothek Augsburg
StadtAA   Stadtarchiv Augsburg
StadtAN   Stadtarchiv Nördlingen
Urg.   Urgicht
VD16   *Das Verzeichnis der im deutschen Sprachbereich erschienenen Drucke des 16. Jahrhunderts (VD16) . . .*, Stuttgart 1983— (in print and on-line form)
VD17   *Das Verzeichnis der im deutschen Sprachraum erschienenen Drucke des 17. Jahrhunderts* (in on-line form)

Prologue: The Witch at the Smithy

1. Candlemas in February, the feast of the Purification of the Virgin, counts as the end of the long ritual winter cycle. It was also believed to be a night on which witches held sabbaths. See Stephen Wilson, *The Magical Universe. Everyday Ritual and Magic in Pre-modern Europe*, London and New York 2000, pp. 25–50; Bob Scribner, *Popular Culture and Popular Movements in Reformation Germany*, London 1987, pp. 1–48; Scribner, *Religion and Culture in Germany (1400–1800)*, London 2001, pp. 302–22; and for England, Ronald Hutton, *The Triumph of the Moon. A History of Modern Pagan Witchcraft*, Oxford 1999; Hutton, *The Rise and Fall of Merry England. The Ritual Year 1400–1700*, Oxford 1994.
2. SAS, Dep. 30, Rep. VI, Pak. 254, Marchtaler Hexenprozesse 1581–1628 (1657), 3–23 March 1627, Ursula Götz.
3. See, for example, the influential interpretations of Keith Thomas, *Religion and the*

Decline of Magic, London 1971, Harmondsworth 1973; Alan Macfarlane, *Witchcraft in Tudor and Stuart England: A Regional and Comparative Study*, London 1970.

4. P.G. Maxwell-Stuart, ed. and trans., *Martin Del Rio. Investigations into Magic*, Manchester and New York 2000, pp. 118–19 (Bk 3, part 1, qu. 1). The *Disquisitiones* was first published in 1595 and the full work, dedicated to Prince-Archbishop Ernst of Bavaria, was published in three volumes between 1599 and 1600. Del Rio took his final vows as a Jesuit in 1600. Maxwell-Stuart, *Del Rio*, editor's Introduction.

5. Heinrich Kramer and James Sprenger, *The Malleus Maleficarum*, ed. and trans. Montague Summers, London 1928; New York 1971, p. 140 (Part II, qu. 1, ch. 13); Wolfgang Behringer and Günter Jerouschek, eds, *Der Hexenhammer*, trans. W. Behringer, G. Jerouschek and W. Tschacher, Munich 2000, p. 474: Kramer says the trial took place in the town of Thann in upper Alsace. Records of it do not survive. (It is now accepted that the book was written solely by Kramer; see Behringer et al., eds, *Der Hexenhammer*. The edition by Summers is deficient, and so all quotations are given in the modern German critical edition as well, which has an excellent scholarly apparatus.)

6. Johannes Geiler von Keisersberg, *Die Emeis*, Strasbourg, Johannes Grenninger, 1517, preached during Lent 1508, p. 47r. He added that women in childbed are often served by people who engage in all kinds of superstitious activities; and in a final dig against the costly practices of childbed festivities, he claimed that numerous visits in childbed only serve to strengthen such nonsense. I am grateful to Susan Karant Nunn for this reference.

7. Maxwell-Stuart, ed. and trans., *Del Rio*, p. 130 (Bk 3, part 1, qu. 4, section 8); Jean Bodin, *On the Demon-Mania of Witches* (1580) trans. and abridged Randy Scott, Toronto 1995, pp. 98 ff., Book 2.1.

8. On fantasy, see Jean Laplanche and Jean-Bertrand Pontalis, 'Fantasy and the Origins of Sexuality', in Victor Burgin, James Donald and Cora Kaplan, eds, *Formations of Fantasy*, London 1987.

9. Torture itself, however, was not finally abolished until many years later: in Bavaria, not until 1808, in Prussia, 1740, and in Austria, 1776: Brian Levack, *The Witch-Hunt in Early Modern Europe*, London and New York 1987, 2nd edn, 1995; Wolfgang Behringer, *Witchcraft Persecutions in Bavaria. Popular Magic, Religious Zealotry and Reason of State in Early Modern Europe*, trans. J. Grayson and David Lederer, Cambridge 1997, pp. 386–7.

10. For a brilliant account of the intellectual break-up of beliefs about witches, see Jonathan Israel, *Radical Enlightenment. Philosophy and the Making of Modernity 1650–1750*, Oxford 2001, pp. 374–405.

11. Behringer, *Witchcraft Persecutions*, p. 387.

12. Ibid., pp. 355–87.

Chapter 1: The Baroque Landscape

1. This point is powerfully made in Wolfgang Behringer, *Hexen. Glaube, Verfolgung, Vermarktung*, Munich 1998.

2. William Monter, 'Witch Trials in Continental Europe 1560–1660', in Bengt Ankarloo, Stuart Clark and William Monter, *Witchcraft and Magic in Europe*, Volume 4: *The Period of the Witch Trials* (Bengt Ankarloo and Stuart Clark, eds, *The Athlone History of Witchcraft and Magic in Europe*, 6 vols, London 1999—), London 2002, pp. 32–3; on appeals, see Gerhard Schormann, 'Die Haltung des Reichskammergerichts in

Hexenprozessen', Hartmut Lehmann and Otto Ulbricht, eds, *Vom Unfug des Hexen-Processes. Gegner der Hexenverfolgungen von Johann Weyer bis Friedrich Spee*, Wiesbaden 1992. Criminal jurisdiction did not always coincide with political authority. In the territory of Würzburg, the areas where supreme authority in criminal jurisdiction (including witchcraft cases) was held by Würzburg extended beyond the area under its political sovereignty.

3. Jeffrey Chipps Smith, *Sensuous Worship. Jesuits and the Art of the Early Catholic Reformation in Germany*, Princeton 2002, pp. 57–76.

4. Martin Luther's German Bible, Revelations 17,Wittenberg 1547 edn.

5. For a general overview of the European witch-hunt, see Behringer, *Hexen*, and Brian Levack, *The Witch-Hunt in Early Modern Europe*, London and New York 1987; and Ankarloo et al., *Witchcraft and Magic in Europe*, vol. 4: *The Period of the Witch Trials*, and amongst the excellent local German studies, see in particular Eva Labouvie, *Zauberei und Hexenwerk. Ländlicher Hexenglaube in der Frühen Neuzeit*, Frankfurt am Main 1991; Rainer Walz, *Hexenglaube und magische Kommunikation im Dorf der Frühen Neuzeit*, Paderborn 1993; Walter Rummel, *Bauern, Herren und Hexen. Studien zur Sozialgeschichte spohheimischer und kurtrierischer Hexenprozesse 1574–1664*, Göttingen 1991; Wolfgang Behringer, *Witchcraft Persecutions in Bavaria. Popular Magic, Religious Zealotry and Reason of State in Early Modern Europe*, trans. J. Grayson and David Lederer, Cambridge 1997; Günter Jerouschek, *Die Hexen und ihr Prozeß. Die Hexenverfolgung in der Reichsstadt Esslingen* (Esslinger Studien vol. 1), Esslingen 1992; Jürgen Michael Schmidt, *Glaube und Skepsis. Die Kurpfalz und die abendländische Hexenverfolgung 1446–1685*, Gütersloh 2000; Johannes Dillinger, *'Böse Leute'. Hexenverfolgungen in Schwäbisch-Österreich und Kurtrier im Vergleich*, Trier 1999.

6. Susanna Burghartz, 'The Equation of Women and Witches', in R.J. Evans, ed., *The German Underworld*, London 1988; Alfred Soman, 'The Parlement of Paris and the Great Witch Hunt (1565–1640)', *Sixteenth Century Journal* 9, 1978, pp. 31–44; E.W. Monter, 'Toads and Eucharists: The Male Witches of Normandy, 1564–1660', *French Historical Studies* 20, 1997, pp. 563–95.

7. See, on these themes in England, Diane Purkiss, *The Witch in History. Early Modern and Twentieth-century Representations*, London 1996, Marion Gibson, *Reading Witchcraft. Stories of Early English Witches*, London 1999, Malcolm Gaskill, 'Women, Witchcraft and Power in Early Modern England: The Case of Margaret Moore', in Jenny Kermode and Garthine Walker eds, *Women, Crime and the Courts in Early Modern England*, London 1994; for Italy, Ruth Martin, *Witchcraft and the Inquisition in Venice 1550–1650*, Oxford 1989, Franco Nardon, *Benandanti e inquisitori nel Friuli del seicento*, Trieste 1999, Guido Ruggiero, *Binding Passions. Tales of Magic, Marriage, and Power at the End of the Renaissance*, New York and Oxford 1993.

8. See, amongst others, Thomas DaCosta Kaufmann, *Court, Cloister & City. The Art and Culture of Central Europe 1450–1800*, London 1995, pp. 166–334; Robert Harbison, *Reflections on Baroque*, London 2000; Germain Bazin, *Baroque and Rococo*, London 1964, 1998; Susan James, *Passion and Action. The Emotions in Seventeenth-century Philosophy*, Oxford 1997; Marc R. Forster, *Catholic Revival in the Age of the Baroque. Religious Identity in Southwest Germany, 1550–1750*, Cambridge 2001.

9. Sebastian Franck, *Weltbuch, spiegel vnd bildniss des gantzen erdtbodens*, Tübingen, V Morhart, 1534.

10. Wolfgang Behringer, 'Weather, Hunger and Fear: Origins of the European Witch Hunts in Climate, Society and Mentality', *German History* 13, 1993, pp. 1–27; Andrew Cunningham and Ole Peter Grell, *The Four Horsemen of the Apocalypse. Religion, War, Famine and Death in Reformation Europe*, Cambridge 2000.

11. *Die Peinliche Gerichtsordung Kaiser Karls V. von 1532 (Carolina)*, ed. Gustav Radbruch, revised by Arthur Kaufmann, Stuttgart 1975; Sönke Lorenz, 'Der Hexenprozess' in Lorenz, ed., *Hexen und Hexenverfolgung im deutschen Südwesten*, Karlsruhe 1994.

12. Wolfgang Behringer, *Mit dem Feuer vom Leben zum Tod. Hexengesetzgebung in Bayern*, Munich 1988.

13. Quentin Skinner, *The Foundations of Modern Political Thought*, 2 vols, Cambridge 1978, pp. 284 ff.

14. Jean Bodin, *Démonomanie des sorciers*, Paris 1580, fo. 11v; trans. from Randy Scott, *On the Demon-Mania of Witches* (abridged), Toronto 1995; and see on Bodin, William Monter, 'Inflation and Witchcraft: The Case of Jean Bodin', and Sydney Anglo, 'Melancholie and Witchcraft: The Debate between Wier, Bodin and Scot', in Brian Levack, ed., *The Literature of Witchcraft*, 12 vols, New York and London 1992, vol. 4.

15. Heinrich Kramer and James Sprenger, *The Malleus Maleficarum*, trans. and ed. Revd Montague Summers, London 1928; New York 1971, Part III, qu. 15, pp. 228–32; Wolfgang Behringer and Günter Jerouschek, eds, *Der Hexenhammer*, trans. W. Behringer, G. Jerouschek and W. Tschacher, Munich 2000, pp. 678–86; and note that there are two question 15s in the original.

16. Nicolas Rémy, *Demonolatry*, ed. and trans. Revd Montague Summers, London 1930, pp. 93–4 (Bk II, ch. ii).

17. Rémy's *Demonolatry* was published in Lyons in 1595 in Latin and issued in the following year at Cologne and Frankfurt; a German translation appeared in Frankfurt in 1598 as *Daemonolatria. Das ist Von Unholden und Zaubergeistern ...* (*Verzeichnis der im deutschen Sprachraum erschienenen Drucke des XVI. Jahrhunderts*, 25 vols, Stuttgart 1983–2000, nos R1090, R1091, R1092; R1093) and was extremely influential in the Holy Roman Empire, possibly even more so than the *Malleus*, Rolf Schulte, *Hexenmeister. Die Verfolgung von Männern im Rahmen der Hexenverfolgung von 1530–1730 im Alten Reich*, 1999; 2nd expanded edn, Frankfurt am Main 2001, pp. 141–3; Jean Bodin's *Démonomanie des sorciers* was translated by Johann Fischart as *Vom Außgelaßnen Wütigen Teuffels heer Allerhand Zauberern/ Hexen vnd Hexenmeistern/ Vnholden/ Teuffels beschwerern/ Warsager etc.*, in 1581 (see Stefan Janson, *Jean Bodin, Johann Fischart: De la démonomanie des sorciers (1580), Vom ausgelassnen wütigen Teuffelsheer (1581) und ihre Fallberichte*, Frankfurt am Main 1980 (Europäische Hochschulschriften 352); I have used the edition of 1586); Peter Binsfeld's *Tractat Von Bekantnuß der Zauberer und Hexen* appeared in German in 1590 (*VD16*, nos. B5531, B5532); Johannes Georg Gödelmann's Latin work of 1591 appeared in German as *Von Zauberern Hexen und Unholden* translated by Georg Nigrinus at Frankfurt in 1592, with the printer Nicolaus Basse who also published the demonological collection, *Theatrum de veneficis* (*VD16*, nos G2486, G2488).

18. See Wolfgang Behringer, 'Falken und Tauben. Zur Psychologie deutscher Politiker im 17. Jahrhundert', in R. Po-Chia Hsia and R.W. Scribner, eds, *Problems in the Historical Anthropology of Early Modern Europe* (Wolfenbütteler Forschungen 78), Wiesbaden 1997. On the role of particular individuals in the Cologne persecutions, jurists amongst them, see Gerhard Schormann, *Der Krieg gegen die Hexen. Das Ausrottungsprogramm des Kurfürsten von Köln*, Göttingen 1992, pp. 68–83; 169–80.

19. Martina Schmid, 'Die Biberacher Scharfrichter', in Sönke Lorenz, ed., *Hexen und Hexenverfolgung im deutschen Südwesten*, Ostfildern bei Stuttgart 1994; Wolfgang Behringer, *Witchcraft Persecutions*, pp. 126 ff.

20. One of the interesting features of the Bavarian case is that the zealots lost in the end. Though a comprehensive mandate against witchcraft was published, no major witch hunts took place after it was issued: Behringer, *Witchcraft Persecutions*, pp. 230–301.

21. Westerstetten presided over probably around a thousand deaths over the course of his career. Behringer, *Hexen*, pp. 56–7 for a handy table of the worst witch-hunters in Germany; and Ankarloo et al., *Witchcraft and Magic in Europe*, vol. 4.

22. On the campaign against Protestants, Götz Freiherr von Pölnitz, *Julius Echter von Mespelbrunn. Fürstbischof von Würzburg und Herzog von Franken (1573–1617)* (Schriftenreihe zur bayerischen Landesgeschichte 17), Munich 1934, pp. 360, 364, 377, 379, 384–430; on building programme pp. 420–3; on administrative reforms, Friedrich Merzbacher, 'Fürstbischof Julius Echter von Mespelbrunn als Gesetzgeber', in *Recht – Staat – Kirche. Ausgewählte Aufsätze*, Vienna 1989, pp. 446–508, Heinzjürgen Reuschling, *Die Regierung des Hochstifts Würzburg 1495–1642. Zentralbehörden und führende Gruppen eines geistlichen Staates*, Würzburg 1984; on the hospital, which was built on the site of the Jewish cemetery and synagogue despite the vigorous protests of the Jewish community, Pölnitz, *Julius Echter*, pp. 283–92; Gottfried Mälzer, *Julius Echter. Leben und Werk*, Würzburg 1989, pp. 36–43; and pp. 78, 92 for the title page of the volume celebrating Echter's thirty-year reign in 1603. The hospital foundation drew indirectly on the model of Lutheran Hesse's two state-run hospitals, built out of the proceeds of expropriating the monasteries, which had also offered refuge for the mentally ill and their families; the Nuremberg City Council gave architectural advice. Louise Gray, 'The Self-perception of Chronic Physical Incapacity among the Labouring Poor. Pauper Narratives and Territorial Hospitals in Early Modern Rural Germany', Ph.D. diss., University of London, 2001; H.C. Erik Midelfort, *A History of Madness in Sixteenth-Century Germany*, Stanford 1999, esp. pp. 366–8 (including reproduction of oil painting of the hospital).

23. These 300 individuals were supposedly executed in one year, 1617. Our source for this figure is the chronicle of the cloth-cutter Jacob Röder, which states that it was proclaimed from the pulpit that 300 witches and magicians had been burnt in that year. Merzbacher, *Die Hexenprozesse in Franken*, p. 45; pamphlets also spread news of the numbers; see *Zwo Hexen Zeitung*, published at Tübingen in 1616, which reports both the Württemberg and Würzburg executions, title page reproduced in Weiß, 'Die Hexenprozesse', p. 335.

24. Götz Freiherr von Pölnitz, *Fürstbischof Julius Echter von Mespelbrunn* (Mainfränkische Hefte 36), Würzburg 1959, p. 20 for banishing of female relatives from court; Friedrich Merzbacher, *Die Hexenprozesse in Franken*, 1957; 2nd edn, Munich 1970, p. 47; Pölnitz claims that Echter personally checked and read the witches' confessions: Pölnitz, *Julius Echter*, p. 303; and that he intervened in one case where he felt that the trial had not been properly conducted, p. 305. He did try to limit the sufferings of those executed by ensuring they were not burnt alive. See also on the Würzburg trials, Elmar Weiß, 'Die Hexenprozesse im Hochstift Würzburg', in Peter Kolb and Ernst-Günter Krenig, eds, *Unterfränkische Geschichte. Band 3: Vom Beginn des konfessionellen Zeitalters bis zum Ende des Dreißigjährigen Krieges*, Würzburg 1995, pp. 327–62; Christel Beyer, '*Hexen-Leut, so zu Würzburg gerichtet'. Der Umgang mit Sprache und Wirklichkeit in Inquisitionsprozessen wegen Hexerei*, Frankfurt am Main 1981 (Deutsche Hochschulschriften, I, Deutsche Sprache und Literatur 948).

25. About thirty children from the orphanage in the Juliusspital were caught up in the trials, a process which may have been strengthened by the practice of placing children suspected of witchcraft in the orphanage. Children also played roles in some of the other Würzburg cases: Weiß, 'Die Hexenprozesse', pp. 350–2. See also Merzbacher, *Die Hexenprozesse in Franken*, pp. 45–8, and Robert Walinski-Kiel, 'The Devil's Children: Child Witch-Hunts in Early Modern Germany', *Continuity and Change* 11, 1996, pp. 171–90.

26. On Loudun, see Sarah Ferber, *Demonic Possession and Exorcism in Early Modern France*, London 2004, Michel de Certeau, *The Possession at Loudun*, 1970; trans. Michael B. Smith, Chicago 1996, 2000, Aldous Huxley, *The Devils of Loudun*, London 1952, and Moshe Sluhovsky, 'The Devil in the Convent', *American Historical Review* 107, 2002, pp. 1379–411.

27. These cases began in earnest in September 1628. Clerics made up half the victims of the executions of the thirtieth to forty-second burnings: Weiß, 'Die Hexenprozesse', pp. 349 ff; Harald Schwillus, *Kleriker im Hexenprozeß. Geistliche als Opfer der Hexenprozesse des 16. und 17. Jahrhunderts in Deutschland*, Würzburg 1992; Schwillus, '"Der bischoff lässt nit nach, bis er die gantze statt verbrennt hat"', *Würzburger Diözesangeschichtsblätter* 49, 1987, pp. 145–54; Schwillus, 'Die Hexenprozesse gegen Würzburger Geistliche unter Fürstbischof Philipp Adolf von Ehrenberg (1623–31)', Diplomarbeit, Bayerische Julius-Maximilians-Universität Würzburg 1987; Elmar Weiß, 'Hexenwahn, Hexenjagd und Hexenprozesse', in Weiß et al., eds, *Geschichte der Brunnenstadt Külsheim*, 2 vols, Külsheim 1992, pp. 130–41.

28. Merzbacher, *Die Hexenprozesse in Franken*, p. 49; Leibniz is the source of the story that Bishop Schönborn of Würzburg asked Spee why he had so many white hairs so young; and Spee replied that this came from the witches, for he had been persuaded of the guilt of none of those he had accompanied to execution: Georg Schwaiger, 'Das Ende der Hexenprozesse im Zeitalter der Aufklärung', in Schwaiger, ed., *Teufelsglaube und Hexenprozesse*, Munich 1988, p. 155.

29. For Echter's programme of education, see also John Doney, 'Reform and the Enlightened Catholic State: Culture and Education in the Prince-Bishopric of Würzburg', Ph.D. diss., Emory University, 1989, esp. pp. 263–83: it is significant that the Landkapitel of Gerolzhofen, which was one of the worst centres of the witch hunt, was also an area where little progress had been made in schooling. In 1612, a visitation noted that only 22 of the 74 communities had schools at all, and most were not well attended. The witch hunt there may have been part of an attempt to at least increase central control, where institutions were weak. On courts, see Hermann Knapp, *Die Zenten des Hochstifts Würzburg. Ein Beitrag zur Geschichte des süddeutschen Gerichtswesens und Strafrechts*, 2 vols, Berlin 1907, Beyer, '*Hexen-leut*', Weiß, 'Die Hexenprozesse', Dietmar Willoweit, 'Gericht und Obrigkeit im Hochstift Würzburg', in Kolb and Krenig, eds, *Unterfränkische Geschichte*; on local government and court systems, see Hildegunde Flurschutz, *Die Verwaltung des Hochstifts Würzburg unter Franz Ludwig von Erthal (1779–1795)* (Veröffentlichungen der Gesellschaft für fränkische Geschichte, Reihe IX, Darstellungen aus der fränkischen Geschichte, 19), Würzburg 1965; Ernst Schubert, *Die Landstände des Hochstifts Würzburg* (Veröffentlichungen der Gesellschaft für fränkische Geschichte, Reihe IX, Darstellungen aus der fränkischen Geschichte, 19), Würzburg 1967.

30. Würzburg's population grew from 9,300 in 1575 to 11,500 in 1617 under Bishop Echter, while middling-sized towns like Gerolzhofen, Ochsenfurt, Karlstadt and Lohr probably numbered between 1,000 and 3,000 inhabitants: Winfried Schenk, 'Die mainfränkische Landschaft unter dem Einfluß von Gewerbe, Handel, Verkehr und Landwirtschaft', in Kolb and Krenig, eds, *Unterfränkische Geschichte*, pp. 558–9.

31. SAW, Domkapitelprotokolle 1627, fo. 18v, 9 Jan. 1627; Domkapitelprotokolle 1617, fo. 197v: see also 108r, 160r, 181v: the woman confessed, and asked for her life, because she had only got into the sect recently. She had been seduced two years earlier.

32. SAW, Domkapitelprotokolle 1627, fo. 90v, 14 April 1627: 'Hilff wider Jhre Nahrungs feindt, vnnd vngezieffer vnnd Hexenwerckh'. Divine intervention and poor harvest had also featured in a miracle at Mühlbach near Karlstadt in Würzburg territory during the

bitter years of the 1590s, when a poor pig-herd with a starving family came upon some flour in the woods. The miracle was celebrated in a woodcut: Walter Strauss, *The German Single-Leaf Woodcut 1550–1600*, 3 vols, New York 1975, vol. 2, p. 494, Bartholomäus Käppeler.

33. This woman's husband had made off with all the couple's money: when caught gambling, he explained 'because his wife had been so long in prison, and he had managed his housekeeping so miserably, he just wanted to be happy once'. Unfortunately for him, he was found in bed at an inn with a woman of loose morals. SAW, Domkapitelprotokolle 1627, fos. 95v, 98r, 112v, 113r, 120r, 132r, 148r, 182r–3r, 200r (22 April 1627–31 Aug. 1627): 'weiln sein weib so lang in genfengnuss gesessen, vnnd Er ein so traurige hausshaltung gefuehrt, einmal lustig zusein'.

34. In Würzburg, as in all mass panics, denunciations by other witches began to count as one of the major sources of evidence against witch suspects. Even so, Würzburg's authorities still tried to operate according to legal systems: they determined that three denunciations should be sufficient to confirm suspicion against an individual; but they also (in line with the provisions of the Carolina) looked for material evidence before a suspect could be imprisoned. See Beyer, '*Hexen-Leut*', p. 177; and see SAW, Gerolzhofen 346 for lists of denunciations of this kind, where one can sense the record-keeper's indecision about how to compile and control the material. The sheer technical difficulties of cross-referencing masses of names created massive problems of information management. In this way, the witch hunt contributed to the sophistication of bureaucratic techniques.

35. SAW, Historischer Verein, f. 20.

36. Merzbacher, *Die Hexenprozesse in Franken*, p. 52; Behringer, *Witchcraft Persecutions* pp. 346, 357–9.

37. SAW, Misc. 2897, 'einen verworrenen Einbiltungs- Kraft und schwäche des Verstands deutlich bermerckht worden'.

38. The witch hunt in Würzburg still awaits its modern historian, and it is beyond the scope of this book to chronicle its history. Excellent recent studies on aspects of the hunt there have been made by Beyer, Schwillus, Walinski-Kiel and Weiß.

39. On the trials, see Robert Dengler, 'Das Hexenwesen im Stifte Obermarchtal von 1581–1756', Ph.D. diss., Erlangen, 1953, H.C. Erik Midelfort, *Witch Hunting in South-western Germany 1562–1684. The Social and Intellectual Foundations*, Stanford 1972, pp. 96–8; on the territory, see *Kreisbeschreibungen des Landes Baden-Württemberg. Der Landkreis Biberach*, 2 vols, Sigmaringen 1987, vol. 1, pp. 111–12 for description of the history of the extent of the territory; and see also *Kartenbeilagen. Statistischer Anhang*, esp. Map 6; and Max Müller, Rudolf Reinhardt and Wilfried Schöntag, eds, *Marchtal. Prämonstratenserabtei. Fürstliches Schloß. Kirchliche Akademie*, Ulm 1992.

40. Dengler, 'Das Hexenwesen', p. 104, for population estimate, which he arrives at using the figures of Abbot Kneer from 1634; my total numbers of executions for both the sixteenth and seventeenth centuries are lower than those of Dengler, who occasionally confuses individuals or adds those cases in the file guilty of crimes other than witchcraft.

41. The old study by Dengler, 'Das Hexenwesen', lists ten cases for the years 1627–57. However, this is misleading. His case numbered 69 'Ursula Schmidt' is in fact identical with Ursula Götz, case numbered 65. Christina Krügner (no. 70) is not from the area, and Jacob Miller's case, 71, for which we have only a condemnation to death, is not necessarily connected to witchcraft at all, as Dengler admits. The trial of Martin Getz concerns bestiality. All these cases occurred in 1627. The case of the boy Hans Hildebrandt (1657) is an isolated incident, so far as we know, not part of a hunt lasting thirty years.

42. Because of the sheer size of the Würzburg trials, it is very difficult to calculate numbers or to establish relationships between the victims. To calculate ages and gender ratios, I have therefore, first, taken a subset of the Würzburg trials, those from Gerolzhofen, and drawn from the material compiled by the Hexensonderkommando, a group of researchers under the SS: see, on the history of this extraordinary collection, Gerhard Schormann, *Hexenprozesse in Deutschland*, Göttingen 1981, pp. 8–16; and Sönke Lorenz, ed., *Himmlers Hexenkartothek. Das Interesse der Nationalsozialismus an der Hexenverfolgung* (Hexenforschung, vol. 4), 2nd edn, Bielefeld 2000; and on its weaknesses, Gerhard Schormann, 'Wie entstand die Kartothek, und wem war sie bekannt?', and Wolfgang Behringer, 'NS Historiker und Archivebeamte im Kampf mit den Quellen. Das Beispiel der Archive Bayerns', in Lorenz, *Himmlers Hexenkartothek*. These can only be rough figures because of errors inherent in the materials compiled by the SS researchers; often the same victim is counted separately under a different name, and so on; but the alphabetization of the names, and the researchers' attempts to record relationships wherever possible, allows us to at least explore the question. The Hexensonderkommando figures for the area under the jurisdiction of Gerolzhofen (within Würzburg) yield totals of 448 women and 93 men tried. In Gerolzhofen, men therefore made up 20.7 per cent of those tried, which accords with the general average of between 20 and 25 per cent in Europe.

   Of the 93 male victims, 38 had close female relatives who were tried for witchcraft. This is certainly an underestimate of the total, because the records do not always indicate whether a female relative had been executed for witchcraft: interestingly, a further 18 men had the same surname as an executed woman. We know that at least 22 of the men were related to other men executed for witchcraft (and another 15 had the same surname). In the Gerolzhofen cases, the pattern seems to be that men were often accused when their female relatives had been accused. Family connections amongst those men accused – even when we do not know of an accused female relative – are very striking (figures computed from Staatsarchiv Koblenz, F215–Zsg.2/1–f (Films), Film No. 17, Gerolzhofen A–Z).

   The same pattern emerges if we take a different subset of the whole Würzburg trials, those where the age of the accused is given: 255 cases, 65 of which concerned men (around 25 per cent). The majority of these cases clearly involved men who were related to women executed as witches, and many of them were men caught up in the witch trials around a decade after the executions of their wives. (Figures computed from Staatsarchiv Koblenz, F215–Zsg.2/1–f (Films), Film No. 62, which contains the 'rough' unalphabeticized and unorganized archival summaries for the whole of the Würzburg archival records, without consideration of the political jurisdictions.)

43. Schwillus, *Kleriker im Hexenprozeß*, p. 28: *Neue Zeitung* 1629.

44. The cases of the clergy have been explored in Harald Schwillus, *Kleriker im Hexenprozeß*, pp. 9–86; and Elmar Weiß, 'Würzburger Kleriker als Angeklagte in Hexenprozessen in den Jahren 1626–1630', *Mainfränkisches Jahrbuch* 40, 1988, pp. 70–94: once individual clergy were interrogated, they named more clergy; while other clerics were denounced because their maids were suspected. There was evidently a preparedness amongst those involved in the trials to believe that clergy could succumb to witchcraft. On the children, Walinski-Kiel, 'The Devil's Children'; and see Weiß, 'Die Hexenprozesse'. (It is also interesting to note that rural mayors and their families were also particularly targeted, a pattern similar to the involvement of clerics and male members of the town elite.) Both these panics, dwarfed by probably over a thousand victims in the 'main' panic, seem to me to

form separate incidents. (Figures computed from Staatsarchiv Koblenz, F215–Zsg.2/ 1–f (Films), Film No. 44.)

45. From the figures for Marchtal, I have excluded the case of Martin Getz, who was guilty of bestiality. SAS, Dep. 30, Rep. VI, Pak. 254, 255.

46. The question of why men were persecuted for witchcraft has been explored by Schulte, *Hexenmeister:* he suggests that higher proportions of men may have been tried for witchcraft in Catholic areas; and examines the link between suspicion of witchcraft and particular craftsmen, such as shepherds and beggars, and the attitudes of demonologists to male witchcraft. Midelfort also suggested that men started to be accused in mass panics as the stereotype of the witch began to break down, which would explain many of the Würzburg cases: Midelfort, *Witch Hunting in Southwestern Germany*. But not every case fits this model. See also Eva Labouvie, 'Men in Witchcraft Trials: Towards a Social Anthropology of "Male" Understandings of Magic and Witchcraft', in Ulinka Rublack, ed., *Gender in Early Modern German History*, Cambridge 2002; on differences in male and female uses of magic, Eva Labouvie, 'Perspektivenwechsel. Magische Domänen von Frauen und Männern in Volksmagie und Hexerei aus der Sicht der Geschlechtergeschichte', in Ingrid Ahrendt-Schulte, Dieter Bauer, Sönke Lorenz and Jürgen Michael Schmidt, eds, *Geschlecht, Magie und Hexenverfolgung* (Hexenforschung vol. 7), Bielefeld 2002; on the connection between legal processes, social roles and the different routes by which men became accused of witchcraft, Ingrid Ahrendt-Schulte, 'Die Zauberschen und ihr Trommelschläger. Geschlechtsspezifische Zuschreibungsmuster in lippischen Hexenprozessen', in Ahrendt-Schulte et al., eds, *Geschlecht, Magie und Hexenverfolung*; and on the connection between male witches and gravediggers, Karen Lambrecht, 'Tabu und Tod. Männer als Opfer frühneuzeitlicher Verfolgungswellen', ibid. See also Lara Apps and Andrew Gow, *Male Witches in Early Modern Europe*, Manchester 2003, for a different and polemical view. Some famous cases concerned powerful individuals: the mayor of Bamberg, Johannes Junius, for example, whose letter to his daughter from prison has survived: Alan Kors and Edward Peters, eds, *Witchcraft in Europe, 400–1700*, 2nd edn, Philadelphia 2001, pp. 348–53. In some village cases, as Labouvie points out in 'Men in Witchcraft Trials', the victims were richer, more powerful villagers whose success was believed to relate to witchcraft; another group consisted of older men who had 'violated masculine roles and patterns of behaviour in some way' (p. 60) and they were more frequently concerned with regulating power in the community. It is clear that trials of men involved slightly different issues; and as Dillinger has pointed out, part of the power of the paradigm of witchcraft was that it could always be applied to different groups and was never equated with a single sociological category: Dillinger, *'Böse Leute'*, esp. pp. 184–233. However, it also seems clear in the cases I have explored that being related to an accused woman was one major factor, though not the only one, that might explain the accusations of men. (Occasionally, it was the case against the man that precipitated the accusation against the woman; this seems to have happened in the sole Nördlingen example.)

47. See, for example, David Sabean, *Power in the Blood. Popular Culture and Village Discourse in Early Modern Germany*, Cambridge 1984, esp. pp. 174–98, for this kind of bureaucratic puzzlement.

48. A. Bechtold, 'Beiträge zur Geschichte der Würzburger Hexenprozesse', *Frankenkalender* 53, 1940, pp. 117–29, 'Die schickelte Amfrau. NB. Von der kommt das ganze Unwesen her', p. 121.

49. On Augsburg, see Bernd Roeck, *Eine Stadt in Krieg und Frieden. Studien zur Geschichte der Reichsstadt Augsburg zwischen Kalenderstreit und Parität*, 2 vols, Göttingen 1989, Lyndal Roper, *The Holy Household. Women and Morals in Reformation Augsburg*, Oxford 1989, Leonhard Lenk, *Augsburger Bürgertum im Späthumanismus und Frühbarock (1580–1700)*, Augsburg 1968, Eugen Liedl, *Gerichtsverfassung und Zivilprozess der freien Reichsstadt Augsburg*, Augsburg 1958, Ingrid Bàtori, *Die Reichsstadt Augsburg im 18. Jahrhundert: Verfassung, Finanzen und Reformversuche*, Göttingen 1969, Etienne François, *Die unsichtbare Grenze. Protestanten und Katholiken in Augsburg, 1648–1806*, Sigmaringen 1991, Paul Warmbrunn, *Zwei Konfessionen in einer Stadt: Das Zusammenleben von Katholiken und Protestanten in den paritätischen Reichstädten Augsburg, Biberach, Ravensburg und Dinkelsbühl*, Wiesbaden 1983, Günter Gottlieb et al., eds, *Geschichte der Stadt Augsburg von der Römerzeit bis zur Gegenwart*, Stuttgart 1984.

50. See, on this case, Roeck, *Eine Stadt in Krieg und Frieden*, vol. 2, pp. 539–53.

51. Behringer, *Witchcraft Persecutions*, pp. 45–7, 122–9.

52. Sources of this kind allow for a clearer glimpse of what we might call 'subjectivity', that is, the way people make sense of their experience individually; and they enable us to construct the background of cases and the biographies of individuals in far greater detail than do the summary records of Würzburg or sixteenth-century Marchtal. For interpretations of witchcraft accusations which set them within the context of village mentalities and conflicts, thus offering indirect insight into subjectivity, see the series of superb rural studies, Walz, *Hexenglaube und magische Kommunikation*; Rummel, *Bauern, Hexen und Herren*, and Labouvie, *Zauberei und Hexenwerk*; and see also Monika Mommertz on magic as one of a whole range of communication processes, 'Handeln, Bedeuten, Geschlecht. Konfliktaustragungspraktiken in der ländlischen Gesellschaft der Mark Brandenburg (2. Hälfte des 16. Jahrhunderts bis zum Dreißigjährigen Krieg)', Ph.D. diss., European University Institute Florence 1997, pp. 268–94; and for unique insight into the symbolism and values of early modern rural culture through witchcraft interrogations, see Norbert Schindler, 'The Origins of Heartlessness: The Culture and Way of Life of Beggars in Late Seventeenth-century Salzburg', in Schindler, *Rebellion, Community and Custom in Early Modern Germany*, trans. Pamela E. Selwyn, Cambridge 2002.

53. StadtAA, Evangelisches Wesensarchiv, nr. 515 Tom I, Acta Die Evangelische Ober-Kirchen-Pfleg oder De ritus ac ceremonias Ecclesiasticas desgl. de disciplinam et censuram ecclesiasticam, 1649–1708, vol. II, nos. 73–81. On the Schiller case, see SSBAugs, 2° Cod. Aug. 288, Schilleriana; and note the song mocking Spitzel's failed exorcism, p. 103, 1671 StadtAA, Strafbuch des Rats 1654–99, p. 390, 7 Feb. 1673; on Spitzel, see his *Die Gebrochne Macht der Finsternuß/ oder Zerstörte Teuflische Bunds- und Buhl-Freundschafft mit den menschen…*, Augsburg 1687, esp. ch. 14, where he castigates the two great sins of parents, namely cursing their poor children and bringing them up badly; and see Dietrich Blaufuß, *Reichsstadt und Pietismus – Philipp Jacob Spener und Gottlieb Spizel aus Augsburg* (Einzelarbeiten aus der Kirchengeschichte Bayerns 53), Neustadt an der Aisch 1977: Spitzel even had contacts with Catholic priests, pp. 257 ff.; and on his relationship to Schiller, pp. 246–52.

54. StadtAA, Reichsstadt, Urg., Juditha Wagner, 9 Nov. 1689 and throughout.

55. See StadtAA, Reichsstadt, Benedict von Paris, Besetzung aller Ämter in der Reichsstadt Augsburg angefangen Anno 1548 fortgesetzt und beendigt bis zur Auflösung der reichsstadtischen Verfaßung Anno 1806.

56. On the witch hunt in Nördlingen, see Gustav Wulz, 'Die Nördlinger Hexen und ihre Richter', in Wulz, *Der Rieser Heimatbote, Heimatbeilage der Rieser Nationalzeitung,*

Nördlingen 1939, nos. 142–5, 147; Wulz, 'Nördlinger Hexenprozesse', in *Jahrbuch des Historischen Vereins für Nördlingen und das Ries* 20, 1937, pp. 42–72; 21, 1938–9, pp. 95–120; Dietmar-H. Voges, 'Reichsstadt Nördlingen', in Sönke Lorenz, ed., *Hexen und Hexenverfolgung im deutschen Südwesten*, Ostfildern 1994, pp. 361–9; Voges, 'Nördlinger Hexenprozesse, – Gesichtspunkte ihrer historischen Bewertung', in Voges, *Nördlingen seit der Reformation. Aus dem Leben einer Stadt*, Munich 1998; Christopher Friedrichs, *Urban Society in an Age of War: Nördlingen, 1580–1720*, Princeton 1979, pp. 206–14; and on Nördlingen, see also Voges, *Die Reichsstadt Nördlingen. 12 Kapitel aus ihrer Geschichte*, Munich 1988.

57. Karl Gundelfinger, another of the city's rotating mayors, was in office between 1589 and 1592, and so also bears considerable responsibility for the trials: Voges, 'Nördlinger Hexenprozesse', p. 71.

58. Klaus Raschzok and Dietmar-H. Voges, '... *dem Gott gnaedig sei*'. *Totenschilde und Epitaphien in der St. Georgskirche in Nördlingen*, Nördlingen 1998, pp. 105–10; Daniel Eberhard Beyschlag, *Beytraege zur Noerdlingischen Geschlechtshistorie. Die Noerdlinger Epitaphien*, 2 vols, Nördlingen 1801–3, vol. 1, pp. 145–50. Röttinger left a legacy to fund scholarships – his father had started out as a furrier, becoming *Stadtamman* (a post whose duties included chairing the city court) in 1549, so Röttinger was certainly continuing the family's social ascent. Interestingly, Röttinger's first wife died in April 1590, just before the executions for witchcraft began. He had also had to help confine his soldier elder brother in a hospital because of insanity in 1579, and this brother had died in 1586, three years before the trials began. The two bereavements, and the effects of coping with an insane elder brother, may all have played their part in Röttinger's behaviour. It is striking that while the elder brother had pursued an active military career, fighting in Hungary, Röttinger had chosen the intellectual path of the law. Röttinger's mother had remarried after his father's death; and it is conceivable that this had made him mistrustful of women. A similar role was played in Esslingen by the Ratsadvokat Daniel Hauff, who was the prime mover in the witch craze there between 1662 and 1666, an episode which only ended with his death by poisoning, possibly plotted by the Council. See Jerouschek, *Die Hexen und ihr Prozeß*; Gisela Vöhringer-Rubröder, 'Reichsstadt Esslingen', in Sönke Lorenz, ed., *Hexen und Hexenverfolgung im deutschen Südwesten*, Ostfildern 1994.

59. With one exception, that of Georg Bin, who was also *Stadtkammerer* (treasurer) at the time and the most senior of the *Beisitzer*, the group charged with carrying out criminal interrogations. This does not suggest that he disapproved of the hunts, but simply that he was burdened with other duties. His wife, however, was later accused of witchcraft but managed to escape.

60. Georg Monninger, *Was uns Nördlinger Häuser erzählen*, Nördlingen 1915; 1984, pp. 124–5: the tablet dates from 1571.

61. Friedrichs, *Nördlingen*, p. 235.

62. Eight of those tried were village women and all were let free, having refused to confess. Voges, *Nördlingen seit der Reformation*, pp. 70, 84–5.

63. Behringer, *Witchcraft Persecutions*, pp. 132–3; these lasted from 1587 to 1594: it is not clear whether the Protestant counts of Öttingen-Öttingen also persecuted witches at this time.

64. Euan Cameron, 'For Reasoned Faith or Embattled Creed? Religion for the People in Early Modern Europe', *Transactions of the Royal Historical Society*, sixth series, 8, 1998, pp. 165–84; plagiarism of Lutheran Gödelmann's attack on Paracelsus by Del Rio: *Del Rio*, p. 170, in Book 6. Evidently, Del Rio also knew the demonology of the Calvinist Daneau well enough to set him and Gödelmann right on points of detail: P.G. Maxwell-

Stuart, ed. and trans., *Martin Del Rio. Investigations into Magic,* Manchester and New York 2000, pp. 135, 213. On Luther's attitude to witchcraft and to magic, see Jörg Haustein, *Martin Luthers Stellung zum Zauber- und Hexenwesen* (Münchener Kirchenhistorische Studien 2), Stuttgart 1990.

65. R.W. Scribner, *Religion and Culture in Germany (1400–1800),* Leiden 2001, p. 335.

66. Maxwell-Stuart, ed. and trans., *Del Rio,* pp. 139–47 (Bk 3, part 1, qu. 4).

67. Reginald Scot, *The Discoverie of Witchcraft* (1584), intro. Montague Summers, New York 1930, 1972; Owen Davies, *Cunning-Folk. Popular Magic and English History,* London 2003, pp. 124–7.

68. For Catholic blessings, see Adolph Franz, *Die kirchlichen Benediktionen im Mittelalter,* 2 vols, Freiburg 1909, vol. 2, pp. 19–45 for weather blessings; and 186–245 for blessings of pregnant women, new mothers and those who die in childbirth; for Protestant attitudes to the sacred in Calvinism, Christopher Elwood, *The Body Broken: The Calvinist Doctrine of the Eucharist and the Symbolization of Power in Sixteenth-century France,* New York and London 1999; on Protestant continuities in belief in the miraculous, R.W. Scribner, '"Incombustible Luther": The Image of the Reformer in Early Modern Germany', *Past and Present* 110, 1986, pp. 38–68; Alexandra Walsham, '"Domme preachers"? Post-Reformation English Catholicism and the Culture of Print', *Past and Present* 168, 2000, pp. 72–123.

69. Maxwell-Stuart, ed. and trans., *Del Rio,* pp. 121 (Bk 3, part 1, qu. 3), 266–7 (Bk 6, section 3), 146 (Bk 3, part 1, qu. 4 section 9 no. 11). On the complexities of Catholic views of magic, see Cameron, 'For Reasoned Faith'.

70. Hedwig Röckelein, 'Marienverehrung und Judenfeindlichkeit in Mittelalter', in Claudia Opitz, Hedwig Röckelein, Gabriela Signori and Guy P. Marchal, eds, *Maria in der Welt. Marienverehrung im Kontext der Sozialgeschichte 10.–18. Jahrhundert,* Zurich 1993, who shows that in sixteen cases, Marian chapels and churches were built on the site of synagogues. These sites were mainly in Bavaria, Franconia, Saxony and Bohemia and include Würzburg, Miltenberg, Ingolstadt, Rothenburg ob der Tauber, Bamberg and Munich. See also J.M. Minty, '*Judengasse* to Christian Quarter: The Phenomenon of the Converted Synagogue in the Late Medieval and Early Modern Holy Roman Empire', in Bob Scribner and Trevor Johnson, eds, *Popular Religion in Germany and Central Europe, 1400–1800,* London 1996. Minty finds thirty-two former synagogues replaced by churches between 1390 and 1520; most of her examples come from Bavaria. In Bamberg, a Marian chapel was built; in Mainz also, a Marian chapel was established in what had once been the synagogue; the Heidelberg synagogue was transformed into a university chapel to Our Lady and in Nuremberg, a church to Our Lady was built out of the proceeds of the goods confiscated by the Council from the Jews murdered in the pogrom of 1350. As Minty points out, this is a clear pattern. For her discussion of the reasons, see pp. 80–4. On Regensburg and its Marian pilgrimage, see Philip Soergel, *Wondrous in his Saints. Counter-Reformation Propaganda in Bavaria,* Berkeley and Los Angeles 1993, pp. 52–61; interestingly, there had been a ritual murder trial in Regensburg in 1478. See also Miri Rubin, *Gentile Tales. The Narrative Assault on Late Medieval Jews,* New Haven and London 1999, esp. pp. 129–31, and R. Po-Chia Hsia, *The Myth of Ritual Murder. Jews and Magic in Reformation Germany,* New Haven and London 1988, pp. 66–85.

71. Midelfort, *History of Madness,* pp. 366–8: Jews had been banished from Würzburg in 1560–61; for the picture of the baptism of the converted Jews in the hospital, Mälzer, *Julius Echter,* p. 40, illustration; p. 64, illus. 67, Dettelbach. Jewish communities in some of the episcopal territories that did hunt witches expanded, though Jews were banned

from episcopal capitals: Jonathan Israel, *European Jewry in the Age of Mercantilism, 1550–1750*, Oxford 1985, pp. 65, 97–100.

72. It is surely suggestive that many places where Marian chapels had been erected over destroyed synagogues – Bamberg, Miltenberg, Würzburg, Weißenburg and Ingolstadt, for example – also saw witch trials. However, there were also many areas which hunted witches but had not erected such chapels. Röckelein identifies sixteen cases of Marian chapels built on demolished synagogues, most of them in Bavaria and Franconia.

73. See, for example, Strauss, *German Single-leaf Woodcut 1550–1600*, 735 Wolfgang Meissner, *Reprobation of Rabbinical and Judaic Apostasy, Confusion and Ignorance in Wittenberg*, Bamberg 1596.

74. Friedrichs, *Nördlingen*, p. 10, n. 11; Voges, *Die Reichsstadt Nördlingen*, pp. 154–74.

75. See, for a brilliant examination of this image and its context, Charles Zika, 'Cannibalism and Witchcraft in Early Modern Europe: Reading the Visual Images', *History Workshop Journal* 44, 1977, pp. 77–106.

Chapter 2: Interrogation and Torture

1. 'in schwarzen hut. mit einem schwarzen federbusch zu Jr bey Tag vf Jren Wiss komen', SAW, Hist. Saal VII, 25/374, fo. 1ff., 21 April 1595, Gertrauta Conradt, Kilian Conradts Witwe.

2. SAW, Hist. Saal VII, 25/374, fo. 2, 21 April 1595, Gertrauta Conradt, 'Man soll Jr die Articul. Was die Apalania Cräfften bekennt fürlesen, Wölle sie es gestehen'.

3. The final 'confirmation' of her confession can be found in SAW, Misc. 1954, I, fos. 129–32, 4 July 1596.

4. *Die Peinliche Gerichtsordung Kaiser Karls V. von 1532 (Carolina)*, ed. Gustav Radbruch, revised by Arthur Kaufmann, Stuttgart 1975.

5. The Carolina attempted to limit the use of torture by specifying that there must be evidence against the victim; and insisting that the advice of legal faculties should be obtained in all difficult cases: Sönke Lorenz, 'Der Hexenprozess', in Lorenz, ed., *Hexen und Hexenverfolgung im deutschen Südwesten*, Ostfildern 1994. These provisions, however, were often overridden during the course of the witch hunt.

6. On torture, see, for a modern investigation of the relation between pain and interrogation, Elaine Scarry, *The Body in Pain. The Making and Unmaking of the World*, Oxford 1985, esp. pp. 28 ff.; however, it is worth pointing out that, whatever we may feel about it, pre-modern societies distinguished very carefully between the torturer and the interrogator; and that their understanding of the role of torture was located in a different understanding of truth and pain in a salvific context. On early modern discourses of pain, see Lisa Silverman, *Tortured Subjects. Pain, Truth, and the Body in Early Modern France*, Chicago 2001; on the history of torture, Edward Peters, *Torture*, Oxford 1985, pp. 74–102; on torture itself, Lorenz, 'Hexenprozess', esp. pp. 77 ff., and Ch. Hinckeldey, ed., *Justiz in alter Zeit*, Rothenburg ob der Taube 1989; and, for an interesting example from 1613 of a town legal adviser who had serious reservations about confessions to witchcraft under torture, see Klaus Graf, 'Hexenverfolgung in Schwäbisch Gmünd', in Sönke Lorenz and Dieter R. Bauer, eds, *Hexenverfolgung. Beiträge zur Forschung – unter besonderer Berücksichtigung des südwestdeutschen Raumes* (Quellen und Forschungen zur europäischen Ethnologie, vol. 15), Würzburg 1993.

7. See Lyndal Roper, *The Holy Household. Women and Morals in Reformation Augsburg*,

Oxford 1989, and Ulinka Rublack, *The Crimes of Women in Early Modern Germany*, Oxford 1999.

8. StadtAN, Hexenprozeßakten, 10 Sept. 1590 and following, Barbara Stecher. Stecher was first interrogated on 5 September, and she confirmed her full confession on 2 November, reconfirming it on 14 January of the following year. She was executed on 25 January 1591, her trial having lasted over four months.

9. The former mint was turned into an eight-cell prison, with two of the cells reserved for witches. Similarly, in Oberdorf in the bishopric of Augsburg in 1590 five blockhouses were seized as additional prisons before a major witch-hunting episode got under way: Wolfgang Behringer, *Witchcraft Persecutions in Bavaria. Popular Magic, Religious Zealotry and Reason of State in Early Modern Europe*, trans. J. Grayson and D. Lederer, Cambridge 1997, p. 128.

10. SSBAugs, Cod. Aug. 289; StadtAA, Reichsstadt, Urg. 1702 Regina Groninger, 16 Jan. 1703; 24 Dec. 1689 Juditha Wagner, testimony of Trostknecht who believed the girl 'too simple' to be a witch.

11. SAS Dep. 30, Rep. VI, Pak. 255, Marchtaler Hexenprozesse, Magdalena Bollmann (née Fuder) 23 April 1747, 'Volkommen starr', 'die straich mit der geweithn beitschen zuverdopplen': these whip strokes were applied in part to her 's.v. hinderen', in part to her back and in part to her arms; 'daher Mann sich genöthtget gesehen, sie Inquisitam durch den ambtsknecht mit einem strickh under denn ärmben binden und auf dem boden die stiegen hinunder biß in dz plockh-Hauß schlaiffen lassen', 16 Oct. 1747, p. 171; 'bey 5 biß 6 Vatter vnser lang', 'hat man ihro mit der geweichten Oster und andern kerzen thails under die naasen thails undter beede grosse zehen gezunden, so sich dann ergeben, dz sie durch ihren blaaß die kerzen widerholter dingen ausszuleschen gesucht', p. 166: four days later, the blisters on her feet were still evident, p. 169.

12. Dietmar-H. Voges, 'Nördlinger Hexenprozesse – Gesichtspunkte ihrer historischen Bewertung', in Voges, *Nördlingen seit der Reformation. Aus dem Leben einer Stadt*, Munich 1998, pp. 84–5; eight of these were from villages around Nördlingen.

13. Nicolas Rémy, *Demonolatry*, ed. and trans. Montague Summers, London 1930, p. xiii (To the Courteous Reader) and p. 48 ff. (Bk 1, ch. xiv).

14. Voges, 'Nördlinger Hexenprozesse', pp. 86, 88; SAN, Allgemeines Staatsarchiv München, Hexenprozeßakten 44, containing a series of impressive letters from Abraham Windeisen from 1617 to 1622 complaining about the unjust imprisonment and interrogation of his wife on suspicion of witchcraft.

15. See Hartmut Lehmann and Otto Ulbricht, eds, *Vom Unfug des Hexen-Processes. Gegner der Hexenverfolgungen von Johann Weyer bis Friedrich Spee*, Wiesbaden 1992; see also Klaus Vogel, 'Wo Sprache endet. Der Bericht des Anton Prätorius über Folter und das Problem der "selektiven Empathie"', in Markus Meumann and Dirk Niefanger, eds, *Ein Schauplatz herber Angst. Wahrnehmung und Darstellung von Gewalt im 17. Jahrhundert*, Göttingen 1997.

16. Behringer, *Witchcraft Persecutions*, pp. 226–300, 303–6, 320. He was supposedly active in Eichstätt between 1624 and 1628 and died in 1630. Kolb appears at interrogations of Waldburga Schmid in 1626, SAW, Misc. 1954, I, fos. 1–28.

17. Rémy, *Demonolatry*, p. 69 (Bk 1, ch. xxiii). Rémy is at pains to insist at the very beginning of his work that judges are immune from the attacks of witches because the God-given office of magistrate is so important that its holders are not tempted, nor do familiars appear to them while in office: see *Demonolatry*, p. 5 (Bk 1, ch. ii), a story which protests rather too much.

18. SAW, Misc. 2896. On Würzburg, see Elmar Weiß, 'Die Hexenprozesse im Hochstift Würzburg', in Peter Kolb and Ernst-Günter Krenig, eds, *Unterfränkische Geschichte*.

Band 3. Vom Beginn des konfessionellen Zeitalters bis zum Ende des Dreißigjährigen Krieges, Würzburg 1995; Harald Schwillus, 'Die Hexenprozesse gegen Würzburger Geistliche unter Fürstbischof Philipp Adolf von Ehrenberg (1623–31)', Diplomarbeit, Bayerische Julius-Maximilians Universität Würzburg; and Schwillus, '"Der bischoff lässt nit nach, bis er die gantze statt verbrennt hat"', *Würzburger Diözesangeschichtsblätter* 49, 1987, pp. 145–54; Christel Beyer, *'Hexen-leut, so zu Würzburg gerichtet'. Der Umgang mit Sprache und Wirklichkeit in Inquisitionsprozessen wegen Hexerei (Europäische Hochschulschriften 1*, vol. 948), Frankfurt am Main, Berne and New York, 1981; A. Bechtold, 'Beiträge zur Geschichte der Würzburger Hexenprozesse', *Frankenkalendar* 53, 1940, pp. 117–29; Friedrich Merzbacher, 'Fürstbischof Julius Echter von Mespelbrunn als Gesetzgeber', in Merzbacher, *Recht – Staat – Kirche. Ausgewählte Aufsätze*, Vienna 1989; Merzbacher, *Die Hexenprozesse in Franken*, 2nd edn Munich 1970.

19. On executioners, see Kathy Stuart, *Defiled Trades and Social Outcasts. Honor and Ritual Pollution in Early Modern Germany*, Cambridge 1999, Helmut Schuhmann, *Der Scharfrichter. Seine Gestalt – seine Funktion*, Kempten 1964, Jutta Nowosadtko, *Scharfrichter und Abdecker. Der Alltag zweier 'unehrlicher Berufe' in der Frühen Neuzeit*, Paderborn 1994, Franz Irsigler and Arnold Lasotta, *Bettler und Gaukler, Dirnen und Henker. Außenseiter in einer mittelalterlichen Stadt. Köln 1300–1600*, Munich 1984, 1989; for diaries, Jürgen Carl Jacobs and Heinz Rölleke, eds, *Das Tagebuch des Meister Franz Scharfrichter zu Nürnberg. Nachdruck der Buchausgabe von 1801*, Dortmund 1980; Samuel Valentin (Gerichtswaibel), *End-Urthel und Verruf Nach Kaiser Caroli Vti Majestaet glorreicher Gedaechtnis, Peinliche Halss-Gerichts-Ordnung verfasst; Aller derjenigen Manns – und Weibspersohnen, so von Einem Hoch-Edlen und Hochweisen Rath des H.R. Reichs Freyen Stadt Augsburg von Anno 1649 bis Anno 1759 vom Leben zum Tod condemnieret und justifizieret worden...*, Augsburg n.d.; and see also the similar listing compiled by the chimney sweep Johann Bausch in 1755: 'Malefizbuch', StadtAA. The Bausch family were known earlier in the century as a family who worked in the dishonourable trade of bailiff; and the beadles might also be indirectly tainted by the dishonour connected with the process of criminal trial, depending on their exact function. By tradition in some areas, the hangman received the clothes of the victim below the waist, the beadle those above.

20. Behringer, *Witchcraft Persecutions*, pp. 126–9, 184–6.

21. SAS Dep. 30, Rep. VI, Pak. 254, Marchtaler Hexenprozesse, Margareta Strenger, 24–26 April 1587; Staatsbibliothek Munich, Handschriftenabteilung, CGM 2026, fos. 64v–65r.

22. The Carolina did consider the case where a criminal did not confess when the accusation against him or her was fully proven, even after this had been pointed out, and even after torture: in such an event punishment should be carried out: *Carolina*, Article 69, p. 59. However, in witchcraft trials this rarely happened. By contrast, steadfast denial despite repeated torture usually prevented condemnation, but few people could endure the levels of torture that were applied in many such cases.

23. The Würzburg cases are full of detailed descriptions of witches' marks. So for example, in the case of Waldburga Schmid, there is a precise description of the two holes found on her feet, big enough to fit a hazelnut. Her shock is palpable: she said 'gottes Sacrament, soll ich dann an disem orth khommen'. After one session of threats and manifestation of the instruments of torture, and one pulling up, she duly confessed. SAW, Misc. 1954, I, fo. 1, Waldburga Schmid, 17 Nov. 1626.

24. StadtAA, Fasz. Hebemmen und Obfrauen, 1548–1813 [Hebammen und Obfrauen 1654–1784, Prod. 1–60, no. 9], Copied Extract from Amtsprotokoll in the case of Sara Eyferle, 9 and 10 Jan. 1675, testimony of Marx Hartmann Executioner, that Eyferle, suspected of being a witch, had twice come to him asking him to inspect her for witches'

marks: he had refused, threatening to throw her downstairs. So also Brigita Herenschmid described how her sister's son had been to see the executioner to find out whether the woman he proposed to marry was a witch: the executioner confirmed that her mother was a witch, but assured him he could marry his intended. StadtAN, Hexenprozeßakten, under Aißlingerin, Verhör über die Schöperlerin, 24 April 1590. On the abiding nature of dishonour from the executioner's touch, see Stuart, *Defiled Trades*, esp. pp. 140–2.

25. 'vnd sich selbs Probieren wollenn, ob sie eine sei', StadtAN, Hexenprozeßakten, Barbara Stecher, 14 Sept. 1590.

26. Lorenz, 'Der Hexenprozess', p. 77. In Augsburg, in a variant of this custom, thieves were forced to wear a special fur coat while being interrogated: Stuart, *Defiled Trades*, pp. 121–48.

27. StadtAA, Urg., Euphrosina Endriss, 20 Dec. 1685, report of Hans Adam Hartman, 5 Feb. 1686.

28. See, for example, Regina Bartholome in Augsburg. I have commented on this case at more length in Lyndal Roper, *Oedipus and the Devil. Witchcraft, Sexuality and Religion in Early Modern Europe*, London 1994, pp. 226–48.

29. SAN, Allgemeines Staatsarchiv München, Hexenprozeßakten 44, 4 Aug. 1620, letter of Abraham Windeisen which describes the use of the technique of tolling bells during interrogation by Dr Mayer.

30. Behringer, *Witchcraft Persecutions*, p. 185. In Würzburg, during interrogation the accused witches had to stand on a red stone etched with the sign of the cross on its corners and in the centre so that they could not become invisible: Weiß, 'Hexenprozesse', p. 342.

31. SAW, Hist. Saal VII, 25/375, fo. 297, Anna Zott, 27–28 July 1616.

32. SAS Dep. 30, Rep. VI, Pak. 254, Marchtaler Hexenprozesse, Ursula Götz, 3 March 1627, witness statements.

33. Ibid., Rosina Baur, 15 June 1587.

34. 'der böss Jr buel zue Jr kommen vor tags, vnnd gesagt, sie soll hinauss gehen. so woll Er sie hinab inn die Post leüthen fueren, da hab es Jm holz ein grossen holenstein vnnd häle, darvnder wöll vnnd Jres willens mit Jr pflegen. (sagen die Gerichts personen es sey wahr, Es hab ein solchere stein in dem holz darunder sich vil schelmen vor Jaren verhalten haben. es wiess aber dass hundert mensch dass orth nit. Jst woll zur Prasumieren wann er sich dahin bracht. hett er Jr den halss vmbdröhet damit er die seel Erhielte Vnnd hett niemandt also erfahren kinden wo sie hinkhommen wäre, Welches aber Gott so die seel Erschaffen vnnd für sie gelitten nit haben wöllen, Vnnd vns denn sinn eingeben, dass wir vmb 5 Vren Wider hinein zue der Inquisition ganngen. da wir ordinarie sonst erst vmb 7 vr vorhin darzue gangen, wie dann da die gerichts personen Jr nit wahr genommen hetten sie doch mir vnnder die hanndt ganngen, war alss dar Jnen *e vestigio* nachganngen', SAW, Misc. 1954, I, 23 Feb. 1590, Anna Hans Schinleders zu Hettingenn, hausfrau, fo. 105.

35. Occasionally they resorted to more direct methods so as not to allow women to escape execution by committing suicide. When Veronica Fritsch threatened to commit suicide by hanging herself by her hair, the authorities simply cut it off. StadtAN, Hexenprozeßakten,Veronica Fritsch, executed 9 June 1598.

36. 'Sie muess mit Im leiden vnnd herrschen', StadtAN, Hexenprozeßakten, Katharina Keßler, 10 April 1591.

37. StadtAN, Hexenprozeßakten, 12 May 1590, Maria Schöpperlin; 'Wolte Gott dz sie Jr herz khunde aufreissen, dz ein Rath dasselbig sehen khünde, wiss dz sie vnschuldig sej, wel sich auch der Oberkhait, vnnd zuuorderst Gott beuelhen', StadtAN, 25 April 1590,

Apollonia Aißlinger; and see also StadtAA, Reichsstadt, Urg., Ursula Gron, 1694, 8 June 1694, 'O Mein Gott dz Sich der himmel nicht aufthut und dz Mann einem nicht in dz Herz sehen kan'.

38. StadtAN, Hexenprozeßakten, 14 May 1590, Apollonia Aißlinger: 'Es sei Ir ebenn Ir herz immer schweher, vnnd ein schwer ding khenne nichts mehr Jnn Jrem herzen finden. sei eben hart bekhümmert. Bite Jmmer Gott soll mit seinen Englen khommen vnd alles recht machen'; 'möchte verdampt werden, oder sein'; 18 May 1590: 'Schrie vnnd dobet sie wüest. khenne nichts glaubenn, wiss nit ob gott bei Ir sei oder nit. Habe nichts gethon, khenne ebenn nit am Christus glauben, oder khain vatter vnnser betten. Seien gedannkchenn In Irem herzen sie seie verdampt. verdampt. verdampt. vnnd wann sie schon shrei Jesus so habs khain verfanng.'

39. Jeffrey Moussaieff Masson, ed., *Sigmund Freud. Briefe an Wilhelm Fliess 1887–1904*, German edn revised and expanded by Michael Schröter, Frankfurt am Main 1986, pp. 237, 240. This connection was noted by Carlo Ginzburg, 'Freud, the Wolf-Man, and the Werewolves', in Ginzburg, *Myths, Emblems and Clues*, trans. John and Anne Tedeschi, London 1990. On the dynamics of transference and counter-transference, see Karl Figlio, 'Oral History and the Unconscious', *History Workshop Journal* 26, 1988, pp. 120–32; and for methodological consideration of the use and limits of psycho-analysis in the interpretation of witchcraft, see Nick Tosh, 'Possession, Exorcism and Psychoanalysis', *Studies in History and Philosophy of Biological and Biomedical Sciences* 33, 2002, pp. 583–96.

40. StadtAN, Hexenprozeßakten, Katharina Keßler, 6–12 April 1591.

41. 'Also dass sie endtmorgens, endtblöst, vnnd gar nackhet scheüzlich befunden, Auch sich darab, ybel gehabt vnnd gannz schwach wordenn', SAS Dep. 30, Rep. VI, Pak. 254, Marchtaler Hexenprozesse, Anna Bernegker, 26 June 1587.

42. SAN, Eichstätt, Hexenprozeßakten 48, Lorenz Fendt, 30 Nov. 1618; 1 Dec. 1618, 'Jr nach dem fürtuoch griffen, vnd gesagt, du Alte huor, must dich heut voglen lassen'; on this case, see Jonathan Durrant, 'Witchcraft, Gender and Society in the Early Modern Prince-Bishopric of Eichstätt', Ph.D. diss., University of London, 2002, pp. 265–79: Durrant is also able to show that some of the sex that went on in the jail was consen-sual, since some accused witches were actively trying to get pregnant, as the only means of deferring execution. This incident, investigated somewhat inconclusively by the authorities, brought a whole series of sexual relationships in the prison to light.

43. SAS Dep. 30, Rep. VI, Pak. 254, Marchtaler Hexenprozesse, Lucia Vischer, 25 April 1587.

44. SAW, Misc. 1954, II, fo. 3, 1603, Walpurg Stainbach: 'Hat dem Maister die hand geben, vnd die pein so er Jhr angethon Verzihen vnd vergeben, hette Jhr recht gethan, dieweil sie so hart gehalten vnd nit bekennen wöllen'; 'hatt lengest gern gestehen dz es darzu kommen wehre, allein sie hette nit gewüsst, wie sie ein anfang machen solte'.

45. '1. Vor 5 Jahren, sey sie im Widtbestandt Zorns weis verfurt worden, vnnd sich Vber redten lassen, Vnd hab sich Jm Zorn Verschworen, Wan sie mit den nachtbehren gestreidten, hab sie gesagt, Wan sies nach gebe, Well sie des bossen sein. Vnnd bringen sie ihr guetter vnd Ir aigner Zorn darzue, Wie auch Jhr eines mahls ein halber Ackher Weinberg Abgelassen Worden.

2. Sagt vor 15 jahren hab sie vf Jhre brun Wisen gegrasset, Wehre ein kleiner mann, in grunen Kleidung khommen, hette sie Neben dem bach gegrast Vnd Wie sie sich Vmbgesehenn, Wehre er hinder ihr gestanden Vnd gesagt, Was sie thet, sie gesagt, Aldo gras ich

Sagt, Er hette zu ihr gesagt, Er Wolt ihr die burden grass Aufhelffen dorauf er sich nider gesezt, Vnd sie die Buertten Aufgefasst vnd fort gehen wollen, der grun gesell gesagt Wartte leg dein bundlein Wider ab, Ich hab noch mehr mit dir zu reden, Vnd sie zur Vnzucht Angemieth, hab sie Jr burdten Wider Abgelegt, hab er ihr guete Wordt geben, hab sie gesagt, es sey schandt, Vnd Sundt, hab er gesagt, es sey kein Sund.', SAW, Hist. Saal VII, 25/375, fo. 313, Barbara Schluchter, 8 March 1617 (Krautheim).

46. However, not all these assets could actually be collected. See Elmar Weiß, 'Die Hexenprozesse im Hochstift Würzburg', in Peter Kolb and Ernst-Günter Krenig, eds, *Unterfränkische Geschichte. Band 3: Vom Beginn des konfessionellen Zeitalters bis zum Ende des Dreißigjährigen Krieges*, Würzburg 1995, pp. 347–8; Carol Karlsen, *The Devil in the Shape of a Woman. Witchcraft in Colonial New England*, New York and London 1987, esp. pp. 77–117; Louise Yeoman, 'Hunting the Rich Witch in Scotland: High-status Witch Suspects and their Persecutors, 1590–1650', in Julian Goodare, ed., *The Scottish Witch-hunt in Context*, Manchester and New York 2002: such cases were rare in Scotland and did not always result in conviction, but were more common in New England trials; Merzbacher, *Hexenprozesse in Franken*, p. 47.

47. See, in particular, Melanie Klein, *Envy and Gratitude and Other Works 1946–1963*, London 1975, 1988.

48. StadtAN, Stadtrechnungen 1590, fo. 327v lists the amounts paid for these meals. On the hangman's meal, see Richard van Dülmen, *Theatre of Horror. Crime and Punishment in Early Modern Germany*, trans. Elisabeth Neu, London 1990, where participation by the victim at the meal is attested for the eighteenth century. In Gerolzhofen, accounts specify the amount that was spent on each witch's 'last meal' (at a cost of 1 lb 18d. per person) and on wine on the day of execution: SAW, Gericht Gerolzhofen 346, fo. 163r. A 'frue Suppen' was held before the execution and a meal after for twenty people for the cost of half a gulden a head, fo. 162r. On similar feasts in village trials, see Walter Rummel, *Bauern, Herren und Hexen*, Göttingen 1991, pp. 183–90.

49. Peter Binsfeld, *Tractat Von Bekantnuß der Zauberer und Hexen*, Trier, Henrich Bock, 1590, pp. 133v–134r.

50. StadtAA, Strafbuch des Rats, 1654–99, pp. 312–14, 23 March 1669; in Nördlingen, too, Maria Schöpperlin was branded with hot iron on her breast at the place of execution because she had killed the fruit of her own body: StadtAN, Nördlinger Urfehdebuch 1587, fo. 112r.

51. Friedrich Spee, *Cautio criminalis oder Rechtliches Bedenken wegen der Hexenprozesse*, trans. Joachim-Friedrich Ritter, 1939; Munich 1982; 2000, p. 101, and on the work and its rhetorical style see Theo G. M. Oorschot, 'Ihrer Zeit voraus. Das Ende der Hexenverfolgung in der *Cautio criminalis*', in Sönke Lorenz and Dieter Bauer, eds, *Das Ende der Hexenverfolgung* (Hexenforschung vol. 10), Stuttgart 1995; see also, on context, Alexander Loichinger, 'Friedrich von Spee und seine "Cautio criminalis"', in Georg Schwaiger, ed., *Teufelsglaube und Hexenprozesse*, Munich 1988; and see Günter Franz, 'Das Geheimnis um den Druck der *Cautio criminalis* in Köln 1632', in Spee, *Cautio criminalis*, 2000. In the second edition of the *Cautio criminalis* there were nine etchings attached (possibly not made specifically for the volume), some of which are reproduced here. These vivid etchings bring to life the sufferings of those enduring torture and probably also played their part in the impact of the book. For an English translation of the work, Friedrich Spee von Langenfeld, *Cautio Criminalis, or a Book on Witch Trials*, trans. Marcus Hellyer, Charlottesville and London 2003.

Chapter 3: Cannibalism

1. Some of them died as a result of the effects of torture. On the panic in the region, see

Wolfgang Behringer, *Witchcraft Persecutions in Bavaria. Popular Magic, Religious Zealotry and Reason of State in Early Modern Europe*, trans. J. Grayson and D. Lederer, Cambridge 1997, pp. 132–4.

2. Twenty-six of thirty-five women (and one man) convicted of being witches are known to have had children. One other was a midwife and had therefore almost certainly had children. Only two had never been married and both were executed at the beginning of the witch panic. One married 'witch' was known to be childless. A further five were married but we have no record of children or miscarriages. It is striking that almost all the condemned witches had been married during their lives. Fourteen were widows and nineteen were married at the time of the trial. The tensions which may have surrounded remarriages and step-relationships might conceivably have played a role: fourteen of the thirty-three marriages were remarriages for husband or wife. See StadtAN, Kriminalakten: 1478, 1534, 1576/89–1598/99 (Hexenprozeßakten); Gustav Wulz, 'Die Nördlinger Hexen und ihre Richter', in *Der Rieser Heimatbote. Heimatbeilage der Rieser Nationalzeitung*, Nördlingen 1939, nos. 142–5, 147; Wulz, 'Nördlinger Hexenprozesse', *Jahrbuch des Historischen Vereins für Nördlingen und das Ries* 20, 1937, pp. 42–72; 21, 1934–9, pp. 95–120; Dietmar-H. Voges, 'Reichsstadt Nördlingen', in Lorenz, ed., *Hexen und Hexenverfolgung im deutschen Südwesten*, Ostfildern 1994, pp. 361–9; Voges, 'Nördlinger Hexenprozesse – Gesichtspunkte ihrer historischen Bewertung', in *Nördlingen seit der Reformation. Aus dem Leben einer Stadt*, Munich 1998; Christopher Friedrichs, *Urban Society in an Age of War: Nördlingen, 1580–1720*, Princeton 1979, pp. 206–14.

3. StadtAN, Hexenprozeßakten, 14 July 1590, Barbara Lierheimer.

4. 'Der böss gaist habs dahin gebracht dz sie es Wider Verlaugnet, geb sich shuldig vnnd welle es Nimer mehr thun. vnd sei alles wahr wass sie Aussgesagt vnnd sonderlich mit Ihrem mann': StadtAN, Hexenprozeßakten, 15 July 1590, Barbara Lierheimer.

5. 'ein Verlogner schelm'; 'Je Vester mann sie Martere Je fester sie liege, man Zwinge sie nur zum liegen': ibid.

6. StadtAN, Hexenprozeßakten, Barbara Lierheimer, see for instance 9 and 10 July 1590; and StadtAN, Stadtrechungen 1590, fo. 174, payment of salary to Lierheimer as civic midwife.

7. Friedrichs, *Nördlingen*, p. 213; 'O Du mein auserwählter Schatz, soll ich mich so unschuldig von Dir scheiden müssen. Das sei Gott immer und ewig klagt. Man nöt(et) eins, es muess eins reden, man hat mich gemartert. Ich bin so unschuldig als Gott im Himmel. Wann ich nur ein Pünktlin um solche Sach wüsst, so wollt ich, dass mir Gott den Himmel versaget'; Wulz, 'Nördlinger Hexenprozesse', p. 67.

8. For example, StadtAN, Hexenprozeßakten: Maria Schöpperlin was the daughter of a councillor and the widow of a councillor. Barbara Wörlin was the widow of the mayor Johann Wörlin, Dorothea Gundelfinger was the widow of the mayor Karl Gundelfinger (who however must have been involved in the persecutions before his death in late 1592), Margaretha Knorz was the daughter of a councillor, Rosina Mair was the widow of a councillor. Margareta Frickinger lived in the town hall. Rebekka Lemp was married to the *Zahlmeister* Peter Lemp. Wulz, 'Die Nördlinger Hexen'; Voges, 'Nördlinger Hexenprozesse'.

9. StadtAN, Hexenprozeßakten, 20 Aug. 1590, Rebekka Lemp.

10. However, belief in witchcraft and in the rightness of the persecution was not uncontested. From the very beginning there were opposing voices. The pastor Friedrich Wilhelm Lutz preached a sermon against the witch craze, for which he had later to account to members of the Council: Wulz, 'Nördlinger Hexenprozesse', pp. 107–9; StadtAN, C. Ammerbacher, 'Allerhand Merkwürdigkeiten der Stadt Nördlingen', 1824, part I, A–L, between p. 424 and p. 425: to my knowledge, no text of this sermon has

survived. Parts of the questioning and his response are recorded on this piece of paper which was presumably removed from an old chronicle. Some spouses insisted on the innocence of their wives; others were unsure, and yet others testified against them.

11. Executions occurred at the Henkelberg: Wulz, 'Nördlinger Hexenprozesse', p. 71; and the 'witches' all concur that the exhumations occurred on the 'Berg' by St Emmeran's. On the topographical history of Nördlingen and on the history of its houses, see Georg Monninger, *Was uns Nördlinger Häuser erzählen*, Nördinglen 1915, 1984; and Dietmar-H. Voges, *Die Reichsstadt Nördlingen. 12 Kapitel aus ihrer Geschichte*, Munich 1988, pp. 154–74.

12. Michel de Montaigne, 'On the Cannibals', trans. M.A. Screech, in *Michel de Montaigne. Four Essays*, London 1995. See Piero Camporesi, *Bread of Dreams. Food and Fantasy in Early Modern Europe*, trans. David Gentilcore, 1980, Oxford 1989, pp. 44–55; and on cannibalism and the New World, see in particular Charles Zika, 'Fashioning New Worlds from Old Fathers: Reflections on Saturn, Amerindians and Witches in a Sixteenth-century Print', in Zika, *Exorcising our Demons: Magic, Witchcraft, and Visual Culture in Early Modern Europe* (Studies in Medieval and Reformation Thought 91), Leiden and Boston 2003, and on images of the New World, for example, Seymour Phillips, 'The Outer World of the European Middle Ages', in Stuart B. Schwartz, ed., *Implicit Understandings. Observing, Reporting, and Reflecting on the Encounters between Europeans and Other Peoples in the Early Modern Era*, Cambridge 1994, p. 62; and Peter Hulme, 'Tales of Distinction: European Ethnography and the Caribbean', in Schwartz, ed., *Implicit Understandings*, p. 172; Inga Clendinnen, 'Franciscan Missionaries in Sixteenth-century Mexico', in James Obelkevich, Lyndal Roper and Raphael Samuel, eds, *Disciplines of Faith. Studies in Religion, Politics and Patriarchy*, London 1987; on the wider significance of the myth and witchcraft, Norman Cohn, *Europe's Inner Demons*, London 1975, pp. 227–8; on violence in sixteenth-century France, see Natalie Zemon Davis, 'The Rites of Violence', *Society and Culture in Early Modern France*, London 1975, pp. 152–88 and p. 324, n.100; Denis Crouzet, 'Die Gewalt zur Zeit der Religionskriege im Frankreich des 16. Jahrhunderts', trans. Annette Böltau and Thomas Lindenberger, in Thomas Lindenberger and Alf Lüdtke, eds, *Physische Gewalt. Studien zur Geschichte der Neuzeit* (1990), Frankfurt am Main 1995. On cannibalism as a motif in representations of witches, see Charles Zika, 'Les Parties du corps, Saturne et le cannibalisme: représentations visuelles des assemblées des sorcières au xvie siècle', in N. Jacques-Chaquin and M. Préaud, eds, *Le Sabbat des sorciers, xve–xviiie siècles*, Grenoble 1993, pp. 389–418; and Zika, 'Cannibalism and Witchcraft in Early Modern Europe: Reading the Visual Images', *History Workshop Journal* 44, 1977, pp. 77–106.

13. The Reverend Montague Summers, trans. and ed., *The Malleus Maleficarum of Heinrich Kramer and James Sprenger* [*sic*], Part I, qu. 11, Part II, qu. 1, ch. 13, pp. 66, 89–9, 140–4, New York 1928; Wolfgang Behringer and Günter Jerouschek, eds, *Der Hexenhammer*, trans. W. Behringer, G. Jerouschek and W. Tschacher, Munich 2000, pp. 286–8, 472–82; for Kelheimer interrogatory, 'Vorgegebenes Frageschema für Hexenprozesse, 1590' (Der Kelheimer Hexenhammer), in Wolfgang Behringer, ed., *Hexen und Hexenprozesse in Deutschland*, Munich 1988; 3rd edn 1995, VI, 'Circa punctum: khinder ausgraben', p. 282, and see Behringer, *Witchcraft Persecutions*, pp. 137–8. The Bavarian 'Gemeine General Instruction' May/June 1590 asks about the injuring of children and the digging up of children and the use of their bones – not however about the cooking and consumption of infant flesh: Behringer, *Mit dem Feuer vom Leben zum Tod. Hexengesetzgebung in Bayern*, Munich 1988, pp. 116 and 145 ff. On the history of these motifs, Cohn, *Europe's Inner Demons*; they also appear in the Berbese cases 1392–1406, where child-flesh is supposedly used to prepare ointments and juice: Hartwig Weber, *Kinderhexenprozesse*, Frankfurt am Main and Leipzig 1991, pp. 120–3, 175–81.

Cannibalism does not appear to have been a theme of the genre of popular literature about child murder. However, there are pamphlets which report large groups of witches preparing cannibalistic meals. See, on such pamphlets from 1609, 1612 and 1627: Joy Wiltenburg, *Disorderly Women and Female Power in the Street Literature of Early Modern England and Germany*, Charlottesville and London 1992, pp. 226–50. Similar to the cases in Nördlingen, the pamphlet of 1609 reports how twenty infanticidal witches had been digging up children at night. Otherwise, this motif appears to be used differently and does not explain its use in Nördlingen. Accusations of cannibalism were not universal in witch hunts. Apparently they were not significant in Lippe: Rainer Walz, *Hexenglaube und magische Kommunikation im Dorf der Frühen Neuzeit. Die Verfolgungen in der Grafschaft Lippe*, Paderborn 1993, pp. 379–88; and although they are mentioned, they do not appear to have been centrally important in the panic in Münster: Sabine Alfing, *Hexenjagd und Zaubereiprozesse in Münster. Vom Umgang mit Sündenböcken in den Krisenzeiten des 16. und 17. Jahrhunderts*, Münster and New York 1991, S. 121; in the electorate of Mainz it was reported that the food at witches' sabbaths did not still hunger and consisted of disgusting things such as knacker's meat, stinking flesh, or baked frogs and toads, but infant flesh does not appear to have been mentioned. As in Nördlingen, the motif of the drinking of stolen wine appears in the Mainz cases, but the silver crockery – mentioned in Nördlingen – revealed itself in Mainz to be skulls. See Herbert Pohl, *Hexenglaube und Hexenverfolgung im Kurfürstentum Mainz. Ein Beitrag zur Hexenfrage im 16. und beginnenden 17. Jahrhundert* (Geschichtliche Landeskunde 32), Stuttgart 1988, p. 265. Cannibalism does however play a role in the cases at Würzburg: SAW Misc. 1954, I, II; Hist. Saal VII, 25/374, 375, 376, 377, etc.; and in Marchtal: SAS Dep. 30, Rep. VI, Pak. 254, Marchtaler Hexenprozesse. For a brief but stimulating psychoanalytic interpretation of the theme of cannibalism in witchcraft, see Cohn, *Europe's Inner Demons*, pp. 259–61. For the image of the child-eating witch in witch trials, see Ingrid Ahrendt-Schulte, *Weise Frauen – böse Weiber. Die Geschichte der Hexen in der Frühen Neuzeit*, Freiburg 1994, pp. 55–61.

14. Not all those women accused of witchcraft were executed. Some were freed, and some were not subjected to torture. Maria Holl is the most famous example of a woman who endured torture without confessing and so was let free. See Lore Sporhan-Krempel, *Die Hexe von Nördlingen. Das Schicksal der Maria Holl. Roman* (1950), Nördlingen 1978–79; Gloria Eschbaumer, *Bescheidenliche Tortur. Der ehrbare Rat der Stadt Nördlingen im Hexenprozess 1593/4 gegen die Kronenwirtin Maria Holl*, Nördlingen 1983. Eleven other individuals were denounced as witches but were not tried, and nine other women were released. For this point I am grateful to Dr Voges. See Dietmar-H. Voges, *Nördlingen seit der Reformation. Aus der Leben einer Stadt*, Munich 1998, pp. 385–6, and Wulz, 'Die Nördlinger Hexen'.

15. Ten supposed witches were related to tanning, leatherworking or similar professional families: for example, Apollonia Aißlinger, daughter of a tanner and married to a tanner; Maria Schöpperlin, married to a leatherworker; Margaretha Humel, widow of a beltmaker; Katharina Keßler, daughter of a leatherworker and married to one; Barbara Kuem, daughter of a cobbler and married to one; Eva Aufschlager, married to a leatherworker; Ursula Klein, twice married to a tanner; Margaretha Knorz, daughter of a pursemaker; Margareth Saugenfinger, the daughter of a leatherworker, was married first to a tanner and then to a leatherworker; Corbiniana Leher was married to a leatherworker. This can partly be explained by the fact that the leather trades were the second most populous in Nördlingen. Their numbers were increasing, growing from 42 to 122 between 1519 and 1567. However, the numerically largest trade in Nördlingen, that of the weavers, was strikingly under-represented amongst those executed as

witches: one woman was the daughter of a linen weaver, and two others came from coarse woollen cloth (Loden) weaving families. Another group worked in various taverns in Nördlingen: Margaretha Getzler was a cook at various inns; Anna Koch had been an innkeeper's wife; Anna Glauner was married to an innkeeper, as was Rosina Mair; Margareta Stahl was the daughter of an innkeeper. Anna Faul was the widow of a baker; Eva Aufschlager and Ursula Klein were daughters of the bakeress and witch Margareth Gnan. Wulz, 'Die Nördlinger Hexen'; Voges, *Die Reichsstadt Nördlingen*; Friedrichs, *Nördlingen*, esp. p. 107; Rolf Kiessling, *Die Stadt und ihr Land*, (Städteforschung A/29), Vienna 1989, pp. 237–47; Ingrid Bátori, 'Herren, Meister, Habenichtse. Die Bürgerschaft der Reichsstadt Nördlingen um 1500', in Walter Barsig et al., eds, *Rieser Kulturtage. Eine Landschaft stellt sich vor* (Dokumentation, vol. VI/1), Nördlingen 1987, p. 262; Bátori, 'Frauen im Handel und Handwerk in der Reichsstadt Nördlingen im 15. und 16. Jahrhundert', in Barbara Vogel and Ulrike Weckel, eds, *Frauen in der Ständegesellschaft*, Hamburg 1991. Thus there was an imaginative connection between the trades with which the witches were connected and the themes of the accusations.

16. StadtAN, Hexenprozeßakten, Ursula Haider, 27 Nov. 1589, Jerg Minderlin. By a dreadful irony, he was later to commit suicide in prison when he was accused of grave robbery and allowing animals to attack corpses in the graveyard, at St Emmeran.

17. Erik Midelfort, *Witch Hunting in Southwestern Germany 1562–1684. The Social and Intellectual Foundations*, Stanford 1972, pp. 36–58; and see also Stuart Clark, 'Protestant Demonology: Sin, Superstition, and Society (*c.* 1520–*c.* 1630)', in Bengt Ankarloo und Gustav Henningsen, eds, *Early Modern European Witchcraft. Centres and Peripheries*, Oxford 1990, pp. 45–82. On the history of Nördlingen's Reformation see Hans-Christoph Rublack, *Eine Bürgerliche Reformation: Nördlingen* (Quellen und Forschungen zur Reformationsgeschichte 51), Gütersloh 1982; Rublack, 'The Song of Contz Anahans: Communication and Revolt in Nördlingen, 1525', in R. Po-chia Hsia, ed., *The German People and the Reformation*, Ithaca, NY, and London 1988, pp. 102–21; Rublack, 'Political and Social Norms in Urban Communities in the Holy Roman Empire', in Kaspar von Greyerz, ed., *Religion, Politics, and Social Protest*, London 1984, pp. 24–60; Friedrichs, *Nördlingen*.

18. 'Jrer selbst leibs geburt, wider die Natur, nit Verschonet', StadtAN, Nördlinger Urfehdebuch 1587, fo. 112r, 10 July 1590.

19. StadtAN, Missivbuch, fo. 47 ff., 1478; Missive, 1478 fo. 140 ff; 176 ff; Wulz, 'Nördlinger Hexenprozesse'. She was however set free. The next case of witchcraft, which also ended without an execution, occurred in 1534. Motifs which appeared in it include a midwife and naked dancing, but no cannibalism: StadtAN, 'Akten in Sachen der Apollonia ... wegen Verdachts der Hexerei 1534'; Urfehdebuch 1533–50, fo. 34.

20. 'Der bess' dug up the child and 'geprotten' it. The 'gefress' lasted four hours. StadtAN, Hexenprozeßakten, 13–14 Nov. 1589; Ursula Haider; 'ein schwarz ding Jnn einer schussel gelegen', StadtAN, Hexenprozeßakten, Anna Koch, Confrontation 15 June 1590, Burckmairin; Apollonia Aißlinger, 18 May 1590, 'schwerz ding gessenn'.

21. StadtAN, Hexenprozeßakten, Katharina Keßler, 6 April 1591; 'nit vil zu dem nachtmal ganngen'; 'Seye nit wild mit vmbganngen, wie die andere', StadtAN, Hexenprozeßakten, Susanna Mair, 28 Sept. 1590; 'hab sie angefochtenn, vnnd allss sie zum nachtmahl ganngen, sie vermaindt Jr sindt werden Jr nit verzigen', StadtAN, Hexenprozeßakten, Barbara Stecher, 5 Sept. 1590; StadtAN, Hexenprozeßakten, 12 Oct. 1590, Barbara Stecher. The theme emerges many times. Another woman related how she had managed to get the Devil to disappear – temporarily – by uttering the name of Jesus, and how she had gone to communion two years earlier, and had felt strange in her

head: 'Jr der Kopf gar fast gedummelt, vnd gerumpelt hab', StadtAN, Hexenprozeßakten, Ursula Haider, 8 Nov. 1589. Immediately after confessing she had attended a meal where child-flesh was served, Barbara Lierheimer volunteered that she had not been to communion for four years: the associative link is plain: StadtAN, Hexenprozeßakten, 8 July 1590, Barbara Lierheimer. See also Maria Schöpperlin, who supposedly gave the Host to the Devil, a confession which she combined with her narrative of child murder: 'Die Kindlein wie Angezaigt. getödt, Auch dz Nachtmal Jme bösen geben', 14 May 1590; she was also believed to have killed her own children.

22. Stephen Greenblatt, *Marvelous Possessions. The Wonder of the New World*, Oxford 1991, pp. 136, 190 note 25; on the motif of Christ in the winepress, R.W. Scribner, *For the Sake of Simple Folk. Popular Propaganda for the German Reformation*, 1981; Oxford 1994, pp. 104–7: interestingly this motif was taken over by the Protestants and reworked so that it becomes the Word which is placed in the hopper; on bleeding hosts, Miri Rubin, *Corpus Christi. The Eucharist in Late Medieval Culture*, Cambridge 1991, pp. 312–16, 135–9, and Charles Zika, 'Hosts, Processions and Pilgrimages in Fifteenth-century Germany', *Past and Present* 118, 1988, pp. 25–64. However, the imagery should not be taken too literally: according to Ursula Haider there was *white* wine at the feasts: StadtAN, Hexenprozeßakten, 25 Nov. 1589.

23. See R. Po-chia Hsia, *The Myth of Ritual Murder. Jews and Magic in Reformation Germany*, New Haven and London 1988; Rubin, *Corpus Christi*; Miri Rubin, *Gentile Tales. The Narrative Assault on Late Medieval Jews*, New Haven and London 1999.

24. Voges, *Die Reichsstadt Nördlingen*, p. 161.

25. According to Haider's testimony one child was eight weeks old: StadtAN, Hexenprozeßakten, Ursula Haider, 25 Nov. 1589; she said that the meat tasted 'wild': 28 Nov. 1589. Margareth Getzler remembered that the child had been a little boy ('ein büeblin'), 5 Feb. 1590; Schöpperlin 'wollte nit wissenn wz dz für ein brats Jm Keller gewesen, so sie gessen habenn' but guessed that it was 'ein hass', 12 May 1590; but two days later she admitted that it was a 'little child' ('kindlein'); 'roast child's little foot/leg' ('Brates kindts füesslin'), Barbara Lierheimer, 14 July 1590; Barbara Stecher, 12 Oct. 1590, remembered a child 'ungeuerlich 6 wuchen alt Worden', called 'Annelin': Katharina Keßler, undated, 'Wass auf Katharinam Keßlerin ausgesagt wird'; Margreta Humlin said it was 'ein Siess fleisch, vnd Stuckhlen gewessen'. Susanna Mair said 'Sie solle zu Jr kommen, sie hab etwas guets zuessenn'; Lierheimer described a 'herrliche malzeit': StadtAN, Hexenprozeßakten, Susanna Mair, 26 Sept. 1590; Barbara Lierheimer, 8 July 1590.

Melanie Klein sometimes terms the stage of oral sadism in infants one of cannibalism: *The Psychoanalysis of Children*, trans. Alix Strachey, London 1932; 1989, pp. 50 and 50n; 130, where Klein points out that this aggression soon comes to be directed against the father as well, and stems from libidinal frustration of oral-sadistic cravings; as she argues (pp. 151, 156–7), in part this is because 'in the cannibalistic phase children equate every kind of food with their objects, as represented by their organs, so that [food] takes on the significance of their father's penis and their mother's breast and is loved, hated and feared like these'. See also, Klein, 'Some Theoretical Conclusions regarding the Emotional Life of the Infant' (1952), in Klein, *Envy and Gratitude and Other Works 1946–63*, London 1975; 1988, pp. 61–93; 'A Contribution to the Psychogenesis of Manic-Depressive States' (1935), esp. p. 287; and 'Weaning' (1936), p. 293 in Klein, *Love, Guilt and Reparation and Other Works 1921–1945*, London 1975, 1988. Klein also explores how, in women who feed their children, these childish primal phantasies are finally resolved and revealed as having been harmless to the mother's breast. Her remarks are illuminating in suggesting why, in some cases, this kind of resolution might not be achieved: Klein, 'The Effects of Early Anxiety-Situations on the Sexual Development of the Girl', in *The Psychoanalysis of Children*, 1989, esp. p. 232 and n.1.

26. 'hab nit fil gesen. sonder sich des Trinckhens vberholffen. dann dz Jm geschmeckht'; 'die mann hab der bess nit gern bei sich, dann sie sauffen sich eben fol, fluechenn, khenne nichts mit Jnen aussrichten, dann es dürst die bader Jmmer, vnnd er khenne Jmer eher. 3 weiber für ein man bekhommen'; 'Sei ein magt schener alß die Ander', StadtAN, Hexenprozeßakten, Jörg Kürschnauer, 6 March 1593. 'Seinß weibs gespann hab sin weib am ersten Jn der Badtstuben herüberzogen. Vnnd nit allwegen Jm beth geschen', StadtAN, 7 March 1593; this was on the day his wife was arrested. Kürschnauer had also said that his wife insulted him as 'useless, either in bed or at table'. On drunkenness, masculinity and the social character of drinking, see B. Ann Tlusty, *Bacchus and Civic Order. The Culture of Drink in Early Modern Germany*, Charlottesville and London 2001; on the man of excess, see Lyndal Roper, *Oedipus and the Devil. Witchcraft, Sexuality and Religion in Early Modern Europe*, London 1994.

27. StadtAN, Hexenprozeßakten, Margaretha Minderlin, 27 Oct. 1598, 'Jtem sie het ein Mann er fraget nichts nach Jhr wer tag vnnd Nacht im Wuerzhauss, vnnd wen sie sein woltte sein muest sie alle guet that von Jhm haben, Er sej der Gross Teufel'.

28. On the myth of Jewish ritual murder see Hsia, *The Myth of Ritual Murder*, and Rubin, *Gentile Tales*. This case also bears striking similarity to waves of persecutions of gravediggers in the wake of plague, documented by Karen Lambrecht, '"Jagdhunde des Teufels". Die Verfolgung von Totengräbern im Gefolge frühneuzeitlicher Pestwellen', in Andreas Blauert and Gerd Schwerhoff, eds, *Mit den Waffen der Justiz. Zur Kriminalitätsgeschichte des späten Mittelalters und der Frühen Neuzeit*, Frankfurt 1993.

29. 'Kain rueh'; 'ein loch vnder der brust gehabt wie ain pfening das sey gar sauber gewest'; 'wan die hen an fach zu faulen so werd das weib an fachen zu fliessen bis die hen erfaul': StadtAN, Hexenprozeßakten, 18 Feb. 1591, Katharina Keßler.

30. 'ellendt worden vnnd ausgesehenn, wie ein Crucifix'; StadtAN, Hexenprozeßakten, Margareth Betsch, '1590', Aussagegen gegen 'Lumpenfreulin' [Barbara Stecher]; 'dem kneblin vber den kopff hinab gefahren mit vermelden wie hond ir ain schenen gross kopfeten bueben, wurt eben eurem fater nach schlagen': Apollonia Aißlinger, 24 April 1590, interrogation concerning Schöperlin/Brückmairin; Apollonia Aißlinger, 24 April 1590, Verhör über die Schöperlin/Brückmairin, Aussagen gegen Burckmairin; Susanna Mair, Akten in Sachen Betsch, 23 Oct. 1590; Katharina Keßler, 18 Feb. 1591.

31. Eucharius Rösslin's widely used *Rosengarten* explained how midwives were to do this when all else failed: Steven Ozment, *When Fathers Ruled. Family Life in Reformation Europe*, Cambridge, Mass., 1983, pp. 110–12; and see, on midwives, Merry Wiesner, 'The Midwives of South Germany and the Public/Private Dichotomy', in Hilary Marland, ed., *The Art of Midwifery. Early Modern Midwives in Europe*, London 1993; and on the horror felt towards those born of dead mothers by Caesarean birth, Jacques Gélis, *History of Childbirth. Fertility, Pregnancy and Birth in Early Modern Europe*, French 1984; Oxford 1991, pp. 236–7.

32. Schöpperlin at first explained that the Devil only took unbaptized children, that is, children who were unbaptized because they had died during or shortly after birth, or miscarriages. She described the eating of her own children or foetuses, and recounted how she had promised the child in her body to the Devil, and her subsequent miscarriage. StadtAN, Hexenprozeßakten, Maria Schöpperlin, 14 May 1590. Barbara Stecher confessed that she had promised the Devil a child which she had carried for twenty-six weeks: 12 Oct. 1590; Barbara Kürschnauer was certain that for the diabolic meals they had collected an 'unbaptized child': 9 March 1593. However, Ursula Haider's confession seems to imply that the children had already been born; and even Schöpperlin's later

confessions apparently indicate that the children had been born. Barbara Stecher described eating a child which she had poisoned when it was six weeks old, and how it had then lain ill for six weeks. For 'exhumation' of the child to be possible, the infant must already have been buried, which would be improbable in the case of the products of a miscarriage. Clearly there is some confusion about whether the 'children' were born or not; as well as some unclarity in the term 'Kindlein' itself, because this word is also used for foetuses which were stillborn before time. It also reveals the fluid nature of what was considered deserving of burial and what was deserving of baptism, a question which was relevant to the passionately debated issue of emergency infant baptism by midwives as well.

Presumably these descriptions arose out of the women's own experiences of miscarriages and were connected to their feelings of mourning and guilt. It is interesting that these women thought they could remember all these miscarriages and the precise age of the 'child'.

33. See Susan C. Karant-Nunn, 'A Women's Rite: Churching and Reformation of Ritual', in Ronnie Po-chia Hsia and Bob Scribner, eds, *Problems in the Historical Anthropology of Early Modern Europe,* Wiesbaden 1997.

34. There were five members of the 'Secret Council' and ten other ordinary members. On the political structure of Nördlingen, see Friedrichs, *Nördlingen,* p. 13. Apart from Georg Bin, who also held office as *Stadtkammerer,* all the ordinary members of the Council as well as some members of the Secret Council can be shown to have taken part in a witch trial. See StadtAN, Steuerbuch 1588–90, fo. 370 ff. for office-holding; together with the lists of those present that head each interrogation record, see Hexenprozeßakten.

35. Johannes Pferinger, mayor and advocate of the fight against the witches, paid 5 fl in tax; StadtAN, Steuerbücher 1588–90: 1588 (366v), 1589 (369v); and in 1591–93 he paid 5 fl. 30 kr: 1591 (367v), 1592 (370v), 1593 (373v); the widow of Caspar Schöpperlin, who had been a councillor, paid by contrast 27 fl. 30 kr.: 1588–90, fo. 67v; Rebekka Lemp's husband Peter Lemp was well-off; Karl Gundelfinger, who was married to Dorothea Gundelfinger, later executed as a witch, was a goldsmith, acted as rotating mayor, and was also involved in witch trials. He paid 6 fl. tax, Steuerbücher 1588 (366v), 1589 (369v), 1592 6 fl. (370r); the brother of Anna Koch, executed for witchcraft, had an inheritance of over 700 fl. from his father and mother. Anna Koch paid 15 fl. tax in 1590 (Wulz, 'Die Nördlinger Hexen'); Apollonia Aißlinger's mother, who died in 1587, was also comfortably off and paid 13 fl. tax (Wulz, 'Die Nördlinger Hexen'). Maria Holl, who did not confess and was let free, was innkeeper at 'zur Golden Krone', for which her husband had paid the sizeable sum of 2,306 fl. in 1586.

36. Dorothea Gundelfinger: see Wulz, 'Die Nördlinger Hexen'.

37. Between 1588 and 1596 there were only twenty-two individuals who had held positions on the Council: StadtAN, Steuerbücher. On the constitution, see Friedrichs, *Nördlingen,* p. 12, esp. n. 14.

38. Sigmund Freud, *Totem and Taboo* (Leipzig and Vienna 1913), in *The Standard Edition of the Complete Psychological Works of Sigmund Freud,* 24 vols, ed. James Strachey in co-operation with Anna Freud, Alix Strachey and Alan Tyson et al., London 1953–74, vol. 13 . Freud developed the idea of the cannibalistic component in the Oedipal love for the parent in his *Three Essays on the Theory of Sexuality* (1905), in Freud, *Standard Edition,* vol. 7, where he argues that the first stage of sexual organization is pregenital and oral, and in *Group Psychology and the Analysis of the Ego* (1921), in Freud, *Standard Edition,* vol. 18, pp. 69–143.

39. StadtAN, Steuerbuch 1594–96, fo. 374v (1596); Friedrichs, *Nördlingen,* pp. 211–12; Wulz, 'Nördlinger Hexenprozesse'.

Chapter 4: Sex with the Devil

1. SAW, Misc. 1954, I, Barbara, Leonhard Hohenberger's wife called Big Head, 3 April 1590, fo. 125 ff.
2. 'er hette gesagt sie seye zu alt darzu', SAW Misc. 1954, II, fos. 9–34, Anna Starr, 11 April 1603; 'Got aber nit gar abgesagt', SAW, Misc 1954, I, fos. 137–50, Affra Mertzler, 5–9 Aug. 1597.
3. See also Richard van Dülmen, 'Imagination des Teuflischen. Nächtliche Zusammenkünfte, Hexentänze, Teufelssabbate', in van Dülmen, ed., *Hexenwelten. Magie und Imagination vom 16.–20. Jahrhundert*, Frankfurt am Main 1987.
4. Henry [*sic*] Boguet, *An Examen of Witches*, French 1590; London 1929, trans. Montague Summers, p. 29.
5. See for instance the love-magic spell recited by Anna Stauder of Augsburg which involves reference to the moon shining upon bodily parts, including 'auf sein gerechte Mannsfeder'. Wolfgang Behringer, *Mit dem Feuer vom Leben zum Tod. Hexengesetzgebung in Bayern*, Munich 1988, p. 209.
6. We meet a variant of Federlin, Federwüsch, amongst Lorraine witches, according to Nicolas Rémy, *Demonolatry*, trans. E.A. Ashwin, ed. Revd Montague Summers, London 1930, p. 30 (Bk I, ch. viii). Witches in Nördlingen and Marchtal frequently met 'Federlin'. In Lorraine, the name Federbusch is found in the archival records too, but only in the German-speaking regions of the Duchy, not in the French-speaking areas: I am grateful to Robin Briggs for this information.
7. SAS Dep. 30, Rep. VI, Pak. 254, Marchtaler Hexenprozesse, Ursula Bayer, 25 June 1586.
8. Winfried Nuber, 'Abtei Marchtal und seine Pfarrei in der Stadt Munderkingen' in Max Müller, Rudolf Reinhardt and Wilfried Schöntag, eds, *Marchtal Prämonstratenserabtei, Fürstliches Schloß, Kirchliche Akademie*, Ulm 1992, p. 128; Max Müller, 'Die Pröpste und Äbte des Klosters Marchtal', in ibid., text of nineteenth-century history of the monastery based on Sebastian Sailer, pp. 76–7 for biography of Frei.
9. 'gar schen bekhommen, nit fil bart gehabt vnnd gesehen wie Jr buel', StadtAN, Hexenprozeßakten, Maria Schöpperlin, 12 May 1590; SAN, Hexenprozeßakten 48, Catherine Puzel, 5 July 1623; SAW, Misc. 1954, I, Walpurg Stainbach von Lauda, 26 Jan. 1603, fo. 226 ('Sey ein schöner Junger man gewest, wie ein schöner Junger Pfarrer').
10. StadtAN, Hexenprozeßakten, Maria Marb, 16 Feb. 1590; 'seie der Edel Jnn Jrem Mutter hauß nach Jr Mueter todt kommen. vf dem Abent, begerendt seins willens zusein, wie beschehen. hernacher begert sich Jme zuuersprechen vnd sein zusein, wiewol Jr hertz betruebt gewesen'; and StadtAN, Hexenprozeßakten, Maria Marb, 12 Feb. 1590.
11. SAW, Gericht Gerolzhofen 346, Agnes Heylmann, 30 Aug. 1617.
12. 'gar mit leyßer stim geredt', SAW, Hist. Saal VII, 25/375 fos. 63–5, Hans Duelicken Weib, 3 May 1616.
13. Valentin Groebner, 'Insides Out: Clothes, Dissimulation and the Arts of Accounting in the Autobiography of Mathäus Schwarz (1498–1574)', *Representations* 66, 1999, pp. 52–72.
14. 'Jn einer schönen Manß gestalt .... vnd grün gekleid gewesen', SAW, Misc. 1954, I, fos. 152–72, Ursula, Hans Giller's widow; 'ein Kleiner mahn, in grunen Kleidung', SAW, Hist. Saal VII, 25/375, fo. 313, Barbara Schluchter, 8 March 1617; 'habe solchen von weiten kommen sehen, ein griens kleidt gehabt, ein hohen huedt, vnd ein feder gehabdt', SAW, Hist. Saal VII, 25/375, Anna Deissler/Zöttlin, Einaugichte Schlösserin,

27 July 1616; SAW, 25/375, fo. 271, Margareta Schreyer, 21 June 1617; 'wehr ein schöner Junger gesell mit Einem schwaren barth, Roder Kleydung, grünen Strümpffen vnd schwarzen huet. Roder federn daruff, kommen', SAW, Gericht Gerolzhofen 346, Anna Grauch, 31 Aug. 1617.

15. 'Wann Jr Gott nit zu einem Mann helfften wölle, so solle Jr halt der teüffel darzu helfften'; 'du waist dass ich dich alzeit lieb gehabt habe'; SAW, Misc. 1954, I, fo. 1ff., Waldburga Schmid, 17 Nov. 1626.

16. 'hernacher seyen sie mit ein ander in Jr stuben gangen, sich hindern disch gesezt, wehr Jr vatter vnd Mutter auch dobey gesessen, haben brott vnd wein gehabt, hab die muetter den wein geholt, haben uff ain halbe stundt zue disch gesessen … der böse feindt hab nit viel geredt, sondern hab nuhr Allezeyt gesagt, sie solt gut sach haben', SAW, Gericht Gerolzhofen 346, Anna Grauch, 31 Aug. 1617.

17. Staatsarchiv Basel, Criminalia 4/3, Dilge Glaser, 1532.

18. SAW, Misc. 1954, II, fos. 112–16, Anna Lang, 4 Jan. 1612.

19. 'Sie Angeredt. Wo hin mus fraülen, Vnd gefragt, ob sie kein Mann, hab sie geantwurt Nein (158) daruf er vermelt, sie soll Jn nemen. Wann sie Jme volgen. Wölle Jr helffen. das sie Jr lebtag gnug haben solle, hette sie zu Jme gesagt, er sei Jr zu hüpsch. vnd gefragt, Wo er her sey.' He replied: 'Wölls er Jr nacher wol sagen. Vnd er wölle heint zu Jr komen. Sie hin wider vermelt. bringe mir etwas gutes. hab er gesagt, Jha. Des Nachts sei er zu Jr Jn Kamern komen, sich zu Jr Jns Beth gelegt, Vnd gesagt. kome her. Jch hab dich lieb. Wöl Jr genug geben, sie soll sein sein, Vnd thon Was er sie heisse, Mit Jr gebulet hette ein kalte scham (158v) gehabt, vnd sich der Spitz Hutlen genant', SAW, Misc. 1954, II, fo. 157v, Barbara Herpolt, 18 March 1602.

20. 'gefatterin weylen ihr so ein bösen man habt, will ich euch ein andern dagegen geben, hatte sie gesagt Ja Wann sie ihr ein frommen geben wolt, so wolt sie ihnen nehmen vnd zu frieden sein'. SAW, Hist. Saal VII, 25/376, fo. 38, Margaretha Schmid, 9 Feb. 1618.

21. 'er wolte ihr guet tag schaffen'; 'Wan sie danoch Wüßte dz es Wahr Wehre er ihr solches starck versprochen', SAW, Hist. Saal VII, 25/375, fos. 275–8, Margareta Limpart, 23 June 1617.

22. 'das sie wider vmbkert. zu ruckh vnnd widerumb, Jn Allerlay gedannkchen haimgangen', SAS Dep. 30, Rep. VI, Pak. 254, Marchtaler Hexenprozesse, Margareta Moll, 25 June 1590, and see record of his death; and also Hans Hepp, 27 July 1586, for his trial.

23. SAW, Gericht Gerolzhofen 346, 25 April 1618, Hans Holz, 25 April 1618, fo. 102r ff.

24. SAS Dep. 30, Rep. VI, Pak. 254, Marchtaler Hexenprozesse, Conrad Schreyer, 13 June 1587. Just how difficult it could be for men to fit their stories into the template of diabolic seduction by a devil who was commonly conceived as male is evident in such cases as that of Cunz Dübner. He first encountered the Devil in male form and only later did he appear in female form for sexual congress. Dübner consistently denied that he had ever committed harmful deeds of any kind, thus distancing himself from the core allegations of witchcraft. His marriage had been unhappy and his wife had been executed. SAW, Gerolzhofen 346, Cunz Dübner, 23 Feb. 1618, fo. 96r ff.

In only one case have I encountered female witches whose stories concern lesbianism: Staatsarchiv Basel Stadt, Criminalia 4/12, Elsbeth Hertner von Riehen, 28 July–14 Aug. 1647. Two *Gutachten* on the case (memorials of advice) have survived. White spirits of the dead appeared to her advising her to lie with a woman, her *Basen*. Parts of her fragmentary story sound like encounters with a mysterious stranger, in this case a woman, who later turns out to be a devil; there was also a tailor who she said appeared nightly to her, but whom others could not see.

25. SAS Dep. 30, Rep. VI, Pak. 254, Marchtaler Hexenprozesse, Martin Getz, 2 Aug. 1627.

Getz was not from Marchtal but had fled to a relative in the jurisdiction of Marchtal once the allegations came out.

26. StadtAN, Hexenprozeßakten, Maria Schöpperlin, 12 May 1590; StadtAA, Urg., Ursula Gron, 14 July 1694; SAW, Misc. 1954, II, Walpurg Stainbach von Lauda, 26 Jan. 1603, fo. 5v.

27. SAW, Misc. 1954, I, Walpurg Schmid, 17 Nov. 1626: the Devil has only one foot and was quite black; Margareta Hainrich, Praunen Jäger's wife, 3 April 1590: Devil has horse feet; SAW, Hist. Saal VII, 25/376, fo. 38, Margaretha Schmid, 19 Feb. 1618: Devil's shame and breast hard; SAW, Misc. 1954, II, fos. 9–34, Anna Starr, 11 April 1603: Anna Starr punningly called her Devil 'Beelzebock' and he did indeed appear to her in the form of a white goat; SAW, Hist. Saal VII 25/375, fo. 271, Margareta Schreyer, 21 June 1617: left foot like a goat's foot; SAW, Misc. 1954, I, fo. 137 ff., 5–9 Aug. 1597, Affra, widow of Michel Mertzler: Devil has cat feet; StadtAA, Urg., Ursula Gron, 14 July 1694: Devil has pig's snout.

28. See Diane Purkiss, *The Witch in History. Early Modern and Twentieth-century Representations,* London 1996, Marion Gibson, *Reading Witchcraft. Stories of Early English Witches,* London 1999, Marion Gibson, *Early Modern Witches. Witchcraft Cases in Contemporary Writing,* London 2000, Barbara Rosen, *Witchcraft in England 1558–1618,* Amherst 1969, 1991.

29. 'Dilge wie kompt es dz du dich also übel gehebst, wie kanstu also thun', Staatsarchiv Basel, Criminalia 4/3, Dilge Glaser, 1532; SAW, Misc. 1954, II, fo. 109, Kethe, wife of Claus am Stein, 30 May 1611.

30. On melancholy, the Devil and temptation to commit suicide, see Vera Lind, *Selbstmord in der Frühen Neuzeit. Diskurs, Lebenswelt und kultureller Wandel,* Göttingen 1999, esp. p. 159 ff.; and on punishments, p. 31 ff.: the Carolina treated suicide as punishable but attempted to limit the practice of confiscation of the suicide's property, a limitation which many local law codes did not observe.

31. 'Denn wann die Weiber in Widerwertigkeit/ Arbeitseligkeit/ oder Betrübnuß gerathen/ entstället ihnen das Gemuth/ insonderheit/ wenn kein Trost/ Rath noch Hulff vorhanden/ diese gelegnheit durchforschet der Teuffel/ vnd vnder gestalt einer erdichter Peronen/ verheischet er mit wunderbarlichem Betrug/ Hulff/ Rath / vnd Beschirmung', Peter Binsfeld, *Tractat Von Bekantnuß der Zauberer und Hexen,* Trier, Heinrich Bock, 1590, fo. 38.

32. Martin Montanus, *Schwankbücher,* ed. Johannes Bolte, Bibliothek des literarischen Vereins Stuttgart 217, Tübingen 1899, *Gartengesellschaft,* ch. 85.

33. 'glater geschmirter wort', SAW, Misc. 1954, II, fo. 109, Kethe, wife of Claus am Stein, 30 May 1611.

34. SAW, Hist. Saal VII, 25/376, fos. 44–9, Barbara Dämeter, 21 Feb. 1618; Margaretha Schmid also said that she felt no seed enter her body, and that the Devil was hard like wood, and icy cold: SAW, Hist. Saal VII, 25/376, 9 Feb. 1618, fo. 38 ff.

35. SAW, Hist. Saal VII, 25/375, fos. 250–3, 26–27 Aug. 1617. 'Ihr Bulschafft hab offt Vnzucht mir ihr getriben, seie sein manlich Kliedt ir in den Leib kommen, hab ir ihres mans Wesen beser gefallen dan eß gar kalt gewesen hab ein geringe freudt darob gehabt, doch ir vnzucht bei einer halben stunden gewehret.'

36. SAS Dep. 30, Rep. VI, Pak. 254, Marchtaler Hexenprozesse, Lucia Vischer, 25 April 1587; 'seiner muottwillen gahr hesslich mit Jr Pflogennm Also dass sie sich darob gar vbel gehalten', SAS Dep. 30, Rep. VI, Pak. 254, Marchtaler Hexenprozesse, Lena Gräter, '1586'.

37. 'vnd wan der boess gaist Lang gnug die vnkeusche werck mit Jr triben hab sie vßgespeyen, hab er Alls dan von Jr weichen müßen.' SAS Dep. 30, Rep. VI, Pak. 254, Marchtaler Hexenprozesse, Anna Moll, 30 Oct. 1593. The elder Anna Moll, executed in 1586, said that she had only one eye because she had once refused the Devil sex and in

revenge he had plucked it out. Vivid and personally revealing as this detail appears to be, it repeated a confession made earlier by other accused witches and was almost certainly borrowed from it. For details of the Moll family see SAS Dep. 30, Rep. VI, Pak. 254, Marchtaler Hexenprozesse, Margareta Moll, 25 June 1590; Hans Hepp, 27 July 1586; Anna Moll, 8 Aug. 1586; Anna Moll, 30 Oct. 1593; Michel Moll, 30 Oct. 1593; there is no record of the execution of Anna Hiert in 1586. Incest also emerged as a theme in other Marchtal trials: Katharina Mundinger confessed to incest with her brother-in-law: SAS Dep. 30, Rep. VI, Pak. 254, Marchtaler Hexenprozesse, Katharina Mundinger, 25 June 1590.

38. Rémy, *Demonolatry*, p. 19 (Bk I, ch. vi). Interestingly, marriages with devils also appear in the confessions of women in the Lorraine archival records, but only from the German-speaking regions to the north-east of the Duchy. I am grateful to Robin Briggs for this information.

39. See Susanna Burghartz, 'Rechte Jungfrauen oder unverschämte Töchter? Zur weiblichen Ehre im 16. Jahrhundert', in Karin Hausen and Heide Wunder, eds, *Frauengeschichte – Geschlechtergeschichte*, Frankfurt 1992; Ulrike Strasser, *State of Virginity: Gender, Religion, and Politics in an Early Modern Catholic State*, Ann Arbor 2003.

40. 'Jnn Jr muetter küchin das erst mal wie ein handtwerckhsmann zue Jr kommen. Schwarz Claidt ganngen. auff dem huedt ein Feder. vnd gais füeß gehabt. Er aber auch schwarz gewest. Sey Jr muetter darbey gewessen vnd begert soll vnzucht mit Jm treiben, Aber lang nit thain wöllen, welches aber Jr muetter eben haben wollen, Sey also genöttigt worden. Vnnd hab das werckh der laiblichen vnzucht anfänglich mit Jme volnzogen, darauff Jr muetter hinweg gangen vnd gelacht', SAN, Eichstätt, Hexenprozeßakten 42, Barbara Weis, 25 March 1590. See also SAW, Hist. Saal VII, 25/375, fo. 297 v, Anna Zott, 27 July 1616, for similar laughter by the *Lehrmeisterin* when the seduction is completed.

41. SAW, Hist. Saal VII, 25/375, fo. 271, Margaret Schreyer, 21 June 1617. See also SAW, Hist. Saal, 25/375, ff. 275–8, 23 June 1617 Margreta Limpart for a similar confession.

42. SAS Dep. 30, Rep. VI, Pak. 254, Marchtaler Hexenprozesse, Margretha Selg [1586]; Hans Hepp and Anna Moll, 8 Aug. 1586.

43. SAS Dep. 30, Rep. VI, Pak. 254, Marchtaler Hexenprozesse, Anna Mayer, 8 June 1587; Anna Glenzinger 10 June 1587; see also for example Juliane Laub [1590], who killed a child shortly after it was born, and Anna Spatenmeyer, who dug up the bodies of children in the cemetery at Saulgart, 10 June 1587.

44. 'Damals hette er sie Jn Jrem Beth gebulet, sein Scham seie gar heiss gewesen, hette katzen füß. vnd ein Natur. Wie ein ander Man gehabt, Doch sie nit recht gesehen, Wie er Jn allem beschaffen Darauf sie gefragt, Weil dann Jrem an zeigen nach. Jr Bul an seinem Natur beschaffen, Wie ein ander Mann, Warumb sie nit schwanger worden', SAW, Misc. 1954, I, fo. 137 ff., 5–9 Aug. 1597, Affra, widow of Michel Mertzler.

45. Charles Stewart, 'Dreams and Desire in Ancient and Early Christian Thought', in Daniel Pick and Lyndal Roper, eds, *Dreams and History*, London 2003.

46. Heinrich Kramer and James Sprenger [*sic*], *The Malleus Maleficarum*, ed. and trans. Revd Montague Summers, 1928; 1971, pp. 21–9 (Part I, qu. 3), and see p. 112 ff. (Part II, qu. 1, ch. 4); Wolfgang Behringer and Günter Jerouschek, eds, *Der Hexenhammer*, trans. W. Behringer, G. Jerouschek and W. Tschacher, Munich 2000, pp. 177–92, 396–411. This is also the line taken by Peter Binsfeld, who argues that as devils do not have bodies, they cannot generate children themselves: *Tractat*, fos. 51–52v, translation of Latin version.

47. Rémy, *Demonolatry*, Bk I, ch. vi, p. 20; and see pp. 11–27; 'Vechselkind', Jean Bodin, *De*

la démonomanie des sorciers, Paris 1580, fo. 106r; 'Vnnd vil schwerer dann andere Kinder seind/ wieuol sie stäts Mager bleiben/ vnnd wol drey Saügammen zu Todt saugten/ eh sie etwas feißt würden …' Jean Bodin, *Vom Außgelaßnen Wütigen Teuffels heer Allerhand Zauberern/ Hexen vnd Hexenmeistern/ Vnholden/ Teuffelsbeschwerern/ Warsager …*, trans. Johann Fischart, Strasbourg, B. Jobin, 1586, p. 359; and see Stefan Janson, *Jean Bodin, Johan Fischart: De la démonomanie des sorciers (1580), Vom ausge-lassnen wütigen Teuffelsheer (1581), und ihre Fallberichte* (Europäische Hochschulschriften 352), Frankfurt am Main 1980; Florence M. Weinberg, *Gargantua in a Convex Mirror. Fischart's View of Rabelais*, New York 1986.

48. Bodin, *Vom Außgelaßnen …*, p. 359; and compare the passage in the French, Bodin, *Démonomanie*, fos. 106 ff.

49. There is a further version of this story in Paul Frisius's *Von deß Teuffels Nebelkappen*, reprinted in Abraham Saur, *Theatrum de veneficis*, Frankfurt, Nicolaus Basse, 1586, pp. 225 ff. In this version, the child is taken to Neuhausen to be weighed by the reluctant mother, who does not wish to part with the monster. The parents are a servant of a cleric and his cook, who have a secret marriage. The original story may well date back at least to Luther. David Meder, *Acht Hexen predigten*, Leipzig, Valentin am Ende Erben, 1615, fos. 73r–74r, also tells the story, ascribing it to Luther, Tischreden and commentaries on Genesis 6. On Frisius, see Charles Zika, 'Appropriating Folklore in Sixteenth-Century Witchcraft Literature: The *Nebelkappe* of Paulus Frisius', in Zika, ed., *Exorcising our Demons. Magic, Witchcraft and Visual Culture in Early Modern Europe*, Leiden and Boston 2003.

50. Binsfeld, *Tractat*, p. 52v: 'mit hulff eins Menschen/ in dem sie den Samen von den Mannen/ mit schändtlichem vnderleigen empfahen/ vnd noch schändtlicher mit den Weiberen vermischendt von sich geben/ aber alles auß sonderlicher ordnung Gottes/ damit der also empfangen vnd geboren wirdt/ nicht des Teuffels Kindt sey/ sonder deß Menschen/ von welchem der Samen genommen ist'.

51. Francesco Maria Guazzo, *Compendium maleficarum*, ed. and trans. Montague Summers, London 1929, p. 29 (Bk 1, ch. x); for Glikl's version, see Natalie Zemon Davis, *Women on the Margins. Three Seventeenth-Century Lives*, Cambridge (Mass.) and London 1995, pp. 38–9: the sexes are reversed. A shipwrecked Talmudic scholar takes a savage wife, who, when he sails away and leaves her, tears their son in two, throws half at the ship, and devours the other half.

52. Quoted in Stuart Clark, *Thinking with Demons. The Idea of Witchcraft in Early Modern Europe*, Oxford 1997, p. 190.

53. On early modern contraceptive practices, see Angus McLaren, *A History of Contraception. From Antiquity to the Present Day*, Oxford 1990; 1992, pp. 141–77.

Chapter 5: Sabbaths

1. *Historia von D. Johann Fausten. Text des Druckes von 1587, Kritische Ausgabe*, ed. Stephan Füssel and Hans Joachim Kreutzer, Stuttgart 1988, pp. 60–70; *Die Schedelsche Weltchronik (1493)*, Facsimile edition Dortmund 1978; and see Frank Baron, *Faustus on Trial. The Origins of Johann Spies's 'Historia' in an Age of Witch Hunting* (Frühe Neuzeit. Studien und Dokumente zur deutschen Literatur im europäischen Kontext, vol. 9), Tübingen 1992, pp. 95–109.

2. Augustin Lercheimer (pseudonym of Hermann Wilken also known as Witekind), *Ein*

Christlich Bedencken vnd Erinnerung von Zauberey (1585), in Abraham Saur, ed., *Theatrum de veneficis*, Frankfurt am Main, Nicolaus Basse, 1586, p. 279: 'Ich habs selbs von einem zauberer gehört/ daß er samt andern von N. auß Sachsen gehn Pariis mehr als hundert meil zur hoch zeit vngeladen gefahren sind auff eim mantel/ hab sich aber bald wider davon gemacht/ da sie gemerckt daß man im Saal murmelt/ was das fur gäst waren/ wo die her kämen.' Witekind was an opponent of the witch hunt, though he was extremely concerned about the dangers posed by learned magicians: Baron, *Faustus on Trial*, pp. 57–8, 128; Otto Ulbricht, 'Der sozialkritische unter den Gegnern: Hermann Witekind und sein *Christlich Bedencken vnd Erjnnerung von Zauberey* von 1585', in Hartmut Lehmann and Otto Ulbricht, eds, *Vom Unfug des Hexen-Processes. Gegner der Hexenverfolgungen von Johann Weyer bis Friedrich Spee*, Wiesbaden 1992.

3. On Abraham Saur, the editor of *Theatrum de veneficis*, and a lawyer, see Baron, *Faustus on Trial*, pp. 69–70, 135. Collections like *Theatrum de veneficis* or Sigmund Feyerabend's *Theatrum diabolorum* (1569) were the subject of piracy allegations in the cut-throat competitive world of publishing in Frankfurt. Convinced demonologists like Lambert Daneau, whose work was also anthologized in the volume, argues in his *A Dialogue of Witches*, English edn [London], K.W. [*sic*], 1575, that mostly, sabbaths are illusions (fo. G ii v); and Johnnes Georg Gödelmann, *Von Zauberern Hexen und Unholden*, trans. Georg Nigrinus, Frankfurt 1592 (Latin 1591), also claimed that the pact was an illusion, p. 198 ff., using words such as 'Einbildung' and 'Phantasey'. See Stuart Clark, 'Protestant Demonology: Sin, Superstition, and Society (*c*.1520–*c*.1630)', in Bengt Ankarloo and Gustav Henningsen, eds, *Early Modern European Witchcraft. Centres and Peripheries*, Oxford 1990, and Clark, *Thinking with Demons. The Idea of Witchcraft in Early Modern Europe*, Oxford 1997.

4. See William Monter, 'Inflation and Witchcraft: The Case of Jean Bodin', in Brian Levack, ed., *The Literature of Witchcraft*, 12 vols; vol. 4, New York and London 1992; Sydney Anglo, 'Melancholie and Witchcraft: The Debate between Wier, Bodin and Scot', ibid.; Christopher Baxter, 'Jean Bodin's *De la démonomanie des sorciers*: The Logic of Persecution', in Sydney Anglo, ed., *The Damned Art. Essays in the Literature of Witchcraft*, London 1977.

5. See Stuart Clark, 'Protestant Demonology', and Clark, *Thinking with Demons*; Peter Binsfeld, *Tractat Von Bekantnuß der Zauberer und Hexen*, Trier, Heinrich Bock, 1590, fos. 59v–60v; 61. Those who confessed to witchcraft might occasionally describe their experiences at the Sabbath as an illusion too, though usually they were eventually persuaded of the reality of their experience. See, for an interesting example, Rainer Beck, 'Das Spiel mit dem Teufel. Freisinger Kinderhexenprozesse 1715–1723', *Historische Anthropologie* 10, 2002, pp. 374–415.

6. Nicolas Rémy, *Demonolatry*, ed. and trans. Montague Summers, London 1930, pp. 28–9 (Bk I, ch. vii).

7. SAW, Hist. Saal VII, 25/376, 21 Feb. 1618, Barbara Dämeter von Sülzheym, ff. 44–9: 'wan der böse feindt hab aussfahren wollen, sey solcher bockh khommen, vor ihrer thür gestanden vnd ein mäkher gethan'; Agnes Haylman had to hold on to the tufts of hair on her goat so she would not fall off, SAW, Gericht Gerolzhofen 346, 30 Aug. 1617, fo. 82v.

8. SAW, Misc. 1954, I, Waldburga Schmid, 17 Nov. 1626, fos. 11r ff.: 'sey hernach biß weilen geschwindt, Je zu zeiten auch langsamb gangen. Jn wehrennden fahrennden hab sie nit gemaint allss ob sie Je in lufft fliehe, sonder mehr eingebildt alss wann sie vff einem wagen fuehre'.

9. For an English example of an allegation that the victim was 'ridden w[i]th a witch' at night, see James Sharpe, *Instruments of Darkness. Witchcraft in England 1550–1750*,

London 1996, p. 177; on the cultural history of flight, see Dieter Bauer and Wolfgang Behringer, eds, *Fliegen und Schweben. Annäherung an eine menschliche Sensation*, Munich 1997, esp. Clive Hart, 'Erotische Implikationen in der Flugdarstellung von der Hochrenaissance bis zum Rokoko', and Andrew Martin, 'Das Bild vom Fliegen, dokumentierte Flugversuche und das Aufkommen von Ansichten aus der Vogelschau zu Beginn der frühen Neuzeit'.

10. On help ales, see Judith Bennett, 'Conviviality and Charity in Medieval and Early Modern England', *Past and Present* 134, 1992, pp. 19–41; and on dancing in this period, Vera Jung, '"Wilde" Tänze – "Gelehrte" Tanzkunst. Wie man im 16. Jahrhundert versuchte, die Körper zu zähmen', in Richard van Dülmen, ed., *Körper-Geschichten*, Frankfurt am Main 1996.

11. SAW, Misc. 1954, I, Waldburga Schmid, 17 Nov. 1626, fos. 12r ff.: 'Nach solcher malziet heb man an zu danzen, eins vmb dass ander vmb, stoß ie eins dass ander hin vnd wider, der teuffel, Stoß vnd beiß wie er zu khom'.

12. 'lauter boese buben lieder', SAW, Gerolzhofen 346, Maria Gleichmann, 15 July 1617, fo. 74r.

13. Eberhard Happel, *Größte Denkwürdigkeiten der Welt oder Sogenannte Relationes Curiosae*, selections and ed. Uwe Hübner and Jürgen Westphal, p. 144. Happel's massive five volumes were produced between 1683 and 1691.

14. SAS Dep. 30, Rep. VI, Pak. 254, Marchtaler Hexenprozesse, 26 June 1627, Anna Traub, wife of Thoma Traub, 'Huckers Anna'.

15. SAW, Hist. Saal VII, 25/376, Margaretha Schmid, 9 Feb. 1618 fo. 40v, dance took place at Gerolzhofen, 'vffm marckh beym bronnen wo man kess vnd buttern feyl hatt'; SAW, Gerolzhofen 346, Anna Grauch, 31 Aug. 1617, fo. 90; SAW, Gerolzhofen 346, Elisabeth Brand, 7 Feb. 1617, fo. 11v, Michelau. SAW, Gerolzhofen 346, fos. 19r–34v contains a fascinating synopsis of the chief points of the witches' confessions, showing that witches had confessed to dances occurring in such locations as the market-place at Gerolzhofen by the fountain, by the town hall in Reyschofen, under the lime tree in the village, and so on. Several mention seeing dances and fires on Waldburgis Eve.

16. But by the seventeenth century, some cases provide a more elaborated sabbath description that corresponds more closely to the theological concerns of demonologists' accounts. So, for example, SAS Dep. 30, Rep. VI, Pak. 254, Marchtaler Hexenprozesse, 23 March 1627, Ursula Götz briefly described a sabbath where a big tall man appeared who sometimes transformed himself into a goat and whom others kissed. She was baptized in the name of the Devil and the cross made with the chrism at the time of her true baptism was ripped out.

17. SAW, Gerolzhofen 346, Maria Gleichmann, 15 July 1617, fos. 70v–71r, 'Clausen Pfrimb, sey gahr frölich, dann er gahr Reich sey, Vnnd Verachte die Arme Leüth, Reth mit Keinem Armen Menschen, hab an den Zusammen Kunfften grossen gewalt, Veracht die Arme, Vermin eß müße alles nach seinem Kopff gehen, Sein Buhle sey schwartz, Vnnd Wie ein Stattliche burgers fraw, gekleidt'; SAW, Hist. Saal VII, 25/376, Margaretha Müller, 22 Feb. 1618: 'sey noch Jung vnndt lustig hab mit gedanzet hab ein hübsche Jungen buhle hab ein gelbes kleid an'; another from Michelau 'sey gar ein Vormacher hab ein gutes muth vndt ain köstlichen buhlen hab ein gelb kleidt an'; SAW, Misc. 1954, I, Waldburga Schmid, 17 Nov. 1626, fo. 15r.

18. SAW, Misc. 1954, I, Waldburga Schmid, 17 Nov. 1626, fo. 12r: 'Vnd bey solchen Mahlzeiten sitzen gemainiglich die reichen bey einander, vnd die Armen gelten eben so wol nit vil daraussen. So conversia mann auch von aller handt sachen, vnd es werde den leüthen, vnd sonderlichen den frauen, die ehr abgeschnitten.' On the relationship between gossip, insults and witch trials, see Rainer Walz, *Hexenglaube und magische*

Kommunikation im Dorf der Frühen Neuzeit: die Verfolgungen in der Grafschaft Lippe, Paderborn 1993.

19. SAS Dep. 30, Rep. VI, Pak. 254, Marchtaler Hexenprozesse, 'Urteil 1587', and see earlier in the file, his case, 13 June 1587.

20. 'Lieber warumb tantzt die welt jung vnnd alt? Des fleisches lust vnnd kützel zu büssen/ vnnd zu erfüllen/ einer dem andern nach dem fleisch zu dienen/ die augen (wo es ye nit mehr sein mag) an andern leutten auffs böß zu ersettigen', Melchior Ambach, *Von Tantzen/ Vrtheil/ Auß heiliger Schrifft/ vnd den alten Christlichen Lerern gestelt*, Frankfurt 1564, fo. B i v; B iv r.

21. Cyriakus Spangenberg, 'Vom Tanz', in Ria Stambaugh, ed., *Teufelbücher im Auswahl*, 5 vols, Berlin 1970–80, vol. 2, p. 162; the Dance Devil naturally featured amongst the Devil Books, excoriating the sins of dancing: for example Florian Daul's *Tantzteuffel: Das ist/wider den leichtfertigen/unverschempten Welt tantz/* …, Frankfurt 1567, in Stambaugh, *Teufelbücher*, vol. 2, was also included in Feyerabend's bumper collection of *Teufelbücher*, Lyndal Roper, 'Drinking, Whoring and Gorging', in *Oedipus and the Devil. Witchcraft, Sexuality and Religion in Early Modern Europe*, London 1994, p. 155. Ambach made the sexual connotations of dancing explicit, condemning what he called 'venereal dancing' and describing how, at dances, 'people practise easygoing, whorish gestures, touch married women and virgins with unchaste hands, kiss one another with whorish embraces; and the bodily parts, which nature has hidden and covered in shame, are uncovered by lechery'. 'Leichtfertige/ hürische geberden übet man nach süssem seytenspil/ vnnd vnkeuschen liederen: da begreifft man frawen vnd junckfrawen mit vnkeuschen henden: man küst einander mit hürischem [Biv v] vmbfahen: vnd die glider/ welche die natur verborgen vnnd scham bedeckt hat/ entblöst offtmals geylheyt vnd vnder dem manttele einer kurzweil vnnd spiles/ wirdt schand vnnd laster bedeckt', Ambach, *Von Tantzen* …, fo. B iv r–v. But a refutation of Ambach's work by Pastor Jacob Ratz soon appeared: *Vom Tanzenn/ Obs Gott verpotten hab/ Obs sünd sey/ Vnd von andern erlaupten kurzweilen der Christen/ als/ Spielen/ Singen/ Trincken/ Jagen usw. Mit verlegung/ des Falschen vnd onbescheyden urteils/ M. Melcher Ambach/ Predigers zu Franckfort/ vom Tanzen/ geschrieben*, n. p., 1565.

22. Johannes Praetorius, *Hexen-, Zauber- und Spukgeschichten aus dem Blocksberg*, 1669, ed. Wolfgang Möhrig, Frankfurt am Main 1979, p. 64; Jean Bodin, *De la démonomanie des sorciers*, Paris 1580, p. 88; Bodin, *Vom Außgelaßne Wütigen Teuffels heer Allerhand Zauberern/ Hexen vnd Hexenmeistern/ Vnholden/ Teuffels beschwerern/ Warsagern* …, trans. J. Fischart, Strasbourg, B. Jobin, 1586, p. 308: 'machen die Leut Rasend vnnd wütig/ vnd die Weiber mißgebären'; and on Fischart's translation and reworking of Bodin, see Stefan Janson, *Jean Bodin, Johann Fischart: De la démonomanie des sorciers (1580), Vom ausgelassnen wütigen Teuffelsheer (1581) und ihre Fallberichte* (Europäische Hochschulschriften 352), Frankfurt am Main 1980.

23. Rémy, *Demonolatry*, p. 63 (Bk I, ch. xix). On Carnival and popular culture, see Peter Burke, *Popular Culture in Early Modern Europe*, London 1978, pp. 182–5; the theme was not just a trope of art, but was apparently enacted in Bologna, as we know from an account of 1506; and see Edward Muir, *Ritual in Early Modern Europe*, Cambridge 1997, pp. 81–4 for an analysis of Brueghel's painting: as he shows, Carnival sports a large codpiece and engages in games and violence; Lent carries a fish skeleton and represents discipline and control.

24. Rémy, *Demonolatry*, p. 61 (Bk I, ch. xvii).

25. Bernhard Albrecht, *Magia*, Leipzig 1628, pp. 196–7.

26. Praetorius, *Hexen-, Zauber- und Spukgeschichten*, p. 62.

27. H.C. Erik Midelfort, *A History of Madness in Sixteenth-Century Germany*, Stanford

1999, pp. 25–79; and on the connection between moralism, dance and the figure of the witch, see also Ingrid Ahrendt-Schulte, 'Die Zauberschen und ihr Trommelschläger. Geschlechtsspezifische Zuschreibungsmuster in lippischen Hexenprozessen', in Ingrid Ahrendt-Schulte, Dieter Bauer, Sönke Lorenz and Jürgen Michael Schmidt, eds, *Geschlecht, Magie und Hexenverfolgung* (Hexenforschung vol. 7), Bielefeld 2002.

28. Francesco Maria Guazzo, *Compendium maleficarum*, ed. and trans. Montague Summers, London 1929, p. 37ff. (Bk 1, ch. xii); Pierre de Lancre, *Tableau de l'inconstance des mauvais anges et demons*, 1612; Paris 1613, p. 121: 'On y voit de grandes chaudieres pleines de crapaux et impres, coeurs d'enfants non baptisez, chair de pendus, & autres horribles charognes, & des eaux puantes, pots de graisse et de poison, qui se preste & se debite a cette foire, comme estant la plus precieuse & commune marchandise qui s'y trouue'. On De Lancre, see Margaret M. McGowan, 'Pierre de Lancre's *Tableau de l'inconstance des mauvais anges et demons*: The Sabbat Sensationalised', in Sydney Anglo, ed., *The Damned Art. Essays in the Literature of Witchcraft*, London 1977.

29. StadtAN, Hexenprozeßakten, Margaretha Stahl, 22 Nov. 1593.

30. SAW, Hist. Saal VII, 25/376, Barbara Dämeter von Sülzheym, 21 Feb. 1618, fos. 44r–9v; Hist. Saal VII, 25/376, Margaretha Müller, 22 Feb. 1618, fos. 15r–19v.

31. StadtAN, Hexenprozeßakten, Maria Marb, 6 March 1590.

32. 'Raupp': SAS Dep. 30, Rep. VI, Pak. 254, Marchtaler Hexenprozesse, Anna Bernegker, 26 June 1587: this is an interesting name, suggesting the connection between witchcraft and damage to crops. Elizabeth Weber was given the name 'KinderNärrin' or fool; Ursula Grön, 'hex bestia' and 'teuffelsriech': StadtAA, Strafbuch des Rats 1654–99, p. 546, 17 Nov. 1685, p. 659, 27 July 1694. Barbara Fischer's devil was called Hennendreckheler, Strafbuch des Rats 1633–53, fo. 237, 23 July 1650, Maria Braun's, 'hunds cäsperle', Strafbuch des Rats 1615–32, p. 499, 30 Dec. 1625.

33. 'Milch aus den Eutern der Kue vnd Schafe (vnd also auch Butter vnd Käse/ so daraus könten gemacht werden)', David Meder, *Acht Hexen predigten*, Leipzig, Valentin am Ende Erben, 1615, fo. 55v.

34. SAS Dep. 30, Rep. VI, Pak. 254, Marchtaler Hexenprozesse, Ursula Götz, 23 March 1627; Anna Traub, 26 June [1627]. On *Kellerfahren*, see Jonathan Durrant, 'Witchcraft, Gender and Society in the Early Modern Prince-Bishopric of Eichstätt', Ph.D. diss., University of London, 2002, pp. 188–91; and on the structure of farmhouses in the Würzburg region, Konrad Bedal, 'Bauen und Wohnen in Dorf und Kleinstadt vor 1650', in Peter Kolb and Ernst-Günter Krenig, eds, *Unterfränkische Geschichte*. vol. 3: *Vom Beginn des konfessionellen Zeitalters bis zum Ende des Dreißigjährigen Krieges*, Würzburg 1995. Animals and humans were normally housed under the same roof, sometimes with the dwelling above the stall, sometimes alongside. In areas of viticulture, important in Franconia, animals might not be kept; but cellars were especially important.

35. StadtAN, Hexenprozeßakten, Barbara Stecher, 14 Oct. 1590.

36. See Hermann Heidrich, 'Grenzübergänge. Das Haus und die Volkskultur in der frühen Neuzeit', in Richard van Dulmen, ed., *Kultur der einfachen Leute. Bayerisches Volksleben vom 16. bis zum 18. Jahrhundert*, Munich 1983. This connection is evident, too, in anthropological accounts. See, for an interesting comparison showing how cannibalism and fears about fertility were evident in the Rwandan genocide, Christopher C. Taylor, *Sacrifice as Terror. The Rwandan Genocide of 1994*, Oxford and New York 1999, pp. 99–149. I am grateful to Bernd Weisbrod for this reference.

37. This document is reprinted in Wolfgang Behringer, ed., *Hexen und Hexenprozesse in Deutschland*, Munich 1988 (4th edn 2000), pp. 285–99.

38. McGowan, 'Pierre de Lancre's *Tableau de l'inconstance des mauvais anges et demons*'.

39. Henry [*sic*] Boguet, *An Examen of Witches*, trans. E.A. Ashwin, ed. Revd M. Summers, London 1929; Rémy, *Demonolatry*, p. ix.
40. Rémy, *Demonolatry*, p. ix; for details of German editions, see Editor's Introduction, p. xxx.
41. Indeed, just how parasitic the relationship between entertainment and witchcraft could be is shown by the work of Charles Zika on depictions of witches in sixteenth- and seventeenth-century art. See Sigrid Schade, *Schadenzauber und Magie des Körpers*, Worms 1983; and Charles Zika, 'Fears of Flying: Representations of Witchcraft and Sexuality in Sixteenth-Century Germany', 'She-man: Visual Representations of Witchcraft and Sexuality', 'Dürer's Witch, Riding Women and Moral Order', 'The Wild Cavalcade in Lucas Cranach's *Melancholia* Paintings: Witchcraft and Sexual Disorder in Sixteenth-Century Germany', 'Body Parts, Saturn and Cannibalism: Visual Representations of Witches' Assemblies in the Sixteenth Century', and other essays in Charles Zika, *Exorcising our Demons: Magic, Witchcraft, and Visual Culture in Early Modern Europe* (Studies in Medieval and Reformation Thought 91), Leiden and Boston 2003. So too, saucy witches straddle the painted ceiling of a sixteenth-century Nuremberg house (now in the Fembo-haus Museum) alongside boys pushing hoops with sticks or farmyard animals; here witches are a domestic decorative motif. Pamphlet accounts of earlier Augsburg trials include *Warhaffte Historische Abbild: und kurtze Beschreibung, was sich unlangst in … Augsburg … Zugetragen…*, Augsburg 1654; *Warhaffte Beschreibung des Urthels …*, Augsburg 1666 (not a local case); *Relation Oder Beschreibung so Anno 1669 … von einer Weibs/Person …*, Augsburg 1669. Sometimes the same broadsides were simply re-used: the sheet of the trial of Anna Ebeler recycles the woodcuts which were used in the broadsheet for the trial of Maria Bihlerin (reproduced, Behringer, *Witchcraft Persecutions in Bavaria. Popular Magic, Religious Zealotry and Reason of State in Early Modern Europe*, trans. J. Grayson and D. Lederer, Cambridge 1997, p. 329), which itself contains images which are clearly taken from another broadsheet about possession.
42. For further detail, see Euan Cameron, *The Reformation of the Heretics. The Waldenses of the Alps 1480–1580*, Oxford 1984, pp. 107–13.
43. Miri Rubin, *Corpus Christi. The Eucharist in Late Medieval Culture*, Cambridge 1991, pp. 359–60; Rubin, *Gentile Tales. The Narrative Assault on Late Medieval Jews*, New Haven and London 1999.
44. The motif of weather-making does not play a central role in the trials I have investigated, though it does occasionally appear. In Marchtal, women were questioned in relation to one particularly bad storm; in Würzburg, the motif regularly occurs; but it does not have the emotional centrality of the other motifs and it is usually dwarfed by the long lists of animals which have been harmed. Witches were certainly believed to cause bad weather and hail sermons regularly dealt with witchcraft; while church bells were rung to ward off evil influences in bad weather.
45. 'dz licht mit der handt Vfm Rück halten müßen', SAW, Gerolzhofen 346, Maria Gleichmann, 15 July 1617, fo. 74v.
46. Sebastian Franck, *Weltbuch: Spiegel vnd Bildtnisz der gantzen Erdtbodens*, Tübingen, V. Morhart, 1534, fo. Li v.
47. StadtAN, Hexenprozeßakten, Susanna Mair, 26 Sept. 1590.

Womanhood

1. All three women were interrogated and the scribe noted that no torture was used:

however, the confessions of all three are so similar and the story has such a feel of folk tale that the story must have been tortured from them. Staatsarchiv Basel Stadt, Criminalia 4/3; Dilge Glaser, Jte Lichtermut, Agnes Salat, 1532. Dilge claimed that four women were present, including her mother. On the Basel cases, see Catherine Huber, 'Die Hexenprozesse in Basel im 16. und 17. Jahrhundert', Lizentiatsarbeit, Basle, 1989. A very similar story is repeated in Johann Gödelmann's *Von Zauberern Hexen und Unholden* (Latin 1591), trans. Georg Nigrinus, Frankfurt 1592, Nicolaus Bassaeus, p. 83, about two witches from Berlin, executed in 1553, who made hail to destroy the fruit, and also stole the little child of a woman neighbour, dismembered and cooked it.

Chapter 6: Fertility

1. 'Vnnd den fürhang vm dem sechs Wochen Beth hin Wegk gethann, Vnnd zu ir gesagt, sie sole sich Jhm Verhaissen, vnd sein sey, Er Wolt sie nit verlassenn … Wie sie Jme zugesagt, hab er sich zu ir Jns beth gelegett, vnd vnzucht mit ir Getriben, hab die Kleidung Anbehalden', SAW, Hist. Saal VII, 25/375, fos. 289–92, Magdalena Winder, 8 Feb. 1617. So also Anna Lang broke the taboo on staying in bed, and when she went outside to feed the animals, met the Devil. Thereafter she fell sick: SAW, Misc. 1954, II, fos. 112–16, Anna Lang, 4 Jan. 1612. Margaretha Schmid, also recovering after birth, fed her child after having sex with the Devil and it sickened and died: SAW, Hist. Saal VII, 25/376, fo. 38v ff., Margaretha Schmid, 9 Feb. 1618.
2. StadtAN, Hexenprozeßakten, Margreta Knorz, testimony of Madalena Mincker, 4 Sept. 1593: 'Jrem khind sei es Jnn der Wickhelbinden widerfahrenn, alß sie aber Jnn Khindsbandenn gelegenn. sei die alt Knörzin onne Angesprochenn khommen, vor Jr gehauret, biß sie dz Khindt gehabt, alß sie aber 3 wuchen zu der Kindbeth alt gewest, so seie dz Khindt wordenn, alß wan es khein häutlin hette, solches bej 2 Jarn getribenn, alles ann Jme gelummelt auch ann hand Vnnd fueßen erkhrummbt, Gemelte Knörzin hab Jr auch Wein vnd Apffel gebracht, vonn welcher sie auch die millich genommen des gelts halben aber uneinig wordenn, darauf gemelte Knerzin Vermelt es werde sie nach wol gereihen, darauff sej Jr khindt, 3 1/2 Jar armetselig gewest.'
3. SAS Dep. 30, Rep. VI, Pak. 254, Marchtaler Hexenprozesse, Juliana Laub, wife of Theuss Weckhenmann [1590]; SAS Dep. 30, Rep. VI, Pak. 255, Marchtaler Hexenprozesse, Catharina Schmid, 1745, undated miscellaneous testimony.
4. 'das es Jnn fünf tagen weder gesauget noch gessen noch gewinnet sey gelegen wie manns gelegt sie hex sey Offtermaln komen. Etwan öpfeler gebracht vnd habs vngern gesehenn das sie soliches segnen hab lassen'. SAS Dep. 30, Rep. VI, Pak. 254, Marchtaler Hexenprozesse, Margaretha Menz, wife of Bastion Schilling, 5 May 1588.
5. Christian Pfister, *Bevölkerungsgeschichte und historische Demographie 1500–1800* (Enzyklopädie Deutscher Geschichte, vol. 29), Munich 1994, p. 29; Stefan Breit, *'Leichtfertigkeit' und ländliche Gesellschaft. Voreheliche Sexualität in der Frühen Neuzeit*, Munich 1991, p. 56.
6. Friedrich Merzbacher, 'Fürstbischof Julius Echter von Mespelbrunn als Gesetzgeber', in *Recht – Staat – Kirche. Ausgewählte Aufsätze*, Vienna 1989, pp. 446–508, pp. 469–71.
7. For a brilliant account of how these ordinances created a new Counter-Reformation gender order, see Ulrike Strasser, *State of Virginity: Gender, Religion, and Politics in an Early Modern Catholic State*, Ann Arbor 2003. Breit points out that such controls on marriage could put the couple who had sex but were prevented from marrying into alliance with the Church, *'Leichtfertigkeit'*, pp. 301 ff. For the monastery of Ottobeuren, Govind Sreenivasan has shown that from the late sixteenth century onwards, the

monks and local richest peasantry pursued a policy of strictly limiting the total number of households and attempting to consolidate farms. The effects of this policy were to push out the children who did not inherit, forcing them to make their living elsewhere, while concentrating power and resources in the hands of the lucky child who did inherit the farm. See Govind Sreenivasan, *The Peasants of Ottobeuren 1487–1723. A Rural Society in Early Modern Europe*, Cambridge 2004. For rural Hohenlohe, Thomas Robisheaux has shown that property was increasingly being concentrated in the hands of a few. Because of shortage of land, the age at which couples married rose: men from Langenburg married around 24 between 1610 and 1619, but the mean rose to over 26 by 1680–89, while women's age at marriage remained around 24 throughout the seventeenth century, Thomas Robisheaux, *Rural Society and the Search for Order in Early Modern Germany*, Cambridge 1989, p. 115; and see David Sabean, *Property, Production and Family in Neckarhausen 1700–1870*, Cambridge 1990, and Sabean, *Kinship in Neckarhausen 1700–1870*, Cambridge 1998.

8. Christopher Friedrichs, *Urban Society in an Age of War: Nördlingen, 1580–1720*, Princeton 1979, pp. 35–45: numbers of citizen households remained broadly constant from 1579 to the 1620s. The year 1579 is the first for which we have records for numbers of baptisms and these show a decline from then until the 1620s, pp. 46, 48.

9. Ibid., p. 64.

10. Merry Wiesner, *Working Women in Renaissance Germany*, New Brunswick 1986; Wiesner, 'Guilds, Male Bonding and Women's Work in Early Modern Germany', *Gender and History* 1, 1989, pp. 125–37; Kathy Stuart, *Defiled Trades and Social Outcasts. Honour and Ritual Pollution in Early Modern Germany*, Cambridge 1999, pp. 200–5; Lyndal Roper, *The Holy Household. Women and Morals in Reformation Augsburg*, Oxford 1989.

11. E.A. Wrigley and Roger Schofield, *The Population History of England, 1541–1871*, Cambridge 1981; Ernest Benz, 'Population Change and the Economy', in Sheilagh Ogilvie and Bob Scribner, eds, *Germany. A New Social and Economic History*, 2 vols, London 1996, vol. 2, p. 54; Jan de Vries, 'Population', in Thomas Brady, Jr., Heiko A. Oberman and James D. Tracy, eds, *Handbook of European History 1400–1600*, Grand Rapids, Michigan 1994–5; 1996, 2 vols, vol. 1: on average, for every year marriage is delayed from 18 to 25, there is a reduction of 0.4 children; and for a recent overview, Pier Paolo Viazzo, 'Mortality, Fertility and Family', in David I. Kertzer and Marzio Barbagli, eds, *The History of the European Family*, Vol. 1: *Family Life in Early Modern Times*, New Haven and London 2001. In Nördlingen between 1611 and 1625, Friedrichs has calculated, the average age of first marriage for women was 25; and he is able to show that this increased over the course of the seventeenth and early eighteenth centuries, rising to as high as 30 between 1691 and 1730 (p. 69). And, as we have seen, his figures for population as a whole suggest that there had been rapid population growth in the fifteenth and sixteenth centuries, as the population rose from 5,000 in 1459 to somewhere between 7,000 and 11,000 by 1579. But from 1579 onwards, when the first figures are available, baptisms were on the decline (pp. 46–8). For an excellent demonstration of the close relationship between age of marriage and overall numbers of children, see, for Laichingen, Hans Medick, *Weben und Überleben in Laichingen 1650–1900. Lokalgeschichte als Allgemeine Geschichte* (Veröffentlichungen des Max-Planck Instituts für Geschichte, vol. 126), 1996, 2nd edn, Göttingen 1997, pp. 337–54.

12. Bernd Roeck, *Eine Stadt in Krieg und Frieden. Studien zur Geschichte der Reichsstadt Augsburg zwischen Kalenderstreit und Parität* (Schriftenreihe der historischen Kommission bei der bayerischen Akademie der Wissenschaften 37), 2 vols, Göttingen 1989, vol. 1, pp. 311, 414: the figures are compiled for the year 1622. In the village of

Laichingen after 1650, by contrast, Hans Medick has shown that it was paradoxically the families of the day labourers who had the lowest child mortality while innkeepers had the highest; child mortality up to the age of five was exceedingly high in all social groups. He relates this to the practice of longer breast-feeding amongst the poorer groups, and the need for women's labour in small and middling peasant households: Medick, *Weben und Überleben*, pp. 355–83.

13. Wolfgang Behringer, 'Weather, Hunger and Fear: Origins of the European Witch Hunts in Climate, Society and Mentality', *German History* 13, 1993, pp. 1–27; Hartmut Lehmann, 'The Persecution of Witches as Restoration of Order', *Central European History* 21, 1988, pp. 107–21.

14. Thomas Robisheaux, 'The Peasantries of Western Germany, 1300–1750', in Tom Scott, ed., *The Peasantries of Europe from the Fourteenth to the Eighteenth Centuries*, London 1998. For a brilliant account of eighteenth-century peasant life, see Rainer Beck, *Unterfinning. Ländliche Welt vor Anbruch der Moderne*, Munich 1993.

15. SAW, Misc. 1954, I, fos. 55–86, Sabina Pforinger, 14 Sept. 1626; Misc. 1954, II, fos. 9–34, Anna Starr, 11 April 1603.

16. Susanna Burghartz, 'Rechte Jungfrauen oder unverschämte Töchter? Zur weiblichen Ehre im 16. Jahrhundert', in Karin Hausen and Heide Wunder, eds, *Frauengeschichte – Geschlechtergeschichte*, Frankfurt 1992; Strasser, *State of Virginity*; and on controls on pre-marital sexuality, see Michael Mitterauer, *Ledige Mütter. Zur Geschichte illegitimer Geburten in Europa*, Munich 1983, pp. 58 ff.

17. *Die Peinliche Gerichtsordung Kaiser Karls V. von 1532 (Carolina)*, ed. Gustav Radbruch, revised by Arthur Kaufmann, Stuttgart 1975, article 131, pp. 84–5; Richard van Dülmen, *Frauen vor Gericht. Kindsmord in der Frühen Neuzeit*, Frankfurt 1991, p. 17; and on the emotional and social meanings of infanticide, see Ulinka Rublack, *The Crimes of Women in Early Modern Germany*, Oxford 1999, pp. 163–96.

18. The correspondences are broad, with peaks in witch-hunting not necessarily coinciding with peaks in infanticide prosecution: in Württemberg, for instance, the worst period for infanticide convictions was the last quarter of the seventeenth century (van Dülmen, *Frauen vor Gericht*, pp. 58–75); in Augsburg the correlation is closer, with nine convictions for infanticide between 1640 and 1699 (StadtAA, Strafbücher des Rats) and a further eight suspected; van Dülmen cites a total of fifteen executions between 1620 and 1786, but he also counts only thirteen executions for witchcraft, though there were seventeen; in Nördlingen, there were very few cases and no executions until the 1590s, that is, around the time of Nördlingen's witch panic; and cases continued regularly through the seventeenth century, Alfons Felber, *Unzucht und Kindsmord in der freien Reichsstadt Nördlingen vom 15. bis 19. Jahrhundert*, Bonn 1961, pp. 95–100.

19. Pfister, *Bevölkerungsgeschichte*, pp. 86 ff.; and see Sreenivasan, *Peasants of Ottobeuren*.

20. There are few statistics before 1700 for numbers of those never marrying. It seems that in the early sixteenth century the proportion of those marrying was very high: figures from the bishopric of Speyer suggest that 90 per cent of the adult population were married. By contrast, in the Genevan upper class, the proportions of spinsters aged fifty and up rose from 1.7 per cent in the mid-sixteenth century to over 30 per cent at the end of the eighteenth century, quadrupling in the course of the seventeenth century. Pfister, *Bevölkerungsgeschichte*, pp. 83–4. In towns, proportions rose as high as 20 per cent, partly because of the large numbers of unmarried servants. For early modern Wildberg in Württemberg, Sheilagh Ogilvie estimates the proportion of lifelong spinsters as between 10 and 15 per cent. As she shows, unmarried women were crucial to the economy: Sheilagh Ogilvie, *A Bitter Living. Women, Markets, and Social Capital in Early Modern Germany*, Oxford 2003, esp. pp. 41–2.

21. Behringer, 'Weather, Hunger and Fear'; Lehmann, 'The Persecution of Witches'. Figures for the Würzburg region suggest rapid population growth in the first half of the sixteenth century, and even a population growth rate of 15 per cent overall during the years of Echter's reign (1573–1617), Winfried Schenk, 'Die mainfränkische Landschaft unter dem Einfluß von Gewerbe, Handel, Verkehr und Landwirtschaft', in Peter Kolb and Ernst-Günter Krenig, eds, *Unterfränkische Geschichte. Band 3: Vom Beginn des konfessionellen Zeitalters bis zum Ende des Dreißigjährigen Krieges*, Würzburg 1995, pp. 522–44.

22. See n. 8 above; Friedrichs's figures also show that total wealth was falling slightly until the early 1590s; but it is hard to judge this trend in the absence of figures from before 1579. Friedrichs, *Nördlingen*, p. 113.

23. Brian Levack, *The Witch-hunt in Early Modern Europe*, 1987; 2nd edn London and New York 1995, p. 190 (ch. 7); Bengt Ankarloo, Stuart Clark and William Monter, *Witchcraft and Magic in Europe*, 6 vols; vol 4: *The Period of the Witch Trials*, London 2002, pp. 22–44; Wolfgang Behringer, *Witchcraft Persecutions in Bavaria. Popular Magic, Religious Zealotry and Reason of State in Early Modern Europe*, trans. J. Grayson and David Lederer, Cambridge 1997, pp. 115–211; and on the 1590s more generally, see Andrew Cunningham and Ole Peter Grell, *The Four Horsemen of the Apocalypse. Religion, War, Famine and Death in Reformation Europe*, Cambridge 2000.

24. Pfister, *Bevölkerungsgeschichte*, p. 14. For population loss in Würzburg territory, see Schenk, 'Die mainfränkische Landschaft', p. 544. Even so, the demographic system could show considerable flexibility in coping with crisis: in Hesse, the population losses, severe as they were, had been made good to such an extent that Hesse was sending companies of mercenaries to America to fight in the eighteenth century. See Charles Ingrao, *The Hessian Mercenary State: Ideas, Institutions, and Reforms under Frederick II, 1760–1785*, Cambridge 1987; John Theibault, *German Villages in Crisis. Rural Life in Hesse-Kassel and the Thirty Years' War 1580–1720*, Atlantic Highlands, NJ, 1995. In Bavaria too, the dramatic falls in population resulting from the Thirty Years War were met with a drop in the age at which women married and a corresponding demographic recovery. Numbers of those marrying increased sharply, but it was not until the 1670s that recovery was accomplished: Peter Schlögl, *Bauern, Krieg und Staat. Oberbayerische Bauernwirtschaft und frühmoderner Staat im 17. Jahrhundert*, Göttingen 1988, pp. 70–81; and for Laichingen in Württemberg, see Medick, *Weben und Überleben*, pp. 337–77. See also John Theibault, 'The Demography of the Thirty Years' War Revisited: Günther Franz and his Critics', *German History* 15, 1997, pp. 1–21.

25. Whereas before the war, numbers of baptisms had regularly exceeded 1,500, after 1650 they hovered between 600 and 700, gradually rising towards 1,000 by the end of the century. Demographic recovery slowed in 1693–95 in the wake of a provisioning crisis and there was another severe demographic crisis in 1704 when the city was besieged by Bavarian and French troops, Etienne François, *Die unsichtbare Grenze. Protestanten und Katholiken in Augsburg 1648–1806*, Sigmaringen 1991, pp. 40–1; table 1, pp. 246–7.

26. There had been an isolated trial resulting in the execution of one woman and her daughter in 1625; see Roeck, *Eine Stadt*, vol. 2, pp. 539–53. The 1650s saw three executions, the 1660s two, the 1670s one, the 1680s seven and the 1690s four. This is mirrored in numbers of cases which did not lead to execution: eighteen such trials were held in the three decades 1650–79; but twenty were held in the 1680s and 1690s.

27. It is very difficult to explain why cities like Augsburg were at first immune from witch-hunting but then began to hold trials in the second half of the seventeenth century. Part of the answer might lie in increasing immigration from the countryside and a growth in the size of the Catholic population after the Thirty Years War: it may be that immigrants from the countryside brought with them witchcraft beliefs and that there were

therefore more people willing to denounce others. However, belief in magic and witch-craft had been strongly evident in Augsburg from at least the second half of the sixteenth century; and there were many criminal trials in which sorcery and magical beliefs figured, but these had not resulted in witchcraft trials, even though the regions surrounding these cities were engaging in mass panics. See, in general, Bernd Roeck, 'Christliche Idealstaat und Hexenwahn. Zum Ende der europäischen Verfolgungen', *Historisches Jahrbuch* 108, 1988, pp. 379–405; and for Augsburg, Roeck, *Eine Stadt*, vol. 2, pp. 550–2; Lyndal Roper, *Oedipus and the Devil. Witchcraft, Sexuality and Religion in Early Modern Europe*, London 1994; Wolfgang Behringer, *Mit dem Feuer vom Leben zum Tod. Hexengesetzgebung in Bayern*, Munich 1988, pp. 205–15; StadtAA, Strafbücher des Rats; Urgichtensammlung. It seems more likely that the demographic and social crisis, together with the decline in civic power in the years after the war, made people see the hand of the Devil at work in human affairs, and made anxieties about popu-lation seem apocalyptic in significance. This sombre religious mood was shared by many in the social group from which councillors were drawn. It was coupled with an anxious concern for the religious fate of individuals and an interest in psychology. For Esslingen, see Günter Jerouschek, *Die Hexen und ihr Prozess. Die Hexenverfolgung in der Reichsstadt Esslingen*, Esslingen 1992: here, the major panic in which 32 people were executed and a total of 60 were tried took place between 1662 and 1665, though there had been eight executions before the Thirty Years War as well. Most of them came from villages ruled by Esslingen. In Rothenburg, which had not executed any witches before 1650, there were two executions after 1650; and 30 cases in the sixty years 1650–1709 compared with 34 in the century from 1549 to 1650: Alison Rowlands, *Witchcraft Narratives in Germany. Rothenburg, 1561–1652*, Manchester 2003. In Nuremberg, there had been some executions for witchcraft in 1536 and in the 1590s. Twelve complex cases involving diabolism were prosecuted after 1650: Birke Grießhammer, ed., *Drutenjagd in Franken 16.–18. Jahrhundert* (1998), 2nd edn, Erlangen 1999, pp. 133–41; Hartmut Heinrich Kunstmann, 'Zauberwahn und Hexenprozeß in der Reichsstadt Nürnberg', D. Jur. diss, Johannes Gutenberg-Universität Mainz, 1970.

28. See, on the persistence of the late age of marriage, Josef Ehmer, 'Marriage', in David I. Kertzer and Marzio Barbagli, eds, *The History of the European Family*, vol. 2: *Family Life in the Long Nineteenth Century, 1789–1913*, New Haven and London 2002. Changes took place unevenly, however, and some historians have doubted whether a single pattern existed. David Sabean has found that in the village of Neckarhausen the mean age of women at first marriage in the early eighteenth century was 24, rising to 26 in the late eighteenth century and still at 26 in the mid-nineteenth century. Averages hide important variations: in the late eighteenth century, a significant number of women delayed mar-riage until their thirties and forties, so that illegitimacy rose; but another group of women married early, around age 20, and these marriages were especially likely if the couple were linked by kin; though in the early nineteenth century, this group of women were also older. Sabean, *Kinship in Neckarhausen*, pp. 217–18, 530. Illegitimacy rates changed in the eighteenth century. In the late eighteenth century, the illegitimacy rate in Augsburg increased dramatically: between 1700 and 1729, just over 2 per cent of all baptisms were of illegitimate children; in 1750–59 the figure reached 4.3 per cent, climbing to over 6 per cent in 1780–89. François, *Die unsichtbare Grenze*, 42. In Nördlingen, the mean age of first marriage for women rose, reaching 30 between 1691 and 1730, Friedrichs, *Nördlingen*, p. 69. On the late eighteenth-century rise in illegitimacy rates in Bavaria, see W.R. Lee, 'Bastardy and the Socioeconomic Structure of South Germany' (1977), repr. in Robert I. Rotberg, ed., *Population History and the Family. A Journal of Interdisciplinary History Reader*, Cambridge, Mass. and London 2001, p. 244.

29. The advent of computer technology, the use of sophisticated back-projection methods for population estimates, the exploitation of tax records and the systematic linking and analysis of baptismal, wedding and funeral registers have enabled modern historians to discover more than contemporaries could ever have known about population.

30. *Die göttliche Ordnung in der Veränderung des menschlichen Geschlechts, aus der Geburt, dem Tode und der Fortpflanzung desselben erwiesen,* 2 vols, 3rd edn, Berlin 1765. For the intellectual context of this work, see Marion W. Gray, *Productive Men, Reproductive Women. The Agrarian Household and the Emergence of Separate Spheres during the German Enlightenment,* New York 2000.

31. The Malthusian model, however, has recently come in for some attack. See Sreenivasan, *Peasants of Ottobeuren.*

32. Johann Süssmilch, *Die göttliche Ordnung in den Veränderungen* ..., 2 vols, 3rd edn, Berlin, 1765, vol. 1, pp. 499–515.

33. Ibid., vol. 2, pp. 316–17 and ff. 'Ungluckliche Kinder, ... die an der Brust enweder durch Erdruckung der Ammen oder der Muetter, oder auf andre Weise umgekommen sind' vol. 1, p. 551: he also thought the numbers of children who perished in this way was declining.

34. For blessings to protect against the weather, and to protect women in childbirth and pregnancy, see Adolph Franz, *Die kirchlichen Benediktionen im Mittelalter,* 2 vols, Freiburg 1909, esp. vol. 2; and on the cycle of the ritual year, designed to foster abundance and fertility, Stephen Wilson, *The Magical Universe. Everyday Ritual and Magic in Pre-modern Europe,* London and New York 2000.

35. Laura Gowing, 'Secret Births and Infanticide in Seventeenth-century England', *Past and Present* 156, 1997, pp. 87–115; for Germany, van Dülmen, *Frauen vor Gericht,* pp. 62–72; there were almost no prosecutions for infanticide before the sixteenth century, and punishments for the crime (in Protestant areas, for which van Dülmen has figures) reach their height in the last decades of the seventeenth century and the first decades of the eighteenth. On images of infanticidal mothers in popular ballad, Tom Cheesman, *The Shocking Ballad Picture Show. German Popular Literature and Cultural History,* Oxford 1994, pp. 119–60.

36. Ulrike Strasser, 'Bones of Contention: Cloistered Nuns, Decorated Relics, and the Contest over Women's Place in the Public Sphere of Counter-Reformation Munich', *Archiv für Reformationsgeschichte* 90, 1999, pp. 255–88; 'Cloistering Women's Past: Conflicting Accounts of Enclosure in a Seventeenth-century Munich Nunnery', in Ulinka Rublack, ed., *Gender in Early Modern German History,* Cambridge 2002; Strasser, *State of Virginity,* ch. 4.

37. Heinrich Kramer and James Sprenger [*sic*], *The Malleus Maleficarum,* ed. and trans. Revd Montague Summers, London 1928; New York 1971 Part I, qu. 6, pp. 46–7; Wolfgang Behringer and Günter Jerouschek, eds, *Der Hexenhammer,* trans. W. Behringer, G. Jerouschek and W. Tschacher, Munich 2000, pp. 236–8.

38. The authorship of the *Malleus* is now attributed solely to Kramer (also known as Institoris), who seems to have exploited the idea that Sprenger was involved in its composition as a way of securing the legitimacy of the work. Though Sprenger was mentioned in the Bull which accompanied the *Malleus,* it is possible that he did not share Kramer's views; he certainly seems to have tried to control and discipline Kramer's activities. For the most recent, definitive account see Wolfgang Behringer and Günther Jerouschek, '"Das unheilvollste Buch der Weltliteratur"? Zur Entstehungs- und Wirkungsgeschichte des Malleus Maleficarum und zu den Anfängen der Hexenverfolgung', in Behringer and Jerouschek, eds, *Hexenhammer.* On Kramer's involvement in real witch hunts, see Eric Wilson, 'Institoris at Innsbruck: Heinrich

Institoris, the *Summis Desiderantes* and the Brixen Witch-Trial of 1485', in Bob Scribner and Trevor Johnson, eds, *Popular Religion in Germany and Central Europe, 1400–1800*, London 1996. On Kramer, see Peter Segl, ed., *Der Hexenhammer. Entstehung und Umfeld des Malleus maleficarum von 1487*, Cologne and Berlin 1988.

39. In the *Malleus* itself, there is comparatively little direct Marianism: Part II, qu. 2, ch. 6 on exorcisms does not mention Mary; and the praise of good women in Part I, qu. 6, is brief on Mary. Kramer was, however, involved in the infamous Jewish ritual murder trial surrounding the 'martyr' Simon of Trent (Behringer and Jerouschek, '"Das unheilvollste Buch …", pp. 41–3. Sprenger's *The Institution and Approbation of the Confraternity of the Most Holy Rosary which was first erected at Cologne on 8 September 1475*, appeared at Cologne in 1475. Behringer and Jerouschek argue that Sprenger's Marian piety does not square with the hatred expressed in the pages of the *Malleus* (p. 40); but this combination is certainly evident in later works of demonology. For instance, Del Rio, *Marian Blossoms* (1598) is a collection of the demonologist's sermons; in 1607, his *A Work About Mary (Opus Marianum)* appeared, P.G. Maxwell-Stuart, ed. and trans., *Martin Del Rio. Investigations into Magic*, Manchester and New York 2000, pp. 5, 8; Pierre Crespet wrote on witchcraft, belonged to the Catholic League, and wrote on the Virgin; the Catholic Friedrich Forner published numerous sermons on both Mary and on witchcraft and superstition: Stuart Clark, *Thinking with Demons. The Idea of Witchcraft in Early Modern Europe*, Oxford 1997, p. 439; and on the way Catholics linked witches with heretical attacks on the chief elements of the faith, Marianism included, see pp. 534–5; see also, on Marian themes and possession in Kramer, Walter Stephens, *Demon Lovers. Witchcraft, Sex and the Crisis of Belief*, Chicago 2002, pp. 335–40.

40. Lyndal Roper, 'Exorcism and the Theology of the Body', in *Oedipus and the Devil*; on Canisius, see David Lederer, *A Bavarian Beacon. Spiritual Physic and the Birth of the Asylum, 1495–1803*, forthcoming; and see Marina Warner, *Alone of All her Sex. The Myth and Cult of the Virgin Mary*, London 1976.

41. Roper, *Oedipus and the Devil*, pp. 171–98; and see, on France, Denis Crouzet, 'A Woman and the Devil: Possession and Exorcism in Sixteenth-Century France' (trans. Michael Wolfe), in Michael Wolfe, ed., *Changing Identities in Early Modern France*, Durham, NC, and London 1997; Michel de Certeau, *The Possession at Loudun*, 1970; trans. Michael B. Smith, Chicago 1996, 2000; Moshe Sluhovsky, 'The Devil in the Convent', *American Historical Review* 107, 2002, pp. 1379–411; Jonathan Pearl, *The Crime of Crimes: Demonology and Politics in France 1560–1620*, Waterloo, Canada 1999; and Sarah Ferber, *Demonic Possession and Exorcism in Early Modern France*, London 2004.

42. Maxwell-Stuart, *Del Rio*, p. 267 (Bk 6, ch. 2, qu. 3, section 3).

43. Ibid., p. 121 (Bk 3, Part 1, qu. 3, section 2).

44. Stuart Clark, 'The "Gendering" of Witchcraft in French Demonology: Misogyny or Polarity?', *French History* 5, 1991, pp. 426–37; and Robin Briggs, 'Women as Victims? Witches, Judges and the Community', *French History* 5, 1991, pp. 438–50.

45. Götz Freiherr von Pölnitz, *Julius Echter von Mespelbrunn. Fürstbischof von Würzburg und Herzog von Franken (1573–1617)* (Schriftenreihe zur bayerischen Landesgeschichte 17) Munich 1934, pp. 289, 414, 429.

46. See Bridget Heal, 'A Woman Like Any Other? Images of the Virgin Mary and Marian Devotion in Nuremberg, Augsburg and Cologne c. 1500–1600', Ph.D. diss., Courtauld Institute of Art/Royal Holloway, University of London, 2001.

47. Merry Wiesner, 'Luther and Women: The Death of Two Marys', in Jim Obelkevich, Lyndal Roper and Raphael Samuel, eds, *Disciplines of Faith. Studies in Religion, Politics and Patriarchy*, London 1987, p. 299; and see Susan Karant-Nunn and Merry E.

Wiesner, eds and trans., *Luther on Women. A Sourcebook*, Cambridge 2003, Stephen Ozment, *When Fathers Ruled. Family Life in Reformation Europe*, Cambridge, Mass., 1983.

48. David Lederer is currently researching Catholic priests and tolerated concubinage in early Counter-Reformation Bavaria.

49. Götz Freiherr von Pölnitz, *Fürstbischof Julius Echter von Mespelbrunn* (Mainfränkische Hefte 36), Würzburg 1959, p. 20 (female relations banned from court); Pölnitz, *Julius Echter*, pp. 345–7 (convents); pp. 384 ff. (concubinage).

50. On the culture of motherhood in early modern Europe, see Olwen Hufton, *The Prospect Before Her*, London 1995, pp. 173–216; Eva Labouvie, *Andere Umstände. Eine Kulturgeschichte der Geburt*, Cologne, Weimar and Vienna 1998; Laura Gowing, *Common Bodies. Women, Touch and Power in Seventeenth-Century England*, London 2003, pp. 193–203.

51. See, on these customs, Alfons Birlinger, *Volksthümliches aus Schwaben. Sitten und Gebräuche*, 2 vols, Freiburg im Breisgau 1861–62.

52. Ekkhard Struckmeier, '"Vom Glauben der Kinder im Mutter-Leibe". Eine historisch-anthropologische Untersuchung frühneuzeitlicher luthersiche Seelsorge und Frömmigkeit im Zusammanhang mit der Geburt', Ph.D. diss, Bielefeld 1995, pp. 185 ff.; Eva Labouvie, 'Geburt und Tod in der Frühen Neuzeit. Letzter Dienst und der Umgang mit besonderen Verstorbenen', in Jürgen Schlumbohm, Barbara Duden, Jacques Gélis and Patrice Veit, eds, *Rituale der Geburt. Eine Kulturgeschichte*, Munich 1998: Labouvie finds such customs as the carrying of the dead child by all the village women to the graveyard; the burial of miscarriages and children born dead in houses; and special rituals, even in Protestant areas, for women who died in childbirth.

53. Walter Strauss, *The German Single-leaf Woodcut 1550–1600*, 3 vols, New York 1975, vol. 2, pp. 635, 637: Lucius was active as a printer in Wittenberg.

54. For a slightly different interpretation of the Tintoretto, see Jill Dunkerton, Susan Roister and Nicholas Penny, *Dürer to Veronese. Sixteenth-Century Painting in the National Gallery*, London 1999, pp. 104–6; Tom Nichols, *Tintoretto. Tradition and Identity*, London 1999, pp. 137–9: it may have been commissioned for Tommaso Rangone, who might have intended it as a gift for Rudolf II or for his predecessor Maximilian II. Rangone had interests in medicine, astronomy and the classics, and may have viewed himself as able to extend human life. Svetlana Alpers, *The Making of Rubens*, New Haven and London 1995, p. 118.

55. Giulia Bartrum, *Albrecht Dürer and his Legacy. The Graphic Work of a Renaissance Artist*, London 2002, p. 116: the original has now been returned to the Kunsthalle in Bremen.

56. Gowing, 'Secret Births and Infanticide'.

57. See James Marrow and Alan Shestack, eds, *Hans Baldung Grien. Prints and Drawings*, Chicago 1981, Figure 29, Urs Graf, copy after *Fortuna*, Germanisches Nationalmuseum Nuremberg. For a discussion of fatness and *Nemesis*, see Charles W. Talbot, 'Baldung and the Female Nude', in Marrow and Shestack, eds, *Hans Baldung Grien*. There is another interesting image by Baldung Grien which may, as Talbot argues, owe something to Dürer's *Nemesis* of a nude woman holding an apple from *c.* 1525. Her hair too is bound and she proffers an apple. Her legs are crossed and her pudenda are clearly visible. Talbot is troubled by the combination of female fatness, beauty and sexuality, but these representations seem to me to be entirely at one with an aesthetic of the mature, fertile woman. They suggest, indeed, that the woman may be in the early stages of pregnancy. Another image which borrows from Dürer is that attributed to Hans Glaser of the faithlessness of Fortune: here she is

represented looking in a mirror and holding peacock feathers as a symbol of vanity
and debauchery: Strauss, *The German Single-leaf Woodcut*, vol. 1, p. 366. And there is
a further remarkable parody of Dürer's image by Niklaus Manuel Deutsch: here,
Nemesis has been tranformed into a naked witch in the prime of life, who sits with
flowing hair astride a globe holding a skull and an hourglass, and brewing a concoc-
tion on her knee. As Koerner argues, the skull held aloft by the witch is a self-portrait
of Manuel Deutsch; Bartrum, *Albrecht Dürer*, no. 179, pp. 228–9; Joseph Koerner, *The
Moment of Self-Portraiture in German Renaissance Art*, Chicago and London 1993, p.
419.

58. Jeffrey Chipps Smith, *Sensuous Worship. Jesuits and the Art of the Early Catholic
    Reformation in Germany*, Princeton 2002, pp. 143–55; the iconography of the Church
    was intensely Marian. For other examples of Last Judgment depictions which include
    fleshy, fertile women, see Joachim von Sandrart's *Das jüngste Gericht*, Waldhausen 1675,
    reproduced in Christian Klemm, *Joachim von Sandrart. Kunstwerk und Lebenslauf*,
    Berlin 1986, p. 276. On Rubens and flesh, see Alpers, *The Making of Rubens*, pp. 118–29.
    She argues that Rubens accommodates men to the same image of female fleshliness.
    Rubens himself, interestingly enough, complained in writing about the flabby, shape-
    less bodies of the modern age and regretted the loss of the beautiful bodies of antiquity.
    Alpers, *The Making of Rubens*, p. 126. Rubens himself is in many ways a good example
    of the intersection of the extreme moralism and the fascination with the flesh charac-
    teristic of both Protestantism and the Counter-Reformation. His father, Jan Rubens,
    almost certainly a Calvinist, had left Antwerp because of his faith, but had fled to
    Catholic Cologne, where the family lived as Catholics. Jan had later become involved
    in an adulterous affair with the Lutheran Anna of Saxony, wife of William of Orange,
    which led to his imprisonment and ruin and disgrace for the family. There could hardly
    have been a more searing illustration of the disastrous power of sexual passion; nor is
    it perhaps surprising that depiction of flesh should have become such an important
    theme in the artist's work.

59. Strauss, *German Single-leaf Woodcut*, vol. 2, p. 609; and on Lorck, see p. 595: Lorck
    worked for the Imperial Court and was knighted by the Emperor in 1564. He had visited
    Constantinople in 1555, and the architecture of the city in the woodcut clearly shows
    Eastern influences. Though Lorck worked in a Catholic milieu, he was also closely
    involved with the Protestant printer Sigmund Feyerabend of Frankfurt, who dedicated
    a volume to him.

60. On Lutheran prayers, Struckmeier, '"Vom Glauben der Kinder im Mutter-Leibe"',
    pp. 19 ff.; on Catholic religious cures for barrenness, Hufton, *Prospect*, pp. 175 ff.; on pil-
    grimage, Rebekka Habermas, *Wallfahrt und Aufruhr. Zur Geschichte des
    Wunderglaubens in der Frühen Neuzeit*, Frankfurt and New York 1991, pp. 54–61; the
    majority of the pilgrims to Hohenpeißenberg were women and most were aged
    between 35 and 40.

61. *Luthers Werke*, Weimarer Ausgabe, vol. 10, part II, p. 275, *Vom ehelichen leben* (1522),
    p. 296; Wiesner, 'Luther and Women', p. 295.

62. See Karant-Nunn and Wiesner-Hanks, *Luther on Women. A Sourcebook*, pp. 171–2. The
    same thing is evident in the late sixteenth- and seventeenth-century genre of the house-
    hold management books, where fertility in the natural and human worlds is a key
    value. See Gray, *Productive Men, Reproductive Women*.

63. Karl Wegert, *Popular Culture, Crime and Social Control in Eighteenth-Century
    Württemberg*, (Studien zur Geschichte des Alltags 5), Stuttgart 1995, p. 45; and on the
    meanings of pregnancy in early modern Germany, Ulinka Rublack, 'Pregnancy, Childbirth
    and the Female Body in Early Modern Germany', *Past and Present* 150, 1996, pp. 84–110.

64. Jacques Gélis, *History of Childbirth. Fertility, Pregnancy and Birth in Early Modern Europe* (French 1984), trans. R. Morris, Oxford 1991; Labouvie, *Andere Umstände*, esp. pp. 198–259 on the collective culture of celebration. She argues that this culture gradually disintegrated in the last third of the eighteenth century, pp. 268–78. For ordinances in Nördlingen on childbed festivities, see Dietmar-H. Voges, *Nördlingen seit der Reformation. Aus dem Leben einer Stadt*, Munich 1998, pp. 105–7. Ulinka Rublack has suggested that the protection offered to women in pregnancy and childbirth in sixteenth- and seventeenth-century Germany, in part through the rituals surrounding childbed, may be connected with the relatively low level of deaths in childbed until the eighteenth century: Rublack, 'Pregnancy, Childbirth and the Female Body', pp. 84–110. On midwives, see Eva Labouvie, *Beistand in Kindsnöten. Hebammen und eine weibliche Kultur auf dem Land (1550–1910)*, Frankfurt and New York 1999; and on the role of the collective of village women in appointing the midwife, pp. 149–59. For England, see Gowing, *Common Bodies*, pp. 149–76.
65. Wegert, *Popular Culture*, pp. 45–6.
66. Ibid., p. 52.
67. Koerner, *The Moment of Self-Portraiture*, p. 324.
68. So, in a woodcut of 1513 of the Three Fates, a subject closely connected to witchcraft, we see the female body in three stages of life: the young woman, with loose, flowing hair, indicating that she is yet to be married, the woman in her child-bearing years, full bosomed, with large stomach, her hair secured under a wifely wimple. The old woman is a terrifying figure, her flesh no longer voluptuous but tautly shrunken, reduced to muscle. Her flowing hair allies her with images of old witches. The connection between images of the ages of woman and images of witches can be found as early as 1497, in Dürer's very influential image now known as *The Four Witches*, which shows four naked mature women seen from different angles with a devil and human bones; though interestingly it was the seventeenth-century artist Joachim von Sandrart, active in Augsburg 1670–73, who first claimed the women were witches. Bartrum, *Albrecht Dürer*, p. 227; Karl Arndt, Josef Bellot et al., eds, *Augsburger Barock*, Augsburg 1968.
69. See Marrow and Shestack, eds, *Hans Baldung Grien*, p. 114.
70. See Koerner, *The Moment of Self-Portraiture*, p. 328; he quotes the figure of 5,000 dead in this panic. The numbers are almost certainly a gross exaggeration, and are taken from an article by L. Levrault of 1835, based on an eighteenth-century manuscript since lost; despite Levrault's references to over 300 trial records, Reuss in his authoritative study of 1871 could find only a thirtieth of these. Rodolphe Reuss, *La Sorcellerie au seizième et au dix-septième siècles particulièrement en Alsace* (1871), repr. Steinbrunn-le-Haut 1987, p. 121 n. 1.
71. Sigrid Schade, *Schadenzauber und die Magie des Körpers. Hexenbilder der frühen Neuzeit*, Worms 1983. On images of witches, see in particular the forthcoming study by Charles Zika, *The Appearance of Witchcraft. Images and Cultural Meaning in Sixteenth-Century Europe*, London 2005; and Zika, 'Cannibalism and Witchcraft in Early Modern Europe: Reading the Visual Images', *History Workshop Journal* 44, 1977, pp. 77–106, and *Exorcising Our Demons: Magic, Witchcraft, and Visual Culture in Early Modern Europe* (Studies in Medieval and Reformation Thought 91), Leiden and Boston 2003.
72. Koerner, *The Moment of Self-Portraiture*, pp. 330–1. Koerner offers a brilliant interpretation of the sexual dimensions of these images, pp. 317–62, though his concentration on the interpretative concept of the male gaze seems to me to limit his understanding of the wider cultural sources and resonances of these images. It also leads him to underplay the importance of the themes of reproduction, fertility and ageing in Baldung's work.

73. Jean Bodin, *De la démonomanie des sorciers*, trans. R. Scott, *On the Demon-Mania of Witches (1580)* (abridged), Toronto 1995, p. 169, Book 3.5; similar accusations that nuns were involved in sexual congress with evil spirits occasionally surfaced in Reformation polemic: Helmut Puff, *Sodomy in Reformation Germany and Switzerland 1400–1600*, Chicago and London 2003, p. 150; Johannes Praetorius, *Hexen-, Zauber- und Spukgeschichten aus dem Blocksberg*, 1668, ed. Wolfgang Möhrig, Frankfurt am Main 1979, p. 94.

74. Hans Behaim; Tobias Stimmer, *Die Lebensalter des Menschen*, Basel, second half of the sixteenth century, in Heide Wunder, *'Er ist die Sonn, sie ist der Mond'. Frauen in der Frühen Neuzeit*, Munich 1992, pp. 34–55; Jost Amman, *The Ages of Man*, in Strauss, *German Single-leaf Woodcut 1550–1600*, pp. 30–31, also used for a calendar printed in 1614; and Michel Manger, ibid., p. 671, calendar for 1589. See also, on these images, Peter Borscheid, *Geschichte des Alters*, Munich 1987; 1989, pp. 38–41.

75. Mary Lindeman, *Medicine and Society in Early Modern Europe*, Cambridge 1999; Danielle Jacquart and Claude Thomasset, *Sexuality and Medicine in the Middle Ages* (French 1985), trans. Matthew Adamson, Oxford 1988; Gowing, *Common Bodies*, pp. 78–81.

76. Elmar Weiß, 'Die Hexenprozesse in der Zent Grünsfeld', *Wertheimer Jahrbuch* 1979–1980, pp. 33–63; p. 44. The idea that they stole milk from cows could be linked to stealing milk from nursing mothers: see Lambert Daneau, *A Dialogue of Witches*, trans. attributed to Thomas Twyne, London 1575, on witches: 'I have seene them, who with onely laying their handes upon a nurses breastes, haue drawne forth all the milke, and dryed them up', fo. Eiv v, also quoted in Johann Gödelmann, *Von Zauberern Hexen und Unholden*, p. 83; and see Jacob Freyherr von Liechtenberg, *Ware Entdeckung und Erklärung aller fürnembster Artickel der Zauberey*, in Abraham Saur, ed., *Theatrum de veneficis*, Frankfurt am Main, Nicolaus Basse, 1586, p. 314.

Chapter 7: Crones

1. Reginald Scot, *The Discoverie of Witchcraft* (1584), intro. Montague Summers, New York 1930; 1972, p. 4; and see Erik Midelfort on Weyer, *A History of Madness in Sixteenth-Century Germany*, Stanford 1999, pp. 196–217.

2. These figures have been compiled from the microfilms of the Hexensonderkommando card files, Staatsarchiv Koblenz, F215–Zsg.2/1–f (Films), Film No. 62, which contains summary records of the Würzburg cases. They can therefore only be impressionistic, because of the inaccuracies inherent in the team's work; and because only rarely was an executed witch's age given. Nor have the records been sorted into the political units to which the researchers assigned them in this film, as they are in the alphabeticized records compiled from the 'raw' archival case material from Würzburg. I have not used, for instance, Film 17 (Gerolzhofen) or Film 44 (Würzburg) to calculate figures because these contain pro-formas which ought, in principle, to note ages of victims systematically, but are less reliable. At around 25 per cent, the proportion of male witches is roughly in line with proportions of male victims generally at this time, which lay globally between 20 and 25 per cent. (Because of the particular circumstances of the cases at the Juliusspital in Würzburg, which involved children, I have not included them in the figures.) Of the women, seventeen were aged under thirty, and thirty-three were aged between thirty and forty.

3. In only two cases can we establish nothing at all about the victim's age. In only four of the thirty-four cases do we know that the victims were younger women: one was a young unmarried woman, one was aged thirty-eight, one married in 1579 and was pregnant during her trial, and one had a child who married in 1601, which suggests that she may have been of a slightly younger age group than most of the other witches. Another woman, Veronica Fritsch, had married in 1585, thirteen years before she was tried in 1598, and so may have been in her late thirties. Only one woman was identified as a widow. Figures derived from StadtAN, Hexenprozeßakten, and from information in Gustav Wulz, 'Die Nördlinger Hexen und ihre Richter', *Der Rieser Heimatbote, Heimatbeilage der Rieser Nationalzeitung*, Nördlingen 1939, Nos. 142–5; 147.

4. In three cases we know that the accused was a single woman. In one case, all that can be established is that the accused had had a miscarriage. Figures compiled from SAS Dep. 30, Rep. VI, Pak. 254, Marchtaler Hexenprozesse.

5. In the literature on witchcraft it has been usual to provide figures on the numbers of widows amongst those accused. Erik Midelfort also comments on 'the commonplace observation that widows and spinsters were most commonly accused of witchcraft, far out of proportion to their numbers in society', *Witch-hunting in South-western Germany, 1562–1684. The Social and Intellectual Foundations*, Stanford 1972, p. 185. Midelfort perceptively linked the witch persecutions to changes in family structure in the sixteenth century, and in particular to the higher proportion of women who remained unmarried. However, he takes the significant factor to be whether a woman was protected by a man or not; and so he considers widows and spinsters to be analogous. It seems however more likely that the important point is the reproductive status of the woman, not her marital status; that is, the numbers of accused witches who had been mothers and were now menopausal. Some elderly single women took on a similar role in society, caring for young children. By contrast, I consider young, never-married spinsters as forming a distinct group. The themes of their trials tended to be rather different.

6. In one case, a woman was executed with her mother. In another, the woman had been seduced by an older woman, who was a 'classic' witch, aged 64. Two women in their thirties were executed with Maria Fleck in a complex case from 1685: the older woman had seduced the younger two and they also allegedly 'corrupted' a young boy who set his stepmother's house on fire. Figures compiled from StadtAA, Reichsstadt, Strafbücher des Rats; Urgichtensammlung.

7. Eva Labouvie, *Zauberei und Hexenwerk. Ländlicher Hexenglaube in der Frühen Neuzeit*, Frankfurt am Main 1991, pp. 172–3; Labouvie is able to use indirect evidence of age, such as age of children, to calculate probable age. For Mainz, Herbert Pohl can provide figures only for Dieburg: here the average age was 55. Herbert Pohl, *Hexenglaube und Hexenverfolgung im Kurfürstentum Mainz. Ein Beitrag zur Hexenfrage im 16. und beginnenden 17. Jahrhundert* (Geschichtliche Landeskunde 32), Stuttgart 1988, p. 218; Rainer Walz also finds that women over 50 predominated in the trials in Lippe, but links this to their status as widows or to the conflicts unleashed by remarriages; Rainer Walz, *Hexenglaube und magische Kommunikation im Dorf der Frühen Neuzeit. Die Verfolgungen in der Grafschaft Lippe*, Paderborn 1993, pp. 299–305; and see, for an overview, Alison Rowlands, 'Witchcraft and Old Women in Early Modern Germany', *Past and Present* 173, 2001, pp. 50–89. These figures are in stark contrast with the numbers of women over the age of 40 in the population in general: 15 per cent of the population of Lautern in 1601 were aged over 40; 24 per cent of the population of Zurich were aged over 40 in 1637: Peter Borscheid, *Geschichte des Alters*, Munich 1987; 1989, p. 25.

8. Walz, *Hexenglaube und magische Kommunikation*, p. 300; and see, on witchcraft and

age, Rowlands, 'Witchcraft and Old Women': Rowlands argues that the age of the woman at trial is misleading, because suspicions and rumours that a particular woman was a witch often circulated for decades before the accusation. However, it is surely significant that it is when the woman can no longer bear children that she seems to become a credible witch and is actually brought to court. Moreover, it is the trial itself which often, though not always, provides evidence for the longevity of the suspicions. Hindsight thus plays an important role, as accusers start to reinterpret the past in the light of a variety of suspicions that finally crystallize at the time the case is brought.

9. Borscheid claims that the image of the mill of age, in which old people pass through a mill producing young and beautiful men and women, became popular around 1600: Borscheid, *Geschichte des Alters*, p. 40; this imagery exploits much older images of the Host Mill, in which Christ's body passes through the mill, producing hosts.

10. See also the images of *The Men's Bath* (1497) and *The Women's Bath* (1496) by Dürer.

11. On old age, see the path-breaking article by Lynn Botelho, 'Old Age and Menopause in Rural Women of Early Modern Suffolk', in Lynn Botelho and Pat Thane, eds, *Women and Ageing in British Society since 1500*, Harlow 2001. Botelho argues that old age was perceived to begin at age fifty in women, and that it was primarily related to the observable physical changes that follow from menopause. The cessation of fertility, she argues, was not regarded as a key index of ageing and no great significance was attached to it: medical writers, she points out, had very little to say about menopause either. However, this book takes a different line. The witchcraft images show, for the most part, a woman who does not have the attributes of advanced old age such as a bent back, toothless gums, extremely wrinkled skin. Instead, she is clearly infertile. On old age in general, see Borscheid, *Geschichte des Alters* and on the connection between old age in women, the menopause and witchcraft accusations see Edward Watts Morto Bever, 'Witchcraft in Early Modern Württemberg', Ph.D. diss., Princeton 1983.

12. Fredericus Petrys Gayer, *Viereckichtes Eheschaetzlein. Da ist: die vier Gradus der Eheleute*, Erfurt, Johann Beck, 1602, esp. fos. C iiir. ff., D viiv ff., and E iiv.

13. Alison Stewart, *Unequal Lovers: A Study of Unequal Couples in Northern Art*, New York 1977.

14. See for example his woodcut, *Three Fates* (1513), in which the older woman is most clearly a witch, his *Ages of Women*, Leipzig, 1544, and his *Death and the Ages of Women* (Prado, Madrid, c. 1541–44).

15. In Hans Weiditz's *Wetterhexe* of 1530, the witch is dressed but she has flying hair, and the artist hints at her sagging breasts.

16. See, on crossed legs and on the sexually provocative stance, Charles W. Talbot, 'Baldung and the Female Nude', in James H. Marrow and Alan Shestack, eds, *Hans Baldung Grien, Prints and Drawings*, Chicago 1981; and on Manuel Deutsch, see Joseph Leo Koerner, *The Moment of Self-Portraiture in German Renaissance Art*, Chicago and London 1993, pp. 417 ff.

17. See Marrow and Shestack, eds, *Hans Baldung Grien. Prints and Drawings*, pp. 278–9.

18. See for example the extraordinary image by De Gheyn of envy as a witch with snake-like hair and sagging breasts; and see Arthur Henkel and Albrecht Schöne, eds, *Emblemata. Handbuch zur Sinnbildkunst*, Stuttgart 1967, pp. 1570–1; see also Charles Zika, *Exorcising our Demons: Magic, Witchcraft, and Visual Culture in Early Modern Europe* (Studies in Medieval and Reformation Thought 91), Leiden and Boston 2003, pp. 475–6.

19. Johann Fischart, *Flöh Hatz, Weiber Tratz*, ed. Alois Haas, Stuttgart 1967; 1982, p. 49 and 51:

und zindt shir an der Alten Fläschen
Ir alt Cavern
zusamt dem Loch
Daraus der stinckend Atam Kroch
and see following verses.

20. Hans Jacob Christoph von Grimmelshausen, *Simplicissimus* (1669), afterword by Volker Meid, Stuttgart 1961; 1996, white alabaster breasts, p. 378; 'hierüber fieng sie an zu lachen, daß man ihr alle vier Zähn sahe, die sie noch im Maul hatte', p. 379; 'Bisse mir vor hitziger Begierde schier die undter Lefzen herab', p. 380; '*Rick su mir mein Herz*', p. 381.

21. Hans Jakob Christoph von Grimmelshausen, *Lebensbeschreibung der Erzbetrügerin und Landstörzerin Courasche*, ed. Klaus Haberkamm and Günter Weydt, Stuttgart 1971; 1998, p. 89.

22. 'Er kam, meinem Wunsch nach, mit völligem Wind in den gefährlichen Port meiner sattsamen Begierden angesegelt, und ich traktierte ihn wie etwan die Circe den irrenden Ulyssem', ibid., p. 113. Grimmelshausen includes a knowing reference to Simplicissimus's description of the same encounter in *Simplicissimus*, Book 5, ch. 6 (p. 484) – a nice shifting of perspective which also advertises the other work.

23. 'Dass ich damals den siebenzehenden Teil meiner vorigen Schönheit bei weitem nicht mehr hatte, sondern ich behalfe mich allbereit mit allerhand Anstrich und Schminke, deren er mir nicht wenig, sondern einer grossen Menge abgeleckt', *Courasche*, p. 114.

24. 'Daß ich den guten Simplen glauben gemacht, die Unfruchtbare hätte geboren', ibid., p. 115.

25. Grön had actually twice been imprisoned for debauchery before she was accused of witchcraft. The lengthy trial transcript is in StadtAA, Reichsstadt, Urg., Ursula Grön 1694, 25 May 1694.

26. 'hette Verdient dz Mans Lebendig Verbrandt', StadtAA, Reichsstadt, Urg., Ursula Grön 1694, 25 May 1694, testimony of Hans Lutz, 7 July 1694.

27. 'alwo vil khinder vnd schwangere Weiber sich befinden', StadtAA, Reichsstadt, Urg., Ursula Grön 1694, 25 May 1694, Michael Schmidt.

28. 'es schiesse Jhm in dem ganz verzehrten Leib herumb Wie ein Pfeil so aber gleich Wider Vergehe dz arme . . . seye Wie ein Kugel, Mache bürzel Wan es im bett lige', ibid., Anna Melchior Schuster, 8 July 1694; and 24 May 1694; and see confrontation between Grön and Schuster, 8 June 1694, where Schuster alleged 'Es kommen von diesem stein Wurff her. Dz Kindt wann die schmerzen an es kommen. Schreye iezo Fallen die Stein mir in die Fueß. Daß arme Kindt so 10 Jahr alt Wäre, habe den geruch verlohren, seye wie ein Kugel so Krumb, der Fuß seye wie ein Kinds Kopf geschwollen und der ubrige Leib nehme ab'.

29. 'der ort der geschwulst ist steinhärth, Wie Mans selbst gefühlt', StadtAA, Reichsstadt, Urg., Ursula Grön 1694, 25 May 1694, testimony 8 July 1694.

30. 'bald brot, baldt apfel', StadtAA, Reichsstadt, Urg., Ursula Grön 1694, 25 May 1694, testimony of Hans Lutz, 26 May 1694: Lutz said that Grön had been pursuing his grandson, offering him now bread, now apples, in a context of enmity between himself and her. Jacobina Bader also reported her children receiving gifts of food from Grön, 26 May 1694; Margaretha Schroff's child died after having been given bread by her, 7 July 1694, Margaretha Schroff.

31. 'man habs nicht gern, Wann alte Weiber den Kindern brodt und apfel geben', StadtAA, Reichsstadt, Urg. Ursula Grön, 1694, 8 June 1694. As Grön put it earlier, 'die alte Weiber seyen in der Welt eben veracht, und heiß es du alte Hex du alter Teuffel', 8 June 1694.

32. 'immer umb die brauth gutschen herumbgelauffen'; and see also StadtAA, Reichsstadt,

Urg., Ursula Grön, 1694, 8 June 1694, testimony of Hans Jerg Lang, 7 July 1694.

33. 'als sie nun mit ein ander schaffen gegangen, habe sich auch ihr Man nit recht Wol auff befunden', StadtAA, Reichsstadt, Urg., Ursula Grön 1694, testimony of Euphrosina Eppenstein, 24 May 1694; Eppenstein also believed that Grön had appeared to her that night, possibly as an illusion.

34. She left very few possessions, as the inventory of her goods indicates. Her social isolation and desire for human connection is evident from her attempt to bequeath her cash to the five clerics at the Franciscan church and the gaolkeeper and his staff, StadtAA, undated letter of Eisenmeister; and see her final appeal at the end of her second interrogation, 8 June 1694, where she tried to use her money to get the authorities to give her better provisions. An important element of her story may be that she had no grandchildren, and so people might also have expected her to envy other women. This pattern is evident in several cases discussed in this book, such as Catharina Schmid (1745 Marchtal), Ursula Götz (1627 Marchtal), and it undoubtedly played a role; but it cannot be generalized. It does not, for instance, apply to the Nördlingen cases, to many of the Marchtal trials, or to many of the Würzburg prosecutions.

35. 'wie alla bastar': the witness thought this happened 'durch ein verblindtnus', StadtAA, Urg., Ursula Grön 1594, testimony of Hans Jerg Lang, 24 May 1694.

36. SAS Dep. 30, Rep. VI, Pak. 254, Marchtaler Hexenprozesse, Kundschaft aus Saulgart 1617, Conradt Weggeman.

37. SAW, Hist. Saal VII, 25/375, fo. 271, Margareta Schreyer, 21 June 1617; Hist. Saal VII, 25/375 fos. 63–5, Hans Dülicken Weib, 3 May 1616.

38. Margareta Streng (mother: Walpurg Keppeler); Margareta Haller (mother: Christina Berger); Anna Moll (mother: Anna Hiert); Anna Graeter and Maria Lepp (mother: Barbara Miller; aunt, Lena Graeter); Anna Windholz (mother: Ursula Bayer); and for the eighteenth century, Maria Dornhauser (mother: Catharina Schmid); Anna Oberländer (mother: Maria Bingasser); information derived from SAS Dep. 30, Rep. VI, Pak. 254, 255, Marchtaler Hexenprozesse.

39. Maria Knorz, whose daughters were Eva Aufschlager and Ursula Klein. One daughter was fifty, the other had been married for thirty years. StadtAN, Hexenprozeßakten. Interestingly, the motif of the mother and daughter who are both witches was also made much of in popular illustrated broadsides about witches. See Charles Zika, *Appearances of Witchcraft. Visual Culture and Print in Sixteenth-Century Europe*, London 2005, ch. 7.

40. Ludwig Walter, 'Pater Sebastian Sailer – Der schwäbische Mundartdichter aus Marchtal', Max Müller, Rudolf Reinhardt and Wilfried Schöntag, eds, *Marchtal. Prämonsstratenserabtei, Fürstliches Schloss, Kirchliche Akademie*, Ulm 1992, pp. 256–7.

41. 'Trauerlied auf ein altes Weib', in *Sebastian Sailers Schriften im schwäbischen Dialekte*, ed. Sixt Bachmann 1819; reprint and additional introduction, Franz Georg Brustgi, Reutlingen 1976, pp. 285 ff.

42. The linking of old women with owls is a common trope: see, for instance, *Ages of Man* by Jost Amman. The owl is also, of course, linked with the night and with witchcraft.

43. On the literature of the man of excess, see Lyndal Roper, *Oedipus and the Devil. Witchcraft, Sexuality and Religion in Early Modern Europe*, London 1994, pp. 145–67; on the open-mouthed woman, see for instance the painting by Peter Huys, *Woman Enraged*; for interpretation see Simon Schama, *The Embarrassment of Riches. An Interpretation of Dutch Culture in the Golden Age*, London 1987, pp. 432–3.

44. See the trial of Catharina Schmid in 1745, SAS, Dep. 30, Rep. VI, Pak. 255.

45. Johann Evangelista Schöttle, *Geschichte von Stadt und Stift Buchau samt dem stiftischen*

Dorfe Kappel. Beschreibung und Geschichte der Pfarrei Seekirch mit ihren Filialen Alleshausen, Brasenberg und Tiefenbach, 1884; Bad Buchau 1977, pp. 541–2.

46. During his illness another priest had been drafted in to help. Ibid., p. 537.

Chapter 8: Family Revenge

1. The letter of Justus Junius, former mayor of Bamberg, to his daughter is translated in Alan Kors and Edward Peters, eds, *Witchcraft in Europe 400–1700: A Documentary History*, 2nd edn, Philadelphia 2001; on the protean nature of witchcraft, see Johannes Dillinger, *'Böse Leute'. Hexenverfolgungen in Schwäbisch-Österreich und Kurtrier im Vergleich*, Trier 1999.

2. On trials of children for witchcraft, see Wolfgang Behringer, 'Kinderhexenprozesse. Zur Rolle von Kindern in der Geschichte der Hexenverfolgung', *Zeitschrift für historische Forschung* 16, 1989, pp. 31–47; Robert Walinski-Kiel, 'The Devil's Children: Child Witch-Trials in Early Modern Germany', *Continuity and Change* 11, 1996, pp. 171–90; Rainer Walz, 'Kinder in Hexenprozessen. Die Grafschaft Lippe, 1654–1663', in Jürgen Scheffler, Gerd Schwerhoff and Gisela Wilbertz, eds, *Hexenverfolgung und Regionalgeschichte. Die Grafschaft Lippe im Vergleich* (Studien zur Regionalgeschichte 4), Bielefeld 1994; Hartwig Weber, *Kinderhexenprozesse*, Frankfurt am Main and Leipzig 1991, and Hartwig Weber, *'Von der verführten Kinder Zauberei'. Hexenprozesse gegen Kinder im alten Württemberg*, Sigmaringen 1996.

3. Hugh Cunningham, *Children and Childhood in Western Society since 1500*, London 1995, p. 61. He also allows that the decline in the belief in original sin was gradual, and that Christianity continued to be important.

4. J. H. Plumb, 'The New World of Children', in Neil McKendrick, John Brewer and J.H. Plumb, eds, *The Birth of a Consumer Society. The Commercialization of Eighteenth-century England*, London 1982, p. 312.

5. Helmut Baier, 'Die evangelische Kirche zwischen Pietismus, Orthodoxie und Aufklärung', in Günther Gottlieb et al., eds, *Geschichte der Stadt Augsburg*, Stuttgart 1984, p. 524; James van Horn Melton, *Absolutism and the Eighteenth-century Origins of Compulsory Schooling*, Cambridge 1988, esp. pp. 24–50. So also Francke's initial project, on which the Augsburg movement was modelled, had been centred on Francke's school in Halle in 1695 for poor children and beggars; and Francke visited Augsburg, where he held catechism classes in the Armenkinderhaus. On Pietist pedagogy, see Hartmut Lehmann, 'Die Kinder Gottes in der Welt', in Martin Greschat, ed., *Zur neueren Pietismusforschung*, Darmstadt 1977.

6. Melton, *Absolutism*, pp. 64, 68.

7. 'gleich Wie Wir Kinder Jhm keine schandt zugezogen so solle Er ein solches Jhnen auch nicht thun und keine nehmen die aller naglers gesellen hur Wäre', StadtAA, Urg., Margaretha Wagner 1694, 20 Nov. 1694, testimony of Philippina Fischer.

8. StadtAA, Hochzeitsprotokolle, 30 April 1628, p. 253; 21 Jan. 1629, p. 337; 19 Oct. 1670, p. 310 (Tobias Wagner); 12 May 1669, p. 189; Archiv der evangelisch-lutherischen Gesamtkirchenverwaltung, Taufbuch Hl. Kreuz 1607–80, pp. 455, 495.

9. StadtAA, Hochzeitsprotokolle, 5 July 1676, fo. 83r; Archiv der evangelisch-lutherischen Gesamtkirchenverwaltung, Trauungsbuch Hl. Kreuz 1597–1792, p. 169, 14 July 1676; Taufbuch Hl. Kreuz 1607–80, p. 523, 27 June 1677.

10. StadtAA, Steuerbücher, 1675, 80c (vom Diepolt); 1676, 83d; 1677, 83c (Vom Schmidhaus); 1679, 83b; 1680, 83a; 1681, 82d; 1687, 76a; 1688, 79b; 1692, 73c.

11. 'albers Mägdlen ... halsstärrig vnd ganz ungeluhrnig', StadtAA, Juditha Wagner, 1694, Ludwig Wagner testimony, 2, 3 Dec. 1689; 'plumpes vngeschikhtes, vngelehrsames Mägdlen', 'vngehorsamb', testimony Hans Christoph Esslinger, 2, 3 Dec. 1689; 'hallstärrig vnd ain verstokhts Mensch', testimony Esaias Johannes Wagner, 2, 3 Dec. 1689; 'albers, ungescheides Mägdlen', testimony Ludwig Wagner, 14 Dec. 1689.

12. StadtAA, Anna Juditha Wagner 1689, testimony of Esaias Johannes Wagner, 24 Dec. 1689, 'gaist'.

13. 'willig'; 'wohhin she selbst zukommen verlangt', StadtAA, Urg. Anna Juditha Wagner, 2 Nov. 1689.

14. StadtAA, Urg. Anna Juditha Wagner, 5 Nov. 1689.

15. Thomas Max Safley, *Charity and Economy in the Orphanages of Early Modern Augsburg*, Boston 1997, pp. 184, 305.

16. Staatsbibliothek München, Cgm 2026, fo. 65r–v; StadtAA, Johann Bausch, Malefizbuch, 1755, p. 231.

17. StadtAA, Strafbuch des Rats 1654–90, p. 595, 3 May 1689.

18. StadtAA, Urg. Anna Juditha Wagner, 26 Nov. 1689. Extract Bürgermeister Protokolle; interrogation of Jacob Schmid, his master and fellow apprentice: this is almost certainly wrongly dated and probably took place a month later. The Orphanage Father was not asked about the probable identity of the boy until 14 Dec., when he said he was most likely Jacob Schmidt. Juditha had only mentioned misleading a boy on 7 Dec. The report from the mayor dated 26 Nov. was not presented to the Council until 3 March 1690 and on 4 March they determined on further questioning; StadtAA, Urg., Anna Juditha Wagner 1694, 7 March 1690 (interrogation of Jacob Schmidt by the mayor; testimony of Hans Andreas Miller and other witnesses); 11 March 1690 (interrogation of Jacob Schmidt); 22 March 1690 (interrogation of Jacob Schmidt and confrontation).

19. Etienne François, *Die unsichtbare Grenze. Protestanten und Katholiken in Augsburg 1648–1806*, Sigmaringen 1991, pp. 167–78, 275–8: the difference between the two confessions' naming strategies was to become increasingly marked during the eighteenth century.

20. 'Durch welchen Gottes hand gross wunder hat gethan
    Alles anligen, ia Teueffel muessen weichen
    Durch hand auf legen und H. Creitz zeichen'.
    SSBAugs, 2° Cod. Aug. 127, fos. 252r, 255v, 262r.

21. Lyndal Roper, *Oedipus and the Devil. Witchcraft, Sexuality and Religion in Early Modern Europe*, London 1994, pp. 171–98; David Lederer, *A Bavarian Beacon. Spiritual Physic and the Birth of the Asylum, 1495–1803*, forthcoming.

22. Baier, 'Die evangelische Kirche'; and this would have been evident to Protestants and Catholics even more clearly as the numbers of Catholic baptisms and weddings began regularly to outstrip the Protestants by quite a long way. See François, *Die unsichtbare Grenze*, pp. 246–52. These figures were collected and published at the time, so confessional demography was a subject very much present in seventeenth- and eighteenth-century Augsburgers' consciousness. On the Salzburg refugees, see Mack Walker, *The Salzburg Transaction. Expulsion and Redemption in Eighteenth-Century Augsburg*, Ithaca, NY 1992; and for their impact in Augsburg, see in particular François and Baier as above.

23. SSBAugs, 2° Cod. Aug. 127, fo. 208.

24. Gottlieb Spitzel, *Die Gebrochne Macht der Finsternuß/ oder Zerstörte Teuflische Bunds- und Buhl-Freundschafft mit den menschen ...*, Augsburg 1687; SSBAugs, 2° Cod. Aug., 127, fos. 250, 278; Christoph Ehinger, *Daemonologia oder etwas neues vom Teufel*, Augsburg 1681; Dietrich Blaufuss, *Reichsstadt und Pietismus – Philipp Jacob Spener und*

Gottlieb Spizel aus Augsburg (Einzelarbeiten aus der Kirchengeschichte Bayerns 53), Neustadt an der Aisch 1977, p. 27. This was not unusual: in 1664, the evangelical synod had ordered prayers to be said for a woman in one of the city's hospitals who was 'continually plagued' with satanic temptations, StadtAA, Evangelisches Wesensarchiv, nr 517 Tom II, 1664, Susanna Waffenschmid.

25. See SSBAugs, 2° Cod. Aug. 288; StadtAA, Strafbuch des Rats 7 Feb. 1673, p. 390; Blaufuss, *Reichsstadt und Pietismus*, pp. 88 ff.; 246 ff.

26. StadtAA, Strafbuch des Rats 1654–99, p. 503, 4 April 1682.

27. 'Sie habe ia sagen Muessen, der Herr Spitzel hab nicht nachlassen wollen; Sie seye nicht die Hexenregel; Herr Spitzel habe es verstanden sie habe mit dem Teueffel zuthun gehabt, wie es auch anderen angefochtenen Personen gemacht, dz Er Sie zu hexen machen wollen, so theils schon todt seyen', StadtAA, Evangelisches Wesensarchiv, nr. 515 Tom I, Acta Die Evangelische Ober-Kirchen-Pfleg oder De ritus ac ceremonias Ecclesiasticas desgl. de disciplinam et censuram ecclesiasticam, 1649–1708, vol. II, nos. 73–81. Margaretha Wagner, interestingly, was aware of the problem of falling into the Church's hands when witchcraft accusations were being made: in her case, the synod of ministers also considered the accusations of witchcraft against her, and asked her to bring proof of her innocence from the Council. Wagner was no fool. She knew that if she tried to procure such a document she would be likely to find herself catapulted into a full criminal trial, with the Council testing out whether she was a witch or no with the use of torture. She wisely omitted to bring the requisite documentation.

28. StadtAA, Urg., Anna Juditha Wagner 1689, first interrogation 5 Nov. 1689, the Devil guided her hands.

29. StadtAA, Urg., Anna Juditha Wagner 1689, 9 Nov. 1689, Rosina Esslinger, statement before the mayor; 3 Dec. 1689 and 14 Dec. 1689, Rosina Esslinger.

30. Jakobina Miller, Juditha's mother, was from a local family. Her father was a weaver. StadtAA, Hochzeitsprotokolle 12 May 1669, fos. 189v–190r.

31. StadtAA, Urg., Juditha Wagner, testimony 2, 3 Dec. 1689, Hans Christoph Esslinger: he said his mother was named Sara Schiffeler and had died nine years ago; his brother, nine or ten years ago. Rosina Esslinger, 3 Dec. 1689, said her brother had died nine years ago and her mother before him, about ten years ago: see also testimony of 9 Nov. 1689.

32. StadtAA, Urg., Anna Juditha Wagner 1689, second interrogation, 7 Dec. 1689, qu. 17: she volunteered this information which was not directly relevant to the question. Rosina commented on it on 14 Dec. 1689; Esaias commented further on 24 Dec. 1689.

33. StadtAA, Urg., Anna Juditha Wagner 1689, 14 Dec. 1689, Dr Daniel Feldt, Daniel Mayr.

34. StadtAA, Urg., Caspar Mayer 1685, Maria Fleck 1685; Strafbuch des Rats 17 Nov. 1685, pp. 543–4. The case was described in Spitzel's *Die Gebrochne Macht der Finsternuß*. There are also numerous accounts of the trials in manuscript chronicles.

35. StadtAA, Chroniken 32, Chronik des Ludwig Hainzelmann 1629–60, 26 Sept. 1642: the chronicler who noted the story and other tales which featured the Devil kept the German School at Augsburg, an interesting example of the connection between children's mental worlds and stories of witchcraft.

36. 'Weis fleckhen, Blau flekhlen, belz fleckhlen, Grien fleckhlen, dz schwarze habe man aus lassen miessen, dan es der teuffel nit habe leiden wollen', StadtAA, Urg., Anna Juditha Wagner 1689, second interrogation 7 Dec. 1689, qu. 19; and see third interrogation 20 Dec. 1689, qu. 57; testimony 24 Dec. 1689 of Trostknecht. The prayer can be found in StadtAA, Urg., Maria Fleck 1685, third interrogation, qu. 113.

37. StadtAA, Strafbuch des Rats 1654–99, p. 541, 15 Nov. 1685; 'Malefizbuch', Johann Bausch, p. 231.

38. StadtAA, Urg., Anna Juditha Wagner 1689, 3 Dec. 1689, Rosina Esslinger.

39. 'vnder disen frag stuckh hat die verhaffte 3 mahl abscheulich den Mundt gekrumbt vnd mit den Zähnen den Mundt zusammen gezogen, auch verschidentlich die farb geEndert, vnd da man die vrsach dessen befragt, sagt sie, der teuffel Regiere so lauth vnd erschrökhenlich daraussen vor diser thür, vnd wolle nicht haben, dz sie mehrers bestehen solle, welches er öffters daroben auch thue vnd schire offt dz feur, vnd da sie eben heut ad locum examinis habe gefuehrt werden wollen, habe der teuffel Jhr gesagt, sie solle nichts bekhennen, wan man sie schon starkh anstrengen werde, oder er wolle sie zerreissen', StadtAA, Urg., Anna Juditha Wagner 1689, second interrogation, 7 Dec. 1689, qu. 45.

40. In understanding the processes at work here, the psychoanalytic concept of projective identification might be useful. Through her physical comportment and lurid stories, Juditha communicated her pain and misery to her interrogators, arousing strong emotions in them. Negative projective identification features strongly throughout the dynamics of the case, as Juditha and those around her projected unacknowledged parts of themselves on to others, who were then associated with witches and the Devil.

41. See, for example, James Sharpe, *Instruments of Darkness. Witchcraft in England 1550–1750*, London 1996, pp. 190–210, on possession and attention-seeking.

42. For a similar argument in the case of the possessions at Loudun, see Michel de Certeau, *The Possession at Loudun*, 1970; trans. Michael B. Smith, Chicago 1996, 2000.

43. 'Sie habe mit dem teuffel khein unzucht getriben, da Jhr aber gesagt worden, warümben sie dan der Abrahamb Esslinger auff den schneider fleckh nakhendt ligen angetroffen, sagt vnd fragt sie, Jhr herren thuet mir ia nichts, vnd da Jhr gesagt worden, solle die Wahrheit bekhennen, gestehet sie, dz dortmahlen der teuffel in gestalt aines klainen hueren buebens bey Jhr gewesen, sie mit der glatten an der s.v. Scham, oder bull, wie sies genendt, angetast, geküzlet, auff sie gelegen, vnd Jhr in die s.v. bull ain schwarze woll gestekht, dz sie etlich zeit, bis sie solche heraus gethan, nit mehr dz wasser lassen khönnen, es habe Jhr dises gar wohl gethan, da sie aber dz wöllen herausthuen wollen, habe der teuffel sie schlagen wollen ... sie habe aber kheinen menschen geschadt', StadtAA, Anna Juditha Wagner 1689, third interrogation, 20 Dec. 1689, qu. 62 and 63.

44. 'von den bösen Leithen sehr vbel zuegericht und gemacht worden sye, daß Sye S.V. das Wasser nit lassen khönnen, und also elendigklich Crepieren müessen', StadtAA, Urg., Juditha Wagner 1689, report of Mayor Joseph Adrian Imhoff, 16 Feb. 1690.

45. Melanie Klein, *The Psychoanalysis of Children*, trans. Alix Strachey, London 1932; 1989, esp. pp. 174–5; Klein, *Envy and Gratitude and Other Works 1946–63*, London 1975; 1988, esp. p. 288, and Klein, *Love, Guilt and Reparation and Other Works 1921–1945*, London 1975; 1988, esp. pp. 188–9.

46. Ulinka Rublack, 'Pregnancy, Childbirth and the Female Body in Early Modern Germany', *Past and Present* 150, 1996, pp. 84–110.

47. StadtAA, Johann Bausch, Malefizbuch, 1755, p. 252.

48. StadtAA, Urg., Anna Juditha Wagner 1689, inquiries to be made concerning Juditha's stepmother's reputation 'in der stille', 8 Nov. 1689; Note on 'Item 11', passed to Mayor Imhoff, since Mayor Amman had not carried out the order, on 13 Dec. 1689; Note on Extraordinai Bekhantnus of 4 Jan. 1690 that the report was asked for again on 12 January 1690; finally supplied on 16 February 1690. By contrast, the Council asked the mayor to find out about Ernst Scheich on 12 January 1690 following Juditha's interrogation on 4 January and the report was tabled at the Council on 16 Feb. 1690. Juditha reaffirmed her earlier confessions, including that her step-grandmother was a witch, on 24 December 1689 and again on 4 January 1690 and confirmed the truth of her confessions in general on 29 April 1690. The relevant extracts are summarized as a document in Urg., Margaretha Wagner 1695.

49. StadtAA, Urg. Margaretha Wagner 1694, Bürgermeisteramtsprotokolle, 18 Nov. 1694.
50. 'gar schlechten gemächlin', StadtAA, Urg., Anna Juditha Wagner 1689, 16 Feb. 1690, Bürgermeisteramtsprotokolle.
51. StadtAA, Urg., Margaretha Wagner 1694, 20 Nov. 1694, witness statements, Anna Maria Find; Philippina Wagner; 26 Nov. 1694, witness statements, Daniel Herz; Joseph Herz; Johanna Silbereissen; Elisabetha Dreschsel; Susanna Vaigeler; 14 Dec. 1689, witness statements, Anna Maria Fischer née Prax.
52. StadtAA, Urg., Margaretha Wagner 1694, 20 Nov. 1694, Esaias Wagner.
53. StadtAA, Urg., Margaretha Wagner 1694, 11 Jan. 1690, Margaretha Gauss.
54. StadtAA, Urg., Margaretha Wagner 1694, 4 Dec. 1694, first interrogation, conclusion, 'dass Sie aber nicht greinen könne, seye daher dz Jhr herz so betrübt seye'.
55. StadtAA, Urg., Margaretha Wagner 1694, 20 Nov. 1694, Philippina Fischer.
56. StadtAA, Urg., Margaretha Wagner 1694, confrontation 5 Jan. 1695, Philippina Fischer, ad 32.
57. StadtAA, Urg., Margaretha Wagner 1694, first interrogation, 4 Dec. 1694, qu. 24; testimony 22 Dec. 1689, Caspar Reuschlin; Maria Duerst.
58. They were probably from the Mehrer family who belonged to the Mehrer, that is, the group who socialized with and intermarried with the patriciate.
59. 'es werde Jhr die Zunge noch aus dem Halß faulen', StadtAA, Urg., Margaretha Wagner 1694, confrontation 5 Jan. 1695, Philippina Fischer; and ad 63, 'Sie seye selbst ein Juden und Christen huer'.
60. Her name disappears from the tax records for ever, so presumably she did actually leave town.
61. Albert Haemmerle, *Evangelisches Totenregister zur Kunst- und Handwerksgeschichte*, Augsburg 1928, p. 106.
62. StadtAA, Bürgermaisteramtsprotokolle (AC), 25 Feb. 1670–8 March 1674, p. 135, 26 June 1671. Esais Wagner claimed that Mayor Jenisch had written this down in 1671 when he had first brought the case and had accepted reconciliation: 'Weilen Esaias Wagner als der Stieffsohn seine hande nicht Will in seiner Stiefmutter bluth Waschen', StadtAA, Urg., Margaretha Wagner 1694, confrontation 5 Jan. 1695.
63. StadtAA, Urg., Anna Juditha Wagner 1689, 24 Dec. 1689, witness statement Esaias Wagner. Mr Beckh was almost certainly Deacon Mathäus Friedrich Beck or Boeck, deacon at the Franciscans from 1678 to 1696 (Horst Jesse, *Die evangelische Kirche 'Zu den Barfüssern' in Augsburg*, Pfaffenhofen 1982, p. 74), which would have been the Wagner family's parish church once they moved in 1677 to the tax district Vom Schmidhaus from Vom Diepolt.
64. 'Bittet endtlich dass man sie doch in disen stublen lassen wolle da sie iezt seie, vnd Jn kein finsters lege, dan die anfechtungen seie Jr gar zu gros', StadtAA, Urg., Anna Juditha Wagner 1689, first interrogation 5 Nov. 1689, conclusion.
65. Jesse, *Die evangelische Kirche 'Zu den Barfüssern' in Augsburg*, pp. 53–4.
66. 'Sie wolle gern vnder des henckhers handt sterben, als dz sie wider hinaus khomen solte, dan sie sonsten wider in dz alte vble leben fallen möchte', StadtAA, Urg., Anna Juditha Wagner 1689, fourth interrogation 24 Dec. 1689, conclusion. As she left, she did, however, ask for a 'gnädiges Vrthel'.
67. StadtAA, Urg., Anna Juditha Wagner 1689, first interrogation, 5 Nov. 1689, Juditha volunteered the information about her stepmother; 14 Dec. 1689, Rosina confirmed the pains although in her earlier statements she had not mentioned them; 20 Dec. 1689, third interrogation, qu. 54, 55, 72, Juditha denies harming her stepmother and says her father told her to say this; 24 Dec. 1689, Esaias Wagner insisted on the serious nature of Rosina's pains; and on 24 Dec. 1689, after confrontation with her father,

Regina revoked her accusation that her father told her to say this and repeated that she had certainly caused her 'mother' pains and spread something on her bed and shirt.

68. StadtAA, Urg. Anna Juditha Wagner 1689, 2 Dec. 1689, witness testimony, Esaias Wagner mentions much tumult ('vngestüme') which he had heard in the house during the lifetime of his first wife, and which he now thought must have been caused by Christele and Juditha; 24 Dec. 1689, he mentioned this again; fourth interrogation with confrontation, 24 Dec. 1689, weeping, Juditha confessed to causing the 'vngestüme' in the house which her father had described.

69. 'Seye Ihme leid genug dz Sie Ihm sein tochter verfuehrt', StadtAA, Urg., Margaretha Wagner 1694, confrontation 5 Jan. 1695.

Chapter 9: Godless Children

1. 'Indessen ist observiert worden, dz sye bey allen fragstuckh, wo sonderbahr kein grose instanz auf die haubt puncten in materia veneficii et Sodomia gemacht worden, mit sich selbst zulachen angefangen, auch öffters gar in hellster geschätter ausgebrochen, hat sich auch bey diser verhöre gar zue geschwäzig vnd muthwellig aufgefiehrdt', StadtAA, Urg., Regina Groninger, fourth interrogation, 16 Jan. 1703, ad 77.

2. Regina's father had married her stepmother in 1699, on 22 Feb (StadtAA, Hochzeitsprotokolle, 1595–1700, fo. 125); and it was not long after the new marriage that Regina's case had first come to the atttention of the church authorities. Regina's natural mother had married her father on 25 Aug. 1686 (fo. 183). A brother was also born, Johann Conrad, on 9 January 1697 (Archiv der evangelisch-lutherischen Gesamtkirchenverwaltung Augsburg, Taufbuch Barfüsserkirche 1694–1734); and it was probably he (her 'natural brother', *leibliches bruderlein*, as the questioner put it, asking whether she had not felt pity, StadtAA, Urg., Regina Groninger, first interrogation, 17 May 1702, qu. 6) whom she supposedly killed. If the child was indeed eighteen months old when it died, and if the death happened, as alleged, five years before the case was brought to trial in 1702, this would date the death to about six months before the arrival of the stepmother.

   The pattern of live births in Regina's family is surprising. Regina would have been an only child until she was nearly ten years old, so she may well have felt jealous of her new brother and therefore susceptible to believing that she was responsible for his death. We do not know exactly when Regina's mother died (the death registers for the parish begin only in 1701), but it was most likely in 1698, since Regina's father stated in May 1702 that she had died 'four years ago', adding that Regina had been twelve when her mother died. So the child's death almost certainly happened not long after Regina's mother had died, when Regina would have been coming to terms with her loss and would, in some sense, have been replacing her mother in a maternal role.

   Regina's stepmother also had a child by her previous marriage, Matthaeus Jeronymus, born in 1692 (Archiv der evangelisch-lutherischen Gesamtkirchenverwaltung Augsburg, Taufbuch Hl. Kreuz 1649–1724, p. 131, 7 Sept. 1692); and perhaps this made family dynamics in the Groninger household particularly difficult. It is not quite clear whether Groninger had any live children by his second wife. In the record of the case, however, there is reference only to one stepbrother, named Hieronymus, who was aged seven when the stepmother joined Groninger (this Hieronymus must be the child christened as Matthaeus Jeronymus, since the dates match and there are no other baptismal records for children of the stepmother's previous marriage). I have found no record in the Barfüsserkirche baptismal register for any further Groninger children.

3. '(der fast täglich zue Jhr kome, sich vber sye vnd Jhren ganzn leib herlege, vnd also trukhe dz ihr S.V. dz Kott zum leib ausgehe) … Der habe Er Ihr ein ding wie eine spindel spizig im vorderen leib gesteckht, WaVon sye grosen schmerzn empfunden, habe doch nicht verspihrt, dz ihr etwas in dem leib gelaßen worden wehre, Vnd wan er also mit Jhr zuthun gehabt, da habe es wohl bey 1/4 stundt gewehrt', StadtAA, Urg., Regina Groninger, first interrogation, 17 May 1702, qu 4. At the end of her long answer to this question, she added that intercourse with the Devil happened 'in a very dark place, and that no one was there but she and he, where he committed the usual indecency, and when all was finished, he let her float in her bed again … There was a table here, and it was quite dark, so that one could not see the sky.'

4. 'Jm Vbrigen seye seine gestalt, nicht wie eines Menschen gewest, der Kopf seye schwarz vnd wie eine Kugel so rund gewesen, Woran doch weder gesicht, augen noch naasen oder anders gesehen worden, Zu dem habe Er ganz dürr mager ärmb gehabt, Vnd Clauen, so ganz spizig wahren, habe fiess gehabt, wie ein gaiss, ybrigens geendt wie ein Mensch.' StadtAA, Urg., Regina Groninger, first interrogation, 17 May 1702, qu. 4. As she went on to explain, he never used her name but only called her 'du'.

5. It is remarkable to have such an account of intercourse from the early eighteenth century. Regina's description does draw on some elements of diabolic cliché – in many accounts given by witches the Devil has tell-tale goat's feet, a sure sign of his real identity. Claws, too, are frequently shown in paintings of the Devil. But her account of her sexual relations with the Devil was unusual, because whereas most adults who confessed to witchcraft spoke of 'having to do with' the Devil and described their seduction in terms which seldom mention bodily processes directly, Regina's description strains to recount her physical sensations as precisely as possible, resisting conventional terms for intercourse or body parts. The Devil puts 'something' into her front body, and it is sharp like a spindle – itself an interesting simile because spindles were objects strongly associated with women's work in this period. There may also be elements of fairy tale: the spindle makes an appearance in the story of Sleeping Beauty, which could have been known in Augsburg at this time. A version of the tale was performed in Upper Germany around 1400 in a Shrovetide play, a printed version appeared in Italian in 1630, and the tale was included in Perrault's collection in French of 1697. I am grateful to Ruth Bottigheimer for this information. Regina's description also has something in common with children's fantasies of parental intercourse as described by Klein, where aggressive elements are strong and excremental themes play a role. (Melanie Klein, *The Psychoanalysis of Children*, trans. Alix Strachey, London 1975 (1932); 'The Psychoanalytic Play Technique: Its History and Significance', in Klein, *Envy and Gratitude and Other Works 1946–1963*, ed. H. Segal, London 1975, 1988. It is of course impossible to know whether Regina's description should be regarded as a version of a fantasy of parental intercourse, or as a description of an actual sexual experience. But it would, I think, be wrong to explain the entire case as the result of sexual abuse without taking into account how Regina symbolized what she was conveying. On this issue, for a different view, see Evelyn Heinemann, *Witches. A Psychoanalytical Exploration of the Killing of Women*, trans. Donald Kiraly, London 2000, pp. 108–15.

6. The records of these sessions of questioning are contained in SSBAugs, 2° Cod. Aug. 289, Acta puncto maleficii et tentationis diabolicae, Incomplete Acta, Ein mit Satanischen Versuchung gequältes Mägdlein Regina Groningerin genannt betr. In Anno 1700 und 1702, 25 Aug. 1700, 20 Sept. 1700, 6 Oct. 1700, 27 Jan. 1702.

7. As the scribe went on to note, 'schir etwas Verdächtig sein, vnd fast scheinen wollen, es mießte Jhr Eine suborration vel ex insticta diabolio, oder anderorth beygekommen sein', and, he noted, she had finally admitted that the *Eisenmutter* had told her she would face interrogation that day. StadtAA, Urg., Regina Groninger, 16 Jan. 1703.

8. Interestingly, the Protestant cleric Christoph Schifflin who interrogated Regina entertained the possibility that she might have been sexually assaulted by a young lodger, Hummel, with whom she shared a bedchamber, and asked her about this directly: Regina emphatically denied it. SSBAugs, 2° Cod. Aug. 289, 20 Sept. 1700, qu. 30 ff.

9. 'unter die Obrigkeitliche Justiz zunehmen', SSBAugs, 2° Cod. Aug. 289, 52; and see also, for example, 'gegen die Kinder die Justiz fürzukehren, dass Sie nicht auch um die Seele kommen', 69; 'disen seinen Sohn in die Richterliche Justiz zunehmen, mithin ihm für grösserm Unglück zu seyn', 43.

10. SSBAugs, 2° Cod. Aug. 289, 127. These four children were aged between seven and ten and the request was made on 6–7 April 1724. Importantly for the course of the case, most of the other children involved in the trial were aged under 14, the age of full legal responsibility. Gottfried Betz claimed to be 19 years old when first questioned, but records showed he was only 17 in 1724: even so, he had been seduced four years before, and so had been under the age of 14 at the time.

11. On their housing, SSBAugs, 2° Cod. Aug. 289, 139, 144, 152; and see discussions in Council (unpaginated) appended to Cod. Aug. 289; total costs, Cod. Aug. 289, 239. A further two boys were denounced by their mothers for witchcraft in 1728, transferred to the Catholic workhouse and subjected to beatings for their godlessness. They were finally freed in 1730. According to the Council Minutes, Gottfried Betz was still confined in the hospital as late as 1729: StadtAA, Reichsstadt, Ratsbuch 1729, 30 April 1729, 322.

12. On child witches, see Wolfgang Behringer, 'Kinderhexenprozesse. Zur Rolle von Kindern in der Geschichte der Hexenverfolgung', *Zeitschrift für historische Forschung* 16, 1989, pp. 31–47; Robert Walinski-Kiel, 'The Devil's Children: Child Witch-trials in Early Modern Germany', *Continuity and Change* 11, 1996 pp. 171–90; Rainer Walz, 'Kinder in Hexenprozessen. Die Grafschaft Lippe 1654–1663', in Jürgen Scheffler, Gerd Schwerhoff and Gisela Wilbertz, eds, *Hexenverfolgung und Regionalgeschichte: die Grafschaft Lippe im Vergleich* (Studien zur Regionalgeschichte 4), Bielefeld 1994; Hans Sebald, *Der Hexenjunge. Fallstudie eines Inquisitionsprozesses*, Marburg 1992; Hartwig Weber, *Kinderhexenprozesse*, Frankfurt am Main and Leipzig 1991; and Weber, '*Von der verführten Kinder Zauberei'. Hexenprozesse gegen Kinder im alten Württemberg*, Sigmaringen 1996.

13. See, on the town in the eighteenth century, Leonhard Lenk, *Augsburger Bürgertum im Späthumanismus und Frühbarock (1580–1700)* (Abhandlungen zur Geschichte der Stadt Augsburg 17), Augsburg 1968; Ingrid Bàtori, *Die Reichsstadt Augsburg im 18. Jahrhundert. Verfassung, Finanzen und Reformversuche* (Veröffentlichungen des Max-Planck-Instituts für Geschichte 22), Göttingen 1969; Franz Herre, *Das Augsburger Bürgertum im Zeitalter der Aufklärung* (Abhandlungen zur Geschichte der Stadt Augsburg 6), Augsburg 1951; Etienne François, *Die unsichtbare Grenze. Protestanten und Katholiken in Augsburg 1648–1806* (Abhandlungen zur Geschichte der Stadt Augsburg 33), Sigmaringen 1991.

14. There was, however, a reference to a 'Lutheran boy' in 1728, SSBAugs, 2° Cod. Aug. 289, 237, after the main episode was over. Part of the background to the religious atmosphere of the period is the expansion of the Catholic community, which had first been a small minority but which after the demographic disaster of the Thirty Years War grew

steadily, until by 1810 Catholics greatly outnumbered Protestants. See François, *Die unsichtbare Grenze.*

15. On the bear, *Grundmässiger Bericht/ Von dem Hergang und Verlauff/ einer Jn Dess Heil. Reichs. Stadt Augspurg in der Evangelischen Kirche zu den Parfüssern ... Enstandener Unordnung,* Augsburg, Joh. Christoph Wagner, 1697: an accusation strenuously denied by the Lutherans, who published all the testimonies of those present, denying the incident; on the riot, Helmut Baier, 'Die evangelische Kirche zwischen Pietismus, Orthodoxie und Aufklärung', in Gunther Gottlieb et al., eds, *Geschichte der Stadt Augsburg,* Stuttgart 1984, p. 521; on exorcism, Lyndal Roper, *Oedipus and the Devil. Witchcraft, Sexuality and Religion in Early Modern Europe,* London 1994, pp. 171–98; François, *Die unsichtbare Grenze;* Roeck, *Eine Stadt in Krieg und Frieden;* and on catechisms and the story of the donkey, R.P. Marco Eschenloher, *Kinderlehren/ Oder Leichtbegreiffliche Auslegungen Uber den gantzen Römisch-Katholischen Catechismum/ Vorlängst offentlich bey Wochentlicher Kinder-Versamblungen an denen Sonntägen vorgetragen ...,* Augsburg Johannes Stretter, 1706, with an Approval from 1701, pp. 39; 36.

16. SSBAugs, 2° Cod. Aug. 103, 525.

17. Our source for the case is a lengthy précis of all the documents from the case, drawn up by one of the Protestant jurists involved, Christian Friedrich Weng. I have been able to uncover little about Weng. In 1730, Weng ordered the legal system of the city, going through the archives, a task suggesting he was held in regard and that he was skilled in ordering and dealing with documents, StadtAA, Reichsstadt, Ratsbücher 34, 26 Oct. 1730, pp. 168–9; this work, 'Augsburger Statuarrecht', is a systematic description of the local legal system in Augsburg and is the most important compilation of law for the town to that point, highly praised for its learning and accuracy by Eugen Liedl in his *Gerichtsverfassung und Zivilprozess der Freien Reichsstadt Augsburg* (Abhandlungen zur Geschichte der Stadt Augsburg 12), Augsburg 1958, p. 110 (Liedl terms it a private work, but it was evidently ordered by the Council and at least four copies of the manuscript exist). Weng wrote other works too, such as the 'Extractus der Stadt Augspurgischen Raths Erkantnussen 1392–1734', in SSBAugs, 2° Cod. S.114, and 'Annales augustani Ecclesiastici Evangelici Inprimis', testifying to his historical interests. The records of the interrogation of the children are missing from the Augsburg archive. I have drawn on the Council Minutes from the period for confirmation of Weng's summaries.

18. See, esp., Memorial of Catholics, 3? April 1724, text in Weng, SSBAugs, 2° Cod. Aug. 289, fos. 162–4. The Catholics wanted to take a further sixteen children into custody in addition to the number – almost certainly seven – who were there already. The conduct of the case was further complicated by the decision to refer the whole matter to the Emperor, and then to the law faculty at Heidelberg, because no final decisions could be taken.

19. Dietrich Blaufuß, *Reichsstadt und Pietismus – Philipp Jacob Spener und Gottlieb Spizel aus Augsburg* (Einzelarbeiten aus der Kirchengeschichte Bayerns 53), Neustadt an der Aisch 1977, pp. 38, 281, 289; Gottlieb Spitzel, *Die Gebrochne Macht der Finsternuß/ oder Zerstörte Teuflische Bunds- und Buhl-Freundschafft mit den menschen ...,* Augsburg 1687.

20. Records of the votes of individual councillors which have survived together with SSBAugs, 20 Cod. Aug. 289, unpaginated, show that confessional allegiance was not always straightforward, and that 'mixed majorities' were sometimes achieved.

21. See Stuart Clark, 'Protestant Demonology: Sin, Superstition, and Society (*c.* 1520–*c.* 1630)', in Bengt Ankarloo and Gustav Henningsen, eds, *Early Modern European Witchcraft. Centres and Peripheries,* Oxford 1990, and Stuart Clark, *Thinking with Demons,* Oxford 1997; H.C. Erik Midelfort, *Witch Hunting in Southwestern Germany 1562–1684,* Stanford 1972, pp. 30–67.

22. 'Obrigkeitliche verwahrung'; SSBAugs, 2° Cod. Aug. 289, 25; Cod. Aug. 103, 525, 'und ist so weit kommen, dass selbst Eltern ihre leibliche zahrte Kinder, der Obrigkeit angezeigt, auch allenfallss zur lebens Straff ubergeben haben'. The exception were three vagabonds who got caught up in the case; but interestingly, their names soon disappeared, and they were able convincingly to deny witchcraft. One of the parents paid tax on a house worth 1,500 gulden, another was worth 1,800 gulden, both very substantial sums; another had goods worth 100 gulden, and two orphan siblings were worth 800 gulden. SSBAugs, 2° Cod. Aug. 289, 124.

23. As Gottfried Betz, one of the accused children, described it: 'Das Pulver . . . habe wie ein Mausskoth oder Linsenkörnlein ausgesehen', SSBAugs, 2° Cod. Aug. 289, 87.

24. Ibid., 97; 49, 71–2, 82, 83, 142.

25. Steingruber, ibid., 26–7; Kuttler, ibid., 12; Weng, 'welche in jedem schlechten bettzeug armer Leuthe, die ihre Sachen nicht allezeit so gar reinlich halten, können gefunden werden', 108; Betz, 5, 72. The Betzs' cousins made the same complaints: Magdalena Neumayr suffered headaches while her husband was plagued with toothache; and they, too, had lived in marital disunity for a year. When the Betz children advised them to shake out their beds, they discovered glass splinters, bones, little black balls as if from a goat, and a bit of a sausage, all of which they took to the Jesuits for advice.

26. Of the around thirty children who became seriously involved in the panic, we know that five had step-parents. One other boy and three siblings from one family had lost their mother and were being brought up by a relative. The same patterns of hostility to the fecund relationships of adults in authority could be found amongst these children without step-parents: so one of the siblings supposedly attacked the pregnant *Hausmeisterin* of the place where he was lodged, using a diabolic powder, 'dass das Kind in Muter Leib abstehe' (SSBAugs, 2° Cod. Aug. 289, 170). However, equally striking is the fact that in three of the families where classic attacks on the parents' beds were carried out (accounting for ten of the 'diabolic children'), the parents were not so far as we know step-parents. It is difficult to be certain, because step-parents were often consistently described as the 'father' and 'mother' of their stepchildren. On antagonisms between step-relations in villages in this period, David Sabean, *Property, Production and Family in Neckarhausen 1700–1870*, Cambridge 1990, pp. 131 ff., 233 ff.; and Sabean, *Kinship in Neckarhausen 1700–1870*, Cambridge 1998, p. 30 ff. and throughout.

27. SSBAugs, 2° Cod. Aug. 289, 70; and on witchcraft and children's play, see Rainer Beck, 'Das Spiel mit dem Teufel. Freisinger Kinderhexenprozesse 1715–1723', *Historische Anthropologie* 10, 2002, pp. 374–415.

28. SSBAugs, 2° Cod. Aug. 289, 72. According to Bartholome Stegmann, David Kopf also took a sheep and put it in the press; again suggesting a half-understood concrete symbolization of central religious imagery in which Jesus is not the shepherd but a sheep.

29. On Christ in the winepress and the host mill, see Miri Rubin, *Corpus Christi. The Eucharist in Late Medieval Culture*, Cambridge 1991, pp. 312–16; and for its reworking in Protestant woodcuts, R. W. Scribner, *For the Sake of Simple Folk. Popular Propaganda for the German Reformation*, Cambridge 1981; revised edn. Oxford 1994, pp. 105–7. The processes of symbolization at work seem rather like what Hanna Segal describes in patients who are unable to dream properly. See here the work of Hanna Segal on concrete thinking and the absence of symbolization. Hanna Segal, *Dream, Phantasy and Art*, London 1991. Witchcraft can be seen as comprising a vivid symbolic system, well suited to expressing psychic conflict; though we would also consider it to be a delusional system. Here, as witchcraft began to lose credibility, the symbol formation also became impaired.

30. SSBAugs, 2° Cod. Aug. 289, 92.

31. 'dass das Mägdlein ganz mit blut überloffen, und das blut aus Nasen, Mund und Ohren geschossen', SSBAugs, 2° Cod. Aug. 289, 49: 'der Satan habe sie bey der Nacht gekusst, und in die Ohren geblasen, bringe ihr auf dem Tanz das essen, und esse mit ihr, greiffe ihr überal hin, als an das herz nicht', 49–50; 'the child did not have as much hair as previously: one did not know where it had got to': 'das Kind habe nicht mehr so vil haar, wie vorhin, man wisse nicht wo hin es kommen', ibid., 50; 134.

32. 'Ihr Tod werde von der Muter aushüngerung herkommen ... der Vater geb ihr doch noch bissweilen von der Suppen, so dem Hund aufgebracht werde', ibid., 136; 'mehr als 1 Tag dem Kind nichts zuessen gegeben zuhaben und doch crepiere es nicht', ibid. Throughout, the father is regularly referred to as the 'stepfather' of the child. It is possible that his wife was also the stepmother of the girl. She is only described as the child's 'mother', but occasionally he is described as the girl's 'father', so this is not conclusive. The girl was listed by the Lutherans amongst those to be punished, and she would have been taken into custody in 1724 had she not died.

33. On orphanages, Thomas Safley, *Charity and Economy in the Orphanages of Early Modern Augsburg*, Boston 1997, p. 235; Bernhard Stier, *Fürsorge und Disziplinierung im Zeitalter des Absolutismus. Das Pforzheier Zucht- und Waisenhaus und die badische Sozialpolitik im 18. Jahrhundert* (Quellen und Studien zur Geschichte der Stadt Pforzheim 1), Sigmaringen 1988; and Sandra Cavallo, *Charity and Power in Early Modern Italy. Benefactors and their Motives in Turin, 1541–1789*, Cambridge 1995; and on the idea of order in the Reformation, see Lyndal Roper, *The Holy Household. Women and Morals in Reformation Augsburg*, Oxford 1989.

34. For Kopf's account of the games, SSBAugs, 2° Cod. Aug. 289, 41; on the riot, see *Specification, Deren In Augspurg aufgestandenen/ und nach Friedberg aussgestrettnen Schuh-Knechten, nach ihrem Tauff- und Zunahmen, wie auch Geburts- und Lehr-Stadt ...*, Augsburg 1726; Wolfgang Zorn, *Augsburg. Geschichte einer deutschen Stadt*, Augsburg 1972, p. 228; and for journeymen's concerns about pollution in this period, Kathy Stuart, *Defiled Trades and Social Outcasts. Honor and Ritual Pollution in Early Modern Germany*, Cambridge 1999, pp. 189–221; on similar kinds of revolt, Robert Darnton, *The Great Cat Massacre and Other Episodes in French Cultural History*, Harmondsworth 1984, pp. 79–104; and on guild mentality, and the Imperial Ordinance of 1731 designed to deal with such problems, Mack Walker, *German Home Towns. Community, State and General Estate, 1648–1817*, Ithaca, NY and London 1971; 1998; pp. 73–107; for the schedule of beatings, SSBAugs, 2° Cod. Aug. 289, 160–1; and on Kopf's story about the beatings he had endured, ibid., 201–4.

35. For her insistence on a trial, SSBAugs, 2° Cod. Aug. 289, 115; Jewess's wimple, ibid., 45–6; parents' reaction: 'Weil sie Zwar der Ruefin der Zauberey nicht verdächtig halten, und villeicht von ihr keine Verführung zu besorgen hätten, der gemeine Ruef aber wider sie gehe', ibid., 126. Similarly, only one adult, the maid of the Trichtler family, claimed that she had suffered harm from the seamstress. The maid was repeatedly questioned, but no other adults came forward to allege that they, too, had been victims of the seamstress.

36. Ibid., 50; 134–6. The council authorities who had urged her to modify the child's food intake were questioned, and they said they had advised a 'diet'. This widely held view about the connection between moderate diet and disciplined habits was also reflected in the food provided for the inmates of Augsburg's orphanages. See Safley, *Charity and Economy*, p. 192.

37. SSBAugs, 2° Cod. Aug. 289, 89; 'das Zeichen habe ihr der böse feind hineingedruckt, so ihr nicht weh gethan, it. ihr mit seinen händen oder Klauen an dem Leib hineingelangt, so ihr wohl gethan, und Unzucht mit ihr getrieben. Wegen der Corruption des Leibes ist sie, um ihr nicht erst Nachdencken zu machen, nicht befragt worden', ibid., 91–2; 'widernatürlich', 102; tickling, 92. But in this case, Weng thought the mother should be jailed for twenty-four hours for false accusation, 105.

38. 'incorrigible'; 'zu obgedachter Unzucht verleitet'; SSBAugs, 2° Cod. Aug. 289, 174; 175. At first she had been punished by being smacked on her hands and admonished by the priest, but this had not helped and she had continued to masturbate; 172; 'an ihnen selbst gemolken, und Unzucht getriben', 174, 177; they had 'einander unzüchtig gemolken, und wie Ludwig gesagt, an einander gedruckt, wie die hund, wan sie läuffig sind', 177. Two other boys were also involved; 'man solle dise unzüchtige incorrigible Kinder separieren, mit Ruthen wohlempfindlich züchtigen und 14. Tag alternis diebus mit Wasser und brod speissen', 177. The Council determined that all the masturbating children should be punished (*castigiert*) and that Gruber should be separated from the other children the 'schlimmsten' children; guards should 'ihre Schuldigkeit beobachten', 178.

39. SSBAugs, 2° Cod. Aug. 289, 179: 'die Kinder hierdurch am Leib und Gemüth sehr fatigiert, und in ihren Phantasien gestärckt werden'. The different views of the new deputies (as ever, one Catholic, one Protestant) became a confessional issue, with the Catholic jurists inclining to the view of the old deputies that the children should not sleep at night – indeed, the outgoing deputies claimed this had been the children's own request because they feared the Devil's nocturnal assaults – while the Protestants agreed with the advice of the new deputies. The Catholics prevailed.

40. The exception among the group of seven masturbating children was Juliana Trichtler, who was pronounced fully improved. Eight children were in the group of those still seeing the Devil (six of them named as having masturbated); but even these eight children were resisting his blandishments, refusing to go on sabbaths and calling on the name of Jesus and making the sign of the cross whenever the Devil appeared. SSBAugs, 2° Cod. Aug. 289, 184. David Kopf and Gottried Betz, who were kept in prison apart from the other children, showed no improvement.

41. One child said the Devil made another body for him which stayed in the room, SSBAugs, 2° Cod. Aug. 289, 187–8; two of the three girls had been guilty of masturbation, 181.

42. 'im alten Luderleben verharrende [Kinder]'; 'durch so schlechte kost, dass sie kaum zuleben haben…[illegible]ten zur besserung gebracht werden', SSBAugs, 2° Cod. Aug. 289, 188; 'nicht alle actus und freuden diser unglückseeligen Leuthen in der realite sondern in illusionen, phantasien und Träumen vilmahlen bestehen', 189; 'ihnen nach und nach ihre böse Einbildungen und Phantasien aus dem Sinn [zu] bringen, und sie hergegen zu aller wahren Gottesforcht an[zu]führen', 121. Gottfried Betz and David Kopf were the last children to be let out. All the children were to be given spiritual advice and their spiritual development was to be monitored. The boys were to be taught trades.

43. SSBAugs, 2° Cod. Aug. 289, 210–19; and the Council discussed whether the last two godless children, Betz and Kopf, should be taught a trade. StadtAA, Reichsstadt Ratsbuch 1728, 20 Apr. 1728, p. 300. Betz was, however, refused citizenship: Ratsbuch 1729, 30 Apr. 1729, p. 322.

44. Isabel V. Hull, *Sexuality, State and Civil Society in Germany, 1700–1848*, Cornell 1996, and Thomas W. Laqueur, *Solitary Sex. A Cultural History of Masturbation*, New York 2003.

45. Samuel Tissot's famous *Onania* was published in 1758 but was not translated into German until 1785. However, there was a seventeenth-century literature which dis-

cussed the sin of masturbation; and Karl Braun shows that a concern with masturbation was typical of Pietists in Germany. Among the writers whose works on masturbation were influential were the Swiss Calvinist Johann Friedrich Osterwald, *Traité contre l'impureté*, 1707; Amsterdam (in German) 1717, the compiler of the English work *Onania* (1710?; first extant copy from fourth edition of 1717; 1736 first German edition) and the Saxon Pietist Christian Gerber who wrote *Unerkannte Sünden der Welt* (1692) in which, however, the sin of Onan means coitus interruptus. See Karl Braun, *Die Krankheit Onania. Körperangst und die Anfänge moderner Sexualität im 18. Jahrhundert*, Frankfurt 1996.

46. See for example Jean Bodin, *De la démonomanie des sorciers*, Paris 1580, fo. 108r, on those who give their seed to Moloch; while as Braun notes, Johann Ellinger in a treatise on witchcraft similarly says that the Devil often stole the seed of 'Samenflüssigen Leuten/ dessgleichen von stummen Sündern und Weichlingen', quoted in Braun, *Die Krankheit Onania*, 159; Johannes Ellinger, *HexenCoppel/ Das ist Vhralte Ankunfft vnd grosse Zunfft Der Vnholdseligen Vnholden oder Hexen*, Frankfurt 1629, p. 47.

47. Gottlieb Spitzel, *Die Gebrochne Macht der Finsternuß*, p. 45.

48. In 1699, Christina Haber had been freed after having been accused of killing babies and newly parturient mothers. She worked as a 'lying-in maid' (*Kindbettkellerin*) and came from the nearby village of Lechhausen. This case followed the classic pattern of accusations brought against older, rural women who worked as lying-in maids when mothers and babies died in childbed. StadtAA, Reichsstadt, Strafbuch des Rats 1654–99, 12 Dec. 1699, 725. Elisabetha Memminger, accused at about the same time, was not so lucky: she died in prison and her body underwent the dishonouring rituals of execution, carried publicly through the streets on the 'shame cart' and buried under the gallows since it was thought there was sufficient proof that she was a witch: Strafbuch des Rats 1654–1699, 722–3. In the 1701 case, a young girl had been bewitched to death. The accused, probably an old woman at the time of the case, who was cited together with her daughter, died shortly after, in 1703: Steuerbücher 1703, fo. 89a. The man who brought the case, Andreas Huber, was described as a spice merchant and he paid 10 gulden tax in 1700–2, a not inconsiderable sum: Steuerbücher 1700, fo. 86b, 1702 fo. 85c; but even so, for him these must have been hard times, for he had paid as much as 60 gulden in 1699, Steuerbuch 1699, fo. 86b. For the case, see Urg. 1701b 3, 6 Aug. 1701; Verbrecher Buch 1700–1806, 31, 20 Aug. 1701.

49. SSBAugs, 2° Cod. Aug. 289, 154; 169, 'Er es aus der Erfahrung wisse, dass dergleichen Kinder aus Unverstand mehr bekennen als wahr seye'. When the Council did not supply such a certificate, Kuttler got one from the priest at Pfersee, a village near Augsburg. The whole Kuttler family had been caught up in the allegations in a major way: Kuttler's three sons and one daughter all confessed to involvement in witchcraft and were taken into custody; so Kuttler's secpticism marked a significant shift. Kuttler petitioned again in Feb. 1726, 182. Similarly, when the Council came to take Joseph Reischle aged 10 or 11 in 1725, into custody, his mother informed them that he was in Ancona in Italy. This boy had also confessed to being one of the godless children back in 1723, but had added that he was now free of the evil. He had been listed by the Catholic jurists as one of those who should be taken into custody; and by the Protestants as one who should be whipped. It seems likely that his mother had made sure the boy was out of reach of the Council's justice – a far cry from the hard-line attitude of some parents convinced of the reality of witchcraft at the start of the panic: 56, 161, 170.

50. For the Council's refusal, SSBAugs, 2° Cod. Aug. 289, 175, 21 April 1725: the matter had to await the arrival of the opinion of the Heidelberg Law faculty; 'evil imaginings', 195, 199.

51. See, in particular, Donald W. Winnicott, *Playing and Reality*, London 1971.
52. There were some wonderful exceptions, carefully noted by Weng: one child insisted his devil was called Jesus, another claimed that the Devil had boiled him in oil; while one child said the Devil had come down the chimney on a donkey.

Chapter 10: A Witch in the Age of Enlightenment

1. SAS Dep. 30, Rep. VI, Pak. 255, Marchtaler Hexenprozesse, Catharina Schmid 1745 for the records of the case. Georg Holl's girl is referred to as his daughter, named Maria; but when she was finally interrogated as Maria Glanzing, she said she was an orphan.
2. *Kreisbeschreibungen des Landes Baden-Württemberg. Der Landkreis Biberach*, 2 vols, Sigmaringen 1987, 1990, I, p. 403: a census of 1719 lists 52 *Lehenleute* and 13 *Beisitzer*. These would be heads of household. In 1746, there were 59 and 8 respectively; in 1769, 55 and 15. In 1719 there were also 29 unmarried sons; in 1746, 66, and in 1769, 52. A census of 1833 lists 68 families, giving a total of 482 souls.
3. Johann Evangelista Schöttle, *Geschichte von Stadt und Stift Buchau samt dem stiftischen Dorfe Kappel. Beschreibung und Geschichte der Pfarrei Seekirch mit ihren Filialen Alleshausen, Brasenberg und Tiefenbach*, Bad Buchau 1977, reprint of 1884 edn, pp. 511–12; Hans Günzl, *Das Naturschutzgebiet Federsee*, 1983, 2nd edn, Karlsruhe 1989.
4. This may have been the terrible fire of 1714, in which forty-two of the village houses were destroyed, *Landkreis Biberach*, I, p. 401.
5. 'unansehnlich', SAS Dep. 30, Rep. VI, Pak. 255, Marchtaler Hexenprozesse, Catharina Schmid 1745, 15 May 1745, p. 59.
6. Indeed, he insisted that she be set free forthwith: SAS Dep. 30, Rep. VI, Pak. 255, Marchtaler Hexenprozesse, Catharina Schmid 1745, Gutachten, 16 Aug. 1745; torture was threatened and applied on 10 (pp. 198 ff.) and 12 July 1745 (pp. 206 ff.) and following.
7. 'es habe die Erste blaue mähler under den boden getragen, so ihro ihr man geschlagen', SAS Dep. 30, Rep. VI, Pak. 255, Marchtaler Hexenprozesse, Catharina Schmid 1745, 12 June 1745, p. 140; and see 22 May 1745, pp. 78 ff.; 'Wann eben ain mann seiner sach nicht selb-sten nach gehe, und alles an seinen bueben henckhe, so gehe es nicht anderst, vnd hernach müssen die böse leüth daran schuldig sein.' SAS Dep. 30, Rep. VI, Pak. 255, Marchtaler Hexenprozesse, Catharina Schmid 1745, 24 May 1745, p. 90, and see also pp. 110–11.
8. 'da hast du 2 kiechlein, so solltest du auch können Kiechlein bachen', SAS Dep. 30, Rep. VI, Pak. 255, Marchtaler Hexenprozesse, Catharina Schmid 1745, 8 May 1745, p. 8.
9. Unpaginated document 24 July 1745, SAS Dep. 30, Rep. VI, Pak. 255, Marchtaler Hexenprozesse, Catharina Schmid 1745.
10. 'fast ohnerhörten halsstarrigkeit', SAS Dep. 30, Rep. VI, Pak. 255, Marchtaler Hexen-prozesse, Catharina Schmid 1745, 10 July 1745, p. 199, qu. 240.
11. A final session of supplementary queries was put to her on the insistence of the legal adviser from Biberach: SAS Dep. 30, Rep. VI, Pak. 255, Marchtaler Hexenprozesse, Maria Dornhauser 1745.
12. 'von diser sund so Rain seye als ein Kind in Muetter leib', SAS Dep. 30, Rep. VI, Pak. 255, Marchtaler Hexenprozesse, Catharina Schmid 1745, 3 July 1745, p.m., p. 179; 'so ohnschuldig als der liebe gott ahn dem Creiz', 7 July 1745, p. 190; 'damit sie desto bälder zu der Marter Cron kome, ... und werde ihre ohnschuldt noch nach dem todt heraus komen', 10 July 1745, p. 200; pp. 210, 363.
13. SAS Dep. 30, Rep. VI, Pak. 255, Marchtaler Hexenprozesse, Catharina Schmid 1745, 23 Nov. 1745, p. 241.
14. SAS Dep. 30, Rep. VI, Pak. 255, Marchtaler Hexenprozesse, Maria Dornhauser, 1745, 7 Dec. 1745, pp. 1–4, 4–12.

15. 'hartnäckigkeit', SAS Dep. 30, Rep. VI, Pak. 255, Marchtaler Hexenprozesse, Maria Dornhauser 1745, Gutachten von Sättelin, 3 March 1746. I have not found a record of the execution itself, but it is clear from SAS Dep. 30, Rep. VI, Pak. 255, Marchtaler Hexenprozesse, Magdalena Bollman, 1747, that it had taken place.

16. SAS Dep. 30, Rep. VI, Pak. 255, Marchtaler Hexenprozesse, Maria Dornhauser 1745, Gutachten von Sättelin, 3 March 1746.

17. Wolfgang Behringer, *Witchcraft Persecutions in Bavaria. Popular Magic, Religious Zealotry and Reason of State in Early Modern Europe*, trans. J. Grayson and D. Lederer, Cambridge 1997, pp. 347 ff.: witch burnings were held in 1740, 1749 and 1751 at Burghausen, 1750 in Straubing, and 1749, 1752, 1754 and 1756 at Landshut; there was also a trial for witchcraft at Kempten in 1775 but there is no record of an execution. For a brilliant study of eighteenth-century witch-hunting in a village near Zürich, see David Meili, 'Hexen in Wasterkingen. Magie und Lebensform in einem Dorf des frühen 18. Jahrhunderts', Ph.D. diss., Zürich 1979.

18. SAS Dep. 30, Rep. VI, Pak. 254, Marchtaler Hexenprozesse, Margaretha Menz 5 May 1588; Julianne Laub, before 7 July 1590; 'sie habe ein so schönes Kind zue welt gebohren'. Cadus also blamed Schmid for the subsequent deterioration of her marriage: SAS Dep. 30, Rep. VI, Pak. 255, Marchtaler Hexenprozesse, Catharina Schmid 1745, unpaginated document, 24 July 1745.

19. SAS Dep. 30, Rep. VI, Pak. 255, Marchtaler Hexenprozesse, Catharina Schmid 1745, unpaginated document, 6 Nov. 1745.

20. 'sie wolten gern das ding hätte ein mahl ein End. Die schmidin möchte schuldig oder ohnschuldig seyn, es wäre noth es könte eines nicht ein mahl ruehig schlaffen', SAS Dep. 30, Rep. VI, Pak. 255, Marchtaler Hexenprozesse, Catharina Schmid 1745, 24 May 1745, pp. 153–4, 153–6.

21. The same pattern is evident in the miracle books which record miraculous cures at shrines: the eighteenth-century accounts become more literary: Rebekka Habermas, 'Wunder, Wunderliches, Wunderbares. Zur Profanisierung eines Deutungsmusters in der frühen Neuzeit', in Richard van Dülmen, ed., *Arbeit, Liebe, Ehre. Studien zur historischen Kulturforschung*, Frankfurt am Main 1988.

22. This was a long process, starting in at least the sixteenth century, but becoming increasingly exclusive. See David Sabean, *Property, Production and Family in Neckarhausen 1700–1870*, Cambridge 1990; and Sabean, *Kinship in Neckarhausen 1700–1870*, Cambridge 1998; Thomas Robisheaux, *Rural Society and the Search for Order in Early Modern Germany*, Cambridge 1989; Govind Sreenivasan, *The Peasants of Ottobeuren 1487–1723. A Rural Society in Early Modern Europe*, Cambridge 2004; and on agriculture and village dynamics, Rainer Beck, *Unterfinning. Ländliche Welt vor Anbruch der Moderne*, Munich 1993.

23. Father Modest Schwazenberger established a village school in summer for 7- to 14-year-olds in 1664: Schöttle, *Geschichte*, p. 532; and from 1736 on, the post of schoolteacher was incorporated into that of *Messmer*. Nicholas Paul acted as both from 1736 to 1773, pp. 541–2.

24. Max Müller, 'Die Pröpste und Äbte des Klosters Marchtal', in Max Müller, Rudolf Reinhardt and Wilfried Schöntag, eds, *Marchtal Prämonstratenserabtei, Fürstliches Schloß, Kirchliche Akademie*, Ulm 1992, pp. 65–110, esp. p. 73; Haberkalt, however, came from Überlingen, outside the region.

25. *Landkreis Biberach*, I, pp. 400–2.

26. See SAS Dep. 30, Kloster Marchtal, Alleshausen, 41, RS lade 2 Fasz. 5, AS Rep VI Schublade 6, A, B, H for lists of those involved. The names – Schreyer, Burckhmayer, Walz, Heckenberger, Sauter and so on – are familiar village names, also to be found amongst those who were harmed by witchcraft.

27. See Andrea Polonyi, 'Die Übertragung des heiligsten Kreuzpartikels von Rom nach

Marchtal. Zum Erscheinungsbild barocker Reliquienverehrung'; Ludwig Walter, 'Pater Sebastian Sailer – Der schwäbische Mundartdichter aus Marchtal'; Konstanin Maier, 'Der schwäbische Meister der "geistlichen Wohlredenheit". Chorherr Sebastian Sailer (1714–1777) von Marchtal'; Karl Butscher, 'Das leben eines Chorherrn auf einer inkorporierten Pfarrei der Abtei Marchtal', all in Müller et al., eds, *Marchtal*. On the importance of relics and pilgrimage in the region, see Marc Forster, *Catholic Revival in the Age of the Baroque. Religious Identity in Southwest Germany, 1550–1750*, Cambridge 2001; and on pilgrimages in the sixteenth century in Bavaria, Philip Soergel, *Wondrous in his Saints. Counter-Reformation Propaganda in Bavaria*, Berkeley and Los Angeles 1993.

28. Joachim von Pflummern, 'Die religiösen und kirchlichen Zustande der ehemaligen Reichsstadt Biberach unmittelbar vor Einführung der Reformation', ed. Andreas Schilling, *Freiburger Diözesanarchiv* 19, 1887, pp. 1–191.

29. *Landkreis Biberach*, I, pp. 686 ff., 698 ff.

30. 'wan die hab zu haus nicht wohl ausgesegnet werde', SAS Dep. 30, Rep. VI, Pak. 255, Marchtaler Hexenprozesse, Catharina Schmid 1745, 23 Nov. 1745, p. 244.

31. SAS Dep. 30, Rep. VI, Pak. 255, Marchtaler Hexenprozesse, Catharina Schmid 1745, 23 Nov. 1745, p. 238; and see, for example, rituals conducted on 12 July 1745, p. 206.

32. SAS Dep. 30, Rep. VI, Pak. 255, Marchtaler Hexenprozesse, Maria Dornhauser, 4 Jan 1746, pp. 148–9.

33. Stuart Clark, in his brilliant *Thinking with Demons. The Idea of Witchcraft in Early Modern Europe*, Oxford 1997, has characterized demonology as a fundamentally binary system of meanings, full of inversions; but whereas demonology of the sixteenth and seventeenth centuries was vivid and dynamic, the oppositions in this period have become formulaic and repetitive.

34. 'Zeug solle sich dessen nicht erschrökhen lassen, weillen Gott der Allmächtige ein Gerechter Gott, so dieJenige nicht straffe, welche die Gerechtigkeit befördern helffen', SAS Dep. 30, Rep. VI, Pak. 255, Marchtaler Hexenprozesse, Catharina Schmid 1745, 8 May 1745, p. 23.

35. SAS Dep. 30, Rep. VI, Pak. 255, Marchtaler Hexenprozesse, Catharina Schmid 1745, 29 May 1745, p. 102.

36. Johann Jaupffbaur, for instance, began by stating that Schmid had never caused him harm. His father had suffered misfortune, and had died twenty-six years ago, but did not blame Schmid for this. His daughter had sickened a year ago, and Schmid's daughter had been unusually solicitous about her health – she had said she would recover, and had given her a piece of bread. When they had journeyed to get the girl blessed, the pastor had said the illness was caused by 'Malefiz'. Schmid had wished her well, had given her food, and had worried about her health: Jaupffbaur strung these apparently harmless stories together because they were the classic details that 'proved' the girl had been the victim of Schmid's malevolence. But this Jaupffbaur was careful not to say. SAS Dep. 30, Rep. VI, Pak. 255, Marchtaler Hexenprozesse, Catharina Schmid 1745, 3 July 1745, pp. 175–6.

37. SAS Dep. 30, Rep. VI, Pak. 255, Marchtaler Hexenprozesse, Catharina Schmid 1745, 15 May 1745, pp. 66–7; and on these pilgrimages and on Steinhausen, see Forster, *Catholic Revival*, pp. 77–9; and also on Steinhausen, Georg Bischof and Hugo Schnell, *Wallfahrtskirche Steinhausen*, 1937; Regensburg 1997 (Schnell, Kunstführer 203); Otto Beck, *Kunst und Geschichte im Landkreis Biberach*, Sigmaringen 1985, pp. 203–6; and see more generally, Jeffrey Chipps Smith, *Sensuous Worship. Jesuits and the Art of the Early Catholic Reformation in Germany*, Princeton 2002, pp. 367–92.

38. SAS Dep. 30, Rep. VI, Pak. 255, Marchtaler Hexenprozesse, Maria Dornhauser 1745, 7 Dec. 1745, pp. 18–19.

39. 'ia wan er aber einen argwohn gehabt, und wider etwas böses in dem dorf beschehen, habe er es gebeichtet', SAS Dep. 30, Rep. VI, Pak. 255, Marchtaler Hexenprozesse, Catharina Schmid 1745, 12 and 14 June, p. 158.

40. Forster, *Catholic Revival*; SAS Dep. 30, Rep. VI, Pak. 255, Marchtaler Hexenprozesse, Catharina Schmid 1745, 1 June 174, p. 114.

41. SAS Dep. 30, Rep. VI, Pak. 255, Marchtaler Hexenprozesse, Catharina Schmid 1745, 8 May 1745, p. 16; and pp. 52–3. Engler was a man of substantial means, paying the second-highest tax assessment in Alleshausen in 1733: SAS Dep. 30, Bd. 1961, 1733. By contrast, Blasi Schmid was listed as a mason, paying the second-lowest basic rate of tax with no asset tax, and Joseph Schmid was listed as a mere *Beisitzer*.

42. 'sie habe aber Vermaint es geschehe nuhr zu disem End damit man keinen bösen argwohn über sie und ihre Muetter haben solle', SAS Dep. 30, Rep. VI, Pak. 255, Marchtaler Hexenprozesse, Maria Dornhauser, 4 Jan. 1746, p. 147.

43. 'Jnquisita seye schon 74 Jahr alt und werde natürlicher weis ohn das bald sterben miessen, solle allso vill lieber ihre missethatten bekönnen, berewen', SAS Dep. 30, Rep. VI, Pak. 255, Marchtaler Hexenprozesse, Catharina Schmid 1745, 3 July 1745, p. 180, qu. 196.

44. Correspondence of Sättelin with Marchtal, 28 Dec. 1745; 4 March 1746; interrogation of Catharina Schmid 26 Feb. 1746, SAS Dep. 30, Rep. VI, Pak. 255, Marchtaler Hexenprozesse, Maria Dornhauser 1745.

45. SAS Dep. 30, Rep. VI, Pak. 255, Marchtaler Hexenprozesse, Catharina Schmid 1745, 10 Nov. 1745, p. 217, permission sought from provincial for torture. Under the new abbot Edmund Sartor who took office in 1746 the trials eventually stopped, but not before they reached their climax with the execution of the condemned witches. The Oberamtmann Frei from Underkingen eventually brought the trials to a halt but there was another trial which did not result in execution in 1757. As late as 1771, however, Sebastian Sailer, poet and member of the order, could defend the trials and execution as fully warranted. Winfried Nuber, 'Abtei Marchtal und seine Pfarrei in der Stadt Munderkingen', in Müller et al., eds, *Marchtal*, p. 142.

46. There was however a trial in Kempten in 1775, Behringer, *Witchcraft Persecutions* pp. 352–4; the last execution for witchcraft in Western Europe took place in 1782, in Glarus, Switzerland.

47. 'Jez Weiß ichs, woher mein ungluckh kombt, dz ich disen winter muss so vil weh! ausstehen', SAS Dep. 30, Rep. VI, Pak. 255, Marchtaler Hexenprozesse, Catharina Schmid 1745, 8 May 1745, p. 13.

48. There was also a miracle involving the saint. In 1661, when a storm lasting over ten days had threatened the monastery with destruction, St Tiberius's head was seen in the clouds and the storms dispersed in harmless rain. This event was commemorated in a picture in the monastery church. Müller et al., eds, *Marchtal*, p. 228, and Ill. 24.

49. 'mann solle Es nicht auskommen lassen, Tibery werde nicht von Marchtal herauf kommen, und Es ihro eingeben, alleinig Es seye nit anderst gewesen, als wann man es durch trompeter in dem ganzen dorff liessen ausblasen', SAS Dep. 30, Rep. VI, Pak. 255, Marchtaler Hexenprozesse, Catharina Schmid 1745, 15 May 1745, pp. 64–5.

50. Erik Midelfort, 'Johann Joseph Gassner and Franz Anton Mesmer: Exorcism and Enlightenment', unpublished paper, American Historical Association Dec. 1995; and Adolph Franz, *Die kirchlichen Benediktionen im Mittelalter*, 2 vols, Freiburg 1909 esp. vol. 2, pp. 574–615; and see also Philip Wheeler, ed., *The Roman Ritual in Latin and English*, Milwaukee 1952, pp. 168–9.

51. See on Gassner's career and on his connections to Mesmer, and on Mesmer's to Charcot and Freud, Midelfort, 'Johann Joseph Gassner and Franz Anton Mesmer', 'Natur und Besessenheit: Physikalische Erklärungen von Besessenheit von der

Melancholie bis zum Magnetismus', Arbeitskreis für interdisziplinaere Hexenforschung, Weingarten, 1999, 'Der Teufel und die Psychologie, aber welche Psychologie? Oder: Charcot, Freud und die Hexen', unpublished papers, and 'Charcot, Freud, and the Demons', in Kathryn E. Edwards, ed., *Werewolves, Witches and Wandering Spirits. Traditional Belief & Folklore in Early Modern Europe* (Sixteenth Century Essays & Studies 62), Kirksville, Missouri 2002; and, for the wider intellectual context, Behringer, *Witchcraft Persecutions*, pp. 355–87. See also David Lederer, *A Bavarian Beacon. Spiritual Physic and the Birth of the Asylum, 1495–1803*, forthcoming. Here my thinking on the origins of psychoanalysis has been greatly influenced by conversations with Ruth Harris.

52. The authorities claimed that suitable women were not available to undertake this examination, the customary way of proceeding. Resorting to the executioner was a further humiliation. Draft headed bey urtell, undated. SAS Dep. 30, Rep. VI, Pak. 255, Marchtaler Hexenprozesse, Catharina Schmid.

53. 'die S.v. scham seye von ein 74 Jährigen dürr und Magers weib gahr zu gros zu fet und zu aufgeschwollen nicht anderst, als wan sie inn alle tag und nacht öffters mit einem Mans bild bey haltete' SAS Dep. 30, Rep. VI, Pak. 255, Marchtaler Hexenprozesse, Catharina Schmid 1745, 23 Nov. 1745, p. 236; and pp. 231–2.

54. 'Man schäme sich einem 74 Jährig weib der läy sachen vor zu tragen, Inquisita solle bekennen ob sich niemahls mit disem barbierer flayschlich versündiget habe'; 'ay behiete gott mit dem barbierer sindigen, das wäre wohl eins!', SAS Dep. 30, Rep. VI, Pak. 255, Marchtaler Hexenprozesse, Catharina Schmid 1745, 11 Dec. 1745, p. 339 qu. 532; p. 342.

55. 'Närrisch Magdlein, ich bin dem Mann vill zu vill schuldig, ich muess machen dass ich mit ihm auskome', SAS Dep. 30, Rep. VI, Pak. 255, Maria Dornhauser, 11 Dec. 1745, p. 41; 'Jhr under Röckh und hembdt uber sich gehöbt, der barbierer aber seine hosen eröffnet und fallen lassen'; 'ihre mutter habe einen so erschöckhlich grosen Nabels', SAS Dep. 30, Rep. VI, Pak. 255, Marchtaler Hexenprozesse, Catharina Schmid 1745, 11 Dec. 1745, p. 344.

56. 'was die tochter gesagt habe und sie das leben verrschult habe, wolle sie nicht mehr endern, es seye Jhro lieb wan sie Jhr medlin mit inn dem himell nehmen könne, wan das Mägdlein vill bekönnt habe wolle sie nicht darwider streitten', SAS Dep. 30, Rep. VI, Pak. 255, Marchtaler Hexenprozesse, Catharina Schmid 1745, 30 Dec. 1745, p. 351.

57. SAS Dep. 30, Rep. VI, Pak. 255, Marchtaler Hexenprozesse, Catharina Schmid 1745, 8 Jan. 1746, p. 358. There was one further interrogation in response to further unease on the part of Sättelin, on 26 Feb. 1746 (record filed under Maria Dornhauser): Schmid still refused to supply the confessions which the court had wanted, that she had caused the illnesses of particular individuals.

Epilogue

1. Walter Scherf, *Das Märchen Lexikon*, 2 vols, Munich 1995, pp. 271, 306, 548–9, 684–5; and see Ruth Bottigheimer, *Grimm's Bad Girls and Bold Boys. The Moral and Social Vision of the Tales*, New Haven and London 1987.

2. Children are also cast out in Giambattista Basile's story of Nenillo and Nennella from the mid-seventeenth century: Giambattista Basile, *The Pentameron*, trans. Sir Richard Burton, London 1952.

3. Charles Zika, *Exorcising Our Demons. Magic, Witchcraft and Visual Culture in Early Modern Europe* (Studies in Medieval and Reformation Thought 91), Leiden and Boston 2003, pp. 411–44, 445–79.

4. Demons' houses usually contain nuts, milk or cheese; but seventeenth-century images of Schlaraffenland do contain houses with roofs of pancakes, so the gingerbread house may not be a pure nineteenth-century invention. See illustration no. of Schlaraffenland, *c.* 1650.

5. Martin Montanus, *Schwankbücher*, ed. Johannes Bolte, Bibliothek des literarischen Vereins Stuttgart 217, Tübingen 1899, 'Gartengesellschaft' ch. 5, p. 260 ff., Ein schoene history von einer frawen mit zweyen kindlin; Madame d'Aulnoy, *Les Contes des fées* (1697), 2 vols, Paris 1997; Charles Perrault, *Contes* (1697), ed. Gilbert Rouger, Paris 1967, pp. 187 ff.

6. This volume contained the Hansel and Gretel story. Here it is interesting to note that another gruesome fairy tale, that of Bluebeard, which was included in Perrault's fairy tales, was modified by the Grimms in ways that made it less disturbing to its middle-class readers' sensibilities: Mererid Puw Davies, *The Tale of Bluebeard in German Literature: From the Eighteenth Century to the Present*, Oxford 2001, pp. 119–31.

7. Kurt Ranke, with Hermann Bausinger et al., eds, *Enzyklopaedie des Märchens. Handwörterbuch zur historischen und vergleichenden Erzählforschung*, 11 vols, Berlin 1975, entry on Hansel and Gretel by Walter Scherf, vol. 6, pp. 498–510; p. 505.

8. Heinz Rölleke, ed., *Brüder Grimm Kinder- und Hausmärchen*, Stuttgart 1980, 1997 with Afterword by Rölleke; Heinz Rölleke, *Grimms Märchen. Ausgewählt und mit einem Kommentar versehen*, Frankfurt 1998; Bruno Bettelheim, *The Uses of Enchantment. The Meaning and Importance of Fairy Tales*, London 1976; Marina Warner, *From the Beast to the Blonde. On Fairy Tales and their Tellers*, London 1988; *Enzyklopaedie des Märchens*, entry on Hansel and Gretel by Walter Scherf; Scherf, *Das Märchen Lexikon*; Basile, *The Pentameron*; Bottigheimer, *Grimm's Bad Girls and Bold Boys*; Walter Scherf, 'Die Hexe im Zaubermärchen', in Richard van Dülmen, ed., *Hexenwelten. Magie und Imagination*, Frankfurt 1987; Robert Darnton, 'Peasants Tell Tales: The Meaning of Mother Goose', in Darnton, *The Great Cat Massacre and Other Episodes in French Cultural History*, Harmondsworth 1984.

9. Josef Ehmer, 'Marriage', in David I. Kertzer and Marzio Barbagli, eds, *The History of the European Family*, vol. 2: *Family Life in the Long Nineteenth Century, 1789–1913*, New Haven and London 2002, p. 290.

10. See Simon Schama, *Landscape & Memory*, London 1995; Joseph Koerner, *Caspar David Friedrich and the Subject of Landscape*, London 1990; 2nd edn 1995, esp. pp. 151–78. But the forests were also being chopped down and tamed. Humanists praise the ordered, pastoral character of the forest, and Altdorfer depicts a verdant, leafy landscape. In some images of witches, the artist places the witch near a tree, or she gestures towards a woodland scene; but witches were more often believed to gather on top of mountains or in desolate scenery rather than forests in particular.

11. Jack Zipes, *The Brothers Grimm. From Enchanted Forests to the Modern World*, New York and London 1988, p. 15.

12. Jack Zipes, *The Oxford Companion to Fairy-Tales*, Oxford 2000, pp. 199 ff.

13. Abraham Saur, *Theatrum de veneficis*, Frankfurt am Main, Nicolaus Basse 1586; *Theatrum diabolorum*, Frankfurt 1569, Sigmund Feyerabend (VD16, no. F904); and on the publishing history of these books and the allegations of piracy which surrounded them, Frank Baron, *Faustus on Trial. The Origins of Johann Spies's 'Historia' in an Age of Witch Hunting*, Tübingen 1992, esp. pp. 69 ff.

14. *Historia von D. Johann Fausten. Text des Druckes von 1587. Kritische Ausgabe*, ed. Stephan Füssel and Hans Joachim Kreutzer, Stuttgart 1988, pp. 86 ff.; the story is then re-used by the indefatigable Guazzo as evidence of the Devil's power: Francesco Maria Guazzo, *Compendium maleficarum*, ed. and trans. Montague Summers, London 1929, p. 8 (Bk 1 ch. 3).

15. Though there is a comparable character in a seventeenth-century version of Faust. On the very different understanding of marriage in the sixteenth-century *Faust* and the author's moral, the dangers of the unmarried state, see Maria E. Müller, 'Poiesis und Hexerei. Zur "Historia von D. Johann Fausten"', in Günther Mahal, ed., *Die 'Historia von D. Johann Fausten' (1587)*, Vaihingen an der Enz 1988.

16. Regina Habermas, ed., with Tanja Hommen, *Das Frankfurter Gretchen. Der Prozess gegen die Kindsmörderin Susanna Margaretha von Brandt*, Munich 1999.

17. The development of regional dictionaries is interesting in this connection. In Swabia, Johann Christoph Schmid's dictionary of Swabian dialect in written form had been published in 1831. It was eventually succeeded by Hermann Fischer's vast seven-volume Swabian dictionary, thus completing a process of dialect transcription begun by Sebastian Sailer of Marchtal, with his rhyming dialect dramas performed in the monasteries of his corner of southern Germany. Fischer's dictionary was itself heir to the original scholarly collection of Adelbert Keller, who had been instrumental in the Litterarischer Verein, which republished much of the literature of the sixteenth and seventeenth centuries. Keller had issued a printed call for help with his Swabian dictionary in 1854, the year the first volume of the Grimm dictionary was published. H. Fischer, *Schwäbisches Wörterbuch*, 7 vols, Tübingen 1904, pp. iii–iv.

Bibliography

Manuscript Primary Sources

Stadt- und Staatsbibliothek Augsburg (SSBAugs).
   2° Cod. Aug. 127, 288, 289.
Staatsarchiv Basel Stadt, Criminalia.
Staatsarchiv Koblenz, F215–Zsg.2/1–f (Films), Film No. 17, 44, 62.
Staatsarchiv Nürnberg (SAN), Allgemeines Staatsarchiv München, Hexenakten
   (Eichstätt).
Staatsarchiv Sigmaringen (SAS), Dep. 30, Rep. VI, Pak. 254, 255, Marchtaler
   Hexenprozesse; Alleshausen, 41, RS lade 2 Fasz. 5, AS Rep. VI Schublade 6, A, B, H.
Staatsbibliothek München.
   Handschriftenabteilung, CGM 2026.
Stadtarchiv Augsburg (StadtAA).
   Evangelisches Wesensarchiv.
   Reichsstadt.
   Urgichtensammlung, Steuerbücher, Strafbücher des Rats, Bürgermeisteramtsprotokolle,
      Chroniken, Schätze, Hochzeitsprotokolle, Ratsbücher, Benedict von Paris, Besetzung
      aller Ämter in der Reichsstadt Augsburg angefangen Anno 1548 fortgesetzt und
      beendigt bis zur Auflösung der reichsstädtischen Verfaßung Anno 1806.
Archiv der evangelisch-lutherischen Gesamtkirchenverwaltung Augsburg.
   Taufbücher.
Stadtarchiv Nördlingen (StadtAN).
   Bestand Stadtgericht, Kriminalakten: 1478, 1534, 1576/89–1598/99 (= Hexenprozeßakten).
   C. Ammerbacher, 'Allerhand Merkwürdigkeiten der Stadt Nördlingen', 1824, Teil I, A–L.
   Missivbuch, Urfehdebücher, Stadtrechnungen Steuerbücher.
Staatsarchiv Würzburg (SAW).
   Domkapitelprotokolle.
   Gericht Gerolzhofen 346; Historischer Saal VII, 25/374, 375, 376, 377.
   Historischer Verein f. 20, Misc. 1954 I and II, 2896, 2897.

Printed Primary Sources

Albrecht, Bernhard, *Magia*, Leipzig 1628.
Ambach, Melchior, *Von Tantzen/ Vrtheil/ Auß heiliger Schrifft/ vnd den alten Christlichen
   Lerern gestelt*, Frankfurt 1564.

Basile, Giambattista, *The Pentameron*, trans. Sir R. Burton, London 1952.

Binsfeld, Peter, *Tractat Von Bekantnuß der Zauberer und Hexen*, Trier, Heinrich Bock, 1590.

Bodin, Jean, *Vom Außgelaßnen Wütigen Teuffels heer Allerhand Zauberern/ Hexen vnd Hexenmeistern/ Vnholden/ Teuffelsbeschwerern/ Warsagern* ..., trans. J. Fischart, Strasburg, B. Jobin 1586.

Bodin, Jean, *De la démonomanie des sorciers*, Paris 1580.

Bodin, Jean, *On the Demon-Mania of Witches (1580)* (abridged), trans. R. Scott, Toronto 1995.

Boguet, Henry [*sic*], *An Examen of Witches* (French 1590), London 1929, trans. E.A Ashwin, ed. Revd Montague Summers.

Daneau, Lambert, *A Dialogue of Witches*, trans. attributed to T. Twyne, [London], K.W., 1575.

Daul, Florian, *Tantzteuffel: Das ist/wider den leichtfertigen/unverschempten Welt tantz/* ..., Frankfurt 1567.

D'Aulnoy, Madame, *Les Contes des fées* (1697), 2 vols, Paris 1997.

Del Rio, Martin, *Martin del Rio, Investigations into Magic*, ed. and trans. P.G. Maxwell Stuart, Manchester and New York 2000.

Ehinger, Christoph, *Daemonologia oder etwas neues vom Teufel*, Augsburg 1681.

Ellinger, Johannes, *HexenCoppel/ Das ist Vhralte Ankunfft vnd grosse Zunfft der Vnholdseligen Vnholden oder Hexen*, Frankfurt 1629.

Eschenloher, R.P. Marco, *Kinderlehren/ Oder Leichtbegreiffliche Auslegungen über den gantzen Römisch-Katholsichen Catechismum/ Vorlängst offentlich bey Wochentlicher Kinder-Versamblungen an denen Sonntägen vorgetragen* ..., Augsburg, Johannes Stretter, 1706.

Fischart, Johann, *Flöh Hatz, Weiber Tratz*, ed. Alois Haas, Stuttgart 1967, 1982.

Franck, Sebastian, *Weltbuch: spiegel vnd bildtnisz des gantzen erdtbodens*, Tübingen, V. Morhart, 1534.

Frisius, Paulus, *Von deß Teuffels Nebelkappen*, reprinted in Abraham Saur, ed., *Theatrum de veneficis*, Frankurt am Main, Nicolaus Basse, 1586.

Gayer, Fredericus Petrys, *Viereckichtes Eheschaetzlein. Da ist: die vier Gradus der Eheleute*, Erfurt, Johann Beck, 1602.

Geiler von Keisersberg, Johannes, *Die Emeis*, Strasbourg, Johannes Grenninger, 1517.

Gödelmann, Johannes Georg, *Von Zauberern Hexen und Unholden* (Latin 1591), trans. Georg Nigrinus, Frankfurt 1592.

Grimm, Jacob and Wilhelm, *Brüder Grimm Kinder- und Hausmärchen*, ed. Heinze Rölleke, Stuttgart 1980, 1997.

Grimm, Jacob and Wilhelm, *Grimms Märchen, Ausgewählt und mit einem Kommentar versehen*, ed. Heinz Rölleke, Frankfurt 1998.

Grimmelshausen, Hans Jacob Christoph von, *Lebensbeschreibung der Erzbetrügerin und Landstörzerin Courasche*, ed. Klaus Haberkamm and Günter Weydt, Stuttgart 1971, 1998.

Grimmelshausen, Hans Jacob Christoph von, *Simplicissimus*, 1669; afterword by Volker Meid, Stuttgart 1961, 1996.

Grundmässiger Bericht/ Von dem Hergang und Verlauff/ einer Jn Dess Heil. Reichs. Stadt Augspurg in der Evangelischen Kirche zu den Parfüssern ... Enstandener Unordnung, Augsburg, Joh. Christoph Wagner, 1697.

Guazzo, Francesco Maria, *Compendium maleficarum*, ed. and trans. Montague Summers, London 1929.

Happel, Eberhard, *Größte Denkwürdigkeiten der Welt oder Sogenannte Relationes Curiosae*, ed. U. Hübner and J. Westphal, 1683–91.

Historia von D. Johann Fausten. Text des Druckes von 1587, Kritische Ausgabe, ed. Stephan Füssel and Hans Joachim Kreutzer, Stuttgart 1988.

Khueller, Sebastian, *Kurtzer/Warhafftige/ vnd summarischer weiss beschirbne Historia/ von einer Junckfrawen/ wölche mit dreissig vnnd etlichen bösen Geistern/ leibhafftig bessessen* ... [Munich, Adam Berg, 1574?].

Kramer, Heinrich, *Der Hexenhammer*, ed. W. Behringer and G. Jerouschek, trans. W. Behringer, G. Jerouschek and W. Tschacher, Munich 2000.

Kramer, Heinrich and James Sprenger [*sic*], *The Malleus Maleficarum of Heinrich Kramer and James Sprenger*, ed. and trans. Revd Montague Summers, London 1928; New York 1971.

Lancre, Pierre de, *Tableau de l'inconstance des mauvais anges et demons*, 1612; Paris 1613.

Lercheimer, Augustin (pseudonym of Hermann Wilken, also known as Witekind), *Ein Christlich Bedencken vnd Erinnerung von Zauberey*, 1585, in Abraham Saur (ed.), *Theatrum de veneficis*, Frankfurt am Main, Nicolaus Basse, 1586.

Liechtenberg, Jakob Freiherr von, *Ware Entdeckung vnnd Erklärung aller fürnembster Artickel der Zauberey*, in Abraham Saur (ed.), *Theatrum de veneficis*, Frankfurt am Main, Nicolaus Basse, 1586.

Luthers Werke, Weimar edition, vol. 10, part II, p. 275, *Vom ehelichen leben*, 1522, p. 296.

Meder, David, *Acht Hexen predigten*, Leipzig, Valentin am Ende Erben, 1615.

Montaigne, Michel de, 'On the Cannibals', trans. M.A. Screech, in *Michel de Montaigne. Four Essays*, London 1995.

Montanus, Martin, *Schwankbücher*, ed. Johannes Bolte, Bibliothek des literarischen Vereins Stuttgart 217, Tübingen 1899.

Osterwald, Johann Friedrich, *Traité contre l'impureté*, 1707 Amsterdam (in German) 1717.

Die Peinliche Gerichtsordnung Kaiser Karls V. von 1532 (Carolina), ed. Gustav Radbruch, revised by Arthur Kaufmann, Stuttgart 1975.

Perrault, Charles, *Contes* (1697), ed. Gilbert Rouger, Paris 1967.

Pflummern, Joachim von, 'Die religiösen und kirchlichen Zustande der ehemaligen Reichsstadt Biberach unmittelbar vor Einführung der Reformation', ed. Andreas Schilling, *Freiburger Diözesanarchiv* 19, 1887, pp. 1–191.

Praetorius, Johannes [= Schultze, Hans], *Hexen-, Zauber- und Spukgeschichten aus dem Blocksberg* (1668), ed. Wolfgang Möhrig, Frankfurt am Main, 1979.

Ratz, Jacob, *Vom Tanzenn/ Obs Gott verpotten hab/ Obs sünd sey/ Vnd von andern erlaupten kurzweilen der Christen/ als/ Spielen/ Singen/ Trincken/ Jagen usw. Mit verlegung/ des Falschen vnd onbescheyden urteils/ M. Melcher Ambach/ Predigers zu Franckfort/ vom Tanzen/ geschrieben*, n. p. 1565.

Relation Oder Beschreibung so Anno 1669 ... von einer Weibs/Person ..., Augsburg 1669.

Rémy, Nicolas, *Demonolatry*, trans. E.A. Ashwin and ed. Revd Montague Summers, London 1930.

Sailer, Sebastian, *Sebastian Sailers Schriften im schwäbischen Dialekte*, ed. Sixt Bachmann, 1819; reprint and additional introduction, Franz Georg Brustgi, Reutlingen 1976.

Saur, Abraham, *Theatrum de veneficis*, Frankfurt am Main, Nicolaus Basse, 1586.

Schedel, Hartmut, *Die Schedelsche Weltchronik (1493)*, Facsimile edn, Dortmund 1978.

Scot, Reginald, *The Discoverie of Witchcraft*, 1584; intro. Revd Montague Summers, New York 1930, 1972.

Specification, Deren In Augspurg aufgestandenen/ und nach Friedberg aussgestrettnen Schuh-Knechten, nach ihrem Tauff- und Zunahmen, wie auch Geburts- und Lehr-Stadt ..., Augsburg 1726.

Spee, Friedrich, *Cautio Criminalis oder Rechtliches Bedenken wegen der Hexenprozesse*, trans. J.-F. Ritter, 1939; Munich 1982, 2000.

Spitzel, Gottlieb, *Die Gebrochne Macht der Finsternuß/ oder Zerstörte Teuflische Bunds-und Buhl-Freundschafft mit den menschen . . .*, Augsburg 1687.

Stambaugh, Ria (ed.), *Teufelbücher im Auswahl*, 5 vols, Berlin 1970–80.

Süssmilch, Johann, *Die göttliche Ordnung in den Veränderungen des menschlichen Geschlechts, aus der Geburt, dem Tode und der Fortpflanzung desselben erwiesen*, 2 vols, 3rd edn. Berlin 1765.

Valentin, Samuel (Gerichtswaibel), *End-Urthel und Verruf Nach Kaiser Caroli Vti Majestaet glorreicher Gedaechtnis, Peinliche Halss-Gerichts-Ordnung verfasst; Aller derjenigen Manns – und Weibspersohnen, so von Einem Hoch-Edlen und Hochweisen Rath des H.R. Reichs Freyen Stadt Augsburg Von Anno 1649 bis Anno 1759 vom Leben zum Tod condemnieret und justifizieret worden . . .*, Augsburg n.d.

Secondary Sources

Ahrendt-Schulte, Ingrid, *Weise Frauen – böse Weiber. Die Geschichte der Hexen in der Frühen Neuzeit*, Freiburg 1994.

Ahrendt-Schulte, Ingrid, 'Die Zauberschen und ihr Trommelschläger. Geschlechtsspezifische Zuschreibungsmuster in lippischen Hexenprozessen', in Ingrid Ahrendt-Schulte, Dieter Bauer, Sönke Lorenz and Jürgen Michael Schmidt (eds), *Geschlecht, Magie und Hexenverfolgung* (Hexenforschung vol. 7), Bielefeld 2002.

Alfing, Sabine, *Hexenjagd und Zaubereiprozesse in Münster. Vom Umgang mit Sündenböcken in den Krisenzeiten des 16. und 17. Jahrhunderts*, Münster and New York 1991.

Alpers, Svetlana, *The Making of Rubens*, New Haven and London 1995.

Anglo, Sydney, 'Melancholie and Witchcraft: The Debate between Wier, Bodin and Scot', in Brian Levack (ed.), *The Literature of Witchcraft*, 12 vols, New York and London 1992, vol. 4.

Ankarloo, Bengt and Henningsen, Gustav (eds), *Early Modern European Witchcraft. Centres and Peripheries*, Oxford 1990.

Ankarloo, Bengt, Stuart Clark and William Monter, *Witchcraft and Magic in Europe*, 6 vols, vol. 4: *The Period of the Witch Trials*, London 2002.

Apps, Lara and Andrew Gow, *Male Witches in Early Modern Europe*, Manchester 2003.

Arndt, Karl, Josef Bellot et al. (eds), *Augsburger Barock*, Augsburg 1968.

Baier, Helmut, 'Die evangelische Kirche zwischen Pietismus, Orthodoxie und Aufklärung', in Gunther Gottlieb et al. (eds), *Geschichte der Stadt Augsburg*, Stuttgart 1984.

Baron, Frank, *Faustus on Trial. The Origins of Johann Spies's 'Historia' in an Age of Witch Hunting* (Frühe Neuzeit. Studien und Dokumente zur deutschen Literatur und Kultur im europäischen Kontext, vol. 9), Tübingen 1992.

Bartrum, Giulia, *Albrecht Dürer and his Legacy. The Graphic Work of a Renaissance Artist*, London 2002.

Bàtori, Ingrid, 'Frauen im Handel und Handwerk in der Reichsstadt Nördlingen im 15. und 16. Jahrhundert', in Barbara Vogel and Ulrike Weckel (eds), *Frauen in der Ständegesellschaft*, Hamburg 1991.

Bàtori, Ingrid, 'Herren, Meister, Habenichtse. Die Bürgerschaft der Reichsstadt Nördlingen um 1500', in Walter Barsig et al. (eds), *Rieser Kulturtage. Eine Landschaft stellt sich vor* (Dokumentation, vol. VI/1), Nördlingen 1987.

Bàtori, Ingrid, *Die Reichsstadt Augsburg im 18. Jahrhundert. Verfassung, Finanzen und*

Reformversuche (Veröffentlichungen des Max-Planck-Instituts für Geschichte 22), Göttingen 1969.

Bauer, Dieter and Wolfgang Behringer (eds), *Fliegen und Schweben. Annäherung an eine menschliche Sensation,* Munich 1997.

Baxter, Christopher, 'Jean Bodin's *De la démonomanie des sorciers:* The Logic of Persecution', in Sydney Anglo (ed.), *The Damned Art. Essays in the Literature of Witchcraft,* London 1977.

Bazin, Germain, *Baroque and Rococo,* London 1964, 1998.

Bechtold, A., 'Beiträge zur Geschichte der Würzburger Hexenprozesse', *Frankenkalendar* 53, 1940, pp. 117–29.

Beck, Otto, *Kunst und Geschichte im Landkreis Biberach,* Sigmaringen 1985.

Beck, Rainer, 'Das Spiel mit dem Teufel. Freisinger Kinderhexenprozesse 1715–1723', *Historische Anthropologie* 10, 2002, pp. 374–415.

Beck, Rainer, *Unterfinning. Ländliche Welt vor Anbruch der Moderne,* Munich 1993.

Bedal, Konrad, 'Bauen und Wohnen in Dorf und Kleinstadt vor 1650', in Peter Kolb and Ernst-Günter Krenig, eds, *Unterfränkische Geschichte,* vol. 3: *Vom Beginn des konfessionellen Zeitalters bis zum Ende des Dreißigjährigen Krieges,* Würzburg 1995.

Behringer, Wolfgang, 'Falken und Tauben. Zur Psychologie deutscher Politiker im 17. Jahrhundert', in Ronnie Po-chia Hsia and Robert W. Scribner (eds), *Problems in the Historical Anthropology of Early Modern Europe* (Wolfenbütteler Forschungen 78), Wiesbaden 1997.

Behringer, Wolfgang, *Hexen. Glaube, Verfolgung, Vermarktung,* Munich 1998.

Behringer, Wolfgang (ed.), *Hexen und Hexenprozesse in Deutschland,* Munich 1988; 4th edn 2000.

Behringer, Wolfgang, 'Kinderhexenprozesse. Zur Rolle von Kindern in der Geschichte der Hexenverfolgung', *Zeitschrift für historische Forschung* 16, 1989, pp. 31–47.

Behringer, Wolfgang, *Mit dem Feuer vom Leben zum Tod. Hexengesetzgebung in Bayern,* Munich 1988.

Behringer, Wolfgang, 'NS Historiker und Archivbeamte im Kampf mit den Quellen. Das Beispiel der Archive Bayerns', in Sönke Lorenz (ed.), *Himmlers Hexenkartothek. Das Interesse der Nationalsozialismus an der Hexenverfolgung* (Hexenforschung, vol. 4), Bielefeld 2000.

Behringer, Wolfgang, 'Weather, Hunger and Fear: Origins of the European Witch Hunts in Climate, Society and Mentality', *German History* 13, 1993, pp. 1–27.

Behringer, Wolfgang, *Witchcraft Persecutions in Bavaria. Popular Magic, Religious Zealotry and Reason of State in Early Modern Europe,* trans. J. Grayson and D. Lederer, Cambridge 1997.

Behringer, Wolfgang and Günter Jerouschek (eds), *Der Hexenhammer,* trans. W. Behringer, G. Jerouschek and W. Tschacher, Munich 2000.

Bennett, Judith, 'Conviviality and Charity in Medieval and Early Modern England', *Past and Present* 134, 1992, pp. 19–41.

Benz, Ernest, 'Population Change and the Economy', in Sheilagh Ogilvie and Bob Scribner (eds), *Germany. A New Social and Economic History,* 2 vols, London 1996.

Bettelheim, Bruno, *The Uses of Enchantment. The Meaning and Importance of Fairy Tales,* London 1976.

Bever, Edward Watts Morto, 'Witchcraft in Early Modern Württemberg', Ph.D. diss., Princeton 1983.

Beyer, Christel, *'Hexen-leut, so zu Würzburg gerichtet'. Der Umgang mit Sprache und Wirklichkeit in Inquisitionsprozessen wegen Hexerei* (Europäische Hochschulschriften, I, Deutsche Sprache und Literatur, vol. 948), Frankfurt am Main, Berne and New York 1981.

Beyschlag, Daniel, *Beytraege zur Noerdlingischen Geschlechtshistorie. Die Noerdlinger Epitaphien*, 2 vols, Nördlingen 1801–3.

Birlinger, Alfons, *Volksthümliches aus Schwaben. Sitten und Gebräuche*, 2 vols, Freiburg im Breisgau 1861–62.

Blauert, Andreas, ed., *Ketzer, Zauberer, Hexen. Die Anfänge der europäischen Hexenverfolgungen*, Frankfurt am Main, 1990.

Blaufuß, Dietrich, *Reichsstadt und Pietismus – Philipp Jacob Spener und Gottlieb Spizel aus Augsburg* (Einzelarbeiten aus der Kirchengeschichte Bayerns 53), Neustadt an der Aisch 1977.

Blécourt, Willem de, 'Witch Doctors, Soothsayers and Priests. On Cunning Folk in European Historiography and Tradition', *Social History* 19, 1994, pp. 335–52.

Borscheid, Peter, *Geschichte des Alters*, Munich 1987, 1989.

Botelho, Lynn, 'Old Age and Menopause in Rural Women of Early Modern Suffolk', in Lynn Botelho and Pat Thane (eds), *Women and Ageing in British Society since 1500*, Harlow 2001.

Bottigheimer, Ruth, *Grimm's Bad Girls and Bold Boys. The Moral and Social Vision of the Tales*, New Haven and London 1987.

Braun, Karl, *Die Krankheit Onania. Körperangst und die Anfänge moderner Sexualität im 18. Jahrhundert*, Frankfurt 1996.

Breit, Stefan, *'Leichtfertigkeit' und ländliche Gesellschaft. Voreheliche Sexualität in der Frühen Neuzeit*, Munich 1991.

Briggs, Robin, *Communities of Belief. Cultural and Social Tensions in Early Modern France*, Oxford 1989.

Briggs, Robin, *Witches and Neighbours: The Social and Cultural Contexts of European Witchcraft*, London 1996.

Briggs, Robin, 'Women as Victims? Witches, Judges and the Community', *French History* 5, 1991, pp. 438–50.

Burghartz, Susanna, 'The Equation of Women and Witches', in R.J. Evans (ed.), *The German Underworld*, London 1988.

Burghartz, Susanna, 'Rechte Jungfrauen oder unverschämte Töchter? Zur weiblichen Ehre im 16. Jahrhundert', in Karin Hausen and Heide Wunder (eds), *Frauengeschichte – Geschlechtergeschichte*, Frankfurt 1992.

Burke, Peter, *Popular Culture in Early Modern Europe*, London 1978.

Butscher, Karl, 'Das Leben eines Chorherrn auf einer inkorporierten Pfarrei der Abtei Marchtal', in Max Müller, Rudolf Reinhardt and Wilfried Schöntag (eds), *Marchtal Prämonstratenserabtei, Fürstliches Schloß, Kirchliche Akademie*, Ulm 1992.

Cameron, Euan, 'For Reasoned Faith or Embattled Creed? Religion for the People in Early Modern Europe', *Transactions of the Royal Historical Society*, sixth series, 8, 1998, pp. 165–84.

Cameron, Euan, *The Reformation of the Heretics. The Waldenses of the Alps 1480–1580*, Oxford 1984.

Camporesi, Piero, *Bread of Dreams. Food and Fantasy in Early Modern Europe*, trans. D. Gentilcore, Oxford 1980, 1989.

Cavallo, Sandra, *Charity and Power in Early Modern Italy. Benefactors and their Motives in Turin, 1541–1789*, Cambridge 1995.

Certeau, Michel de, *The Possession at Loudun*, 1970; trans. M.B. Smith, Chicago 1996, 2000.

Cheesman, Tom, *The Shocking Ballad Picture Show. German Popular Literature and Cultural History*, Oxford 1994.

Clark, Stuart, 'The "Gendering" of Witchcraft in French Demonology: Misogyny or Polarity?', *French History* 5, 1991, pp. 426–37.

Clark, Stuart, 'Protestant Demonology: Sin, Superstition, and Society (*c.* 1520–c. 1630)', in Ankarloo, Bengt and Gustav Henningsen (eds), *Early Modern European Witchcraft. Centres and Peripheries,* Oxford 1990.

Clark, Stuart, *Thinking with Demons. The Idea of Witchcraft in Early Modern Europe,* Oxford 1997.

Clendinnen, Inga, 'Franciscan Missionaries in Sixteenth-century Mexico', in James Obelkevich, Lyndal Roper and Raphael Samuel (eds), *Disciplines of Faith. Studies in Religion, Politics and Patriarchy,* London 1987.

Cohn, Norman, *Europe's Inner Demons,* London 1975.

Crouzet, Denis, 'Die Gewalt zur Zeit der Religionskriege im Frankreich des 16. Jahrhunderts', in Thomas Lindenberger and Alf Lüdtke (eds), *Physische Gewalt. Studien zur Geschichte der Neuzeit,* trans. A. Böltau and T. Lindenberger, Frankfurt am Main 1990, 1995.

Crouzet, Denis, 'A Woman and the Devil: Possession and Exorcism in Sixteenth-Century France' (trans. Michael Wolfe), in Michael Wolfe (ed.), *Changing Identities in Early Modern France,* Durham, NC and London 1997.

Cunningham, Andrew and Ole Peter Grell, *The Four Horsemen of the Apocalypse. Religion, War, Famine and Death in Reformation Europe,* Cambridge 2000.

Cunningham, Hugh, *Children and Childhood in Western Society since 1500,* London 1995.

DaCosta Kaufmann, Thomas, *Court, Cloister & City. The Art and Culture of Central Europe 1450–1800,* London 1995.

Darnton, Robert, *The Great Cat Massacre and Other Episodes in French Cultural History,* Harmondsworth 1984.

Davies, Mererid Puw, *The Tale of Bluebeard in German Literature: From the Eighteenth Century to the Present,* Oxford 2001.

Davies, Owen, *Cunning-Folk. Popular Magic in English History,* London 2003.

Davis, Natalie Zemon, *Society and Culture in Early Modern France,* London 1975.

Dengler, Robert, 'Das Hexenwesen im Stifte Obermarchtal von 1581–1756', Ph.D. diss., Erlangen 1953.

Dillinger, Johannes, *'Böse Leute'. Hexenverfolgungen in Schwäbisch-Österreich und Kurtrier im Vergleich,* Trier 1999.

Doney, John, 'Reform and the Enlightened Catholic State: Culture and Education in the Prince-Bishopric of Würzburg', Ph.D. diss., Emory University 1989.

Dülmen, Richard van, *Frauen vor Gericht. Kindsmord in der Frühen Neuzeit,* Frankfurt 1991.

Dülmen, Richard van (ed.), *Hexenwelten. Magie und Imagination vom 16.–20. Jahrhundert,* Frankfurt am Main 1987.

Dülmen, Richard van, *Theatre of Horror. Crime and Punishment in Early Modern Germany,* trans. E. Neu, London 1990.

Durrant, Jonathan, 'Witchcraft, Gender and Society in the Early Modern Prince-Bishopric of Eichstätt', Ph.D. diss., University of London 2002.

Ehmer, Josef, 'Marriage', in David I. Kertzer and Marzio Barbagli (eds), *The History of the European Family,* vol. 2: *Family Life in the Long Nineteenth Century, 1789–1913,* New Haven and London 2002.

Elwood, Christopher, *The Body Broken: The Calvinist Doctrine of the Eucharist and the Symbolization of Power in Sixteenth-century France,* New York and London 1999.

Eschbaumer, Gloria, *Bescheidenliche Tortur. Der ehrbare Rat der Stadt Nördlingen im Hexenprozess 1593/4 gegen die Kronenwirtin Maria Holl,* Nördlingen 1983.

Felber, Alfons, *Unzucht und Kindsmord in der freien Reichsstadt Nördlingen vom 15. bis 19. Jahrhundert,* Bonn 1961.

Ferber, Sarah, *Demonic Possession and Exorcism in Early Modern France*, London 2004.

Figlio, Karl, 'Oral History and the Unconscious', *History Workshop Journal* 26, 1988, pp. 120–32.

Fischer, H., *Schwäbisches Wörterbuch*, 7 vols, Tübingen 1904.

Flurschutz, Hildegunde, *Die Verwaltung des Hochstifts Würzburg unter Franz Ludwig von Erthal (1779–1795)* (Veröffentlichungen der Gesellschaft für fränkische Geschichte, Reihe IX, Darstellungen aus der fränkischen Geschichte 19), Würzburg 1965.

Forster, Marc, *Catholic Revival in the Age of the Baroque. Religious Identity in Southwest Germany, 1550–1750*, Cambridge 2001.

François, Etienne, *Die unsichtbare Grenze. Protestanten und Katholiken in Augsburg 1648–1806* (Abhandlungen zur Geschichte der Stadt Augsburg 33), Sigmaringen 1991.

Franz, Adolph, *Die kirchlichen Benediktionen im Mittelalter*, 2 vols, Freiburg 1909.

Freud, Sigmund, *The Standard Edition of the Complete Psychological Works of Sigmund Freud*, 24 vols, ed. James Strachey in co-operation with Anna Freud, Alix Strachey and Alan Tyson et al., London 1953–74.

Friedrichs, Christopher, *Urban Society in an Age of War: Nördlingen, 1580–1720*, Princeton 1979.

Gaskill, Malcolm, 'Women, Witchcraft and Power in Early Modern England: The Case of Margaret Moore', in Jenny Kermode and Garthine Walker (eds), *Women, Crime and the Courts in Early Modern England*, London 1994.

Gélis, Jacques, *History of Childbirth. Fertility, Pregnancy and Birth in Early Modern Europe* French 1984; trans. R. Morris, Oxford 1991.

Gibson, Marion, *Early Modern Witches. Witchcraft Cases in Contemporary Writing*, London 2000.

Gibson, Marion, *Reading Witchcraft. Stories of Early English Witches*, London 1999.

Gijswijt-Hofstra, Marijke, Levack, Brian and Porter, Roy, *Witchcraft and Magic in Europe*, Volume 5: *The Eighteenth and Nineteenth Centuries*, in Bengt Ankarloo and Stuart Clark, eds, The Athlone History of Witchcraft and Magic in Europe, 6 vols, London 1999–, London 1999.

Ginzburg, Carlo, *Ecstasies. Deciphering the Witches' Sabbath*, trans. R. Rosenthal, London 1990.

Ginzburg, Carlo, *Myths, Emblems and Clues*, trans. J. and A. Tedeschi, London 1990.

Ginzburg, Carlo, *The Night Battles. Witchcraft and Agrarian Cults in the Sixteenth and Seventeenth Centuries*, trans. J. and A. Tedeschi, London 1983.

Gottlieb, Günter, et al. (eds), *Geschichte der Stadt Augsburg von der Römerzeit bis zur Gegenwart*, Stuttgart 1984.

Gowing, Laura, *Common Bodies. Women, Touch and Power in Seventeenth-Century England*, London 2003.

Gowing, Laura, 'Secret Births and Infanticide in Seventeenth-century England', *Past and Present* 156, 1997, pp. 87–115.

Graf, Klaus, 'Hexenverfolgung in Schwäbisch Gmünd', in Sönke Lorenz and Dieter R. Bauer (eds), *Hexenverfolgung. Beiträge zur Forschung – unter besonderer Berücksichtigung des südwestdeutschen Raumes* (Quellen und Forschungen zur europäischen Ethnologie, vol. 15), Würzburg 1993.

Gray, Louise, 'The Self-perception of Chronic Physical Incapacity among the Labouring Poor. Pauper Narratives and Territorial Hospitals in Early Modern Rural Germany', Ph.D. diss., University of London 2001.

Gray, Marion W., *Productive Men, Reproductive Women. The Agrarian Household and the Emergence of Separate Spheres during the German Enlightenment*, New York 2000.

Greenblatt, Stephen, *Marvelous Possessions. The Wonder of the New World*, Oxford 1991.

Grießhammer, Birke (ed.), *Drutenjagd in Franken 16.–18. Jahrhundert*, 1998; 2nd edn Erlangen 1999.

Groebner, Valentin, *Defaced. The Visual Culture of Violence in the Late Middle Ages*, trans. P. Selwyn, Cambridge, Mass. 2004.

Groebner, Valentin, 'Insides Out: Clothes, Dissimulation and the Arts of Accounting in the Autobiography of Mathäus Schwarz (1498–1574)', *Representations* 66, 1999, pp. 52–72.

Habermas, Rebekka, *Wallfahrt und Aufruhr. Zur Geschichte des Wunderglaubens in der Frühen Neuzeit*, Frankfurt and New York 1991.

Habermas, Rebekka, 'Wunder, Wunderliches, Wunderbares. Zur Profanisierung eines Deutungsmusters in der frühen Neuzeit', in Richard van Dülmen (ed.), *Arbeit, Liebe, Ehre. Studien zur historischen Kulturforschung*, Frankfurt am Main 1988.

Habermas, Regina (ed.) with Tanja Hommen, *Das Frankfurter Gretchen. Der Prozess gegen die Kindsmörderin Susanna Margaretha von Brandt*, Munich 1999.

Haemmerle, Albert, *Evangelisches Totenregister zur Kunst- und Handwerksgeschichte*, Augsburg 1928.

Harbison, Robert, *Reflections on Baroque*, London 2000.

Hart, Clive, 'Erotische Implikationen in der Flugdarstellung von der Hochrenaissance bis zum Rokoko', in Dieter Bauer and Wolfgang Behringer (eds), *Fliegen und Schweben. Annäherung an eine menschliche Sensation*, Munich 1997.

Haustein, Jörg, *Martin Luthers Stellung zum Zauber- und Hexenwesen* (Münchener Kirchenhistorische Studien 2), Stuttgart 1990.

Heal, Bridget, 'A Woman Like Any Other? Images of the Virgin Mary and Marian Devotion in Nuremberg, Augsburg and Cologne *c.* 1500–1600', Ph.D. diss., Courtauld Institute of Art/Royal Holloway, University of London 2001.

Heidrich, Hermann, 'Grenzübergänge. Das Haus und die Volkskultur in der frühen Neuzeit', in Richard van Dülmen, ed., *Kultur der einfachen Leute. Bayerisches Volksleben vom 16. bis zum 18. Jahrhundert*, Munich 1983.

Heinemann, Evelyn, *Witches. A Psychoanalytical Exploration of the Killing of Women*, trans. D. Kiraly, London 2000.

Henkel, Arthur and Albrecht Schöne (eds), *Emblemata. Handbuch zur Sinnbildkunst*, Stuttgart 1967.

Herre, Franz, *Das Augsburger Bürgertum im Zeitalter der Aufklärung* (Abhandlungen zur Geschichte der Stadt Augsburg 6), Augsburg 1951.

Hinckeldey, Ch. (ed.), *Justiz in alter Zeit*, Rothenburg ob der Taube 1989.

Hsia, Ronnie Po-chia, *The Myth of Ritual Murder. Jews and Magic in Reformation Germany*, New Haven and London 1988.

Huber, Catherine, 'Die Hexenprozesse in Basel im 16. und 17. Jahrhundert', Lizentiatsarbeit, Basel 1989.

Hufton, Olwen, *The Prospect Before Her*, London 1995.

Hull, Isabel V., *Sexuality, State and Civil Society in Germany, 1700–1848*, Ithaca, NY 1996.

Hulme, Peter, 'Tales of Distinction: European Ethnography and the Caribbean', in Stuart B. Schwartz (ed.), *Implicit Understandings. Observing, Reporting, and Reflecting on the Encounters between Europeans and Other Peoples in the Early Modern Era*, Cambridge 1994.

Hutton, Ronald, *The Rise and Fall of Merry England. The Ritual Year 1400–1700*, Oxford 1994.

Hutton, Ronald, *The Triumph of the Moon. A History of Modern Pagan Witchcraft*, Oxford 1999.

Huxley, Aldous, *The Devils of Loudun*, London 1952.

Ingrao, Charles, *The Hessian Mercenary State: Ideas, Institutions, and Reforms under Frederick II, 1760–1785*, Cambridge 1987.

Irsigler, Franz and Arnold Lasotta, *Bettler und Gaukler, Dirnen und Henker. Außenseiter in einer mittelalterlichen Stadt. Köln 1300–1600*, Munich 1984, 1989.

Israel, Jonathan, *European Jewry in the Age of Mercantilism, 1550–1750*, Oxford 1985.

Israel, Jonathan, *Radical Enlightenment. Philosophy and the Making of Modernity 1650–1750*, Oxford 2001.

Jacobs, Jürgen Carl and Heinz Rölleke (eds), *Das Tagebuch des Meister Franz Scharfrichter zu Nürnberg. Nachdruck der Buchausgabe von 1801*, Dortmund 1980.

Jacquart, Danielle and Claude Thomasset, *Sexuality and Medicine in the Middle Ages* (French 1985), trans. M. Adamson, Oxford 1988.

Jacques-Chaquin, Nicole and Maxime Préaud, *Le Sabbat des sorciers en Europe (xve–xviiie siècles)*, Grenoble 1993.

James, Susan, *Passion & Action. The Emotions in Seventeenth-century Philosophy*, Oxford 1997.

Janson, Stefan, *Jean Bodin, Johan Fischart: De la démonomanie des sorciers (1580). Vom ausgelassnen wütigen Teuffelsheer (1581), und ihre Fallberichte* (Europäische Hochschulschriften 352), Frankfurt am Main 1980.

Jerouschek, Günter, *Die Hexen und ihr Prozeß. Die Hexenverfolgung in der Reichsstadt Esslingen* (Esslinger Studien vol. 1), Esslingen 1992.

Jesse, Horst, *Die evangelische Kirche 'Zu den Barfüssern' in Augsburg*, Pfaffenhofen 1982.

Jung, Vera, '"Wilde" Tänze – "Gelehrte" Tanzkunst. Wie man im 16. Jahrhundert versuchte, die Körper zu zähmen', in Richard van Dülmen (ed.), *Körper-Geschichten*, Frankfurt am Main 1996.

Karant-Nunn, Susan C., 'A Women's Rite: Churching and Reformation of Ritual', in Ronnie Po-chia Hsia and Bob Scribner (eds), *Problems in the Historical Anthropology of Early Modern Europe*, Wiesbaden 1997.

Karant-Nunn, Susan and Merry E. Wiesner (eds and trans.), *Luther on Women. A Sourcebook*, Cambridge 2003.

Karlsen, Carol, *The Devil in the Shape of a Woman. Witchcraft in Colonial New England*, New York and London 1987.

Kiessling, Rolf, *Die Stadt und ihr Land* (Städteforschung A/29), Vienna 1989.

Klein, Melanie, *Envy and Gratitude and Other Works 1946–1963*, ed. H. Segal, London 1975, 1988.

Klein, Melanie, *Love, Guilt and Reparation and Other Works 1921–1945*, ed. H. Segal, London 1975, 1988.

Klein, Melanie, *The Psychoanalysis of Children*, trans. Alix Strachey, London 1932, 1989.

Knapp, Hermann, *Die Zenten des Hochstifts Würzburg. Ein Beitrag zur Geschichte des süddeutschen Gerichtswesens und Strafrechts*, 2 vols, Berlin 1907.

Koerner, Joseph Leo, *Caspar David Friedrich and the Subject of Landscape*, London 1990, 2nd edn 1995.

Koerner, Joseph Leo, *The Moment of Self-Portraiture in German Renaissance Art*, Chicago and London 1993.

Kors, Alan and Edward Peters (eds), *Witchcraft in Europe, 400–1700*, 2nd edn Philadelphia 2001.

Kreisbeschreibungen des Landes Baden-Württemberg. Der Landkreis Biberach, 2 vols, Sigmaringen 1987, 1990.

Kunstmann, Hartmut Heinrich, 'Zauberwahn und Hexenprozeß in der Reichsstadt Nürnberg', D. Jur. diss, Johannes Gutenberg-Universität Mainz, 1970.

Labouvie, Eva, *Andere Umstände. Eine Kulturgeschichte der Geburt*, Cologne, Weimar and Vienna 1998.

Labouvie, Eva, *Beistand in Kindsnöten. Hebammen und eine weibliche Kultur auf dem Land (1550–1910)*, Frankfurt and New York 1999.

Labouvie, Eva, 'Geburt und Tod in der Frühen Neuzeit. Letzter Dienst und der Umgang mit besonderen Verstorbenen', in Jürgen Schlumbohm, Barbara Duden, Jacques Gélis and Patrice Veit (eds), *Rituale der Geburt. Eine Kulturgeschichte*, Munich 1998.

Labouvie, Eva, 'Men in Witchcraft Trials: Towards a Social Anthropology of "Male" Understandings of Magic and Witchcraft', in Ulinka Rublack (ed.), *Gender in Early Modern German History*, Cambridge 2002.

Labouvie, Eva, 'Perspektivenwechsel. Magische Domänen von Frauen und Männern in Volksmagie und Hexerei aus der Sicht der Geschlechtergeschichte', in Ingrid Ahrendt-Schulte, Dieter Bauer, Sönke Lorenz and Jürgen Michael Schmidt (eds), *Geschlecht, Magie und Hexenverfolgung* (Hexenforschung, vol. 7), Bielefeld 2002.

Labouvie, Eva, *Zauberei und Hexenwerk. Ländlicher Hexenglaube in der Frühen Neuzeit*, Frankfurt am Main 1991.

Lambrecht, Karen, '"Jagdhunde des Teufels". Die Verfolgung von Totengräbern im Gefolge frühneuzeitlicher Pestwellen', in Andreas Blauert and Gerd Schwerhoff (eds), *Mit den Waffen der Justiz. Zur Kriminalitätsgeschichte des späten Mittelalters und der Frühen Neuzeit*, Frankfurt 1993.

Lambrecht, Karen, 'Tabu und Tod. Männer als Opfer frühneuzeitlicher Verfolgungswellen', in Ingrid Ahrendt-Schulte, Dieter Bauer, Sönke Lorenz and Jürgen Michael Schmidt (eds), *Geschlecht, Magie und Hexenverfolgung* (Hexenforschung, vol. 7), Bielefeld 2002.

Laplanche, Jean and Jean-Bertrand Pontalis, 'Fantasy and the Origins of Sexuality', in Victor Burgin, James Donald and Cora Kaplan (eds), *Formations of Fantasy*, London 1987.

Lederer, David, *A Bavarian Beacon. Spiritual Physic and the Birth of the Asylum, 1495–1803*, forthcoming.

Lee, W.R., 'Bastardy and the Socioeconomic Structure of South Germany' (1997), in Robert I. Rotberg (ed.), *Population History and the Family. A Journal of Interdisciplinary History Reader*, Cambridge, Mass. and London 2001.

Lehmann, Hartmut, 'Die Kinder Gottes in der Welt', in Martin Greschat (ed.), *Zur neueren Pietismusforschung*, Darmstadt 1977.

Lehmann, Hartmut, 'The Persecution of Witches as Restoration of Order', *Central European History* 21, 1988, pp. 107–21.

Lehmann, Hartmut and Otto Ulbricht (eds), *Vom Unfug des Hexen-Processes. Gegner der Hexenverfolgungen von Johann Weyer bis Friedrich Spee*, Wiesbaden 1992.

Lenk, Leonhard, *Augsburger Bürgertum im Späthumanismus und Frühbarock (1580–1700)* (Abhandlungen zur Geschichte der Stadt Augsburg 17), Augsburg 1968.

Levack, Brian, *The Witch-hunt in Early Modern Europe*, London and New York 1987, 2nd edn 1995.

Liedl, Eugen, *Gerichtsverfassung und Zivilprozess der freien Reichsstadt Augsburg* (Abhandlungen zur Geschichte der Stadt Augsburg 12), Augsburg 1958.

Lind, Vera, *Selbstmord in der Frühen Neuzeit. Diskurs, Lebenswelt und kultureller Wandel*, Göttingen 1999.

Lindeman, Mary, *Medicine and Society in Early Modern Europe*, Cambridge 1999.

Loichinger, Alexander, 'Friedrich von Spee und seine "Cautio criminalis"', in Georg Schwaiger (ed.), *Teufelsglaube und Hexenprozesse*, Munich 1988.

Lorenz, Sönke, *Aktenversendung und Hexenprozess*, Frankfurt 1982.

Lorenz, Sönke (ed.), *Hexen und Hexenverfolgung im deutschen Südwesten*, Ostfildern 1994.

Lorenz, Sönke (ed.), *Himmlers Hexenkartothek. Das Interesse der Nationalsozialismus an der Hexenverfolgung* (Hexenforschung, vol. 4), 2nd edn, Bielefeld 2000.

Lorenz, Sönke and Bauer, Dieter, eds, *Das Ende der Hexenverfolgung*, Stuttgart 1995.

Lorenz, Sönke and Bauer, Dieter, eds, *Hexenverfolgung. Beiträge zur Forschung*, Würzburg 1995.

Macfarlane, Alan, *Witchcraft in Tudor and Stuart England: A Regional and Comparative Study*, London 1970.

McGowan, Margaret M., 'Pierre de Lancre's *Tableau de l'inconstance des mauvais anges et demons*: The Sabbat Sensationalised', in Sydney Anglo (ed.), *The Damned Art. Essays in the Literature of Witchcraft*, London 1977.

McLaren, Angus, *A History of Contraception. From Antiquity to the Present Day*, Oxford 1990, 1992.

Maier, Konstantin, 'Der schwäbische Meister der "geistlichen Wohlredenheit". Chorherr Sebastian Sailer (1714–1777) von Marchtal', in Max Müller, Rudolf Reinhardt and Wilfried Schöntag (eds), *Marchtal Prämonstratenserabtei, Fürstliches Schloß, Kirchliche Akademie*, Ulm 1992.

Mälzer, Gottfried, *Julius Echter. Leben und Werk*, Würzburg 1989.

Marrow, James and Alan Shestack (eds), *Hans Baldung Grien. Prints and Drawings*, Chicago 1981.

Martin, Andrew, 'Das Bild vom Fliegen, dokumentierte Flugversuche und das Aufkommen von Ansichten aus der Vogelschau zu Beginn der frühen Neuzeit', in Dieter Bauer and Wolfgang Behringer (eds), *Fliegen und Schweben. Annäherung an eine menschliche Sensation*, Munich 1997.

Martin, Ruth, *Witchcraft and the Inquisition in Venice 1550–1650*, Oxford 1989.

Masson, Jeffrey Moussaieff (ed.), *Sigmund Freud. Briefe an Wilhelm Fliess 1887–1904*, German edn revised and expanded by Michael Schröter, Frankfurt am Main 1986.

Medick, Hans, *Weben und Überleben in Laichingen 1650–1900. Lokalgeschichte als Allgemeine Geschichte* (Veröffentlichungen des Max-Planck Instituts für Geschichte, vol. 126), 1996; 2nd edn, Göttingen 1997.

Meili, David, 'Hexen in Wasterkingen. Magie und Lebensform in einem Dorf des frühen 18. Jahrhunderts', Ph.D. diss., Zürich 1979.

Melton, James van Horn, *Absolutism and the Eighteenth-century Origins of Compulsory Schooling*, Cambridge 1988.

Merzbacher, Friedrich, *Die Hexenprozesse in Franken*, Munich 1957, 1970.

Merzbacher, Friedrich, *Recht–Staat–Kirche. Ausgewählte Aufsätze*, Vienna 1989.

Midelfort, Erik, 'Charcot, Freud, and the Demons', in Kathryn E. Edwards, ed., *Werewolves, Witches and Wandering Spirits. Traditional Belief & Folklore in Early Modern Europe* (Sixteenth Century Essays & Studies 62), Kirksville, Missouri 2002.

Midelfort, Erik, *A History of Madness in Sixteenth-Century Germany*, Stanford 1999.

Midelfort, Erik, *Witch Hunting in Southwestern Germany 1562–1684. The Social and Intellectual Foundations*, Stanford 1972.

Minty, J.M., '*Judengasse* to Christian Quarter: The Phenomenon of the Converted Synagogue in the Late Medieval and Early Modern Holy Roman Empire', in Bob Scribner and Trevor Johnson (eds), *Popular Religion in Germany and Central Europe, 1400–1800*, London 1996.

Mitterauer, Michael, *Ledige Mütter. Zur Geschichte illegitimer Geburten in Europa*, Munich 1983.

Mommertz, Monika, 'Handeln, Bedeuten, Geschlecht. Konfliktaustragungspraktiken in der ländlichen Gesellschaft der Mark Brandenburg (2. Hälfte des 16. Jahrhunderts bis zum Dreißigjährigen Krieg)', Ph.D. diss., European University Institute, Florence 1997.

Monninger, Georg, *Was uns Nördlinger Häuser erzählen*, Nördlingen 1915, 1984.

Monter, E. William, 'Inflation and Witchcraft: The Case of Jean Bodin', in Brian Levack (ed.), *The Literature of Witchcraft*, 12 vols, vol. 4, New York and London 1992.

Monter, E. William, 'Toads and Eucharists: The Male Witches of Normandy, 1564–1660', *French Historical Studies* 20, 1997, pp. 563–95.

Monter, E. William, 'Witch Trials in Continental Europe 1560–1660', in Bengt Ankarloo, Stuart Clark and William Monter, *Witchcraft and Magic in Europe*, Volume 4: *The Period of the Witch Trials*, in Bengt Ankarloo and Stuart Clark (eds), The Athlone History of Witchcraft and Magic in Europe, 6 vols, London 1999—, London 2002.

Muir, Edward, *Ritual in Early Modern Europe*, Cambridge 1997.

Müller, Maria E., 'Poiesis und Hexerei. Zur "Historia von D. Johann Fausten"', in Günter Mahal (ed.), *Die 'Historia von D. Johann Fausten' (1587)*, Vaihingen an der Enz 1988.

Müller, Max, Rudolf Reinhardt and Wilfried Schöntag (eds), *Marchtal. Prämonstratenserabtei. Fürstliches Schloß. Kirchliche Akademie*, Ulm 1992.

Nardon, Franco, *Benandanti e inquisitori nel Friuli del seicento*, Trieste 1999.

Nowosadtko, Jutta, *Scharfrichter und Abdecker. Der Alltag zweier 'unehrlicher Berufe' in der frühen Neuzeit*, Paderborn 1994.

Nuber, Winfried, 'Abtei Marchtal und seine Pfarrei in der Stadt Munderkingen', in Max Müller, Rudolf Reinhardt and Wilfried Schöntag (eds), *Marchtal. Prämonstratenserabtei. Fürstliches Schloß. Kirchliche Akademie*, Ulm 1992.

Ogilvie, Sheilagh, *A Bitter Living. Women, Markets, and Social Capital in Early Modern Germany*, Oxford 2003.

Oorschot, Theo G.M., 'Ihrer Zeit voraus. Das Ende der Hexenverfolgung in der *Cautio criminalis*', in Sönke Lorenz and Dieter Bauer (eds), *Das Ende der Hexenverfolgung* (Hexenforschung, vol. 10), Stuttgart 1995.

Ozment, Steven, *When Fathers Ruled. Family Life in Reformation Europe*, Cambridge, Mass., 1983.

Pearl, Jonathan, *The Crime of Crimes: Demonology and Politics in France 1560–1620*, Waterloo, Canada, 1999.

Peters, Edward, *Torture*, Oxford 1985.

Pfister, Christian, *Bevölkerungsgeschichte und historische Demographie 1500–1800* (Enzyklopädie Deutscher Geschichte, vol. 29), Munich 1994.

Phillips, Seymour, 'The Outer World of the European Middle Ages', in Stuart B. Schwartz (ed.), *Implicit Understandings. Observing, Reporting, and Reflecting on the Encounters between Europeans and Other Peoples in the Early Modern Era*, Cambridge 1994.

Plumb, J.H., 'The New World of Children', in Neil McKendrick, John Brewer and J.H. Plumb (eds), *The Birth of a Consumer Society. The Commercialization of Eighteenth-century England*, London 1982.

Pohl, Herbert, *Hexenglaube und Hexenverfolgung im Kurfürstentum Mainz. Ein Beitrag zur Hexenfrage im 16. und beginnenden 17. Jahrhundert* (Geschichtliche Landeskunde 32), Stuttgart 1988.

Pölnitz, Götz Freiherr von, *Fürstbischof Julius Echter von Mespelbrunn* (Mainfränkische Hefte 36), Würzburg 1959.

Pölnitz, Götz Freiherr von, *Julius Echter von Mespelbrunn. Fürstbischof von Würzburg und Herzog von Franken (1573–1617)* (Schriftenreihe zur bayerischen Landesgeschichte 17), Munich 1934.

Polonyi, Andrea, 'Die Übertragung des heiligsten Kreuzpartikels von Rom nach Marchtal. Zum Erscheinungsbild barocker Reliquienverehrung', in Max Müller, Rudolf Reinhardt and Wilfried Schöntag (eds), *Marchtal Prämonstratenserabtei, Fürstliches Schloß, Kirchliche Akademie*, Ulm 1992.

Puff, Helmut, *Sodomy in Reformation Germany and Switzerland 1400–1600*, Chicago and London 2003.

Purkiss, Diane, *The Witch in History. Early Modern and Twentieth-century Representations*, London 1996.

Raschzok, Klaus and Dietmar-H. Voges, '... *dem Gott gnaedig sei'. Totenschilde und Epitaphien in der St. Georgskirche in Nördlingen*, Nördlingen 1998.

Reuschling, Heinzjürgen, *Die Regierung des Hochstifts Würzburg 1495–1642. Zentralbehörden und führende Gruppen eines geistlichen Staates*, Würzburg 1984.

Reuss, Rodolphe, *La Sorcellerie au seizième et au dix-septième siècles particulièrement en Alsace* (1871), repr. Steinbrunn-le-Haut 1987.

Robisheaux, Thomas, 'The Peasantries of Western Germany, 1300–1750', in Tom Scott (ed.), *The Peasantries of Europe from the Fourteenth to the Eighteenth Centuries*, London 1998.

Robisheaux, Thomas, *Rural Society and the Search for Order in Early Modern Germany*, Cambridge 1989.

Röckelein, Hedwig, 'Marienverehrung und Judenfeindlichkeit in Mittelalter', in Claudia Opitz, Hedwig Röckelein, Gabriela Signori and Guy P. Marchal (eds), *Maria in der Welt. Marienverehrung im Kontext der Sozialgeschichte 10.–18. Jahrhundert*, Zurich 1993.

Roeck, Bernd, 'Christliche Idealstaat und Hexenwahn. Zum Ende der europäischen Verfolgungen', *Historisches Jahrbuch* 108, 1988, pp. 379–405.

Roeck, Bernd, *Eine Stadt in Krieg und Frieden. Studien zur Geschichte der Reichsstadt Augsburg zwischen Kalenderstreit und Parität* (Schriftenreihe der historischen Kommission bei der bayerischen Akademie der Wissenschaften 37), 2 vols, Göttingen 1989.

Roper, Lyndal, *The Holy Household. Women and Morals in Reformation Augsburg*, Oxford 1989.

Roper, Lyndal, *Oedipus and the Devil. Witchcraft, Sexuality and Religion in Early Modern Europe*, London 1994.

Rosen, Barbara, *Witchcraft in England 1558–1618*, Amherst 1969, 1991.

Rowlands, Alison, 'Witchcraft and Old Women in Early Modern Germany', *Past and Present* 173, 2001, pp. 50–89.

Rowlands, Alison, *Witchcraft Narratives in Germany. Rothenburg, 1561–1652*, Manchester 2003.

Rubin, Miri, *Corpus Christi. The Eucharist in Late Medieval Culture*, Cambridge 1991.

Rubin, Miri, *Gentile Tales. The Narrative Assault on Late Medieval Jews*, New Haven and London 1999.

Rublack, Hans-Christoph, *Eine Bürgerliche Reformation: Nördlingen* (Quellen und Forschungen zur Reformationsgeschichte 51), Gütersloh 1982.

Rublack, Hans-Christoph, *Gescheiterte Reformation. Frühreformatorische und protestantische Bewegungen in süd- und westdeutschen geistlichen Residenzen*, Stuttgart 1978.

Rublack, Hans-Christoph, 'Political and Social Norms in Urban Communities in the Holy Roman Empire', in Kaspar von Greyerz (ed.), *Religion, Politics, and Social Protest*, London 1984.

Rublack, Hans-Christoph, 'The Song of Contz Anahans: Communication and Revolt in Nördlingen, 1525', in Ronnie Po-chia Hsia (ed.), *The German People and the Reformation*, Ithaca, NY and London 1988.

Rublack, Ulinka, *The Crimes of Women in Early Modern Germany*, Oxford 1999.

Rublack, Ulinka, 'Pregnancy, Childbirth and the Female Body in Early Modern Germany', *Past and Present* 150, 1996, pp. 84–110.

Ruggiero, Guido, *Binding Passions. Tales of Magic, Marriage, and Power at the End of the Renaissance*, New York and Oxford 1993.

Rummel, Walter, *Bauern, Herren und Hexen. Studien zur Sozialgeschichte spohheimischer und kurtrierischer Hexenprozesse 1574–1664*, Göttingen 1991.

Sabean, David, *Kinship in Neckarhausen 1700–1870*, Cambridge 1998.

Sabean, David, *Power in the Blood. Popular Culture and Village Discourse in Early Modern Germany*, Cambridge 1984.

Sabean, David, *Property, Production and Family in Neckarhausen 1700–1870*, Cambridge 1990.

Safley, Thomas Max, *Charity and Economy in the Orphanages of Early Modern Augsburg*, Boston 1997.

Scarry, Elaine, *The Body in Pain. The Making and Unmaking of the World*, Oxford 1985.

Schade, Sigrid, *Schadenzauber und die Magie des Körpers. Hexenbilder der frühen Neuzeit*, Worms 1983.

Schama, Simon, *The Embarrassment of Riches. An Interpretation of Dutch Culture in the Golden Age*, London and New York 1987.

Schama, Simon, *Landscape & Memory*, London 1995.

Schenk, Winfried, 'Die mainfränkische Landschaft unter dem Einfluß von Gewerbe, Handel, Verkehr und Landwirtschaft', in Peter Kolb and Ernst-Günter Krenig eds, *Unterfränkische Geschichte. Band 3: Vom Beginn des konfessionellen Zeitalters bis zum Ende des Dreißigjährigen Krieges*, Würzburg 1995.

Scherf, Walter, 'Die Hexe im Zaubermärchen', in Richard van Dülmen (ed.), *Hexenwelten. Magie und Imagination*, Frankfurt 1987.

Scherf, Walter, *Das Märchen Lexikon*, 2 vols, Munich 1995.

Schindler, Norbert, *Rebellion, Community and Custom in Early Modern Germany*, trans. Pamela E. Selwyn, Cambridge 2002.

Schlögl, Peter, *Bauern, Krieg und Staat. Oberbayerische Bauernwirtschaft und frühmoderner Staat im 17. Jahrhundert*, Göttingen 1988.

Schmauder, Andreas (ed.), *Frühe Hexenverfolgung in Ravensburg und am Bodensee* (Historische Stadt Ravensburg, 2), Constance 2001.

Schmid, Martina, 'Die Biberacher Scharfrichter', in Sönke Lorenz (ed.), *Hexen und Hexenverfolgung im deutschen Südwesten*, Ostfildern bei Stuttgart 1994.

Schmidt, Jürgen Michael, *Glaube und Skepsis. Die Kurpfalz und die abendländische Hexenverfolgung 1446–1685*, Gütersloh 2000.

Schormann, Gerhard, 'Die Haltung des Reichskammergerichts in Hexenprozessen', in Hartmut Lehmann and Otto Ulbricht (eds), *Vom Unfug des Hexen-Processes. Gegner der Hexenverfolgungen von Johann Weyer bis Friedrich Spee*, Wiesbaden 1992.

Schormann, Gerhard, *Hexenprozesse in Deutschland*, Göttingen 1981.

Schormann, Gerhard, *Der Krieg gegen die Hexen. Das Ausrottungsprogramm des Kurfürsten von Köln*, Göttingen 1992.

Schormann, Gerhard, 'Wie entstand die Kartothek, und wem war sie bekannt?', in Sönke Lorenz (ed.), *Himmlers Hexenkartothek. Das Interesse der Nationalsozialismus an der Hexenverfolgung* (Hexenforschung 4), 2nd edn, Bielefeld 2000.

Schöttle, Johann Evangelista, *Geschichte von Stadt und Stift Buchau samt dem stiftischen Dorfe Kappel. Beschreibung und Geschichte der Pfarrei Seekirch mit ihren Filialen Alleshausen, Brasenberg und Tiefenbach*, 1884, reprint Bad Buchau 1977.

Schubert, Ernst, *Die Landstände des Hochstifts Würzburg* (Veröffentlichungen der Gesellschaft für fränkische Geschichte, Reihe IX, Darstellungen aus der fränkischen Geschichte, 19), Würzburg 1967.

Schuhmann, Helmut, *Der Scharfrichter. Seine Gestalt – seine Funktion*, Kempten 1964.

Schulte, Rolf, *Hexenmeister. Die Verfolgung von Männern im Rahmen der Hexenverfolgung von 1530–1730 im Alten Reich*, 1999; 2nd, expanded, edn, Frankfurt am Main 2001.

Schulze, Sabine (ed.), *Goethe und die Kunst*, Stuttgart 1994.

Schwaiger, Georg (ed.), *Teufelsglaube und Hexenprozesse*, Munich 1988.

Schwillus, Harald, ' "Der bischoff lässt nit nach, bis er die gantze statt verbrennt hat".
   Bemerkungen zu der 1745 veröffentlichten Liste der unter Furstbischof Philipp Adolf
   von Ehrenberg wegen angeblicher Hexerei hingerichteten Menschen', *Würzburger
   Diözesangeschichtsblätter* 49, 1987, pp. 145–54.

Schwillus, Harald, 'Die Hexenprozesse gegen Würzburger Geistliche unter Fürstbischof
   Philipp Adolf von Ehrenberg (1623–31)', Diplomarbeit, Bayerische Julius-Maximilians-
   Universität, Würzburg 1987.

Schwillus, Harald, *Kleriker im Hexenprozeß. Geistliche als Opfer der Hexenprozesse des 16.
   und 17. Jahrhunderts in Deutschland*, Würzburg 1992.

Scribner, Bob, *Popular Culture and Popular Movements in Reformation Germany*, London
   1987.

Scribner, Bob, *Religion and Culture in Germany (1400–1800)*, Leiden 2001.

Scribner, R.W., *For the Sake of Simple Folk. Popular Propaganda for the German
   Reformation*, Cambridge 1981; revised edn, Oxford 1994.

Scribner, Robert W., ' "Incombustible Luther": The Image of the Reformer in Early
   Modern Germany', *Past and Present* 110, 1986, pp. 38–68.

Sebald, Hans, *Der Hexenjunge. Fallstudie eines Inquisitionsprozesses*, Marburg 1992.

Segal, Hanna, *Dream, Phantasy and Art*, London 1991.

Segl, Peter (ed.), *Der Hexenhammer. Entstehung und Umfeld des Malleus maleficarum von
   1487*, Cologne and Berlin 1988.

Sharpe, James, *Instruments of Darkness. Witchcraft in England 1550–1750*, London 1996.

Silverman, Lisa, *Tortured Subjects. Pain, Truth, and the Body in Early Modern France*,
   Chicago 2001.

Skinner, Quentin, *The Foundations of Modern Political Thought*, 2 vols, Cambridge 1978.

Sluhovsky, Moshe, 'The Devil in the Convent', *American Historical Review* 107, 2002,
   pp. 1379–411.

Smith, Jeffrey Chipps, *Sensuous Worship. Jesuits and the Art of the Early Catholic
   Reformation in Germany*, Princeton 2002.

Soergel, Philip, *Wondrous in his Saints. Counter-Reformation Propaganda in Bavaria*,
   Berkeley and Los Angeles 1993.

Soman, Alfred, 'The Parlement of Paris and the Great Witch Hunt (1565–1640)', *Sixteenth
   Century Journal* 9, 1978, pp. 31–44.

Sporhan-Krempel, Lore, *Die Hexe von Nördlingen. Das Schicksal der Maria Holl. Roman*
   (1950), Nördlingen 1978–79.

Sreenivasan, Govind, *The Peasants of Ottobeuren 1487–1723. A Rural Society in Early
   Modern Europe*, Cambridge 2004.

Stephens, Walter, *Demon Lovers. Witchcraft, Sex and the Crisis of Belief*, Chicago 2002.

Stewart, Alison, *Unequal Lovers: A Study of Unequal Couples in Northern Art*, New York
   1977.

Stewart, Charles, 'Dreams and Desire in Ancient and Early Christian Thought', in Daniel
   Pick and Lyndal Roper (eds), *Dreams and History*, London 2003.

Stier, Bernhard, *Fürsorge und Disziplinierung im Zeitalter des Absolutismus. Das
   Pforzheimer Zucht- und Waisenhaus und die badische Sozialpolitik im 18. Jahrhundert*
   (Quellen und Studien zur Geschichte der Stadt Pforzheim 1), Sigmaringen 1988.

Strasser, Ulrike, 'Bones of Contention: Cloistered Nuns, Decorated Relics, and the
   Contest over Women's Place in the Public Sphere of Counter-Reformation Munich',
   Archiv für Reformationsgeschichte 90, 1999, pp. 255–88.

Strasser, Ulrike, 'Cloistering Women's Past: Conflicting Accounts of Enclosure in a

Seventeenth-century Munich Nunnery', in Ulinka Rublack (ed.), *Gender in Early Modern German History*, Cambridge 2002.

Strasser, Ulrike, *State of Virginity: Gender, Religion, and Politics in an Early Modern Catholic State*, Ann Arbor 2004.

Strauss, Walter, *The German Single-Leaf Woodcut 1500–1550*, 4 vols, New York 1945.

Strauss, Walter, *The German Single-Leaf Woodcut 1550-1600*, 3 vols, New York 1975.

Struckmeier, Ekkhard, ' "Vom Glauben der Kinder im Mutter-Leibe". Eine historisch-anthropologische Untersuchung frühneuzeitlicher lutherischer Seelsorge und Frömmigkeit im Zusammenhang mit der Geburt', Ph.D. diss., Bielefeld 1995.

Stuart, Kathy, *Defiled Trades and Social Outcasts. Honour and Ritual Pollution in Early Modern Germany*, Cambridge 1999.

Talbot, Charles W., 'Baldung and the Female Nude', in James H. Marrow and Alan Shestack (eds), *Hans Baldung Grien, Prints and Drawings*, Chicago 1981.

Taylor, Christopher C., *Sacrifice as Terror. The Rwandan Genocide of 1994*, Oxford and New York 1999.

Theibault, John, 'The Demography of the Thirty Years' War Revisited: Günther Franz and his Critics', *German History* 15, 1997, pp. 1–21.

Theibault, John, *German Villages in Crisis. Rural Life in Hesse-Kassel and the Thirty Years' War 1580–1720*, Atlantic Highlands, NJ 1995.

Thomas, Keith, *Religion and the Decline of Magic*, London 1971, Harmondsworth 1973.

Tlusty, Ann B., *Bacchus and Civic Order. The Culture of Drink in Early Modern Germany*, Charlottesville and London 2001.

Tosh, Nick, 'Possession, Exorcism and Psychoanalysis', *Studies in History and Philosophy of Biological and Biomedical Sciences* 33, 2002, pp. 583–96.

Ulbricht, Otto, 'Der sozialkritische unter den Gegnern: Hermann Witekind und sein *Christlich bedencken vnd erjnnerung von Zauberey* von 1585', in Hartmut Lehmann and Otto Ulbricht (eds), *Vom Unfug des Hexen-Processes. Gegner der Hexenverfolgungen von Johann Weyer bis Friedrich Spee*, Wiesbaden 1992.

Viazzo, Pier Paolo, 'Mortality, Fertility and Family', in David I. Kertzer and Marzio Barbagli (eds), *The History of the European Family*, Vol. 1: *Family Life in Early Modern Times*, New Haven and London 2001.

Vogel, Klaus, 'Wo Sprache endet. Der Bericht des Anton Prätorius über Folter und das Problem der "selektiven Empathie"', in Markus Meumann and Dirk Niefanger (eds), *Ein Schauplatz herber Angst. Wahrnehmung und Darstellung von Gewalt im 17. Jahrhundert*, Göttingen 1997.

Voges, Dietmar-H., *Nördlingen seit der Reformation. Aus dem Leben einer Stadt*, Munich 1998.

Voges, Dietmar-H., 'Reichsstadt Nördlingen', in Sönke Lorenz (ed.), *Hexen und Hexenverfolgung im deutschen Südwesten*, Ostfildern 1994.

Voges, Dietmar-H., *Die Reichsstadt Nördlingen. 12 Kapitel aus ihrer Geschichte*, Munich 1988.

Vöhringer-Rubröder, Gisela, 'Reichsstadt Esslingen', in Sönke Lorenz (ed.), *Hexen und Hexenverfolgung im deutschen Südwesten*, Ostfildern 1994.

Vries, Jan de, 'Population', in Thomas Brady, Jr., Heiko A. Oberman and James D. Tracy (eds), *Handbook of European History 1400–1600*, 2 vols, Grand Rapids, Michigan 1994–95; 1996.

Walinski-Kiel, Robert, 'The Devil's Children: Child Witch-Trials in Early Modern Germany', *Continuity and Change* 11, 1996, pp. 171–90.

Walker, Mack, *German Home Towns. Community, State and General Estate, 1648–1817*, Ithaca, NY, and London 1971, 1998.

Walker, Mack, *The Salzburg Transaction. Expulsion and Redemption in Eighteenth-Century Augsburg*, Ithaca, NY, 1992.

Walsham, Alexandra, ' "Domme preachers"? Post-Reformation English Catholicism and the Culture of Print', *Past and Present* 168, 2000, pp. 72–123.

Walter, Ludwig, 'Pater Sebastian Sailer – Der schwäbische Mundartdichter aus Marchtal', in Max Müller, Rudolf Reinhardt and Wilfried Schöntag (eds), *Marchtal. Prämonsstratenserabtei, Fürstliches Schloss, Kirchliche Akademie*, Ulm 1992.

Walz, Rainer, *Hexenglaube und magische Kommunikation im Dorf der Frühen Neuzeit. Die Verfolgungen in der Grafschaft Lippe*, Paderborn 1993.

Walz, Rainer, 'Kinder in Hexenprozessen. Die Grafschaft Lippe 1654–1663', in Jürgen Scheffler, Gerd Schwerhoff and Gisela Wilbertz (eds), *Hexenverfolgung und Regionalgeschichte: die Grafschaft Lippe im Vergleich* (Studien zur Regionalgeschichte 4), Bielefeld 1994.

Warmbrunn, Paul, *Zwei Konfessionen in einer Stadt: Das Zusammenleben von Katholiken und Protestanten in den paritätischen Reichstädten Augsburg, Biberach, Ravensburg und Dinkelsbühl*, Wiesbaden 1983.

Warner, Marina, *Alone of All her Sex. The Myth and Cult of the Virgin Mary*, London 1976.

Warner, Marina, *From the Beast to the Blonde. On Fairy Tales and their Tellers*, London 1988.

Weber, Hartwig, *Kinderhexenprozesse*, Frankfurt am Main and Leipzig 1991.

Weber, Hartwig, *'Von der verführten Kinder Zauberei'. Hexenprozesse gegen Kinder im alten Württemberg*, Sigmaringen 1996.

Wegert, Karl, *Popular Culture, Crime and Social Control in Eighteenth-Century Württemberg* (Studien zur Geschichte des Alltags 5), Stuttgart 1995.

Weinberg, Florence M., *Gargantua in a Convex Mirror. Fischart's View of Rabelais*, New York 1986.

Weiß, Elmar, *Geschichte der Brunnenstadt Külsheim*, 2 vols, Külsheim 1992.

Weiß, Elmar, 'Die Hexenprozesse im Hochstift Würzburg', in Peter Kolb and Ernst-Günter Krenig (eds) *Unterfränkische Geschichte. Band 3: Vom Beginn des konfessionellen Zeitalters bis zum Ende des Dreißigjährigen Krieges*, Würzburg 1995.

Weiß, Elmar, 'Die Hexenprozesse in der Zent Grünsfeld', *Wertheimer Jahrbuch* 1979–80, pp. 33–63.

Weiß, Elmar, 'Würzburger Kleriker als Angeklagte in Hexenprozessen in den Jahren 1626–1630', *Mainfränkisches Jahrbuch* 40, 1988, pp. 70–94.

Wheeler, Philip (ed.), *The Roman Ritual in Latin and English*, Milwaukee 1952.

Wiesner, Merry, 'Guilds, Male Bonding and Women's Work in Early Modern Germany', *Gender and History* 1, 1989, pp. 125–37.

Wiesner, Merry, 'Luther and Women: The Death of Two Marys', in Jim Obelkevich, Lyndal Roper and Raphael Samuel (eds), *Disciplines of Faith. Studies in Religion, Politics and Patriarchy*, London 1987.

Wiesner, Merry, 'The Midwives of South Germany and the Public/Private Dichotomy', in Hilary Marland (ed.), *The Art of Midwifery. Early Modern Midwives in Europe*, London 1993.

Wiesner, Merry, *Working Women in Renaissance Germany*, New Brunswick 1986.

Wilbertz, Gisela, Gerd Schwerhoff and Jürgen Scheffler (eds) *Hexenverfolgung und Regionalgeschichte. Die Grafschaft Lippe im Vergleich* (Studien zur Regionalgeschichte 4), Bielefeld 1994.

Willoweit, Dietmar, 'Gericht und Obrigkeit im Hochstift Würzburg', in Peter Kolb and Ernst-Gunter Krenig, *Unterfränkische Geschichte. Band 3: Vom Beginn des Konfessionellen Zeitalters bis zum Ende des Dreibigjahrigen Krieges*, Würzburg 1995.

Wilson, Eric, 'Institoris at Innsbruck: Heinrich Institoris, the *Summis Desiderantes* and the Brixen Witch-Trial of 1485', in Bob Scribner and Trevor Johnson (eds), *Popular Religion in Germany and Central Europe, 1400–1800*, London 1996.

Wilson, Stephen, *The Magical Universe. Everyday Ritual and Magic in Pre-modern Europe*, London and New York 2000.

Wiltenburg, Joy, *Disorderly Women and Female Power in the Street Literature of Early Modern England and Germany*, Charlottesville and London 1992.

Winnicott, Donald W., *Playing and Reality*, London 1971.

Wrigley, E.A. and Roger Schofield, *The Population History of England, 1541–1871*, Cambridge 1981.

Wulz, Gustav, 'Die Nördlinger Hexen und ihre Richter', in *Der Rieser Heimatbote, Heimatbeilage der Rieser Nationalzeitung*, Nördlingen 1939, Nos. 142–5, 147.

Wulz, Gustav, 'Nördlinger Hexenprozesse', *Jahrbuch des Historischen Vereins für Nördlingen und das Ries* 20, 1937, pp. 42–72; 21, 1934–39, pp. 95–120.

Wunder, Heide, *'Er ist die Sonn, sie ist der Mond'. Frauen in der Frühen Neuzeit*, Munich 1992.

Yeoman, Louise, 'Hunting the Rich Witch in Scotland: High-Status Witch Suspects and their Persecutors, 1590–1650', in Julian Goodare (ed.), *The Scottish Witch-Hunt in Context*, Manchester and New York 2002.

Zika, Charles, *Appearances of Witchcraft. Visual Culture and Print in Sixteenth-Century Europe*, London 2005.

Zika, Charles, 'Cannibalism and Witchcraft in Early Modern Europe: Reading the Visual Images', *History Workshop Journal* 44, 1977, pp. 77–106.

Zika, Charles (ed.), *Exorcising our Demons. Magic, Witchcraft and Visual Culture in Early Modern Europe* (Studies in Medieval and Reformation Thought 91), Leiden and Boston 2003.

Zika, Charles, 'Hosts, Processions and Pilgrimages in Fifteenth-century Germany', *Past and Present* 118, 1988, pp. 25–64.

Zika, Charles, 'Les Parties du corps, Saturne et le cannibalisme: représentations visuelles des assemblées des sorcières au xvie siècle', in Nicole Jacques-Chaquin and Maxime Préaud (eds), *Le Sabbat des sorciers, xve–xviiie siècles*, Grenoble 1993.

Zipes, Jack, *The Brothers Grimm. From Enchanted Forests to the Modern World*, New York and London 1988.

Zipes, Jack, *The Oxford Companion to Fairy-Tales*, Oxford 2000.

Zorn, Wolfgang, *Augsburg. Geschichte einer deutschen Stadt*, Augsburg 1972.

Index

NOTE: Page numbers in italic indicate information is to be found in an illustration or its caption.